PEN

BLOO

Roger Wilkes is a journalist. Born in North Wales in 1948, he was educated in Shropshire and joined the BBC in 1972. He has worked in television and radio in Liverpool, London, Bristol and, now, as a freelance in Manchester. This is his third book.

ROGER WILKES

BLOOD RELATIONS

*Jeremy Bamber and the
White House Farm Murders*

PENGUIN BOOKS

PENGUIN BOOKS

Published by the Penguin Group
Penguin Books Ltd, 27 Wrights Lane, London W8 5TZ, England
Penguin Books USA Inc, 375 Hudson Street, New York, New York 10014, USA
Penguin Books Australia Ltd, Ringwood, Victoria, Australia
Penguin Books Canada Ltd, 10 Alcorn Avenue, Toronto, Ontario, Canada M4V 3B2
Penguin Books (NZ) Ltd, 182–190 Wairau Road, Auckland 10, New Zealand

Penguin Books Ltd, Registered Office: Harmondsworth, Middlesex, England

First published by Robinson Publishing Ltd 1994
Published in Penguin Books 1995
1 3 5 7 9 10 8 6 4 2

Printed in England by Clays Ltd, St Ives plc

ACKNOWLEDGEMENTS

As well as those mentioned in the introduction, my thanks are due to John Arkell, headmaster of Gresham's School; Anthony Arlidge QC; David Blomfield; George Boorman; Wendy Brading, *Evening Gazette*, Colchester; Barbara Bullen, St Nicholas's Hospital, Great Yarmouth; Jan Chamier; Janet Forbes; Jenny Grinter, Essex Constabulary; Margaret Harker; Helene Jones; Trevor Jones; Edmund Lawson QC; David Martin-Sperry; Geoff and Nicola Merriman; Hilary Monahan; Gavin and Shelley Power; Stewart and Eileen Roy; Ewen Smith; Yvonne Smith; Diana Stenson; Jim Stevenson; Paul Terzeon; Canon Eric Turner; Mark Webster; Barbara Wilson; Stella Wiltshire, West Park Hospital, Epsom; David Young, Christ's Hospital, Horsham. I owe a special debt of gratitude to the crime historian Jonathan Goodman and to Nick Robinson for his encouragement and guidance.

Scale 1:25000

INTRODUCTION

THE JURY said he did it: Jeremy Bamber killed five of his own family in cold blood, thinking he could get away with it.

Yet at first the police had believed him when he blamed the killings on his deranged sister. Evidence was destroyed, bodies cremated, case closed. A decent interval of grieving. Then, sensationally, Jeremy Bamber was arrested, questioned, tried and convicted on five counts of murder.

Bamber has served nearly a third of a life sentence, handed down with a recommendation that he should remain in prison for at least twenty-five years. But seven years into his time, Bamber remains a tireless proselytizer for his own innocence; he insists that when the killer set the firestorm in White House Farm on that dreadful night in August 1985, he was home, in bed, alone, asleep. He says it was his sister Sheila, crazy on cocaine, who shot her sleeping twin sons and gunned down her adoptive parents before turning the gun on herself. Jeremy stood to inherit more than £400,000 in the wills of his murdered parents; it was his surviving, dispossessed, scheming and jealous relatives, he says, who set the trap for him and sprang it.

So did he do it? Jeremy Bamber's trial in 1986 lasted nineteen days. The court heard details of an act so dreadful that it seemed beyond the understanding of sane people. In the end, although Bamber was convicted, the jury was split. Ten thought him guilty. Two did not. Even in the face of overwhelming evidence, disbelievers remain. This book re-examines the evidence adduced before the jury and introduces fresh evidence that has come to light since the trial. It tests assumptions, and raises some difficult and disturbing questions about the Bamber family and their seemingly idyllic life lived against the backdrop of an English pastoral. It cracks open the elegant façade of White House Farm to reveal the tormented truth of a landed middle-class family in decay. With its introspective, village setting and Archeresque echoes, the story might have been wrought by any lady crime writer from the Mayhem Parva school of English whodunits. Curiously, one of the great exponents of that genre, Margery Allingham, lived at Tolleshunt D'Arcy for many years; she considered the village 'a little too good to be true' and 'almost complacently picturesque'. She could scarcely have conceived of the slaughter that would engulf White House Farm that harvest night. Moreover, with its subtext of thwarted middle-class ambition, flawed expectation and raw greed, the story outpaces any so-called Aga saga at every turn.

From the outset, Jeremy Bamber has insisted that he didn't do it. He says he was framed. He wants the case to be referred to the Court of Appeal, like the cases of the Guildford Four and the Birmingham Six. In 1991, the Birmingham Six fiasco prompted proposals for a complete overhaul of the criminal justice system; when they were announced in July 1993, they called for an independent appeals tribunal to be set up to investigate alleged miscarriages of justice. An estimated 700 such cases are waiting to be reviewed. Bamber's defence team are unlikely to wait.

Jeremy Bamber wants his case to be referred to the Court of Appeal, and he wants it referred without further delay. He has hired new lawyers. His case has been taken up by a group of campaigners with a record of exposing wrongful convictions and judicial errors. They have fresh evidence.

This account examines that evidence, and is based on a detailed study of the case, transcripts of the trial, statements, depositions and reports, as well as interviews with the principal surviving figures. These include Jeremy Bamber himself, but exclude his former girlfriend Julie Mugford, now married and living abroad. Throughout the text, dialogue, descriptions and other directly quoted matter are authentic, derived from original documentation, transcribed evidence at Bamber's trial, or personal interview. The arguments concerning the blood evidence, on which Jeremy Bamber now bases his case for review, have been marshalled by an organization called Justice for All. I am grateful to the Manchester McKenzie Organization, and in particular its co-principal, James Stevenson, for giving me access to their documentation. Other new material derives from interviews I have conducted with people connected with the case, some of whom have asked not to be named. I am grateful to them nonetheless. I owe a special debt of gratitude to the members of the Bamber family who, after initial misgivings, agreed to talk to me. June Bamber's sister and brother-in-law, Pamela and Robert Boutflour, generously supplied a wealth of material on the family's history and background; their daughter and son-in-law, Ann and Peter Eaton, endured several lengthy interrogations from me with patience and fortitude. So did former Detective Sergeant Stan Jones, now retired, and Nevill Bamber's former secretary at White House Farm, Mrs Barbara Wilson. I am indebted to all these people for their forbearance and hospitality, as I am to others in Essex, London and elsewhere who shared their knowledge of the case in return for anonymity.

The book has been written with the help of Jeremy

Bamber, but not at his bidding; indeed, it is manifestly not the one-sided book in support of his innocence that he might have hoped for. But he knows that I never promised him that. Indeed I have taken into account, and reflected, several points of view, often bearing on the same point or turn of events. You, the reader, can judge for yourself, without my own prejudices or opinions getting in the way. In any case, on the known facts, likelihoods and suppositions, the dispassionate observer might feel that the question of who *really* did it is just too close to call. After all, the terrible events scrutinized here almost certainly happened within the compass of only a few minutes. In those cataclysmic moments, five lives were snuffed out, the lives of the survivors devastated, the life of Jeremy Bamber ruined in the time it took to pump twenty-five bullets into his family. But as you are drawn into the story, and towards your own conclusions, remember: whoever it was who came in the night and killed them all, of those who are left, only Jeremy Bamber knows the truth of it.

PROLOGUE

SHEILA CAFFELL picked her way down from the farmhouse to the rape field, while the twins scampered alongside and waved excitedly at the tractor. Daniel and Nicholas were only six years old, and the husks of rape, ripened to the colour of parchment, tickled their knees as they ran, calling to the little dog, Crispy, to keep up. Sheila smiled. Her twins loved the farm and its fields, the hot, breathy smell of the cattle, the breeze from the estuary brushing their blond, upturned faces. She stood for a moment, tracking the distant purple line between land and sky by shading her eyes with a slender manicured hand.

The barn had been running all day. Harvest at White House Farm drew all the menfolk on to the land; now, in the first week in August, it had drawn Sheila from London to share a holiday there with the twins. This land had once been her birthright. But she had rejected it in favour of a prospect of better times and greater fortune in London, the city she loved and longed for whenever she came home to the farm.

Sheila's life was spinning out of control. A modelling career had foundered in a cauldron of drugs and debt. She had suffered a mental breakdown. Her marriage had failed. Her husband Colin shared custody of Dan and Nick, and she now saw them only at weekends and in the holidays.

Across the flatlands of Essex, the soggy summer of 1985 had been unusually cold and wet. Freak hailstorms had swept in from the sea, devastating whole fields of tender salad crops. But this Tuesday, 6 August, had dawned sunny and dry, an ideal day for harvesting rape. Jeremy Bamber, Sheila's adopted younger brother, had spent most of the day in the cab of the farm's new tractor. It was airless, hot and heavy work. Sheila's arrival with the twins meant a chance to take a break. Jeremy signalled to the farmhand, Len Foakes, to shut down the controls of the huge combine. The din of the engine died.

The twins loved climbing up on to the tractor, and this afternoon the treat was extra-special; Uncle Jem – their name for Jeremy – was at the wheel of a brand-new John Deere tractor that gleamed in the afternoon sunlight. They clambered aboard. Jeremy showed them the smart new cab with its impressive array of dials and slipped another tape into the stereo system. Crispy, the hyperactive shih-tzu, snuffled at the edge of the uncut rape nearby. Sheila watched, not smiling now. Jeremy left the children playing in the cab and jumped down, wiping his brow with the back of a dusty hand. He nodded to his sister, screwing his eyes against the sun. Sheila, with her characteristic vacancy, began to speak, but slowly, haltingly. She and the twins, Jeremy gathered, had been into nearby Tiptree with her mother to do some shopping.

At 28, Sheila was three years older than Jeremy, and she too was adopted. While still a teenager, she had trained in London as a model, meeting with only limited success, under the professional name 'Bambi'. She continued to live in London, much to Jeremy's envious irritation, but paid frequent visits to her adoptive parents, Nevill and June Bamber, at White House Farm.

The farm stands at the seaward fringe of the Regency village of Tolleshunt D'Arcy, six miles from Maldon at the mouth of the River Blackwater.

For more than half the year, a vicious wind whips

across the farm's 350 acres from the estuary, and the hedges lining the lanes around the village of Tolleshunt D'Arcy bend their backs towards the river's mouth. But in August, at the height of the harvest, on this dizzily sunny day, the wind merely rippled across the waves of ripened rape seed towards Pages Lane. This is a narrow private track that leads to White House Farm from the Tollesbury Road.

It was along this track that Jeremy Bamber had gunned his silver Vauxhall Astra hatchback at seven-thirty on that summer's morning. The drive from his small cottage at Goldhanger took less than ten minutes at that early hour; Jeremy Bamber, a fast driver, often did it in little over five. He parked the car alongside the farm pick-up and crossed the yard to the back door. As usual on a working day, Jeremy was dressed for the tractor: he wore a T-shirt, light grey jogging bottoms and dirty white plimsolls. Even scruffily clad, Jeremy Bamber cut a striking figure. He was tall and slender, darkly handsome with full, moist lips and remarkably wide blue eyes which twinkled when he smiled, but which otherwise had a curious blank and unblinking quality. In the kitchen, Jeremy shared coffee with his father. It was a familiar daily routine. Father and son spent about half an hour discussing the progress of the harvest and what was to be done that day. At eight, both men left the house to meet the farmworkers. When Jeremy returned briefly to the farmhouse an hour or so later, Sheila and the twins were having breakfast. Jeremy's mother, June Bamber, sat with them at the kitchen table.

In all its humdrum domesticity, the scene in the kitchen at White House Farm that August morning might have echoed a thousand similar family gatherings throughout middle England. The kettle boiled on the Aga, coffee gurgled in the percolator. In fact, the scene disguised deep divisions within the Bamber clan. For despite appearances, the Bambers were not a family to bond together or to share the familiar intimacies of hearth and home. Meal times, in particular, were strained; Jeremy found himself at odds with both his parents and his sister.

His differences with Sheila went back several years. Indeed, they had never been truly close. The usual bonds between brother and sister – which should have brought them together in spite of an absence of consanguinity – had ceased to develop since their days together at prep school. There had been a time during Jeremy's college days when he had been a regular visitor to Sheila's London flat, for Jeremy relished the glamour of the capital. But by the time he returned from a trip to Australia at the age of twenty, Sheila's marriage had broken down, Dan and Nick had arrived and (as he would observe without a trace of bitterness from his prison cell many years later) 'life was difficult for her'.

Jeremy tried to understand what was happening to Sheila, but he confessed himself defeated by her moods, her bizarre conversation and what he described as her acute paranoia. Neither did he pretend to understand his mother.

June Bamber's deepening interest in religion merely baffled him. She had hung the walls of the farmhouse with framed religious texts, and had, taken to leaving little scribbled notes around the house, mainly biblical quotations about personal behaviour and beliefs. Grace at meal times was strictly observed.

As for his father, Jeremy found him increasingly difficult and intolerant. Nevill Bamber had hoped, naturally, to pass the farm and its associated businesses on to Jeremy. But since leaving school, Jeremy had shown little interest in the land, preferring to travel exotically and expensively, to drift through a series of dead-end jobs and to chase unsuitable women. Only recently had he shown any sign of wanting to settle down and to work for his inheritance. He had returned home to Essex, to lead the life of a prosperous farmer's son, to learn about the land that he would one day call his own. But Nevill Bamber regarded the return of the prodigal with mixed feelings, for he found that Sheila's strange moods, her mother's preoccupation with religion, and Jeremy's baffled indifference to both, meant that the underlying family tensions remained tight as wire.

The twins had been put to bed by the time Jeremy returned to the farmhouse between 8 p.m. and 9 p.m., and from then on Jeremy's is the only account we have of what happened there that evening. He says that he stayed for about half an hour, eating something while standing at the kitchen sink before joining his parents and Sheila at the supper table in the kitchen and listening to their conversation. The talk was about the possibility of Sheila fostering the twins. At one point, Jeremy left the room to check that the drier was still running. Crossing the yard in the fading light, Jeremy spotted the scuts of some rabbits near the potato shed. Instinctively he dashed back into the farmhouse, seized a .22 semi-automatic rifle from his father's den, and grabbed a box of bullets which he tipped out on to the sideboard. Jeremy hurriedly stuffed several rounds into the empty magazine clip, rammed it into its slot and cocked the rifle. But when he ran back into the yard, the rabbits had gone. Jeremy scoured the yard around the barns for a few minutes in the gathering gloom, but he could see no sign of rabbits and he returned to the house without firing a shot. After taking out the unfired round in the breech and putting it in the magazine, Jeremy left the rifle leaning against the kitchen wall, and the magazine lying on top of a wooden settle just inside the back door.

The light was now almost gone, but at White House Farm the working day was still not over. Jeremy made one last run down to the combine, taking an empty trailer from the barn and towing it across to the rape field behind the tractor. He returned to the house on foot at about 9.45 p.m. June, Nevill and Sheila Bamber were still sitting round the kitchen table talking. Jeremy spoke briefly to his father, arranging for Nevill Bamber to pick up the last trailer-load of rape of the day. Then he got into his car and drove home.

According to Jeremy Bamber's account, he would have arrived at his cottage in Head Street, the main road running through Goldhanger, at about ten o'clock. He had worked an exhausting fourteen-hour day, but before turning in he telephoned his girlfriend in London, and he made himself a sandwich and a drink. Then he flopped on to the sofa and half-watched a television programme. At about eleven-thirty, he switched it off and went upstairs to bed.

Whatever the truth of what happened later that terrible night, it was undoubtedly a night that changed Jeremy's life for ever. For at some time in the dead, small hours, someone crept silently up the stairs at White House Farm armed with a rifle. The question of whose finger pulled the trigger in the dreadful bloodbath that ensued is at the heart of the Jeremy Bamber story.

ONE

DAWN was still two hours away when the telephone rang in the control room at Chelmsford police station on Wednesday, 7 August. The duty officer, PC Michael West, lifted the receiver, glancing at the digital clock beside him as he did so. 'Police, Chelmsford. Good morning.'

'I am Jeremy Bamber,' the caller announced in a deep, laconic voice, 'of 9 Head Street, Goldhanger. You've got to help me.' PC West knew that Goldhanger was a village about fifteen miles from Chelmsford, north-east of Maldon. Bamber told him that he had just received a frantic phone call from his father, who lived at White House Farm just outside the nearby village of Tolleshunt D'Arcy. 'Please come over,' his father had pleaded. 'Your sister's gone crazy and she's got the gun . . .' Then the line had gone abruptly dead.

'Who is your sister?' the officer asked.

'Sheila,' Bamber replied. 'I can't remember her surname. Sheila Bamber.'

'How old is she?'

'About twenty-seven. She's had a history of psychiatry. She's been depressed before.' Bamber then said something to the effect that Sheila 'could go mad at anything; she's done it before'.

West asked if Sheila had access to any guns, and Jeremy explained that his father kept a collection of .410s, 12-bores and .22s at the farm. He went on to say that he'd tried ringing the police station at Witham, 'but there was nobody in; so I rang you'. PC West asked

11

Bamber to hold the line, and put the call on hold. Using the radio link between Chelmsford and Witham, PC West contacted PC Robin Saxby, who said he would go to White House Farm at once with his sergeant. West then returned to the telephone and spoke to Jeremy Bamber, who was still on the line.

'Christ,' said Bamber, 'you took a long time.'

West explained he had contacted Witham Police, and that a car was on its way to his father's farm at Tolleshunt D'Arcy. West took a note of the farm's telephone number. During this second conversation, West could sense Bamber's voice growing more urgent and excitable. He was starting to gabble, and his voice rose in pitch.

West asked if Jeremy knew who was in the house. 'My father obviously,' Bamber replied. 'My mother and Sheila.' By now he sounded even more agitated, and gave PC West the impression that he thought the policeman was underestimating the urgency of the matter. 'Look,' Bamber cried, 'when my father rang he sounded terrified. I don't think he's kidding about. He sounded really frightened.'

West asked Bamber if he had tried ringing his father back. Yes, said Bamber, but he couldn't get any reply.

'Will you go to the house and wait for the police officers and liaise with them there?'

'Shall I go now?'

'Yes,' said West, 'the car from Witham won't take long.'

The police were already on their way. As West was making a note of Jeremy Bamber's telephone number at Goldhanger, a marked police Ford Sierra, call sign Charlie Alpha 7, was roaring out of the yard at Witham and heading towards Tolleshunt D'Arcy, some ten miles away. The car contained three police officers: Sergeant Christopher Bews, PC Robin Saxby, and PC Stephen Myall. On the outskirts of the village, the Sierra's headlights picked out a silver Vauxhall Astra travelling ahead along the Tollesbury Road at about 30 m.p.h. As the police car overtook at high speed, the officers noticed that the driver at the wheel of the Astra was a young man in his mid-twenties. A few moments later, when the car turned into Pages Lane, the private road leading to White House Farm, the police were parked and waiting, in the narrow lay-by in front of the farm cottages. Bamber nosed in behind the police Sierra and switched off his lights.

Sergeant Bews hurried over. 'Are you Jeremy Bamber?' The young man nodded. 'What's happened?' asked Bews.

Bamber explained that about thirty minutes earlier, his father, sounding frightened, had telephoned to say that his sister had gone berserk with a gun. Then the phone had gone dead.

'What do you mean: "The phone went dead"? Do you mean it was hung up or your father just stopped talking?'

'It sounded as though someone had put their finger on it to cut it off,' replied Jeremy Bamber.

Bamber told the officers that the house contained five people: his two parents, his sister Sheila and her twin six-year-old sons. Bews asked if there were any guns in the house. 'Oh yes,' said Bamber, 'lots.' There were a few shotguns and two .22 rifles. Sergeant Bews motioned to PC Myall and the two officers started towards the house, leaving PC Saxby and Bamber standing by the police car. In a moment, Bews and Myall returned, and Myall asked Bamber if he thought it likely that Sheila would be in the house with a gun. Bamber replied, 'Oh yes.'

Myall asked, 'Who's she more likely to be annoyed at seeing, you or us?'

'Both of us,' Bamber replied. 'I don't get on with her at all. I don't like her and she doesn't like me.'

Myall looked at Bews and then at Bamber. The officer remembered thinking that the young man seemed remarkably calm, given the circumstances. Myall eyed him up and down. Bamber was warmly and smartly dressed, in trainers, jeans, an open-necked shirt under two crew-necked jumpers and a blue canvas jacket or blouson. 'I think as it's your family,' said PC Myall, 'you ought to come with us.'

'All right,' said Bamber. Leaving Saxby listening out for radio messages in the car, the three walked slowly up the lane towards the back drive. It was two minutes past four.

In a whisper, Sergeant Bews asked Jeremy Bamber if Sheila was likely to go berserk with a gun.

'I don't really know,' Bamber replied. 'She's a nutter. She's been having treatment.'

They walked on. Bews asked, 'Why did your father phone you and not the police – if there was trouble?'

Jeremy Bamber said, 'You've got to understand that he's not the sort of person to get organizations involved. He likes to keep it in the family. The family name and all that. All the treatment Sheila's had has been private. He doesn't even like the National Health Service.'

Bews considered this, then asked, 'Why didn't you dial 999 instead of trying two police stations?'

Bamber said he didn't think it would make any difference, adding, 'I don't know how your system works.' At this point, the group arrived in the farmyard at the side of the house, taking cover behind a wall next to the main barn. From here they had a clear view of one side of the dark, silent house. Bews noted that one light downstairs was on. In the room above, a light shone through drawn orange curtains, and in a neighbouring room he could see a light shining through a pair of green curtains. As they listened, Bews picked up the faint sound of a dog 'not

14

quite barking, not quite whining' from somewhere inside the house. The sergeant turned to Jeremy Bamber, who said, 'That's really strange, the way the dog is barking and my father not coming to see what's happening. Usually he's only got to get the smell of a fox in the back garden and he's out there.'

The doors and all the windows appeared to be closed. The strangely muffled sound of the distressed dog could still be heard, but otherwise there was silence. Hugging the low wall, the huddled group made their way noiselessly into the field at the front of the house. From behind the low hedge fringing the front lawn, they could see the front of the house in total darkness. Jeremy pointed out the windows of his parents' bedroom and the bedroom used by Sheila. Again, the group crouched motionless, watching and listening. Suddenly, in the window above the front door, there seemed to be a movement, a shadow. Bews, Bamber and Myall all ducked down, quickly and instinctively. Three pairs of eyes strained to catch the shadow. After a minute or two, Bews concluded that what they had seen was a momentary reflection in the glass: a trick of the light. But this was not a situation in which to take a chance. On Bews's signal, the three men quietly circled the house until they reached the top of the back drive. Then they ran for all they were worth.

They found PC Saxby sitting patiently in the police car in Pages Lane. Myall, breathless, asked Bamber about Sheila. 'You said your sister was nutty. What did you mean by that?'

'She's a depressive psychopath,' Jeremy replied. 'She's been having psychiatric treatment. She only came out of hospital about six weeks ago.'

Sergeant Bews asked if Sheila could use a gun. 'Oh yes,' said Bamber, 'she used to come target-shooting with me. She's used all the guns before.' And as if to dispel any doubt in the sergeant's mind, he added, 'Something's wrong. The dog doesn't usually make that kind of noise. It's more of a whine than a bark. Something's wrong.'

'I didn't like it,' Bews recalled later. He was now persuaded that Sheila had indeed run amok in this isolated farmhouse, brandishing and shooting one of the guns. On the basis that she was still inside the house, armed and waiting, Sergeant Bews reached for the radio telephone and summoned armed assistance. 'I thought: "There's either nobody in there, or four dead bodies and a nutter with a gun," and I wasn't going to go any further or let any of my men go any further until we'd got expert support from the Tactical Firearms Unit.'

Bews knew that, at that time of night, armed police units would take at least an hour to arrive. In the meantime, he decided to enlist the assistance of Jeremy Bamber. Bews rummaged in the back of his police car and produced a clipboard and a piece of paper. At Bews's request, Bamber drew a plan of White House Farm and its grounds, together with a plan of both the upper and lower floors of the house, showing the position of the doorways and the names of the various rooms. Bews also asked Bamber to list the names of the people he thought were likely to be in the house. This he did:

Sheila Bamber	Sister
June Bamber	Mum
Nevill Bamber	Dad
Daniel Caffell	Twin Boy
Nicholas Caffell	Twin Boy
Small Dog	

On the same piece of paper, Jeremy Bamber also listed the weapons he expected to find in the house:

.22 Rifel [sic] semi auto
3 x Double Barrell [sic] Shotgun
May be 4
.22 Rifel Bolt Action
410 Single Barrel Shotgun
.22 Air Rifel

Sergeant Bews ran his eye down the list. 'Are any of these weapons likely to be loaded?'

'They're all probably loaded,' Bamber replied, 'but the automatic .22 certainly is because I loaded it last night.' He explained that he'd loaded a full magazine before going out in search of rabbits, but that in the event he hadn't fired the rifle. PC Myall asked where the weapon was likely to be. Bamber said he'd left it propped against a wooden settle, or bench, in the vestibule adjoining the kitchen, with a full magazine clip and a box of ammunition lying on a blanket on the settle seat, at about a quarter past ten.

At 5 a.m., an armed squad of officers from Essex Police Tactical Firearms Unit arrived at White House Farm. Bamber told the officer in charge, Sergeant Douglas Adams, about the loaded rifle he'd left in the kitchen the previous evening. As dawn broke over the Blackwater estuary, Sergeant Adams led Bamber back to the farm-yard, asking him to point out various windows at the side of the house. Jeremy indicated the kitchen, where a light was still burning, and above it the room with the orange curtains (the bathroom) and the room with the green curtains (the twins' bedroom). Adams swiftly deployed his men. Sergeant Bews noticed that the whimpering, barking dog had ceased its noise.

Sergeants Bews and Adams explained to Jeremy Bamber that the Tactical Firearms Unit was planning to surround the house and storm it if necessary.

PC Myall asked him if there was anyone living locally

whom he wished to have with him at the scene. Jeremy replied that the only person he wanted to contact was Julie Mugford, his girlfriend, in London. Shortly after 5.30 a.m., accompanied by PC Robert Lay, Jeremy Bamber was allowed to call her from a telephone kiosk in the centre of the village. He told her not to go to work that morning, but to wait for the arrival of a police car which would bring her to Tolleshunt D'Arcy. The call was necessarily brief; Jeremy had only one 10p coin, and PC Lay found he had no change at all on him.

Back at the farm, PC Lay and another officer, PC Alan Batchelor, took it in turns to sit with Jeremy Bamber while the police ringed the house. Bamber, appearing 'calm and unworried', told PC Batchelor that the family always kept a loaded gun in the kitchen in case a fox came into the yard. To Batchelor, and again to PC Lay, Bamber boasted that his father was planning to stand him a £38,000 Porsche. He explained that his father only paid him a labourer's wage and that the Porsche – 'my dream car' – was by way of a perk. PC Lay also found him relatively calm, but saw that from time to time he was on the verge of tears. So the officer tried to keep the conversation away from the events around the farmhouse. The talk turned from cars to caravans. Jeremy explained that he was a partner in the family caravan site at Osea Road, in nearby Heybridge, and that they'd been having problems with break-ins. He and PC Lay discussed the merits of various security measures, such as high fences, guard dogs and closed-circuit cameras.

It was getting light. At White House Farm, Sergeant Adams had established a forward control point inside the main barn and within sight of the kitchen door. From here, Adams was able to shout challenges through a loudhailer, but from inside the house the only response was the frenzied yapping of a small dog. At 6 a.m. he sent for Jeremy Bamber, and asked him to explain in detail what he had earlier told the officers from Witham about where and how the .22 semi-automatic rifle had been left.

Jeremy was apologetic. 'I suppose I should tell you that I took out the magazine . . .' he began.

'I'm not interested in the legal side,' Adams hissed. 'I need to know about that gun.'

Jeremy then reiterated the circumstances under which he'd left the rifle in the house, with a full clip, after his abortive rabbit shoot the night before.

Sergeant Adams could hear more vehicles arriving. He glanced at his watch. A quarter to seven. Trudging back down the side drive to the lane, Adams and Jeremy Bamber saw that two police crew buses had pulled up, and that even more officers carrying rifles and wearing flak jackets were piling out and waiting to be briefed. An officer wearing a peaked cap, Inspector Ivor Montgomery, drew Adams aside. The two men spoke together for a couple of minutes. Adams explained the situation to Montgomery, indicating Jeremy Bamber with a nod of his head and showing him the sketch the young man had drawn of the inside of the house. Montgomery nodded. Stepping across, he introduced himself to Jeremy as the commander of the Tactical Firearms Unit. When his men stormed the house, he added, it would be on his orders.

Montgomery briefly explained what would happen. The armed officers would be divided into two groups: one, to be called the raid group, would storm the house; the other would provide cover and containment. Swiftly and silently, the armed officers were deployed around the farmhouse. All the doors and windows were covered, with the maximum firepower focused on the back door through which the raid group was preparing to enter the kitchen. It was 7.25 a.m.

Jeremy Bamber was escorted away from the forward control point inside the barn and led down the back drive to the second line of police vehicles in Pages Lane. Six armed officers approached the door, keeping themselves close to the wall, and covered by other marksmen crouching out of sight. Montgomery's radio crackled quietly; one of the raid group had managed to peep through the kitchen window and had seen what appeared to be a body. At a given signal, one of the raid group, Acting Sergeant Peter Woodcock, stepped forward and swung a heavy sledgehammer at the kitchen door. It took several shuddering blows. Finally the door swung open.

Four of the raid group moved silently through the vestibule into the kitchen. Another two stayed outside to give covering fire in the event of an ambush. Nevill Bamber was in the kitchen. He was perched on his favourite chair, but it had overturned and now lay on its side beside the Aga cooker. Nevill, in a crouching position and his right arm dangling limply to the floor, appeared to be balanced crazily on the arm of his upturned chair, as if the slightest current of air might bring him crashing to the ground. His body had slumped forward and his badly battered head was buried face-down in the Aga fuel hod. Blood had poured down the side of the hod like red and purple rain on a window. His blue pyjama top was heavily bloodstained, and blood had puddled from the wounds in his head into a deep red pool on the floor. Somehow, his pyjama bottoms had finished up round his knees. More small blood spots were flecked across the floor at the far side of the kitchen, where the telephone stood on one of the worktops. The telephone was off the hook, the receiver lying on the work surface.

What struck the advancing marksmen was that the kitchen had plainly been the scene of a violent struggle: a fight, literally, to the death. The big wooden table in the middle of the room stood laid for breakfast, but chairs and stools had been sent flying across the room, and the floor was littered with broken plates and dishes. Old farming magazines had fallen from the table and lay scrunched and scattered on the ground. A bowl of sugar had been spilled in the mêlée, and now crunched beneath the boots of the police officers as they trod wordlessly around the table with its neat place settings of blue and white cereal dishes. Fragments of glass from the shattered light fitting in the ceiling made a more metallic, grinding sound. PC Laurence Collins motioned to his colleagues to search the rest of the ground floor. The main reception rooms were in darkness, and two other external doors – including the main front door – were locked and bolted from the inside. In Nevill Bamber's downstairs den, across the stone-flagged vestibule from the kitchen, PC Collins looked inside the gun cupboard and saw a double-barrelled 12-bore shotgun and some boxes of ammunition.

Crouched at the foot of the main staircase and using an extending mirror, Collins was able to survey the upstairs landing. He could see a hand protruding from the doorway of one of the front bedrooms. The marksmen moved stealthily up the main staircase, straining to catch the slightest sound of movement, but hearing only a muffled scratching sound, as though a small dog had been left locked up and was trying to get out.

June Bamber was spreadeagled on her back and slightly on her side, her head against the open door. She had been shot in the head several times, including once directly between the eyes. Blood glistened on her throat and stained the bodice of her light-blue nightdress. The bedclothes on the large double bed had been pulled back on the side nearest June Bamber's body revealing blood-spattered sheets and a pillowcase. From beneath the bed came the scratching noise, this time accompanied by a high-pitched whimper. Bending down, PC Collins saw a small dog cowering and trembling with fright. His eye also caught two spent cartridge cases lying on the floor near June Bamber's body. Moving further into the room, he stepped to the foot of the bed and saw another body. It was Sheila Caffell.

She, too, was lying on the floor on her back, and wearing just a bloodstained nightdress. Two bullet wounds could clearly be seen beneath her chin, and blood had run down each side of her mouth. On top of her body lay a .22 rifle, the end of the barrel close to Sheila's chin. Her right hand lay loosely near the trigger. On the floor next to the body lay a single spent cartridge case, a pair of men's blue woollen socks and an open paperback Bible face-down on the carpet.

Down the landing, in the children's room, Nicholas and Daniel lay shot where they had slept, in separate twin beds with the matching pink candlewick covers pulled up to their shoulders. In the left-hand bed, Daniel was lying on his right side facing the wall. In the right-hand bed, Nicholas lay on his back. Both had been shot in the head at point-blank range. While Collins and two colleagues examined the scene in the twins' room, another armed officer, PC Michael Hall, stood in the passageway covering a closed door opposite. On it was a small ceramic sign. It said: Jeremy's Room. Moments later, Inspector Montgomery's personal radio burbled once more: the house was clear. Everyone inside it had been shot dead.

Shortly after 8 a.m., Sergeant Christopher Bews was detailed to tell Jeremy Bamber about the scene of carnage inside the farmhouse. Bews found him sitting in a police car parked on the farm track well away from the house. The sergeant told him that the police had broken in and that everyone inside, his father, mother, sister and two little nephews – his entire family – was dead. Jeremy Bamber didn't reply, but closed his eyes and began to cry.

Bews sat with him for a few moments, then signalled across to PC Robin Saxby. Bews got out of the car and told the constable to sit with Bamber. Saxby slid into the car, and the two men sat for a few moments saying nothing. Then Saxby broke the silence.

'I'm sorry it turned out this way,' he said softly. 'Are you all right?'

Slowly, as a child might, Jeremy replied, 'You said everything would be all right.'

Saxby looked away. 'Yes,' he murmured, 'we obviously hoped that it would.'

After a short silence, Jeremy Bamber spoke again. 'But you said it would be all right.'

'I know,' said Saxby. 'We like to think things will work out.'

The two sat quietly for a short while. Once or twice, the constable asked Bamber if he was feeling all right, and Bamber nodded, sitting hunched in the passenger seat of the police car. Then, to Saxby's relief, the familiar figure of Dr Ian Craig appeared at the car window. Dr Craig had been summoned from his home at nearby Maldon by telephone. He had acted as the local police surgeon for most of his thirty-one years in general practice; he was an experienced man who, having witnessed the appalling scenes inside White House Farm, had now concluded that the massacre had the appearance of murder plus the suicide of Sheila. By the time Dr Craig reached the police car containing Jeremy, the only surviving member of the Bamber family was apparently in a state of shock. The doctor asked him if he was all right. Jeremy said he was, and Dr Craig said he would be back to see him shortly.

In fact it was another half hour before Dr Craig

returned, having examined all five bodies inside the farm-house and certified death by shooting. With Dr Craig was Chief Superintendent George Harris, head of the Chelmsford division of Essex Police. Harris had been roused from his bed shortly after 4 a.m. As the senior police officer at the scene, he had toured the house and seen the carnage for himself.

Seeing Harris approach, Jeremy Bamber got out of the police car and asked if he could go into the house. Harris suggested he stayed where he was for the time being. 'Can't I see my dad?' Jeremy asked.

The officer glanced at PC Saxby, then put a steadying hand on Bamber's shoulder. 'I'm sorry,' he said, 'but both your parents are dead.'

Jeremy sobbed quietly for a few moments. Then he said, 'I want to see him. Why can't my dad come out to see me?'

'Jeremy,' said Harris gently, 'both your parents are dead.'

Dr Craig appeared at Harris's side. The doctor asked Bamber if he had any relatives or friends he wanted to contact.

'I have a girlfriend,' said Bamber. 'She's a lovely girl.'

Harris looked at his watch. It was 9 a.m. 'Can she be contacted now?'

'Yes,' Jeremy replied, 'she's on the phone.'

Harris said he'd arrange for Jeremy to telephone her. But Bamber began to cry again. 'Why can't my dad come out and speak to me?' he sobbed.

Dr Craig suggested to Bamber that they should take a walk. Just then, a police officer came up and offered him a cup of tea. Bamber asked if there was any whisky to stir into it, and Dr Craig fetched a hip flask from his car. Bamber drank, saying it was good whisky. Then the two walked a little way together along Pages Lane. 'Why can't my father come?' Bamber repeated. Gently, Dr Craig explained that his father had been killed. Again, Jeremy Bamber broke down and cried. After a few moments the two men walked on.

Craig thought it might help if Jeremy were simply encouraged to talk. Bamber spoke of Sheila's mental illness and her treatment from a psychiatrist, Dr Ferguson. Sheila had been in a mental hospital six or eight weeks previously, he said. 'They should never have let her out.' He also said that the previous evening, gathered around the supper table, the family had quarrelled over the possibility of having the twins fostered. This was not the first time that the question of the boys' future had been raised, Jeremy explained. Nevill and June Bamber were concerned that Sheila may have been physically abusing the twins.

Dr Craig asked Jeremy if such allegations had been reported to the police or social services. Jeremy said they had not. His parents would never have done such a thing, he explained. 'It would spoil the good name of the family.'

Bamber asked the doctor if he could walk on alone. Craig stopped and watched as the young man turned and walked slowly into the crop field alongside Pages Lane. He didn't notice the small unmarked car that drove up from the Tollesbury Road and parked behind the cluster of police vehicles blocking the lane. Two men got out. The older of the two, a tall man in his early forties and wearing a dark suit, ambled over to Dr Craig. The doctor recognized him as a detective sergeant called Stan Jones.

'What's the score?' Jones had seen the incident book on the front desk at Witham Police Station and knew only that some bodies had been found at the farm. Hearing that murder plus suicide was suspected, he and his immediate boss, Detective Inspector Bob Miller from

Braintree, had driven over to see if they could help with the inevitable paperwork that would be needed for the coroner. Dr Craig drew Sergeant Jones to the side of the track and pointed to Jeremy Bamber, who had walked about a hundred yards into the field. 'That young man has just lost all his family,' said Craig. 'I've just given him some Scotch. Now it looks as though he's being sick.'

Jones looked at the lone figure in the distance, and saw that he was bending forward, as though he was retching. Jones watched him for a moment, then turned to Inspector Miller. 'Come on, Bob,' he said.

The two detectives walked away and up the back drive towards the house. Dr Craig looked over to where Jeremy had been standing and saw that he was walking on and out of sight. When he disappeared behind a hedge, the doctor walked after him, only to meet Jeremy coming back carrying a small bunch of flowers. Dr Craig recognized them as opium poppies. 'It's all right,' said Jeremy Bamber. 'We've got a licence to grow them.'

The two detectives walked into the farmyard and saw that the back door was almost hanging off its hinges. A uniformed constable wrote their names on a form and stood aside. Jones and Miller stepped into the kitchen. There seemed to be people everywhere, mainly top brass from Essex Police. Stan Jones was surprised to see Chief Superintendent George Harris talking to one of his senior detectives, Taff Jones. Harris was a former detective, but it was unusual to see him out on a job and apparently taking personal command, especially in what everyone seemed to be telling Stan Jones was a case of four murders plus a suicide. Jones looked around. There had been mayhem in this kitchen, he thought, surveying the upturned stools and chairs, the broken crockery, the smashed light fitting and the sugar spilled all over the floor. He moved over to where Nevill Bamber's body still sat, slumped on an upturned chair. Blood was everywhere. Such an appalling scene was beyond Stan Jones's experience. It crossed his mind that he might have stayed in the office rather than become embroiled in such a shambles.

Jones and Miller were given a guided tour of the house. They stood at the foot of the twins' beds. One of the little boys still had his thumb in his mouth. Stan Jones had expected more blood, but in this tiny room there was scarcely any. But down the landing, in the main bedroom, he saw that June Bamber's body was heavily bloodstained. There was blood on the pillow and the sheets, and blood on the floor where she'd apparently tried to drag herself out of bed and towards the door. On the far side of the room lay Sheila Caffell. The rifle and the Bible were still in place. There was some blood staining on her turquoise nightdress, but otherwise the body seemed remarkably clean. What struck Stan Jones in particular was the marble whiteness of Sheila's arms and legs.

Downstairs in the kitchen, the head of the CID, Superintendent Taff Jones, a ruddy-faced Welshman in his mid-forties, was giving instructions. Stan Jones caught his eye, and Taff beckoned him over. The sergeant explained that he'd come over to see if there was anything he could do to help. Taff Jones took him aside. This, he said, had all the hallmarks of a terrible tragedy: four shootings followed by the suicide of the young woman, Sheila Caffell. There was, Taff Jones confided, no doubt about who was responsible. He and George Harris had surveyed the scene and both agreed that Sheila had shot her children, her adoptive parents and finally herself. Everyone was dead. The only survivor within the immediate Bamber family was the son, Jeremy. Stan Jones was to take charge of him, and take him home. 'Take someone with you,' said Taff Jones, 'and just get a statement for the coroner.'

Stan Jones walked back down the drive. It had turned out to be a glorious summer's morning. At the corner by the farm cottages, one of the uniformed constables directed Stan Jones to one of the police cars. Jeremy Bamber was sitting in the back seat. Jones got in beside him and introduced himself. Jeremy was sobbing quietly.

'Look,' said the sergeant without any further ceremony, 'they're all dead. You've got to accept that fact.'

Jeremy looked at him. 'You're a hard bastard,' he said.

Stan Jones shrugged. 'If I'm hard, it's for a reason,' he replied.

Jones explained that he would drive Jeremy home to take a formal statement, and to get him away from the grisly scenes inside the farmhouse. One of the armed officers approached, carrying the little dog that had been found whimpering in the main bedroom. It was a shih-tzu. Stan Jones suggested to Jeremy that he should take the dog back with him. But to Jones's surprise, Jeremy insisted that he wouldn't have the animal in his house, damaging all his stereo equipment. 'Get rid of it,' Jeremy snapped. 'Have it put down. I hate the fucking thing.'

The detective was shocked at Jeremy's apparent indifference. 'From that moment,' he recalled, 'Jeremy behaved as though nothing had happened.' For a man who had just learned that his entire family had been slaughtered in almost unimaginable circumstances, he seemed cool, callous and unconcerned. Stan Jones told Jeremy that he and another officer, Detective Constable Mick Clark, would drive him home. But Jeremy insisted on taking his own car and doing his own driving. So the three men climbed into Jeremy's Vauxhall Astra and drove over to Goldhanger. On the way, Jeremy spoke calmly about the killings. His main concern seemed to be to arrange some help for the farmworkers so that they could get on with the day's harvesting.

When they arrived at Bourtree Cottage in Head Street, Jeremy announced that he was starving. Without more ado, he proceeded to cook himself a breakfast of fried bacon, toast and coffee. He ate hungrily in the dining room, watched by Stan Jones and Mick Clark who sat drinking mugs of coffee.

'Right,' Jeremy said at last, pushing away his empty plate and wiping crumbs of toast from his mouth. 'Let's get on with it. I'm ready to start when you are.'

THROUGHOUT the next few days, the detectives took statements, and began to piece together the background of the family that had been almost entirely eliminated that night in White House Farm. It was a complex process, as the family relationships were complex, but it was an essential element in their investigations, as the relations of June and Nevill Bamber would themselves become key figures in the events of the coming weeks.

The detectives' investigations gave them a good general impression of who was who among the family, but it is arguable that the problems they later faced over the case were directly related to their failure to understand those relationships in any depth. The following picture is far more detailed than the one they were able to put together. It is based on very detailed interviews with all the surviving members of the family, and is an essential element in any reassessment of the case.

The Bambers were in general very like other landed East Anglian families of the 1980s, except in one respect – both of the Bamber children, Sheila, who had died alongside her parents, and Jeremy, who was the sole survivor, were adopted.

The essentially East Anglian element of the family lay in June Bamber's background. So too did most of the family's money. June was the daughter of a local landowner, Leslie Speakman.

Of the dozens of wealthy farming dynasties that owned the rich arable farmland of Essex between the wars, the Speakmans were among the wealthiest. In total, Leslie and Mabel Speakman owned or tenanted six farms covering many hundreds of acres of land in the area of the Blackwater estuary. They farmed as tenants at Vaulty Manor Farm, a 100-acre holding between Maldon and the village of Goldhanger which was also their home. In addition, they owned Carbonells Farm, a small manor house dating from the 12th century at Wix, thirty miles away, and tenanted the neighbouring Burnt Ash Farm. They were also tenants of three separate farms in and around the village of Tolleshunt D'Arcy: Gardener's Farm, Charity Farm and – at some 250 acres the biggest of the three – White House Farm. However, although they had money and land in abundance, the Speakmans had no son on whom to settle an inheritance. They had only two daughters, Pamela and June. Fortunately, though, they would see both of them marry farmers. The family tradition – and the family wealth – would be in safe hands.

In 1947, Pamela married Robert Boutflour. On his marriage, Robert accepted his new father-in-law's offer of the tenancy of Carbonells and Burnt Ash Farms at Wix. Robert Boutflour's father, Professor Boutflour, was at that time Principal of the Royal Agricultural College at Cirencester, and in the summer of 1948 young Boutflour asked his father to find him a couple of good agricultural students to come down to Essex to help with the harvest.

The students arrived in the middle of a heatwave in late July. One of them, a tall, well-set young man with a twinkle in his eye and an easy air of self-assurance that belied the fact that he was just twenty-four years old, was Ralph Nevill Bamber. Everyone called him Nevill.

June Speakman met him at a tennis party at Vaulty Manor. As with Robert and Pam Boutflour two summers before, it was love at first sight. Nevill Bamber enthralled June with stories of his exploits during the war when he had trained as a Royal Air Force pilot in Rhodesia. But he'd had an accident when a Mosquito he was flying crashed and he spent weeks in hospital lying on his back encased in plaster. Characteristically, he defied the doctors who'd told him he'd never walk again, and Nevill Bamber returned to the UK on his own two feet, determined to realize a lifelong ambition to become a farmer.

Nevill Bamber and June Speakman courted for little more than a year before marrying at Goldhanger in September 1949. Then in April 1950 they moved into White House Farm at Tolleshunt D'Arcy, a handsome foursquare Georgian farmhouse with walls thick with ivy of the darkest green from which, on a clear summer's day, they could see down to the saltings at Goldhanger Creek on the Blackwater estuary. The owners of the farm, an old-established charity dating from the 16th century, offered the tenancy to Nevill following a ringing endorsement from Nevill's wealthy father-in-law, Leslie Speakman. Once installed at the White House, Nevill Bamber formed a partnership with Speakman and farmed his lands in the Goldhanger area. When Speakman died in August 1975, Nevill continued to farm his lands, becoming a partner with his wife June in a company known as N and J Bamber Ltd.

Another consequence of Leslie Speakman's death was that the ownership of Osea Road Caravan Site was redistributed between the Boutflours and the Bambers. It was the canny Mabel Speakman who had spotted the potential of the site at Osea Road before the Second World War. It ran from the main road from Maldon down to the River Blackwater, a perfect holiday spot for the hundreds of Londoners who joined in the camping craze of the mid-1930s and drove down from the capital with their families to pitch their tents and buy their eggs and potatoes from the Speakmans at Vaulty Manor Farm, a quarter of a mile from the site entrance. In the 1950s the Speakmans bought up neighbouring plots of land, and by the mid-1980s, Osea Road Caravan Site comprised 550 plots.

As well as White House Farm and the Osea Road Caravan Site, the Bambers enjoyed a third source of income. Nevill Bamber was a partner in a cooperative of five local farmers known as North Maldon Growers. At its premises on the outskirts of Goldhanger, the cooperative grew, stored and packed – in bulk – produce such as peas and corn-on-the-cob to sell to local markets and freezer centres.

Both the farms and the business flourished, but Nevill and June had one great sorrow in their life. Although Robert and Pamela Boutflour soon had two children, David and Ann, the Bambers tried for years to begin a family without any success. Eventually in 1958 they adopted a baby girl whom they named Sheila Jean.

Sheila was just seven months old in 1958 when she was adopted through the Church of England Children's Society, an organization that proclaimed June's deep-rooted religious faith. Sheila's natural mother was the daughter of Canon Eric Jay, a one-time senior chaplain to the then Archbishop of Canterbury. Her father was a curate.

It was not until the following year that Nevill and June underwent fertility tests to see where the problem lay. A cyst was discovered on one of June Bamber's ovaries, and after the operation to remove it, June was told that she would never be able to bear children of her own. The news triggered a prolonged bout of severe depression, and she was admitted to Britain's largest private psychiatric clinic, St Andrew's Hospital in Northampton. There she underwent a course of electroconvulsive therapy, from which her consultant reported she made a full recovery. On her discharge from the clinic, June persuaded

Nevill Bamber to submit their names for a second time to the Church of England Children's Society, with a view to adopting another baby.

As a result, on 27 July 1961 Nevill and June Bamber adopted a wide-eyed, gurgling baby boy, aged six months; the child was christened Jeremy Nevill Bamber. (Jeremy had been born illegitimate on Friday 13 January 1961, his father being a former Comptroller of Stores at Buckingham Palace.) Now the Bambers had a family to compete with the Boutflours, though Sheila and Jeremy were far younger than David and Ann Boutflour.

Both of these adopted children, Sheila and Jeremy, would variously be held responsible for the tragedy of White House Farm, and the police very properly collected what evidence they could on both their backgrounds. Most of it initially came from their relatives. It gave them their primary view of the family they were dealing with.

First they concentrated on Sheila.

Sheila and Jeremy both attended Maldon Court, a private preparatory school based in an eighteenth-century town house in the centre of Maldon, about six miles from White House Farm, but from then on they saw less and less of each other, and developed very different personalities and different tastes. At ten, Sheila was sent away to board at another private school, Moira House in Eastbourne. One of her teachers there remembers her as a girl who enjoyed 'the more imaginative and artistic interests' of the school, especially modern dancing. However, Sheila failed to settle, and in January 1971, aged thirteen, she was moved again, this time to the Old Hall School in Hethersett, Norfolk. According to her cousin, David Boutflour, Sheila caused her parents some concern by getting into trouble there. She frequently played truant, disappearing to London to attend parties with school friends.

34

Despite the inevitable warnings, at the age of sixteen Sheila was eventually expelled.

In 1974, Sheila left White House Farm to live in London. She attended an expensive finishing school for three months, then took a job as a trainee hairdresser with a firm called Robert Fielding. This didn't last, and Sheila was sacked after a few months. To make ends meet, Sheila took a succession of menial jobs. In the evenings she attended a secretarial school in London before enrolling on a modelling course at the Lucie Clayton school in London. June Bamber paid the fees.

Sheila's cousin Ann Boutflour, who had married Peter Eaton and settled at Little Totham, remembers Sheila at this time 'as a very attractive girl. She wasn't practical at all, just pretty. A bit of a dumb blonde really, who enjoyed harmless flirtations with men and who always worried about how she looked.' A family friend of the Bambers remembered June's suffocatingly protective attitude towards her daughter, and described Sheila as a naïve girl who could be easily led. This naïvety may have framed a darker aspect of Sheila's teenage years because, according to David Boutflour, she had two abortions.

By 1977, Sheila was pregnant again and planning to marry Colin Caffell, a dreamy-eyed sculptor and potter. The ceremony took place at Chelmsford Register Office. Sheila subsequently miscarried, and on her twenty-first birthday, 18 July 1978, she had a huge row with her husband, accusing him of having a girlfriend. It ended with Sheila smashing her hand through a plate glass window. The wound had to be heavily stitched in hospital. Shortly afterwards, Colin lost his job. Towards the end of 1978, she announced that she was expecting twins. June Bamber gave Sheila and Colin some money to put down as a deposit on a ground-floor flat in Maida

Vale with access to a garden so that there would be a play area for the expected grandchildren.

Sheila duly entered the Royal Free Hospital in Hampstead, north-west London, prior to the birth of twins. The twins were born prematurely on 22 June 1979, and named Daniel and Nicholas. All the relatives who saw the golden-haired little boys doted on them.

Sheila remained close to her adoptive parents, and June Bamber visited her daughter and grandsons in London every couple of weeks or so. But Sheila soon found it difficult to cope with the twins in London. Often she travelled up to White House Farm, and June Bamber paid local girls to act as nannies. Meanwhile June helped Colin Caffell to get another job as a sales representative and paid for a course of driving lessons. When he passed his test, Colin bought a small car. He was now able to drive Sheila and the twins from London to White House Farm to stay with the Bambers. But while the twins were still in nappies, the marriage between Colin and Sheila Caffell was deteriorating. Sheila seemed to be suffering deeper and deeper bouts of depression, and eventually Colin moved out of the flat in Maida Vale and moved in with his new girlfriend.

It was now 1981. Nevill Bamber would regularly drive to London to collect Sheila and the twins. Sheila was depressed about the failure of her marriage, and seemed to enjoy returning to White House Farm to spend time with her adoptive parents. However, June Bamber found her daughter's marital traumas increasingly hard to handle.

June Bamber was a totally committed Christian. For years she had been agonized by her daughter's wayward life in London, most especially by her abortions and her casual approach to her marriage. In June 1982, June had a mental breakdown. According to her psychiatrist, Dr Hugh Ferguson, June was in the grip of a psychosis, as a result of which 'she suffered a distortion of her already strong religious beliefs and tended to see everything in terms of good and evil.' – June Bamber's condition improved under Dr Ferguson's treatment – although her religious fervour remained undiminished – but on 2 August 1983 it was Sheila's turn to seek psychiatric help. When Sheila first consulted her London GP, Dr Myrto Angeloglou, he referred her to an NHS clinic at the Royal Free Hospital. But June and Nevill Bamber intervened, and asked Dr Angeloglou to refer Sheila to Dr Ferguson, since he had already successfully treated June.

When Dr Ferguson examined Sheila at his consulting rooms in Devonshire Place, near Harley Street, he diagnosed a state of acute psychosis. 'It was evident that she had been depressed and unconfident for the previous eighteen months and had an increasing sensitivity about other people,' Dr Ferguson reported. He arranged for Sheila to be admitted without delay to St Andrew's Hospital, Northampton.

During her treatment, Dr Ferguson discovered that Sheila had bizarre delusions about being possessed by the Devil, coupled with complex ideas about having sex with her twin sons. She told Dr Ferguson that she felt as if she was caught up in what she called 'a coven of evil'. These feelings, the consultant explained, appeared to involve her relationship with June Bamber and June's standards of good and evil.

The feelings Sheila expressed were clear symptoms of paranoid schizophrenia. 'Sheila didn't give any impression that she was violent or potentially violent,' Dr Ferguson reported. 'She was bewildered.' She saw June as a threat, felt that June had been over-protective towards her, and found it difficult to express warm feelings towards her.

Sheila's relationship with Nevill Bamber, however, struck the consultant as more trusting and supportive.

Sheila, now divorced from Colin Caffell, with custody of the children shared – Colin looked after them in the week and Sheila at weekends – was conducting an affair with an Iranian called Freddie Emami. 'I believe he baby-sat for her,' was Dr Ferguson's euphemistic assertion. He noted that Sheila's friends in London seemed reason-ably supportive, and that she tried to live independently of her parents. 'But,' he observed, 'I doubt whether she was financially independent.'

Sheila told Ferguson that she knew she was adopted. In 1982, she had decided she wanted to discover the identity of her natural mother and did so through an agency. However she seemed less keen to trace her real father. (Two years later, in the summer of 1985, a few weeks before she died, Sheila met her natural mother when she visited England from her home in Nova Scotia. According to Sheila's natural uncle, Peter Jay, the meeting went very well.)

While at St Andrew's Hospital, Sheila responded to Dr Ferguson's treatment and on 10 September 1983 she was discharged. Dr Ferguson considered that she had made only a partial recovery, but at least she was not deluded or hallucinating. He ordered that Sheila should live at White House Farm for a few weeks before returning to the hurly-burly of life in London.

Throughout 1984, Dr Ferguson continued to treat Sheila as an outpatient. She managed to maintain normal relationships with her family, but the doctor found that she remained vulnerable to unsettled feelings. In Decem-ber 1984, Sheila told Dr Ferguson she felt settled and was about to start work in a shop. She and Freddie spent Christmas together in London.

On the evening of 2 March 1985, the telephone rang at

White House Farm. Nevill Bamber picked up the receiver to hear Sheila's voice, calling from the Maida Vale flat. She was hysterical. She talked all night. Next morning, Nevill Bamber telephoned Dr Ferguson asking him to readmit Sheila to hospital as a matter of urgency because of a major deterioration in her mental state. Later the same day, she was admitted to St Andrew's Hospital for a second time. Hugh Ferguson examined her at once. 'Sheila was found to be psychotic and this time thought that her boyfriend Freddie was the Devil,' he recalled. Sheila said nothing about her parents or her children. 'Her behaviour was more disconnected than before: she laughed inappropriately and was restless. She said she had some religious feelings – she had found God and felt relaxed,' he noted. On 25 March, Sheila wrote from hospital to Ann and Peter Eaton.

Dear Ann and Peter. I expect by now you have got wind of the fact that I am here. I didn't want everyone to know because I thought as usual they would get the wrong end of the stick. I am not in here because I am worrying about my body, so let's get this one perfectly clear. I could never look you straight in the face if you thought that, because it is all so futile. In fact I couldn't possibly be in here for that, because to begin with there is nothing specially terribly wrong with my body. In fact when I had the twins when I was in hospital they decided there was nothing wrong with my cervix and that I quite possibly had a sensitive womb which is why I started off early. So in future with God's blessing I won't have any troubles. I am sorry for saying this but it is important.

The reason I am here is because of general stress and I haven't been taking care of myself. I didn't want to come in but Dad said I should. I asked God into my life so I could understand Mum's moods more and became completely high on his love, so much so that I wanted to join CND thinking I had a calling from God to sort the world's problems out myself. Then I got a thing about the CIA following me. I finally thought a friend was the Devil, so I went through a tough time of unreality. But I am getting over it now and everything will be OK. I'm missing the boys. With love, Sheila.

Sheila had scribbled on the back of the envelope:

PS I have found God in a very simple way.
PPS Please don't tell anyone else in the family I have come here.

Reading this letter, Ann Eaton felt bewildered. Ann's mother, Pamela Boutflour, when consulted, would only hint at what was going on. 'Don't say anything,' she confided, 'but Sheila's not very well at the moment.' Sheila's illness was something that the family preferred to keep quiet.

Hugh Ferguson persuaded Sheila to admit to him that she had used cocaine fairly frequently since Christmas. 'She did not go into depth about drug abuse, except she said she had smoked the cocaine in a social context. She denied using hallucinogenic drugs or amphetamines. Her psychotic condition was not drug-induced, but would certainly be exacerbated by abuse of illicit drugs. I was not aware that she abused alcohol at all.' Once again, Sheila responded to his regime, and was discharged from St Andrew's just over three weeks later, on 29 March.

Dr Ferguson wrote to Sheila's GP, recommending follow-up treatment in London on the NHS. He also urged that her long-term management should include visits from a community psychiatric nurse. In the meantime, Sheila was to continue taking anti-psychotic drugs, in particular a tranquillizer called Haloperidol decanoate

(HCF), which is injected into the muscles and absorbed by the body over a period of time. It reacts chemically within the brain and restores the patient's mental stability. In the treatment of schizophrenia (as in Sheila's case), its main function was to quieten her down and to relieve her anxieties, but without impairing her level of consciousness. Her GP was to inject her once a month with 200 mg of the drug, although three weeks before her death, the dose was halved as she considered she was receiving too much.

On Saturday evening, 3 August 1985, Sheila Bamber turned up at a party given in London by her ex-husband, Colin Caffell, and his new girlfriend Heather. The following day, Sunday, Colin drove her and the twins to Tolleshunt D'Arcy. The visit was apparently her own idea.

On the morning of Tuesday 6 August, Sheila and the twins were seen walking one of the dogs in woods near White House Farm. Julie Foakes, the daughter of one of the farmhands, remembered Sheila skipping about with the children quite happily. That afternoon, Sheila and June Bamber drove over to Tiptree. The two women with the twins in tow visited a clothes shop, where Sheila was remembered by the shopkeeper, Barry Parker, who said Sheila struck him as a strange woman, rather vacant and not taking much interest in things.

Late that evening Pamela Boutflour telephoned her sister June to invite her to Carbonells Farm the following Thursday along with Sheila and the twins. At one point in the conversation June handed the receiver to Sheila. Pamela Boutflour remembered that the conversation with her niece was hard going. She expressed her concern to June when Sheila returned the receiver to her mother. Later Mrs Boutflour described Sheila as sounding like a zombie.

It was the last time she spoke to either June or Sheila.

THREE

WHEN it comes to reconstructing Jeremy's background, I have had the advantage of hearing Jeremy's own recollections, as well as those of his family and friends.

As with Sheila, there is little doubt that, whatever family stress there might have been in later life, Jeremy enjoyed a secure, comfortable childhood at White House Farm. His earliest memories were of the family farms where, as a small child, he played happily with various cats, dogs and farm animals under the surveillance of a succession of au pair girls with names like Ursula and Monica.

He was aware of Sheila – 'my big sis' – who kept an eye on him during his early schooldays, but he was not drawn to her by any strong brotherly instinct. For company, he preferred the sons of neighbouring families who, like his own, farmed the rich, arable land around the Blackwater estuary: two – Ross and Greg – were particular pals. The trio had the run of the family farms, building dens in the warmth and darkness of the barns, and exploring the ancient saltings and marshlands that stretched from the creek at Goldhanger to Shinglehead Point.

Jeremy's childhood memories were largely happy ones. 'In later years, Mum used to comment that I was a happy little boy, especially when I'd got my Lego set out which I played with endlessly. Mum was always around and I felt very secure and loved, though I was quite shy and used to hide under Mum's skirt when strangers came. Dad was a kind man, but was never openly affectionate with anyone.

Even Mum. But I looked upon him as very strong and very wise. I would run to him with scraped knees or bee stings for protection and comfort.'

Grandparents played only a minor part in young Jeremy's life. He'd never known his paternal grandfather; Granny Bamber was a shadowy figure during his childhood. He saw her only once a year, on Boxing Day, when the family paid a visit to her house in Guildford. Most of the old lady's money seemed to Jeremy to be soaked up in the upkeep of this vast family pile, and she wasn't one to spoil her grandchildren with presents. Granny and Grandad Speakman were different. They lived close by at Vaulty Manor, and Jeremy saw them several times a week during his school holidays. Leslie Speakman doted on his adopted grandson, and never missed an opportunity to spoil him with bottles of fizzy pop. Mabel Speakman, on the other hand, regarded such indulgence with haughty disdain. Jeremy thought her cold and distant, and never felt close to her. On birthdays and at Christmas, Granny Speakman never bothered with the ritual of present-buying. Instead, she slipped money to June Bamber, and it was she who chose the gifts, smuggling them back to Vaulty Manor to be wrapped and given to the old lady to bestow on her unsuspecting grandchildren.

As a day boy at Maldon Court, Jeremy had difficulty learning the alphabet, but found that arithmetic came easily; in adulthood, writing and spelling remained his weak points. In 1969, aged eight and a half, Jeremy was sent as a junior boarder to Gresham's School, Holt, on the Norfolk coast. Jeremy was being groomed for responsibility in the well-worn ways of the British middle classes, and like hundreds of small boys boarding for the first time, he felt unhappy and bewildered. 'For me, this was too young an age to be away from home,' he said, 'but once I'd got over the first couple of years, I enjoyed school.'

At eleven, Jeremy went up to the senior school at Gresham's. Here reading and writing remained troublesome, but Jeremy did well in oral work, and showed a certain flair for figures. Overall, however, he was (on his own admission) 'no great scholar'.

The highlight of his time at Gresham's came in his second year in the senior school when girls were admitted for the first time. Their arrival coincided with Jeremy's search for his sexuality. As a small boy, he had registered the normal passing interest in his friends' sisters. Now, at twelve, came his first sexual encounters with girls at school. He found he enjoyed their attention, but recognized that he was also attractive to some of the older boys. 'I'm a bit effeminate,' he cheerfully conceded. 'I'm still accused even now of being gay. But I don't find men at all sexually attractive or interesting. I could never indulge in sex with a man. I'm heterosexual to the core – and fairly conventional at that.

'I had lots of sexual experience with the girls at school, but we never went all the way.' Jeremy counted girls among the best friends of his teenage years, along with Roger and Kenny, his house-mates at Gresham's. They would go cycling together at weekends, criss-crossing the lanes of north Norfolk, or catching a bus into Holt. They were happy, carefree times. 'Insecure? That's one thing I've never been,' he says. 'I've always been confident, verging on the arrogant at times. I'm not proud of that but it's part of my personality.' His headmaster, Mr Logie Bruce-Lockhart, recognized Jeremy's arrogance at an early age. 'He was a rather quiet, prickly sort of boy,' he recalled. 'I believe some of the boys found him irritating in that he could be a relentless tease.' Perhaps it was this incipient arrogance that encouraged Jeremy in one of the few school activities at which he excelled: he joined Gresham's Combined Cadet Force and learned to be a crack shot.

He enjoyed the occasional field trips and summer camps but, as a fifteen-year-old, he regarded the military drill and spit-and-polish regime as too macho and over-regimented. He turned to more introspective pleasures for relaxation. There was a period when he amassed a collection of motor racing stickers. When that craze passed, he moved on to electronics, building radio sets, and inventing gadgets that made buzzing sounds or dimmed lightbulbs.

When they were still small, both Sheila and Jeremy had been told by June that they 'had not grown in Mummy's tummy but had been chosen'. At Gresham's, Jeremy confided to a friend that he was an adopted child. The friend broke the confidence and told other boys, who promptly nicknamed Jeremy 'The Bastard'. The jibe stung deeply.

Despite this, Jeremy still felt that his years at Gresham's were a great experience, and that the school taught him self-sufficiency. It had a proud sporting tradition, but Jeremy was troubled by a knee injury as he grew through adolescence, and glory on the games fields eluded him. The incapacity also meant that he was never at the forefront of school activities and was not made a prefect.

Jeremy's crowd seized any opportunity to buck the system, slipping away, for example, to watch punk bands like the Sex Pistols and The Clash at West Runton Pavilion outside Cromer. But he was not reckoned among the school's front-line rebels. He broke rules occasionally, but was seldom caught and punished only rarely. He remembers being caned only twice in his entire school career. He was not a drinker and smoked only the occasional cigarette.

Drugs, however, were his weakness, and during his

time at school he experimented with what he described later as the full range. He found that he enjoyed cannabis most, being a regular cannabis user since the age of fourteen, smoking mostly his own home-grown variety. At Gresham's, cannabis was almost impossible to obtain.

His favourite subjects were chemistry, mathematics ('We had an inspired maths teacher') and geography. He hated history, dismissing it as propaganda. Ironically, among his clutch of seven O-levels, he found that he had failed his chemistry but passed in history. His teacher in geography was a Mr Walton, a strict disciplinarian, but a man who inspired the growing Jeremy Bamber with vivid descriptions of faraway places that fuelled the boy's wanderlust. Every year, Mr Walton took a group of boys skiing, and during these annual visits to Sauze d'Oulx in the Italian Alps, he was a changed man: kind, warm and friendly, who (Jeremy remembered) handed out cigarettes and bought the boys the occasional gin and orange. It was on such trips that Jeremy determined to see more of the world.

Jeremy discussed this newly nurtured desire to travel with his father. During the school holidays, Jeremy had returned home to Tolleshunt D'Arcy to work on the family farm, but in Jeremy's mind, there had never been any question of him automatically joining his father at White House Farm. Nevill Bamber evidently listened to his son's plans with a philosophical shrug, told him that while he hoped to pass the farm on to him at some stage, he understood his son's wish to try other things first. Perhaps Nevill Bamber shrewdly calculated that it would be better to give the boy his head, and for him to learn for himself that the world could be a hostile place. As Jeremy himself put it: 'Dad wanted me to try other things first, so that I wouldn't have itchy feet or regrets in later life when I'd not be able to leave.'

Jeremy left Gresham's at the age of sixteen with his A-level studies incomplete. He enrolled at Colchester Technical Institute on a one-year A-level crammer course where he thought his chances of passing would be better. He was wrong. He studied for biology and geology and failed both, surrendering to the restlessness that had haunted him throughout his teenage schooldays. 'After spending nine years boarding,' he explained, 'I wanted more freedom.'

For her part, June Bamber at this stage was anxious to foster religious faith and fervour in her adopted son, but Jeremy, now seventeen, was impatient for more worldly pleasures. 'She did try to encourage me to be religious,' he recalled, 'but she used to do that with everyone. This used to get on my nerves at times, more so because I didn't understand why she did it. There's no disputing that in her later years, Mum became obsessive about Christianity. She was a fanatic.'

In 1978, having failed his A-levels at Colchester Tech, Jeremy decided to take himself off to the other side of the world, and spent a year travelling in Australia and New Zealand, finding support from his father's relatives who had settled in New Zealand, including a cousin, Chris Nevill.

In New Zealand Jeremy enrolled on a course to learn sport scuba diving. At this point his money seems to have run out. According to his uncle Robert Boutflour, Jeremy wrote an 'almost threatening' letter to his mother asking her to send £1,500 to cover the course fees. This she did, but subsequent demands for money were refused. According to Boutflour, 'June often said that she wouldn't give Jeremy any more money until he grew up and adopted a responsible attitude to life.' He completed the diving course, returning home with a one-star gold award.

This experience planted in Jeremy Bamber the idea of

47

making a career in deep-sea diving. Attracted by the high salaries paid to qualified divers, he returned to New Zealand to enrol on a course of commercial diving. But his hopes were dashed when he failed the qualifying medical examination because his skull – perhaps as a result of of an injury he suffered in a childhood accident – couldn't stand the deep-water pressures. Crestfallen, Jeremy once more set out for home.

There was talk that Jeremy had been forced to leave New Zealand in a hurry, after a row with Chris Nevill's sister over some money that had been left with her by Nevill Bamber when he had visited his relations in New Zealand a few years before. Jeremy got as far as the Middle East before being forced to ask his parents to send him money to get him home. Instead, they sent him an air ticket.

Jeremy returned to live at White House Farm, but his parents were unable to persuade him to settle. He told them that he didn't want to work the land and instead took a job at the Little Chef roadside restaurant at Rivenhall End. Nevill and June were distraught. They were also at a loss to know what to do about Jeremy's highly unsuitable girlfriend, a married woman nearly ten years older than Jeremy.

French-born Suzette Ford, a striking blonde with a husband and three children, had met Jeremy in 1979, when he was eighteen, in a wine bar in North Hill, Colchester, called the Frog and Beans. In his words – 'it was instant attraction'. Suzette was beautiful, funny and interesting, very different from the teenage girls who used to hang around the bar waiting to be chatted up by the local youths. Jeremy found himself, for the first time, dizzily in love. 'They used to sit in the corner all night, drinking black coffee and gazing into each other's eyes,' a friend reported. While this was happening, Sue Ford's unsuspecting husband stayed at home babysitting. When Geoff Ford found out that his wife was having an affair with Jeremy Bamber, he left.

Jeremy lived at White House Farm during the week, and with Sue Ford in Colchester at weekends, and became a surrogate father to Mrs Ford's three sons, Nicky, who was ten, Ashley, aged four, and two-year-old Jamie. The affair caused Nevill and June Bamber much concern. Jeremy's mother disapproved profoundly, but realized that there was nothing she could do about her son's infatuation but wait for it to fizzle out. However, the grand passion lasted longer than everyone expected. From time to time, Jeremy took Sue and the children over to White House Farm for a meal with his parents, and in January 1982, Sue Ford joined the Bambers and some of their friends at Jeremy's twenty-first birthday party. The celebration was held at an expensive restaurant near Flatford. But on most evenings, Jeremy was to be found at the bar of the Frog and Beans.

Colchester, an Army garrison town, was short on glamour, and for the local would-be jet-setters, the Frog and Beans was the nearest thing in Colchester to the bright lights of London. For Jeremy, the place had an added attraction. He knew the owners, Michael Deckers and Malcolm Waters, and drank largely at their expense in return for produce from the farm. Many a bottle of house wine was uncorked for Jeremy and his cronies in return for sacks of potatoes and supplies of vegetables ferried from Tolleshunt D'Arcy in the boot of Jeremy's car. He discovered that the high life in Colchester was almost self-financing, but realized that the kind of life he lusted for in London didn't come cheap. Another member of his set recalled a conversation about money, and Jeremy's observation that 'It's important to have money when you're young.' Someone pointed out that he would be a wealthy man one day, but Jeremy couldn't wait. 'He wanted a flat in London, he wanted to go out drinking, take people out to dinner, go abroad. He hated having to run to his parents every time he wanted extra cash.'

In the meantime, he was content with the smaller provincial notoriety that accrued from his affair with Sue Ford. It was as though Jeremy had deliberately chosen an older woman in order to taunt his conventional parents and offend their middle-class morality. But while he complained to friends about parental narrow mindedness, Jeremy knew he ran the risk of being disinherited for his pains and made no secret of his willingness to dump his exotic mistress if he was forced to do so.

At White House Farm, Jeremy ran the gauntlet of his mother's fury over the affair. She pointed out that sex before marriage was a sin in the eyes of God. Seizing a Bible she would quote screeds of moralizing scripture while Jeremy, contemptuous, simply screamed his defiance. In the end, the affair fizzled out. Sue Ford, wearying of Jeremy's vanity and arrogance (he made no secret of his philanderings with other women), went back to her husband. The couple moved away to Jersey, while Jeremy, feeling unwelcome at White House Farm, was offered accommodation at a house in Colchester owned by Deckers and Waters.

Although he continued to show little interest in the farm, Jeremy made a point of attending the annual meetings of the Osea Road Caravan Site in which he was an 8 per cent shareholder. It had become a limited-liability company, with June Bamber, her elder sister Pamela Boutflour and Pamela's daughter, Ann Eaton, as directors. June Bamber insisted that her son Jeremy should be given a bigger part to play in the company, and it was at her request that Jeremy was allowed to sit in on the board meetings. His first appearance at such a meeting was on 13 April 1983.

That spring, Jeremy seemed unsure about which direction his career should take, and for several weeks he helped out his father on the farm. Then, suddenly, in the middle of the harvest, in the summer of 1983, he just left and returned to New Zealand. His father was angry and upset. Jeremy came home in late September, as abruptly as he had left.

From this point, Jeremy worked full-time at White House Farm. His parents sought to make him feel comfortable, wanted, and groomed him for his eventual succession as tenant of White House Farm. To some onlookers, the young man's heart wasn't in it. 'He didn't want to be a farmer,' said one close friend of his parents. 'You could see that. He seemed to want the good life. But June and Nevill never stood in his way. He was free to choose what he wanted to do.'

To others, however, both Nevill and Jeremy gave the opposite impression. Nevill Bamber was a shrewd and adventurous farmer. Anticipating a decline in the market for traditional cereals because of over-production, he was the first in the Blackwater area to see the potential of experimental crops such as borage, evening primrose, fenugreek and even opium poppies for use in alternative medicine preparations. This innovative streak was the subject of much approving comment. George Nicholls, a surveyor from Witham who carried out the annual valuation of the farm and its contents for tax purposes, thought it augured well for the future. He described Nevill as 'a happy and considerate gentleman'. When he visited the farm in June 1985 to discuss a rent review, Nevill told him how pleased he was with the way Jeremy was shaping up as a farmer. (Indeed, when – a month after the murders – Nicholls visited the White House to make

51

his annual valuation and stock take, he found the farm generally to be in good heart. He recommended to the landlords that Jeremy would be suitable to take over the tenancy, even though he lacked experience. It was as though Jeremy was poised to take the helm at the White House in just the same way as his father had, thirty-five years before.)

There were of course rewards for Jeremy's efforts. Nevill gave his adopted son the rent-free use of a small farm cottage in the neighbouring village of Goldhanger, together with a company car. Jeremy's salary was fixed at £8,750. This was supplemented in 1984 by a cash bonus of £1,000 and a further £2,500 by way of his director's fee from Osea Road Caravan Site. Jeremy also enjoyed free petrol, insurance, private medical cover, free telephone and bottled gas to heat his cottage. Some said that his income was insufficient to support his flashy lifestyle, but according to Bamber himself, he had just finished furnishing his cottage at the time of his family's death, and had about £1,000 in his deposit account. On these figures, it is hard to support charges that he was living beyond his means.

His lifestyle at his farm worker's cottage at 9 Head Street, Goldhanger, was almost utilitarian. Even so, he evidently enjoyed his new-found independence there, visiting White House Farm only to pick up fresh clothes or to talk farm business with his father. According to one villager, who knew the Bambers for more than twenty-five years, once installed in his cottage Jeremy seemed much more secure and worked regularly on the farm in a responsible way.

By now he had also found himself another girlfriend. This was Julie Mugford, a student teacher at Goldsmiths' College. She used to spend her holidays at the cottage, much to June Bamber's fury. Yet again, though, there was nothing June could do about it, except tell the girl to her face that she was a 'harlot'.

Jeremy attended a few short courses, but he insists that almost everything he knew about agriculture, he gleaned firsthand from his father. 'Dad was a very good farmer, and I learned everything I could from him. It would have caused arguments if I'd have come from college with a head full of ideas. Farming is very much a feel. It's experience with each field, and luck with the weather. I was happy to be Dad's understudy. It worked really well. We both had progressive ideas about diversifying our crop portfolio. In business, Dad would always listen if I picked up new ideas on these various courses.'

However, his father's secretary, Barbara Wilson, saw things somewhat differently. She observed that Jeremy's views about the day-to-day running of the farm were often totally different from Nevill's. Nevill was essentially a sentimental man who clung to reminders of his past. His desk, indeed the entire office at White House Farm, was bulging with personal mementoes such as theatre programmes, old birthday cards, letters and even bills from Gresham's School. 'A little something to remind him of each phase of his life, something he took great pride in, something to look at when he'd retired.' The result was that the office seemed hopelessly cluttered and disorganized.

Jeremy, on the other hand, seemed baffled by such a haphazard system and made no secret of it. 'He joked about installing a computer and making me redundant,' she recalled. Jeremy had written off for computer sales literature, but his father successfully resisted the change until the day he died. Even so, he was acutely aware of Jeremy's disapproval. 'File that, Barbara,' he used to say, 'but I don't know why. Jeremy will throw it all away when he takes over.'

At this time, the family gave Jeremy specific responsibilities at the caravan site, including looking into the problem of security. His uncle Robert Boutflour said: 'We tried to encourage him to take an interest and he was given various tasks like drafting a new brochure, equipping the shop and investigating security on the camp site because there'd been a number of cases of pilfering during the closed seasons.'

A few days after Christmas 1983, Jeremy attended a directors' meeting at Osea Road and agreed to prepare a questionnaire to send to all the caravan owners about facilities on the site. On 9 February 1984 a chalet was burned to the ground. Police were called and suspected arson. Less than a month later, on Friday 2 March, the shop on the site was burned down and destroyed. Once again, arson was suspected. At a board meeting on 7 March, the directors agreed to build a new shop and to hire a Portakabin while the building was under way. Jeremy was to plan the interior layout of the new shop, and to produce some financial projections. This he did with the help of his friend Michael Deckers, who employed Jeremy as a part-time cocktail barman at evenings and weekends. Jeremy was also given the task of advertising the lease of the shop.

During the winter of 1984–5 Jeremy's cousin Ann Eaton prepared a detailed report on the condition of each of the several hundred plots on the Osea Road site. On two or three occasions, Nevill and Jeremy Bamber went with her to take measurements. Then the site manager Jim Carr was taken ill with jaundice, and was still off sick at the beginning of March 1985 when the site was due to open for the season. It was the custom of many of the caravan owners to call at the office during March to pay their annual site fees, so Ann Eaton and her father Robert Boutflour manned the office for the first two weekends of the month. The money collected was paid straight into the bank. For the third and fourth weekends of March, Nevill and Jeremy Bamber were put in charge. At Jeremy's suggestion, the money paid in was placed in the office safe.

On 22 March, the office was burgled and £1,000 stolen from the safe. When Jim Carr mentioned that Jeremy had been running the office that weekend, Douglas Moule, who worked at the site part-time, immediately commented: 'We know who had that, then!' As for Robert Boutflour, the incident strengthened his suspicions of his adoptive nephew. 'I always suspected Jeremy,' he would subsequently tell the police, 'because of his desire for money . . . and my distrust of Jeremy which I couldn't really explain. It was a feeling I had.'

Robert Boutflour's distrust of Jeremy deepened further a few weeks later, at a meeting of the site shareholders on 2 May. Pamela Boutflour suggested rewarding her daughter Ann for all her hard work at the site during Jim Carr's illness and for drawing up a report on each plot. Jeremy at once angrily objected. Robert Boutflour could see a potentially serious family rift opening up, and a few days later he spoke privately to his nephew with a proposition. Jeremy and his cousin Ann could become joint managing directors of the site with their own separate responsibilities. Jeremy appeared responsive. 'I thought,' Boutflour recalled, 'that by giving them joint directorships, they could run the caravan site together to prevent family squabbles.' The older man also discussed with Jeremy what to do about an income for Sheila and the twins. Her modelling career in decline, she was clearly unable to support herself. Sheila was expected to inherit a field on the site owned exclusively by her mother, but in the meantime she owned no shares of her own. Boutflour hinted that Jeremy might care to consider making over some of his shares to his sister. The suggestion was made with considerable circumspection; Boutflour knew that Jeremy and Sheila did not get on together.

For several months in the spring of 1985, Nevill Bamber's cousin, Chris Nevill, stayed at White House Farm on a visit from New Zealand. The visitor told Robert Boutflour's son David that Jeremy didn't have a very high regard for his father and had an even lower regard for his mother. In fact, he treated her with contempt. David Boutflour recalled an occasion in the late 1970s when Jeremy was blatantly rude to her. 'I can't think of any specific reason as to why Jeremy had this contempt,' Boutflour observed, 'although . . . Aunty June was somewhat weak in matters relating to his discipline. This also applied to a lesser extent in relation to my uncle Nevill . . . this lack of discipline caused Jeremy's lack of respect for them both.'

Jeremy himself pinpoints 1978 as the year which saw the rift develop with his mother. 'Mum and me had a great relationship until I was seventeen,' he declared. 'She was a warm, caring, loving Mum, and I always felt close and secure. What changed when I was seventeen I just don't know.' It was the year in which Jeremy left Gresham's and enrolled at Colchester Tech to cram for A-levels. It was the year that Sheila's short marriage broke up and she filed for divorce.

It was also the year that Betty Bamber, June's widowed mother-in-law, moved out of her big old house in Guildford and into White House Farm. This house was both the Bamber family's greatest asset and its most dangerous bone of contention.

When Betty Bamber died in 1981, Nevill Bamber's inheritance included this massive five-storey pile. Called Clifton House, it was designed by Nevill Bamber's grandfather, the architect Ralph Nevill. Clifton House had a private entrance into Castle Park and overlooked the Castle Gardens and the bowling green. Inside, it had hardly changed for generations. When Betty Bamber died, Nevill had visions of turning the house into retirement flats, but in the end he settled for a straightforward conversion. Nevill seems to have felt an obligation towards his niece and nephew, Jackie Wood and Anthony Pargeter, the children of his late sister, Diana. Accordingly, he transferred half ownership of the Guildford house to them, 25 per cent to Jackie, 25 per cent to Anthony, although under inheritance law, brother and sister would have been entitled only to a 25 per cent share between them.

While the shareout of the house at Guildford seemed a satisfactory arrangement to everyone concerned, the deal actually masked a nagging source of friction within the Bamber family. Major alterations to the house were carried out at a cost of some £100,000, much of which was borrowed from Nevill's bank. The work transformed the cavernous old house into five separate flats. (Nevill Bamber, generous to a fault, loaned Pargeter and Jackie a further £25,000 each to finance their share of the alterations.) When the work was complete, a dispute arose about what to do with the flats. Should they be rented out, leased or sold outright? Nevill Bamber, under pressure from his bank to realize a cash return on his expensive investment, wanted to let two of the flats on short leases, but other members of the family wanted to sell the entire property freehold. In the end, all five flats were sold on 99 year leases; the stables were to be converted into a small flat for the Bamber family to use when they liked. Planning permission was due to be be granted in the summer of 1985.

The financial pressure on Nevill Bamber grew more acute during the early spring of 1985. At the beginning of

March, he was heard to complain bitterly that Jeremy had just announced the purchase of an expensive microwave oven and a sunbed. 'Jeremy must have a very friendly bank manager,' Nevill was heard to mutter, 'because he seems to get bank loans without any trouble.'

Such financial pressure was not, however, so unusual for a man involved in major agricultural deals. What was unusual, though, was that Nevill Bamber became increasingly depressed over the summer of 1985, and behaved quite uncharacteristically on the evening of 6 August.

That evening at about 9.30 p.m., Barbara Wilson, the farm secretary, telephoned Nevill Bamber about her daughter's bicycle, which the twins, Daniel and Nicholas, wanted to borrow. It was a small child's bicycle, with stabilizers. 'Would you like me to pop it down now, Mr Bamber?' she said. She lived less than five minutes from the farm by car.

'No, no, just leave it,' said Nevill Bamber. 'I'll pick it up tomorrow.'

Barbara Wilson thought he sounded angry, as though he'd been having an argument when she called. 'It worried me,' she recalls. 'I knew there was something wrong.' However it was the next day that she connected it with an extraordinary conversation that she had had with him only a few weeks before. It was the week of Nevill's 61st birthday, the first week in June. For nearly a month, Barbara Wilson had wondered why Mr Bamber was looking so ill. 'Normally he looked well set up,' she remembered, 'hale and hearty. But I could tell from the look on his face and in his eyes that he was terribly worried.'

Nevill started to stoop and complained of a bad back. He seemed to sigh a lot, something he never did. 'You bring children into the world, and they seem so ungrateful,' Nevill had remarked to Mrs Wilson. Now, in the farm office on this June morning, he seemed particularly unwell. Nevill sat in his usual chair, but he was uneasy and asked Barbara Wilson if she minded him smoking. (Nevill was a moderate smoker, but never smoked in the office, preferring to suck on his favourite mints instead.)

Barbara Wilson opened the window to let the smoke out. 'Strange you should have a cigarette,' she said.

Nevill turned his chair to look at her. 'I very seldom do,' he murmured, 'but I just need one.'

There was some conversation about children. Nevill remarked about their ingratitude, and complained about how much Sheila and Jeremy were costing. Barbara Wilson, who signed the cheques, was aware of Sheila's bills from the London flat, and knew about Jeremy's attitude to money. He had crashed his car the previous November, writing it off. Nevill had been obliged to replace it. 'Jeremy wanted so much money,' Mrs Wilson recalled. 'He thought his father had endless supplies of money, and that because he was a farmer's son he could have anything he wanted.' The talk turned to money. Suddenly, Nevill Bamber said: 'Barbara, we'll have to find a new hiding place for the key to the safe.'

'It was as though he didn't want Jeremy to know where it was,' said Mrs Wilson. They decided to move it from its usual spot to the box in her desk drawer. Barbara Wilson looked into the careworn face of Mr Bamber. It crossed her mind that he might be concealing some terrible personal anguish. Perhaps he had been told he had cancer, she thought. Sometimes in church she would glance at him and he would seem lost, miles away. Odd inquiries merely drew a vague response about back-ache. Barbara Wilson could sense that he was concealing something darker and more dangerous. At that moment, with June sunlight shafting through the office, Nevill

Bamber fixed Mrs Wilson with a steady gaze and said: 'May I ask you something?'

Barbara Wilson nodded. 'Of course.'

'Will you promise me? If anything were to happen to me, will you promise to look after the farm and make sure that everything carries on as normal? Make sure things don't get messed up, that sort of thing?'

Mrs Wilson was stunned. 'Yes,' she said quietly. 'Of course.'

'Promise me.'

'Promise.'

Seizing the moment, she confronted him. 'What's wrong?' she asked. 'Are you seriously ill?'

Nevill Bamber's voice sank to a whisper. 'No,' he replied, 'but I don't think I've got long.'

'What do you mean? If you're not ill, what's wrong?'

Nevill Bamber drew on his cigarette, swallowed deeply and blew a cloud of smoke above his head. 'There's so much to tell, Barbara,' he murmured. 'But I can't bother you with all that. It's not your burden. But if anything were to happen to me, you will promise me you'll do that?'

'Yes, of course I will.'

'Of course,' he added, 'the shooting season's coming up.' Nevill Bamber just sat and looked at her. Then he said, 'Living on a farm is a dangerous business and one never knows what's going to happen . . .' His voice tailed off and he looked away.

'Do you have a premonition?' asked Barbara Wilson.

'Well, perhaps. But one never knows. I could go out one day shooting and you never know, do you? These things do happen. You can never tell.'

FOUR

No sooner had DC Mick Clark started to take down Jeremy's statement than the telephone rang at the foot of the stairs. Jeremy picked up the receiver and heard the voice of his cousin, Ann Eaton.

'It's Ann here.'

Jeremy must have guessed that Ann had heard the news. He simply said, 'I've got no family left.' He sounded upset.

'Yes you have,' said Ann Eaton. 'I'm coming over.'

'Just a minute. I'll have to ask if that's all right.' Jeremy spoke to Mick Clark. Ann heard him say that his first cousin was on the phone. Jeremy told Ann that she could come over. But he added, 'You don't have to because Julie will be here soon.'

'How long will she be?'

'About ten minutes.'

Still in her farm scruff, Ann Eaton hurriedly packed a jar of coffee, some milk, sugar and biscuits into a bag and took one of the workmen's cars to drive over to Goldhanger. On the way, she reflected on the events of the morning.

The first she had known that something was wrong at White House Farm was at 8 a.m., when Betty Howie, a cousin of June Bamber, had phoned her. Betty Howie explained that she had had a call from Jill Foakes at one of the White House Farm cottages. Something was happening at the farm and whatever it was it was bad. Jill Foakes had counted twenty-four police cars in the lane leading to the farm, and had reported the place swarming with police marksmen and dog handlers. Sheila and the twins had been staying at the farm, Jill Foakes had said. Ann Eaton had then telephoned Jill Foakes herself. Yes, it was all true; Jill had also seen Jeremy sitting in one of the police cars drinking a cup of tea.

Ann's next call had been to her parents at Wix. They had heard nothing, so Ann had telephoned the police at Witham. An officer there explained he could tell her nothing over the phone. With a rising sense of panic, Ann had called Betty Howie back. Betty was now distraught. Some reporters had just called at her house to tell her that there had been a multiple tragedy at White House Farm. Ann had frantically tried to call both the farm and Jeremy's cottage, but both numbers just rang out. At about 8.30, Ann had called her parents again, and related what she'd been told by Betty Howie. Eventually she had managed to get through to Jeremy at Goldhanger.

Ann Eaton arrived at Bourtree Cottage at about 10.10. She hurried up the path at the side of the cottage and met Jeremy emerging from the back door. Ann hugged him, and followed him into the cottage. Stan Jones and Mick Clark introduced themselves as detectives from Essex CID. Clark was taking down a statement. Ann sat down on the sofa and listened as Jeremy told her what had happened: Sheila had shot dead her aunt and uncle and the twins before turning the gun on herself. Ann sat shaking her head in bewilderment.

A second car drew up outside, and someone knocked on the door. It was Jeremy's girlfriend, Julie Mugford, who'd been driven up from London by the police. A good-looking brunette of 20, she joined him in an ashen-faced hug. 'Julie was obviously upset as she embraced with Jeremy,' Ann Eaton remembered. Jeremy, too, appeared upset. He would sob for short periods, as if frightened of his emotions. He sat down alongside Ann, and held her hand. Julie sat down too, and took his other hand to comfort him. The tension was almost unbearable; Ann Eaton kept going to the kitchen to make coffee and tea to try to keep herself busy. Meanwhile Jeremy kept talking to the detectives. As the morning wore on, Ann remembered that on least two occasions Jeremy and Julie went upstairs together, as if they wanted to be alone to comfort each other.

At exactly 11 a.m., Ann Eaton's brother, 37-year-old David Boutflour, turned his car into Pages Lane and nosed up towards White House Farm. He was astonished to find a Radio Orwell outside broadcast vehicle parked near the entrance to the farm drive and as many as a dozen other vans and cars littering the lane. At the gate, Boutflour identified himself to a police officer and told him that he wanted to know what the hell was going on. The constable made a call on his personal radio, then asked Boutflour to park to one side to await a police escort up to the house. It was while David Boutflour was waiting that another car appeared from the far end of Pages Lane and crunched to a halt. The driver wound down his window, and Boutflour recognized Francis Seabrook, who farmed the neighbouring Wycke Farm. Boutflour asked if he knew anything, but Seabrook could say only that what he had heard was too horrific to repeat. Presently the constable walked across from the gate and told Boutflour that the family were meeting at Jeremy's cottage. If he were to drive to Goldhanger, they would be able to tell him what had happened. Boutflour reversed his car and sped off down Pages Lane and on to the Tollesbury Road.

He was in Goldhanger in less than five minutes, running up the path and into the cottage through the kitchen door. Through the open door to the sitting room, he could see Jeremy sitting on the settee, heavy-eyed and upset, talking to a detective. By now Boutflour himself, a no-nonsense farmer, was visibly distressed and highly emotional. Ann stepped forward and drew him to one side to tell him what had happened at the farm. Boutflour had scarcely had time to absorb the news when Jeremy came into the kitchen, put his arms round him and hugged him. Boutflour noted that Bamber's eyes had a distant look about them and remembered thinking this was only natural under the circumstances. Boutflour and Julie were dispatched to the Chequers pub, down the street, to fetch lunch. Robert Boutflour appeared with his wife, Pamela, who'd brought some ham. Julie returned from the pub with David Boutflour carrying a big silver tray of sandwiches covered with a cloth. Jeremy, meantime, had finished his statement and was sitting with Ann Eaton on the sofa. Sandwiches were distributed, and coffee prepared. Jeremy ate in silence. The Boutflours spoke in hushed voices about Sheila. How could she have done such an appalling thing? Why?

The detectives listened as the family tried to piece events together. So did Ann Eaton. But her instinctive sympathy for Jeremy was mixed with a sense of unease. She thought of Sheila, the mentally unstable young woman with no knowledge of guns and the slender but weak and unskilled model-girl fingers. It occurred to Ann that she should make a note of Jeremy's version of events. Later, back at Oak Farm, she scribbled notes about the interview on a piece of card.

Jeremy said he had spent the previous day helping with the harvest. At teatime he had returned to the farmhouse to find the family sitting round the kitchen table. Sheila had just been staring and not saying anything. She'd been told that she wasn't a fit mother, and that the twins were going to be fostered.

At this, Ann Eaton had interrupted: 'That's the first

I've heard of that!' She pressed Jeremy for an explanation.

'We knew that Colin had been after custody of the twins,' Jeremy replied, 'and Mum didn't want that to happen. She wanted them near her so that she could see them regularly.' Sheila, Jeremy went on, had been staying in a private clinic in Northampton. Bills totalling £15,000 had been paid by his parents. This couldn't continue, so it had been decided that Sheila would have to leave and go into a National Health Service hospital. As all this was being discussed, Sheila had just continued to stare and to say nothing.

At some point, Jeremy had spotted some rabbits behind the barn and had seized the gun and some ammunition, pausing in the kitchen to load the magazine with bullets. Sheila may have seen him doing this, Jeremy told the detectives, but he hadn't been aware of her showing any interest in what he was doing. She just kept staring. Jeremy described inserting the loaded magazine into the Anschutz .22 rifle. He had done this near the pine settle opposite the downstairs office or den. When he returned, having failed to find any rabbits, the conversation round the table was continuing. Jeremy said he'd left the gun by the settle but was unsure whether or not he'd removed the magazine.

Later, as she picked over Jeremy's story, several things struck Ann Eaton as curious. Why had Jeremy loaded the magazine in the kitchen, where Sheila could see what he was doing, when the actual rifle was propped against the settle near the den? As for the rabbit-shooting episode, Jeremy's answers to questions from the detectives had been strangely vague. He'd seemed unsure about whether or not he had fired the rifle, and – if he had – how many bullets he had used. But most incongruous were Jeremy's protestations about his father. He was telling the police that he and Nevill Bamber had got on well; Ann Eaton knew that this was untrue, mainly because of Jeremy's pursuit of an extravagant lifestyle.

Then there was the business of the phone call in the middle of the night. Jeremy's story was that his father had telephoned to say that Sheila had gone crazy and had got the gun. Then the line had gone dead. Ann Eaton felt that what Jeremy was saying didn't make sense. If Jeremy was still listening when the line went dead, somebody must have broken the connection at White House Farm because otherwise Jeremy would have still been able to hear noises even if Nevill Bamber had dropped the phone. Ann Eaton was struck by Jeremy's apparent nonchalance as he related all this, and thought he was enjoying the experience; later her brother, David Boutflour, said he thought Jeremy had been acting.

Ann also couldn't understand why, in the light of his father's alleged phone call, Jeremy hadn't immediately dialled 999. Jeremy's explanation was that he was uncertain about how urgent matters had become. Why had he rung Julie and not gone straight to White House Farm? Jeremy explained that he'd been frightened that the call might have been a trick by Sheila to lure him to the farm where he too would have been shot. How had Jeremy managed to arrive at the farm after the police car, when he had only a mile or so to travel, and when he was known to be a fast driver at the wheel of a powerful car?

Colin Caffell and his girlfriend Heather Amos arrived from London. Heather was in tears, and Ann Eaton had to comfort her in the kitchen. Colin, too, was very distressed. He kept saying he was unhappy about having left the twins with Sheila at White House Farm the previous Sunday. Apparently, Colin had driven Sheila and the boys up from London, and Sheila hadn't spoken a single word in the course of the journey. At Colin's party the night before, Sheila had been acting very strangely.

The detectives continued to piece together Jeremy's statement. As the interview progressed, the detectives were rehearsing their own theory about the events at White House Farm, telling Jeremy and the listening relatives that they thought Sheila must have had a brainstorm after being told that she wasn't a fit mother and that the twins were to be fostered. They surmised that, having seen Jeremy load the rifle to shoot rabbits the night before, Sheila had seized the opportunity to kill her parents. She had shot the twins so that no one else could take them from her.

Ann Eaton didn't like what she heard. There were too many inconsistencies, too much that was unlikely or simply untrue. The .22 rifle, for example. How had Sheila known how to load and shoot it? According to Jeremy, she had been out shooting rabbits with Nevill Bamber and Nevill's nephew, Anthony Pargeter. Ann Eaton's view, later volunteered to the detectives, was that Sheila didn't know one end of a gun from the other. She asked Jeremy bluntly if he had shown Sheila how to use the gun. Jeremy said he had not.

David Boutflour was also sceptical. Like his sister, he had heard numerous snatches of conversation as Jeremy told his story to the detectives making notes on the settee. Several aspects of the story struck Boutflour as odd. He heard Bamber explaining that he had removed the silencer and the telescopic sight from the Anschutz rifle before the rabbit-shooting episode. He had done so, he said, so that the rifle would fit into the gun cupboard in the den. Boutflour understood that the rifle with a silencer fitted might indeed be too long to fit into such a cupboard. But this didn't explain the removal of the telescopic sight. 'At this moment,' he stated later, 'I thought it odd that he'd taken the telescopic sight off, knowing how long it takes to set it up again. In any case I'd have thought that Jeremy would have used the sight for accuracy when out shooting rabbits.' Moreover, the sight wouldn't have affected the length of the gun, the critical dimension in the would-it-fit debate regarding the gun cupboard.

David Boutflour tackled Jeremy. He asked him about the state of the rifle when he left it in the kitchen after the unsuccessful rabbit shoot. Jeremy said he'd left the magazine in the gun, but that he hadn't left a bullet in the breech. 'Do you mean that you left the loaded magazine in the gun but not a loaded bullet in the breech?' 'Yes,' replied Bamber. 'At that moment,' Boutflour reflected, 'I thought how extremely careless that was, in view of the potential danger that could cause. In hindsight I fail to see how a bullet could not have been in the breech if (as Jeremy had said) he had fired some shots at rabbits, unless he'd removed the magazine and separately removed the bullet that would have been in the breech. In that case, the magazine would not have been left in the gun.'

The afternoon became a kaleidoscopic swirl of movement and conversation. From Colin Caffell, talk of Sheila's Iranian boyfriend Freddie Emami and some supposed link with cocaine; Colin's girlfriend Heather, sitting on the sofa, shocked and seemingly spaced-out; Crispy, June Bamber's shih-tzu dog, somehow, despite Jeremy's antipathy, scampering under the feet of the detectives; a call to the builders to fit a new back door at the farm to replace the one sledgehammered by the police; a discussion about security at the farm and the state of the rooms. Stan Jones and Mick Clark explained there was bloodstaining and general disorder, especially in the kitchen. Jeremy, now head of the household, ordered the destruction of the bloodied carpets and curtains and wrote out an authorization in capital letters on a piece of paper. This was handed to Stan Jones, who said that alarms would be fitted at the farm in case of burglars. At about seven o'clock, Ann Eaton and David Boutflour left the cottage and walked up the street to break the news to Ann's great-aunt Connie Lugg who lived nearby. Mick Clark sat with Jeremy and Julie in the living room while Jones took a statement in the kitchen from Colin Caffell, detailing Sheila's psychiatric history. Caffell told the detective that in his view, there was no way that Sheila would have murdered her own children.

Stan Jones's dilemma was that while he inclined to the view that Jeremy might have been the killer, his instructions were to assume Sheila's guilt and to persuade Colin Caffell to accept the official police view. 'I had to convince Caffell that it was four murders and a suicide,' Stan Jones recalled, 'despite my own personal feelings. Basically, I lied to him about how I really felt.' Colin shook his head. No way could it have been Sheila, he repeated. Caffell and Heather Amos left the cottage shortly before eight, leaving Jeremy and Julie with only the two detectives for company.

'Come on then, Jeremy,' Stan Jones suggested, 'get the bottle out.' The suggestion was characteristic. It was Jones's way of lowering the emotional temperature. Jeremy found some whisky and poured the drinks. 'It was quite an amicable gathering,' Jones recalled. 'No formality, everyone on first-name terms, as though we were part of the family.' Jeremy managed a joke about the detectives drinking and driving. They each swallowed two whiskies. 'I treated him like a newly bereaved individual,' said Jones. 'No way was I coming the heavy copper. It was a PR job. Chat, laugh, joke, trying to lighten things up. In fact, Jeremy was already cheerful enough.'

Jones steered the conversation away from the events of

the day and towards general chit-chat. 'But in my mind, something wasn't right. I kept thinking about the hearty breakfast, his general demeanour, and the feelings of the family that Sheila just couldn't have done it.'

At 8.30 p.m., Jones and Clark said goodnight and left Jeremy and Julie alone at the cottage. At the wheel of his Citroën Dyane, Stan Jones was reluctant to share his early suspicions with Mick Clark. Instead the two men pondered the significance of the debriefing that had been arranged at Witham Police Station for 9 p.m. Detectives were seldom formally debriefed in cases of suicide. Jones and Clark thought the meeting might have been called because so many had died and because the Tactical Firearms people had been involved.

A sizeable crowd of police officers, some uniformed, others not, gathered in the snooker room at Witham. DCI Taff Jones took the chair and announced that in his opinion, the events at White House Farm amounted to a tragic case of four murders and a suicide. Stan Jones glanced round the room, and wondered how many of the others were thinking what he was thinking. The debriefing broke up after half an hour. Meanwhile, less than five miles away at Oak Farm, her home at Little Totham, Ann Eaton was discussing the murders with her father, Robert Boutflour, and her husband, Peter. The farmhouse lights burned late into the night. 'To put it bluntly,' she reported, '[we] were not satisfied with what Jeremy Bamber was telling the police.'

FIVE

ONE of the things that struck Ann Eaton when she visited Jeremy at lunchtime the following day was that he had bought copies of every national newspaper. They lay scattered and open on the living-room floor. The White House Farm massacre was front-page news. The popular tabloids splashed the story: MODEL MURDERS 4 OF HER FAMILY was a typical headline from the *Daily Mail*; FAMILY OF 5 KILLED BY 'SUICIDE MOTHER', reported the *Daily Telegraph*, one of several papers to note that the Bambers were known locally as 'the Archers of D'Arcy' because they resembled the fictional family in the radio soap opera. While the tabloids focused on the 'glittering, glamorous' modelling career that had eluded Sheila, the broadsheets angled their reports on the impact of the massacre on the local farming community. Many of the villagers were in tears, *The Times* reported.

The two CID officers, Stan Jones and Mick Clark, drove over to Goldhanger from White House Farm where they had checked on the progress of the forensic investigation. Arriving at Jeremy's cottage, they found him chatting to Julie and Ann Eaton. Jones noted that Jeremy seemed happy; Ann, too, was struck by his composure. He seemed neither emotional nor distressed. Julie also seemed to be taking events in her stride. The officers mentioned the question of formally identifying the bodies of Jeremy's family. Jeremy refused point-blank. Then, to their amazement, Julie said, 'I'll do it.'

Stan Jones could scarcely contain his surprise. 'Are you sure?' he asked.

'Oh yes,' Julie replied, 'I'll do it.'

No sooner had Julie made her offer than Jeremy announced that he, too, would be out for the afternoon. He was going to Colchester, he declared, to see his solicitor, his accountant and his bank manager. Stan Jones thought this was also odd, and asked Jeremy why he wanted to attend to such matters only a day after the murder of his family. Jeremy explained that his family's finances needed urgent and detailed attention. In the meantime, he was hungry. Ann disappeared into the kitchen to prepare a lunch of toasted sandwiches. Stan Jones telephoned the mortuary in Chelmsford and told them to expect Julie Mugford that afternoon to identify the bodies. At 1.30 the detectives excused themselves and walked down the road for lunch at the Chequers pub.

When the detectives had left, Ann Eaton asked Jeremy about newspaper reports that Sheila had been taking drugs. 'I shouldn't tell you this,' he replied, 'but she was on the hard stuff. That's what she was being treated for.' Ann Eaton was shocked and surprised. She had never noticed any needle marks on Sheila's arms. Jeremy smiled. 'There are much more sophisticated ways of doing it these days. Anyway, they'll soon be able to tell if she was on drugs when they cut into the body's fatty tissue and have it analysed.' Jeremy checked his watch and said he would have to go in order to keep his appointment in Colchester with the family solicitors. The Bambers' accountant, Basil Cock, would also be there. Ann asked if he felt up to going on his own, and offered to go with him, but Jeremy said he was all right and would go alone.

In the low-beamed lounge of the Chequers, a crowd of reporters put down their drinks and swarmed around the CID men, hungry for news. Stan Jones, normally at ease

72

with the press, was in no mood to talk and waved them away. 'Do us a favour,' he snapped, 'we're just trying to get something to eat.' Jones and Clark ordered their food, and took their drinks over to a corner table. The reporters huddled moodily at the bar, throwing the police officers the occasional glance. Stan Jones lit a roll-up, took a slug of Scotch and lemonade, and said, 'Mick, there are too many things not right.'

Mick Clark said, 'I agree.'

The two men reviewed the events of the morning. There was Julie's unsolicited offer to identify the bodies, a task she must have known would be traumatic and upsetting. Stan Jones shook his head. 'That shook me rigid,' he said. Neither detective gave her credit for trying to shield Jeremy from the trauma. Then there was Jeremy and his trip to Colchester to talk money. Such a visit didn't square with Jeremy having just lost all his family, Jones thought. That would surely be the last thing on his mind. Mick Clark agreed. 'I know we all act different,' Stan Jones said, 'but this just doesn't seem real. It doesn't ring true.'

Their sandwiches arrived, and the two men munched in silence for a moment. Then Stan Jones spoke.

'Right,' he said, 'this is where I start talking.'

Jones reminded Clark of the two phone calls Jeremy claimed to have made in the middle of the murder night, one to Julie Mugford and the other to the police at Chelmsford. Stan Jones believed that the order in which those calls were made might be crucial. 'If we could show he'd phoned Julie first,' he explained, 'it would point to Bamber's guilt.' An innocent Bamber, he reasoned, would have called the police without delay, almost certainly dialling 999. In fact, Bamber had telephoned Chelmsford police headquarters, having looked up the number in the telephone directory.

Stan Jones looked at Mick Clark over his glass. 'I'm going to have a go at Julie,' he said.

When they reached the cottage, the detectives saw that Ann Eaton's car was still parked outside. Stan Jones decided to risk taking her into his confidence, knowing that she was not convinced that Sheila was the killer. In the cottage, he drew her aside and explained that he was going to tackle Julie in a subtle way about her story. He would pretend that it was no more than a routine chat, that he needed clarification about the exact times of the two telephone calls for the coroner's report. The whole approach would be as casual as possible. Ann nodded. The CID men ambled into the living room where Julie was sitting on the sofa, smoking a cigarette. After some general pleasantries, Stan Jones sat down and asked her to fix the time that Jeremy had phoned her in the middle of the night.

'About 3 a.m.,' said Julie.

'I need it more accurate than that,' Stan Jones said.

Julie thought for a moment. 'I'm not sure myself,' she said, 'but I may be able to find out.'

She picked up the telephone at the foot of the stairs and dialled the digs in Lewisham, South London, where she lived. Jones heard Julie talking to one of her flatmates, and presently she returned to the living room saying that the call from Jeremy had come at around 3.30 a.m. This didn't square with Jones's theory. For if the call to Julie had gone through at 3.30 a.m., it would have been made after Jeremy's call to the police, which had been logged at 3.26 a.m. But Jones realized that the 3.30 'fix' on the call to Lewisham might not have been absolutely accurate. People are naturally vague about exact times in the middle of the night. So he made a note to double-check with Julie's three other flatmates, some of whom might have been woken by the sound of the ringing telephone.

In the meantime, Sergeant Jones had a more pressing problem. A knock on the cottage door announced the arrival of Jeremy's cousin, a short, spare, bespectacled man in his late thirties, Anthony Pargeter. Pargeter had driven over from his home in Buckinghamshire after telephoning Taff Jones at Chelmsford that morning to challenge the police assumption about Sheila. Taff Jones, resenting what he considered to be unwarranted interference from yet another member of the Bamber clan, had told Pargeter to mind his own business. Pargeter, however, had insisted on driving over to Essex. Stan Jones had received a call at Bourtree Cottage from police headquarters, warning him about Pargeter's arrival. Taff Jones had added an instruction: placate Pargeter and keep him happy.

Apart from his misgivings over Sheila's guilt, Anthony Pargeter had another reason to be worried. He remembered that when he had last visited White House Farm a couple of weeks earlier, he had seen a brand-new Anschutz .22 with telescopic sights and silencer attached in a cupboard in Nevill Bamber's den. Pargeter knew all about such weapons: he had owned a similar rifle since 1980 and had shot in competitions at Bisley. In fact, Pargeter kept his own Anschutz at White House Farm, always removing the bolt and taking it home so that no one else could fire it. Pargeter's .22 was normally kept in its case and lying on a bench in the ground-floor shower room at White House Farm. His two 12-bore shotguns were also stored there. But when he had arrived at the farm on Friday, 26 July, to visit the Bambers with his wife and two children, the Anschutz was missing.

It was Pargeter's aunt, June Bamber, who had suggested that the weapon might be in the gun cupboard in the den. And so it was, lying on the floor of the cupboard inside its case. But it was a second, gleaming Anschutz .22 that caught Pargeter's eye, standing complete with telescopic sight and silencer fitted to the muzzle, its butt resting on the cupboard floor. A 12-bore shotgun stood alongside. Pargeter took the .22 from the cupboard and admired its sleek lines. It was, he told police later, in pristine condition and unmarked. Pargeter paid particular attention to the fitted Parker-Hale silencer and scope. He had recently bought an identical sight for his own Anschutz, and was going to fit it that very afternoon.

Anthony Pargeter replaced the weapon as he had found it, picked up his own rifle and case, laid the case on the floor of the den and drew out the rifle. He was still fitting the sight when Nevill and Jeremy Bamber appeared at the door of the den. Jeremy asked if Anthony had seen the new rifle; Pargeter said he had, and remarked on its quality, saying he thought it was a very good one. Jeremy proudly reached for the rifle, announcing that he was off to shoot vermin in one of the fields, and inviting Pargeter to come along. But Pargeter explained he wanted to finish fitting the new sight to his own Anschutz before trying it out. It would need to be zeroed in. Jeremy and Nevill Bamber left with their new rifle, saying they would join him later.

Pargeter finished the fitting, took some ammunition from the desk in the den, slung the rifle on to his shoulder and strode out across the yard to a spot behind the barns. To zero the weapon in, he set up a piece of wood on the side of one of the haystacks, then fired a single shot and used that as the bullseye for subsequent shots. For an hour or so, the farmyard resounded to the crack of Pargeter's rifle as he fired at least four or five magazines – each containing ten bullets – into the makeshift target. But he was not satisfied with the way his rifle was performing. It appeared to be firing slightly low and to the right.

He was just finishing off when Jeremy appeared and asked how he was getting on. Pargeter told him what he thought of his rifle's performance. 'You try it and see what you think,' he said. Jeremy Bamber took the rifle, inserted a full magazine, and fired all ten bullets into the wooden target from a distance of about twenty-five yards. After inspecting the results, Jeremy called out that he thought the rifle was firing correctly. From where Pargeter was watching, he couldn't see how accurate Jeremy's shots had been. Jeremy handed the rifle back and disappeared into the house. Anthony Pargeter didn't see the new Anschutz again over that weekend, but remembered that it 'easily' fitted in his uncle's gun cupboard with both the sight and silencer attached.

While the two detectives listened to Pargeter's story, Julie sat quiet and nervous, smoking cigarettes. Stan Jones was in no doubt that Pargeter was implying Jeremy's guilt. Now it was Jones's turn to use the telephone. Excusing himself, and quietly closing the living-room door behind him, Jones telephoned the mortuary at Chelmsford and told Detective Inspector Bob Miller that he wasn't convinced that Sheila was responsible. On the contrary, he felt that Jeremy was the murderer. Keeping his voice to scarcely more than a whisper, knowing that Julie and members of the Bamber family were sitting in the next room, he told Miller that he didn't think things were what they seemed. There was silence at the other end of the line, then a gasp.

'Right,' Miller said, 'there's a meeting at the farm at half-past four. I'll see you there.'

A police car arrived to take Julie Mugford to the mortuary at Chelmsford. Ann Eaton went too, and waited for Julie outside the mortuary in the back of the police car. Mick Clark took Julie inside. Surveying the five bodies one by one, she showed no sign of nervousness or emotion. She merely asked why the heads had been shaved. Apart from asking to smoke on the way back to Goldhanger, Julie betrayed no sign of having found the trip an ordeal.

Anthony Pargeter was still at the cottage when Mick Clark dropped Ann and Julie off. A kettle was boiling when Jeremy returned from Colchester. 'He seemed very pleased,' Ann recalled, 'and was smiling. Jeremy told Anthony and I that his father had far more interests than he'd been aware of. Jeremy then started to quote huge figures of what various properties and assets were worth. He also outlined details of his mother's interests in Osea Road Caravan Site and said he knew exactly how much money he'd need to pay death duties in connection with it.' Jeremy kept stressing how important it was to retain all his mother's interests in Osea Road.

Jeremy Bamber went on to say that he'd been notified at the meeting to the effect that he would have to quit White House Farm. Meanwhile, he announced, both Anthony Pargeter and Ann Eaton were beneficiaries in his parents' wills, to the extent of £1,000 and £500 respectively.

Ann Eaton could scarcely believe what she was hearing. Whatever her expectations from the Bambers' estate, she found it hard to comprehend Jeremy's callous indifference to his family's fate. 'Jeremy showed no distress about the previous day's events, or any remorse about leaving the gun by the settle,' she remarked later. Then there were the funerals. Basil Cock would make the arrangements, Jeremy declared, adding that since the bodies 'weren't whole', he wanted his family cremated. 'He insisted he wouldn't have them buried unless they were whole,' said Ann. 'I was shocked because I didn't know what he meant. But he had apparently not seen the bodies at all and couldn't have known what condition they were in.'

Jeremy also announced that his parents' and Sheila's funerals would be held at Tolleshunt D'Arcy while those of the twins would be in London.

At White House Farm, detectives on the case were gathering for a case conference. They sat, rather self-consciously, around the highly polished table in the main dining room. Joining Stan Jones, Mick Clark and Bob Miller were various scenes-of-crime people and the most important man in the room, Home Office pathologist Dr Peter Vanezis. He had conducted the post-mortem examinations on the murdered family. A couple of his students sat attentively at his side, shuffling pieces of paper. One or two detectives glanced at their watches; the meeting had been called by Taff Jones but it was already after 4.30 and there was still no sign of him. Bob Miller took the chair and called for quiet. Everyone sat down. Throats were cleared, cigarettes lit. But before Miller could say any more, Stan Jones weighed in. 'Before we start,' he said, 'I want to say something. I think Jeremy Bamber might have done it.'

Everyone in the room stared hard at Stan Jones. He knew, he said that his was a one-off view, but he had very good reasons for expressing it. What was more, none of the Bamber relations believed Sheila was capable of doing such a thing.

At that moment the dining-room door opened and Taff Jones came in. As he listened to Stan Jones's reasons for suspecting Jeremy Bamber, the detective chief inspector's face grew redder and redder. Everyone in the room sat stock-still and completely silent. Undeterred, Stan Jones pressed on. 'I'd rather say it now, not leave it until another day when it might be too late,' he said. 'Remember this is only day two. You can resurrect a lot of things in one day. Leave it, and you can lose a lot of evidence.'

Stan Jones had said his piece. Taff Jones made his way to a chair and sat down. The sergeant could see from his face, still flushed, that the chief inspector was not persuaded. Indeed, Taff Jones briskly pooh-poohed the theory. It was definitely four murders and a suicide, he insisted. As for Stan Jones, the senior man made it clear that he thought he was completely out of order.

Dr Vanezis reported on the causes of death: in each case, shots to the head, some fired at almost point-blank range. In Sheila's case, the fatal shot had been fired with the weapon apparently pressed beneath her chin. There were traces around the wound that suggested contact. But what struck Stan Jones as he listened to the pathologist's report was the fact that Sheila had been shot not once but twice. At first he thought he had misheard or misunderstood. Then he thought it was a wind-up. You've got to be joking, he thought. Once again he chimed in, telling Taff Jones and Vanezis that two shots to Sheila's brain just didn't make sense. Vanezis began to speak, but the detective chief inspector interrupted him, glaring across at Stan Jones. During the war, he pointed out, people were shot in the head and despite their wound they managed to go further forward before they dropped, in some cases several hundred yards. It was, Taff Jones hissed, a well-known phenomenon.

Stan Jones asked Dr Vanezis about the exact site of the first bullet wound. The pathologist said the first shot had been through the chin and up into the jaw.

'Would that have left her conscious?' asked Stan Jones.

Vanezis was non-committal. 'Not necessarily,' he replied.

Jones was incredulous. It flashed through his mind that detectives tell pathologists too much. They should be told nothing. The police should tell the pathologist to tell *them* what happened. Stan Jones was at a loss to understand how Sheila could have shot herself twice, when the first shot had clearly done so much damage. He blurted out a memory of his own, of the day he'd had excruciating toothache and had staggered into the dentist's surgery in agony, only to be told that the trouble had been caused by one little tooth. Yet half of Sheila's jaw had been shot away. How, Stan Jones asked, could she have possibly shot herself twice?

Later, talking to Mick Clark out in the farmyard, Stan Jones was assailed by an angry Taff Jones. 'Fancy!' he shouted. 'Fancy being influenced by the family!'

Stan Jones raised a quizzical eyebrow. 'Well, better to think these things now, rather than later.'

The chief inspector looked at Mick Clark, then at Stan Jones. 'You're wrong on this one, boy,' he said. 'Just get on with those background statements for the coroner and leave it at that.' Taff Jones turned and stalked off. Stan Jones shot an inquiring glance at Mick Clark. 'Do you think I'm wrong, Mick?'

'No,' said Clark, quietly. 'I don't.'

Bob Miller ambled over. Stan Jones could tell that Miller was undecided. It was typical of Bob, he thought. Although Miller was the senior of the two, it was always him asking Stan Jones for advice, never the other way round. But now Bob Miller had a piece of advice for Stan Jones: 'You've got to go along with what the Guv'nor says. You never know,' he added. 'It might all just go away.'

Later, at Witham Police Station, the team gathered to discuss the position. Stan Jones again pointed out that the person to gain most from the deaths of the Bambers was Jeremy Bamber. But PC Norman Wright, the coroner's officer who'd spent most of the day at the mortuary, said the scene suggested that Sheila was the killer. There was evidence, he said, to show that she was mentally unstable. Furthermore, Dr Vanezis had commented that Sheila had been menstruating, a fact that could have increased the young woman's instability. The meeting broke up inconclusively, but with a vague thought that everyone on the inquiry should take care in case someone else had in fact been responsible.

As he drove home late that evening, Stan Jones was boiling with inner rage. He had convinced himself beyond a shadow of a doubt that Jeremy Bamber had slaughtered five members of his family, and he had managed to persuade Mick Clark to agree. But they were on their own. Taff Jones was beyond the reach of reason. If only Chief Superintendent George Harris hadn't turned up at the house and swallowed Jeremy's story, Taff would have tumbled to him right away. But Taff now saw only what Jeremy wanted him to see, a classic case of tunnel vision. Stan Jones had said his piece, and in return he'd received a public slagging-off. At home, Stan Jones threw off his jacket and poured himself an extra large slug of his favourite Scotch. It had been a diabolical day. And whatever Bob Miller thought, the one certainty was that it wouldn't all just go away.

SIX

ANN EATON left Bourtree Cottage that evening with Anthony Pargeter, and drove over to Oak Farm where she once again made notes of the day's events on a piece of card. When her brother David arrived, the three discussed their suspicions with Ann Eaton's husband Peter. During the day, David had spoken to Jeremy about the fight his father must have put up in the kitchen; Jeremy had remarked about getting two small cuts on his right hand while doing some work on the farm. He had stretched out his palm, but David was too far away to see any marks. He compared his suspicions with those of his sister and her husband. After talking matters over for some hours, they decided to contact the police next morning to alert them to their concern.

First thing on Friday, 9 August, Ann Eaton telephoned Witham Police Station and made an appointment to see a senior detective on the case. She was told to come at once. At 10.15 a.m., Ann – along with her brother David and Anthony Pargeter – confronted Detective Chief Inspector Taff Jones at Essex Police headquarters in Chelmsford. Ann Eaton had prepared a list of questions, but when she started to make notes she was told sharply not to. The chief inspector had with him his detective sergeant, Stan Jones. But it was the senior officer who did the talking. He told the relatives that the rifle was found on Sheila's body without its silencer, and that a total of twenty-five rounds had been fired in the course of the massacre. The magazine attached to the murder weapon held ten rounds. Ann Eaton, realizing that the killer would have had to reload the magazine at least twice, told the detectives that there was no possibility that Sheila could have loaded the magazine herself. Sheila, Ann repeated, had absolutely no knowledge of guns. Asked if three loaded magazines might have been prepared in advance, the officers said there had been only one magazine, the one found fitted to the murder rifle.

The family were at pains to point out some worrying discrepancies to the listening detectives. One concerned Jeremy's statement to the police on the morning of the killings that the rifle wouldn't fit into the gun cupboard in the den if the silencer and telescopic sight were attached. This, the relatives claimed, was untrue. Anthony Pargeter insisted to the officers that the rifle could be stored in the cupboard with the attachments fitted.

The meeting became fractious and broke up in some disarray, with Taff Jones continuing to insist that he was conducting an investigation into four murders and the suicide of Sheila Caffell. Stan Jones, still smarting from the drubbing he'd received at the farm, shepherded the relatives out of the office and into a corridor. As he did so, he muttered apologetically to Ann Eaton about Taff Jones being a good detective, but an arrogant one. Ann looked at him, pained and despairing. The detective sergeant half-smiled, as if to reassure her. 'One of these days,' he said, 'I'll tell you something. But I can't tell you now.'

Pargeter drove Ann Eaton out to Goldhanger, and found Jeremy at home in Bourtree Cottage with Julie Mugford and Nevill Bamber's cousin, Chris Nevill, a tall, rugged-looking New Zealander in his mid-fifties. Chris Nevill was on an extended visit to Britain, and had stayed at White House Farm in the spring.

A fresh batch of that morning's newspapers were lying open in the sitting room. Ann and Jeremy embraced. He started to cry, great, heaving sobs. He asked to see a doctor, and Julie telephoned to Tollesbury. Ann recalled that she had never seen Jeremy so upset and emotional. Presently a doctor arrived and gave Jeremy a sedative.

After lunch, Chris Nevill took charge of the cottage. Ann returned to Oak Farm, while Jeremy drove with Julie to Colchester. Jeremy had fixed a meeting with Peter Eaton and the accountant, Basil Cock, to discuss the question of who would run the farm in future.

Jeremy had already discussed with Peter Eaton the possibility of Peter taking over White House Farm as manager, and had accepted Peter's offer to help get the harvest in. The two had talked briefly that morning about what to do for the best, but people kept arriving at the cottage and the telephone never seemed to stop ringing. Now, in the cloistered calm of the accountant's office, Jeremy talked expansively of what he might and might not do. Peter Eaton listened apprehensively. According to Jeremy, the feoffees, the group of trustees who administered the farm, had already issued him with a notice to quit. Peter Eaton thought this sounded highly unlikely. He also realized that, whatever happened, Jeremy needed to get back to working on the farm. Jeremy offered Peter Eaton the job of farm manager there and then. Eaton accepted. Jeremy added that the job would only be for a year as he was determined to accept the £80,000 that he'd been offered to quit. Peter Eaton was shocked, and pointed out that the feoffees would never just pay money out like that. Jeremy ignored him. Moreover, Jeremy added, the combine harvester was going back. So was the brand-new tractor, which he thought would fetch at least £20,000.

Jeremy then announced that he was going off to pick up Julie. Alone with Basil Cock, Peter Eaton impressed on him the urgency of getting Jeremy back working at the farm. The accountant nodded agreement. Jeremy, he said, seemed to be taking it all very well. Cock was sure that after a few days Jeremy would be back at the farm. In the meantime, it was agreed that Peter Eaton should step in and run it.

'Right,' Eaton said, rising to leave. 'Half-past seven, Monday morning. And I expect Jeremy to be there too.'

Later that afternoon Ann Eaton returned to Goldhanger. Jeremy, back from Colchester, announced he was going away for the weekend. He was sick of the reporters who had been asking questions in the village. He asked Ann to arrange for a security firm to guard White House Farm on Saturday and Sunday nights. Jeremy also confided that he planned to instruct Sotheby's, the London auction house, to value the contents of White House Farm and to store them prior to selling them off. 'I won't go into that house now or ever again,' Jeremy told her. Jeremy said he kept seeing the faces of his murdered family.

At Witham CID office, detectives on the Bamber case were hailing Stan Jones as something of a hero. Word of his one-man stand at the case conference had filtered back, along with details of his confrontation with Taff Jones. But Stan Jones realized that a murder inquiry was no place for heroics; he knew he was out of favour with 'the Guv'nor', and that he could expect to be treated no better than a pariah until Taff Jones's temper cooled. The meeting with the family that morning had been fraught and unpleasant. Certainly, the chief inspector had made no move to patch up his relationship with his detective sergeant. The two men spent the day in a state of armed truce. But then, in the middle of the afternoon, Stan Jones's telephone rang at Witham. It was Taff. 'Be ready in half an hour,' he barked. 'We're going to see Bamber.'

Taff Jones drove. Stan Jones sat glumly in the passenger seat as the car wove its way along the country roads towards Goldhanger. The point of going to see Bamber, Taff explained, was to show Stan Jones that Jeremy had nothing whatsoever to do with the killings. 'I'll show you that you're wrong,' he growled, 'and I'll show you that the family's wrong too. We're going to see Bamber and we're going to get this sorted out one way or another.'

When they arrived at Head Street, the two detectives found Jeremy with Julie, his cousin Ann Eaton and his father's cousin, the New Zealander Chris Nevill. The officers asked Jeremy if he felt well enough to be interviewed again. Jeremy said he'd been sedated by the doctor, who'd prescribed some Valium. He explained that if he 'drifted away' in the course of the interview, it would be the effect of the drugs. But he seemed normal enough, 'quite chatty' in the opinion of Stan Jones. The officers questioned him again about his previous statement, and about how he'd left the rifle and the ammunition on the murder night.

Then Jeremy said, 'Can you guys tell which order they were killed in?'

'What did you ask that for, Jeremy?' Stan Jones asked.

Bamber explained that it affected the various wills.

At this point Ann Eaton asked what would happen to June Bamber's engagement ring: Ann explained to Jeremy that her mother wished to have something belonging to her murdered sister. Jeremy insisted that nothing was to be removed from the farm because 'it's my shrine'. He added that he wanted his mother's engagement ring to be buried with her.

The detectives drew Ann Eaton to one side and told her that the farm was nearly ready to be reoccupied; Jeremy had told them that he wouldn't go back into the house, so the keys would be handed over to her as his closest surviving relative. Taff Jones promised to ring her at home that evening when they were in a position to hand over the keys.

On the drive back to Witham, Taff asked Stan Jones if he felt any happier about Jeremy as a result of the interview. Stan Jones lied and said he felt a little easier. But what about the question of who died first? Wasn't that a strange thing to ask?

Taff Jones disagreed. 'It's quite common for people to ask that,' he said.

'I suppose so,' said Stan Jones, 'but I still think it's strange.'

At about 8 p.m., just as the light was fading, the two detectives returned to White House Farm to hand over the keys to Ann Eaton and her husband Peter. Jones unlocked the back kitchen door and led the way inside. There was still enough evening glow in the sky for the four of them to pick their way through the kitchen without switching on the lights. The Eatons had been warned to expect things out of place in view of the struggle that had taken place there, and Ann noticed that the kitchen table had been moved. So had Nevill Bamber's customary chair. The coal scuttle that used to stand beside the Aga was missing. From the kitchen, they moved into the passage and up the two steps towards the hall. Ann Eaton noticed that the cellar door on the left had been forced: Stan Jones admitted that the damage would have been caused by the police during the search of the house.

They turned right into the lounge. Stan Jones told the Eatons that nothing had happened in this room on the murder night. Ann Eaton surveyed the familiar scene. On the hearth rug lay a child's game. Some drinks mats had fallen out of their basket on one of the small tables and lay scattered on the carpet. On a little coffee table next to the settee she saw a child's toy gun, about five inches long and coloured silver. But what particularly attracted her attention was the cardboard tube that had been left lying beside it. It was a tampon tube, with the cotton loop and some of the cotton tampon itself missing. Ann Eaton wondered why half a tampon should have been left lying in the lounge.

Across the hall in the dining room, coloured crayons and childish drawings on large sheets of paper still lay on the big dining table where the twins, Daniel and Nicholas, had left them.

The Eatons and the police officers walked silently up the stairs on to the front landing and turned right into Nevill and June Bamber's bedroom. Ann was surprised to find that more than half the carpet had been taken up: the detectives explained that the carpet had been heavily bloodstained on both sides of the bed where Sheila and June had been found.

Across the landing, in the room used by Sheila, a large black suitcase stood at the foot of one of the two single beds. On the other bed, Ann noticed several wrapped tampons protruding from a sponge bag. 'I could see they were in a box which had been open,' she stated later. 'I assumed that Sheila was having a period and that the used Tampax container in the lounge had come from the sponge bag.' In the twins' bedroom down the landing, the two beds had been stripped of their mattresses and pillows. Taff Jones murmured that they had been burned. Some of the wallpaper around the bedheads had been ripped off.

Downstairs, the Eatons peered into the shower room and saw that the shower unit had been removed from its bracket and was hanging loose. In Nevill Bamber's office, one of his double-barrelled shotguns stood propped against the wall, the barrels broken away from the stock for safety. Peter Eaton picked up the shotgun and examined it.

By now it was getting dark. Ann Eaton switched on the lights in some of the rooms and Stan Jones showed her how to work the newly installed burglar alarm. Then he handed her the keys to White House Farm. The Eatons stood in the kitchen and thanked the police for their efforts. 'It's all right,' said Ann Eaton when the officers had gone. 'I haven't any funny feelings.'

Early on Saturday morning, Ann Eaton drove alone to White House Farm in her Ford Sierra diesel estate car. She let herself in through the back door, disarmed the burglar alarm and switched off the lights that had been left on all night. On the first full day of her stewardship at White House Farm, she had decided that a partial springclean was in order. She vacuumed the remains of spilt sugar from the kitchen floor and rinsed it down with a mop. She also vacuumed all the other downstairs rooms. It was as she stood at the sink in front of the kitchen window that she noticed some smudges on the inside of the window pane and on the window frame itself. Moreover, on the inside window sill Ann Eaton saw diluted blood marks, the relics – she assumed – of a less-than-thorough clean-up in the kitchen by the police. Also in the kitchen stood three buckets in which washing had been left to soak. Ann noted that among the items of clothing were some of Sheila's bloodstained knickers.

Ann's brother, David Boutflour, arrived at about 11 a.m. Ann pointed out the marks in the kitchen, and the pair discussed the general state of the house. Now that the police had gone, they also determined to make their own search of the property to see if any clues had been missed. They would make a start directly after lunch.

Ann had arranged to meet her parents for lunch at Oak Farm. Later she drove her father, Robert Boutflour, back to White House Farm where David was waiting. Also there was the Bamber family accountant and executor, Basil Cock, who wished to remove some of the family's valuables such as cash, cheque books and cameras. He telephoned the farm secretary, Barbara Wilson, asking her to come over. When she arrived, Mrs Wilson was dabbing tears from her eyes. Meanwhile Ann Eaton had taken the assembled company on a brief tour of the house, telling them what had happened where on the night of the tragedy. In the lounge she pointed to the half-empty cardboard tampon tube lying next to the toy pistol.

While Barbara Wilson and Basil Cock conferred in the office, David Boutflour was considering the gun cupboard beneath the stairs in Nevill's den. The wooden cupboard was about three feet deep, four and a half feet long and about four feet tall at its highest point. The descending line of the stairs made the cupboard an odd shape: at the other end, it tapered down to a height of only about eight inches. The door was made of inch-thick plywood. The door was kept shut by a nylon ball catch instead of a lock. David Boutflour opened the door and looked inside.

Boxes of ammunition were piled on top of one another. To the left a cardboard box was packed with fourteen smaller boxes, each containing twenty-five 12-bore Raker cartridges. Behind this, someone had stored a dartboard which was standing upright with three darts stuck in it. To the right was a bigger box with a see-through cellophane top revealing an electric spray-gun and a length of coiled pipe. On top of this was another box, about a foot square. Boutflour carefully reached inside. In the back left-hand corner, standing on its end, was a Parker-Hale gun silencer, about seven inches long and about an inch in diameter. Lifting it out, he could see that one end was threaded inside while the other end had a knurled threaded sleeve which held the silencer's internal baffles tight. To his sister, bustling in the kitchen nearby, he announced simply, 'I've found the silencer.' Ann came to the kitchen door, and saw her brother scrabbling in the cupboard on his hands and knees.

Boutflour carefully replaced the silencer in the corner of the box. To its right was a white plastic carrier bag. Reaching inside, he pulled out one of a number of clear plastic boxes, each containing fifty rounds of .22 low velocity ammunition. This he also replaced. Lying partly across the top of the carrier bag was a telescopic sight. It was still in the maker's packaging, encased in polystyrene within a gold-coloured cardboard sleeve. Boutflour partially removed the sight from its box for a very brief examination, then pressed it back into its polystyrene casing.

David Boutflour glanced again at the contents of the gun cupboard. By the light of the ceiling lamp burning above in the passage, he recognized the brown canvas case of his uncle's favourite Webley & Scott 12-bore shotgun. There was an old poker made of rusting mild steel with the end bent at ninety degrees like a golf club. This he left untouched, along with the dartboard and darts, the spray-gun and the box that had contained the white plastic bag, the silencer and the telescopic sight. Everything else was carried through into the kitchen.

Brother and sister sat at the kitchen table and took a closer look at the silencer. David told Ann Eaton that the silencer and the telescopic sight belonged to the rifle that had killed the Bamber family. About half-way along its length was a fresh silver-coloured scratch mark about an inch long.

David and Ann's father, Robert Boutflour, had meanwhile been engaged in some investigating of his own. He'd checked every window in the house for signs of forced entry or exit, and had identified a total of six windows which might have been used by an intruder without detection. These included the window in the kitchen, on which Ann had earlier noticed several smudges and smears of watery blood. In the garage, Robert Boutflour found the back door that had been smashed down by the police to gain entry to the house. To his surprise, the door had no bolts. The lock was damaged and there was no sign of any key. Boutflour reported his suspicions to his son and daughter. Later, in his diary, he pointed out that the condition of the lock meant there was no way of telling whether the key had been in the lock on the night of the killings.

The kitchen of White House Farm had taken on the appearance of a small armoury. On the table lay the plastic carrier bag containing the silencer and telescopic sight, plus five full boxes of .22 ammunition, each containing fifty rounds. Stacked against various cupboards and work surfaces were no fewer than five guns and rifles of various shapes and sizes which had been found stored or lying in different parts of the house. David listed them:

- A Webley & Scott hammerless and ejector 12-bore shotgun in its canvas case recovered from the gun cupboard beneath the stairs.
- A BSA Meteor .22 air-gun, found under some old clothes being stored on a turn in the stairway leading from the kitchen to the upstairs landing. This gun, originally the property of the Pargeters, had been given to the Bambers in the late 1970s, ostensibly for Jeremy's use.
- A Webley & Scott single bolt action .410 shotgun, found next to the air-gun, but standing upright behind some old clothes, leaning against the wall with the barrel pointing upwards.

- A Greener double-barrel ejector 12-bore shotgun, stored in a double leather gun case along with
- An older hammer double-barrel 12-bore shotgun. These two weapons were found in the ground-floor shower room, and belonged to Anthony Pargeter who kept them at White House Farm to use when he went shooting there. They were lying on the floor beneath some bric-à-brac behind an old chair. Both were broken down into their component parts.

The Boutflours spent some time carefully loading the weapons, ammunition and accessories into two separate cars. The guns travelled in Ann Eaton's car. Everything else went with her brother David. Once Ann had delivered her father to Vaulty Manor Farm, where he was to spend the night, the entire haul was delivered to the Eatons' farm in Little Totham, where it was spread out on the kitchen table. Peter Eaton, an expert on firearms, sat in his usual chair poring over the weapons. Ann was up and down the stairs to the attic with boxes of jewellery that she had also taken from White House Farm when suddenly David Boutflour pointed to the silencer, exclaiming that there was something on it. Ann reached over to pick it up but her brother said, 'Don't touch it!' Carefully, he took the silencer between his fingers and Ann could see what she took to be a tiny blob of coagulated blood around the exit hole. She could also clearly see a fleck of red paint on the end of the silencer. The colour immediately reminded her of the red paintwork around the Aga oven in the kitchen at White House Farm.

Before going any further, Boutflour stowed the silencer in a locked cupboard in the main bedroom. He, Ann and Peter then sat down to discuss the implications of what they'd found. How could this silencer have found its way into the gun cupboard with blood and paint on it? If

Sheila had gone crazy and, in her brainstorm, had shot four people, surely she wouldn't have stopped to remove the silencer, replacing it in the gun cupboard under the stairs before returning upstairs to shoot herself dead? Would she have done so? Could she have done so?

SEVEN

ROBERT BOUTFLOUR scarcely slept that night. Lying awake, he tried to piece together what he imagined must have happened in the days and weeks leading up to the massacre at the farm. The police had told him very little; Boutflour was gleaning information from the newspapers, from overheard snatches of Jeremy's statement, and from his search of the house itself, above all the finding of the silencer in the gun cupboard. Then there were remembered fragments of conversations with both Jeremy and Boutflour's brother-in-law, the murdered Nevill Bamber. By dawn, Robert Boutflour had convinced himself that he knew who had murdered the family, and how. That Sunday morning, 11 August, Boutflour began to keep a record of events, jotting down notes and recollections. This makeshift journal focused on his adopted nephew Jeremy, and admitted to no finer feelings than a deep and rancorous dislike.

The more Robert Boutflour pondered, the clearer it became. There was Jeremy's infamous world tour, which had taken him to Australia and New Zealand, paid for by Nevill. There was Jeremy's extraordinary disappearance at the height of the harvest in 1983 when he once again returned to New Zealand. There were his bitter recriminations when he failed the medical examination for a deep-sea diving course because of a weak skull, the result – Jeremy claimed – of a crack caused when June Bamber dropped him as a child. Could this have triggered a hatred of his mother? In Boutflour's view at any rate, June certainly had reason to despair of her adopted son:

undiscriminating in his choice of friends, in New Zealand he had taken up with a man recently released from prison, and on his return to England had been seen with a young man who wore a feather in his ear, fuelling suspicions that Jeremy might be gay. Boutflour also recalled what he had heard of Jeremy's enforced stopover in the Far East on his way home from Australia when – 'without a cent in his pocket' – he met two English airline stewards and shared their flat for ten days.

But on his return, Jeremy's attitude to farming had changed. Boutflour recalled Jeremy promising his father that his roaming days were over, and that he would henceforward work on the farm. And yet, Boutflour recorded, 'during all the conversations I've had with Nevill, he not once gave any indication that Jeremy was shaping up to farming. Conversations on the subject usually ended: "I don't know, I think he's more interested in the caravan site."'

'I have since learned,' Robert Boutflour wrote, 'that Nevill had been reduced to tears by Jeremy's attitude and behaviour.' One incident, reported by one of the farm workers, Len Foakes, typified Jeremy's cavalier approach to his responsibilities and reminded Boutflour that Nevill Bamber had had trouble persuading his son to work overtime during evenings and weekends: after accidentally tipping a load of potatoes into a ditch, Jeremy's reaction had been to jump into his car and drive home, leaving everyone else to clear up the muddle.

Boutflour also recalled a conversation with Jeremy after a meeting of the directors of the Osea Road Caravan Site in the spring of 1985. There had been a spate of minor thefts and break-ins. Boutflour had recommended calling in the police rather than the family mounting vigilante-style patrols of their own. Boutflour reasoned that tackling the culprits unarmed might risk being outnumbered; going armed and having to shoot, however, posed problems of a different kind. Then came Jeremy's astonishing rejoinder: 'Oh no, Uncle Bobby. I'd have no trouble in killing anybody. I could easily kill my parents.' To which Boutflour, stunned, had replied, 'Don't be so stupid,' before turning and walking away.

Then there was Jeremy's constant craving for money, and the frequent arguments with his mother which invariably began with Jeremy asking, 'Why won't you let me have more money, Mum?' Boutflour considered Jeremy's position carefully; he realized that his own wife, Pamela Boutflour, gave half her director's fees to Jeremy's cousin, Ann Eaton. June Bamber had used hers to buy Sheila a flat in London and paid most of her bills. Moreover, June made a weekly trip to the flat to deliver food. Jeremy, meanwhile, was expected to earn his keep by reporting for work at the farm at 7.30 each morning. 'These were facts,' Robert Boutflour noted, 'to feed any feelings of envy and greed.'

Boutflour also recalled the burglary at the Osea Road Caravan Site the previous spring. Robert Boutflour had refused to believe that Jeremy could have stooped to robbing his own family. Now, however, he was beginning to think the unthinkable. 'I am convinced that Jeremy has sold his soul to the Devil,' he wrote. 'A consuming greed, envy, and possibly the immediate need for cash to support an already-expensive lifestyle (possibly involving a dependence on expensive drugs such as cocaine) has driven him to take this dreadful crime.'

How had he done it? Robert Boutflour constructed a possible scenario.

- Does he persuade Sheila to help him load a magazine with ammunition for the .22 rifle? Has he obtained a spare magazine so that Sheila can load twenty rounds covered with her fingerprints?

98

- Jeremy leaves his car outside his cottage. He can easily make the journey to the farm on foot. Once at White House Farm, he lets himself in with his own key, and confronts Nevill Bamber with the Anschutz rifle fitted with the silencer. Nevill dies after a struggle in which the end of the silencer is dashed against the mantelpiece. Red paint is ingrained. Jeremy fires a few random shots to make it look like the work of a maniac. The magazine is emptied. He reloads, or seizes the spare magazine that Sheila loaded earlier.

- Jeremy mounts the stairs to his parents' bedroom. His mother is awake. She is harder to kill cleanly, and Jeremy pumps another ten rounds at her, emptying a second magazine.

- Jeremy reloads the magazine himself. He can scarcely believe that he has used so much ammunition. (Boutflour noted that if Sheila was the killer, these are the rounds that must have carried her fingerprints. Jeremy, however, is wearing gloves and leaves no prints.)

- The twins, Nicholas and Daniel, are each dispatched with a single shot to the temple. Bamber possibly fires a second shot into each sleeping child, just to make sure.

- Jeremy moves downstairs to the lounge, where there is a light. He unscrews the silencer and goes upstairs again to Sheila's room. She has taken a sleeping draught prescribed by her doctor and is in a deep slumber. 'Wake up Sheila,' Jeremy calls softly. 'Mummy wants you to say prayers with her. Bring your Bible, give me your arm, I'll help you.' In June Bamber's room, Sheila is still almost comatose. 'Lie down here, darling,' says Jeremy, 'and put the Bible on your chest.' Sheila does so. 'Give me your hand,

Sheila darling.' Jeremy has rested the rifle on the Bible, and now takes Sheila's hands. The left hand is placed at the end of the rifle barrel under her chin. The right hand is positioned on the trigger guard and her thumb pressed on to the trigger. Bang! Sheila has committed suicide!

- Jeremy moves back into Sheila's room, rummages in her toilet bag and removes a single tampon from its box. Downstairs in the lounge, the toy gun is just the thing with which to poke the absorbent tampon from its cardboard cylinder. He uses the tampon to wipe down the silencer, which he places in the gun cupboard.

- Removing his shoes, Jeremy climbs silently over the kitchen sink, carefully removing any traces before slipping through the window and closing it behind him. He checks that the catch has fallen into place, and that the window seems impossible to open from the outside.

- Jeremy slips on to his mother's bicycle and pedals back to Goldhanger, sticking to the unlit farm tracks that keep him well away from any of the neighbouring farms and houses. All these tracks are gravelled, but the route home takes Jeremy a few hundred yards across a muddy field of rape that has already been combined. No light is needed, for there is a good moon that night.

Ann Eaton was back at White House Farm shortly after ten o'clock on Sunday morning, 11 August. On the way, she had collected the Bambers' housekeeper, Jean Bouttell, for there were still cleaning jobs to do in order to restore the house to some sort of normality. There was talk between the two women about why the police had found it necessary to break down the back door when

Jeremy could have presumably supplied them with his own latchkey. Alternatively, Jean Bouttell knew of a spare key that hung in the coal shed. She supposed it was still there, and hurried out into the yard. Moments later, she returned with the key.

After lunch, other family members assembled again at White House Farm. Robert Boutflour, his wife Pamela, son David and his wife Karen, joined Ann Eaton in another systematic search of the farmhouse. On the wall of the hall, near the baize door to the kitchen, David Boutflour now noticed several large bloodstains at about chest height. Blood had dribbled down the wall for about two inches. He also noted about a dozen specks of blood on the main staircase carpet, most of them near the top of the stairs. Meanwhile, Karen Boutflour and Ann Eaton collected up the belongings of Sheila and the twins, placing them in the cupboard in the room that had been used by the two boys.

When Peter Eaton arrived at White House Farm at 7.30 the following morning, as agreed, there was no sign of Jeremy. Over the weekend, Eaton had spoken to a couple of the farmworkers and knew what needed to be done in order to restart the harvest. Orders were issued, the men dispersed. By the time Barbara Wilson arrived for work at her usual time, 9 a.m., the farmhouse stood deserted and silent. Mrs Wilson parked her car and sat looking at the back door for a full fifteen minutes. The thought of turning that knob and going inside alone was unbearable. She started her car again, reversed out and drove back down Pages Lane and into D'Arcy to the home of the housekeeper, Jean Bouttell.

'Jean,' Barbara Wilson said when she opened the door, 'I can't go up there alone. Will you come with me?'

A thin grey haired woman in her late fifties, Jean Bouttell was every inch the sprightly villager, old-fashioned in her ways and dress, a kindly soul who, seeing Barbara standing so troubled on her doorstep, needed no second bidding. The two women drove back to White House Farm, and Jean took Barbara's arm as they walked in together. Although she wasn't expected at the farm that day, Jean Bouttell stayed none the less, busying herself in the kitchen and answering the door to the numerous police and forensic people who continued to call.

Meanwhile, Robert Boutflour and his wife Pamela drove from Vaulty Manor Farm to Maldon Police Station. Robert Boutflour outlined his suspicions to the duty sergeant, who arranged for them to see officers from the local CID that afternoon. Then he and his wife drove over to the farm to meet their daughter Ann.

It had been five days since the discovery of the killings, and it occurred to Ann Eaton over coffee in the kitchen that Jeremy hadn't returned to White House Farm since being sent back to his cottage in Goldhanger on the morning after the massacre. There and then, Ann decided to call Jeremy and ask him over. He said he'd come straight away. Fifteen minutes later, they heard a car draw up in the yard outside. Jeremy had arrived with Julie.

Despite his suspicions, Robert Boutflour was shocked to observe Jeremy in a state of near-collapse. 'He was in a terrible state,' his uncle reported, 'and though dosed with Valium, he was suffering from the "shakes".' Jeremy walked uncertainly into the kitchen and sat in his father's customary chair. Julie followed, and sat with her back to the dresser. Jeremy said he didn't know where anything was – a curious remark, but one that signified to Ann Eaton that he wanted to know where the bodies of his family had been found. Julie sat quietly, saying little. Ann got to her feet and announced that she would take him on a tour of the house.

They moved towards the passage, but Jeremy stopped and asked Julie if she was coming. Julie replied that she didn't want to, then buried her head in her hands and started to cry. Jeremy took her hand, and she rose to follow him, drying her eyes with a tissue. They moved through the passage and down the hall. Jeremy's eyes were staring, and he was as pale as parchment. Ann had to take him by the arm to steer him into the lounge. Jeremy glanced round the room and announced that a number of things were missing. Ann explained that she'd put various pictures away, and that she had stored some other bits and pieces in chests. In the dining room, Jeremy appeared composed. The party moved upstairs, followed by Robert Boutflour. 'Jeremy was very apprehensive about going into the bedroom and Ann had to help him in,' his uncle stated later. 'He was in a shattered state, hardly able to walk or talk.' Ann Eaton agreed. 'Jeremy appeared to be frightened of going into the upstairs bedrooms,' she stated later. He stopped at the open door to his parents' room and refused to cross the threshold. His uncle stepped into the room and pointed out that a huge piece of carpet had been removed by the police, and a different piece inserted to cover the bare boards. Jeremy stood framed in the doorway, staring and saying nothing.

Ann turned and motioned Jeremy across the landing to Sheila's room. Again, Jeremy followed but stopped short at the open door. Ann observed that he looked 'absolutely petrified'. He said nothing, asked no questions. Ann took his arm and pulled him into the room. Still Jeremy said nothing. At the door to the twins' room, Jeremy still seemed hesitant. After a moment, he ducked his head and moved inside, hunching himself up and creeping in on tiptoe. Ann explained that some of the furniture had been rearranged and the bedding changed since the murders.

She noted that he seemed less troubled here than in the two other bedrooms.

After his hesitant tour of the house, Jeremy seemed to recover some of his composure, and returned downstairs to the kitchen for coffee. He became, according to Ann Eaton's recollection, very confident. Robert Boutflour thought his nephew's behaviour positively 'cocky'.

Presently Jeremy got up and went back upstairs, returning to announce that his father's wallet containing four or five hundred pounds and various credit cards was missing. There and then he telephoned Detective Sergeant Stan Jones at Witham to report the wallet's disappearance.

In the lounge, he seized the video-recorder from its position beneath the colour television, and when Ann challenged him he announced that it was his, and carried it out to his car. In the kitchen, Jeremy checked through some letters stored on a shelf above the telephone, pulled one down, tore it open and threw it in the bin. Again, Ann asked what he was doing. Jeremy replied that the letter was for someone who'd been using the farm as an address. Robert Boutflour looked on with a mixture of shock and bubbling anger; finally, his uncle was so disgusted at the young man's demeanour that he made an excuse and announced that he and his wife were leaving.

That afternoon, the Boutflours were interviewed at Witham by Detective Sergeant Stan Jones, who listened as they outlined their suspicions of Jeremy. The couple thought the detective seemed sceptical. He explained that everyone on the case had heard the theory. But all the tests (he didn't say *what* tests) pointed to Sheila as the culprit. At this point, Inspector Miller appeared. He announced that he had just come from a case conference, that 'there was only one more test to be done' and that so far 'all the tests point to Sheila as the person responsible'.

Robert Boutflour fixed the officers with a look of

disbelief. 'I said they'd never be able to convince me that Sheila could possibly have used a rifle to such effect,' he recalled. Then Boutflour detonated the explosive news of what the relatives had uncovered during their own search of White House Farm. Finding the bloodstained and scratched silencer, he exclaimed, would surely justify the police taking a fresh look at the case? Inspector Miller and Sergeant Jones agreed; they would arrange for the silencer to be collected and forensically examined.

It was Sergeant Stan Jones himself who knocked at the door of the Eatons' home, Oak Farm, that evening. Peter Eaton handed him the silencer, still inside a plastic carrier bag. Jones took it out and held it up. He could see what appeared to be congealed blood at the knurled end. Ingrained in the knurl itself was some reddish-brown paint. Looking closer, Jones could make out a scratch mark, ending in a small burr of metal to which a small grey hair, about three-quarters of an inch long, had become attached. Jones agreed with Peter Eaton that the silencer needed microscopic examination; it might prove to be a crucial piece of evidence. But the detective had arrived ill-prepared for his task. The silencer needed expert and careful wrapping in order to preserve the various marks and the single grey hair. In the absence of the proper equipment, the two men improvised. Jones took the cardboard tube from the centre of a roll of kitchen towels and bent one end over and secured it with a clothes peg. Then he slid the silencer into the cardboard cylinder, bending the other end over and securing that with a second peg.

Ann arrived home shortly afterwards, having spent some time with her mother at the vicarage in Tolleshunt D'Arcy discussing funeral arrangements. The vicar, the Rev. Bernard Robson, had agreed that Nevill and June Bamber should be buried at a joint funeral the following

Friday at St Nicholas's Church; Sheila and the twins would be buried later in London. Peter Eaton told his wife that some flowers had been delivered for her that afternoon, and handed her a small envelope. Inside was a card, on which a message had been printed in small capital letters: THANK YOU FOR ALL YOUR LOVING – JEREMY.

EIGHT

'ONE SILENCER with one grey hair attached,' Stan Jones murmured, laying the cardboard tube on Inspector Cook's desk in the CID office at Witham. Ron Cook looked up from his huge pile of papers. He was not impressed. As scene-of-crime officer, his caseload was enormous, and he seemed to have no one to help with all the paperwork it generated. Nearly a week after the Bamber massacre, Cook had already been called out on several new cases. These, in turn, required their own quota of report-writing and statement-taking. Now he looked doubtfully at the cardboard tube with its ends crimped down. 'That silencer's taken a hell of a knock,' Stan Jones was saying. 'Part of the metal's peeled back. The hair's stuck to it on a kind of burr. There's paint on the knurled end,' he added, 'a sort of reddy colour.' Stan Jones slipped a mint into his mouth and crunched down hard; he'd not had a cigarette for several days. 'And as for the hair,' he added, 'what's the betting it belongs to Old Man Bamber?'

Ron Cook pursed his lips. 'Yes, well,' he said. 'That hair could have got there at any time. Bamber lived there. It was his house. It's perfectly feasible. Like the red paint. Could be a perfectly innocent explanation. Gun might have been propped up against that mantelpiece and just fallen down or slipped.' Stan Jones knew that Ron Cook would be difficult to convince because he wouldn't want to subscribe to any theory that wasn't supported by the CID head. And yet there was something in Cook's manner that suggested to Stan Jones that, although he couldn't say so, the detective inspector might at last be wavering. Certainly he had seemed dismissive of the hair, sceptical about the paint. As for the tiny blob of blood on the end of the silencer Cook had merely pointed out that it could be any type of blood, human or animal. Stan Jones felt that while Cook was putting these arguments and challenges in his way, he was doing so not, perhaps, to demolish his theory, but to test it. It was as though Ron Cook himself was summoning up the confidence, the courage, to come over to Stan Jones's side.

Ann Eaton had arranged to drive Julie Mugford to Colchester that morning to order flowers for the funeral. With her small daughter Jane strapped in the back seat, Ann pulled up in her Sierra Estate outside Jeremy's cottage in Goldhanger at about mid-morning and pipped the horn. Julie came out, followed by another young woman, tall and blonde, whom Ann didn't recognize. In the car, Julie introduced this newcomer as Liz Rimington. She was staying at the cottage at Julie's request. Ann reckoned Liz Rimington's age at about twenty. She was well-spoken and told Ann that her parents lived at Manningtree, five miles north of Colchester. Ann Eaton slipped the car into gear and headed out of Goldhanger towards Colchester.

On the way, the three women chatted. Ann mentioned that late the previous evening she'd been called out to White House Farm where the security alarm was ringing out. Helped by a uniformed policeman, she had checked and reset the alarm. There'd been no sign of an intruder. As the women drove on towards Colchester, Liz asked Julie if she was going to call at the travel agency. Ann asked Julie if she was going away on holiday, and was told it was possible. Ann Eaton had the impression that Jeremy was going too, but neither of the other women confirmed this.

Jeremy himself was receiving an unexpected visitor.

Stan Jones had driven out to Goldhanger to conduct an unofficial experiment. The detective wanted to see how he'd respond to a 'social' visit out of the blue. So when Stan Jones knocked on the front door at Head Street at about midday, he was only mildly surprised to be greeted by Jeremy wearing nothing but a towel and announcing that he was just about to step into the shower. Smiling, Stan Jones muttered apologies. Jeremy invited him in, and asked him to wait in the living room while he took his shower and got dressed. There was no one else in the house.

Stan Jones could hear the sounds of Jeremy's showering, and moved quickly. He didn't know what he was looking for, but knew he was trying to find something, anything. There was a clue to be found, but he didn't know where. Silently, he darted from room to room, looking at any pieces of paper left lying around, looking for names on envelopes. There was nothing. Presently Jeremy appeared, showered and shaved, and offered coffee. As he boiled the kettle, he asked about the way the police planned to organize themselves for his parents' funeral. Stan Jones smiled bleakly, and said they'd get something sorted out. The unofficial 'social' visit had been a disappointing failure.

In Colchester, Ann, Julie and her friend Liz visited the florist, Worrall's, to order flowers for the funeral. There was some difficulty over apricot-coloured roses, and Liz promised to call a flower shop in Manningtree to see whether they could supply some. Ann settled the bill and went shopping with her daughter, leaving Julie and Liz to keep a rendezvous with Jeremy elsewhere in Colchester.

That evening, Ann Eaton telephoned Jeremy at his cottage. She was crying. Ann explained that she had just called June Bamber's cousin, 'Aunty' Betty Howie, to discuss arrangements for the funeral and had become very upset. Jeremy immediately jumped into his car and drove over to Oak Farm to comfort his cousin. During the course of the evening, Ann showed Jeremy the flowers he had sent her.

It was the one time that Ann Eaton allowed herself to break down in front of Jeremy. But it was a vulnerability, a sign of weakness, and it vexed her later that she had allowed herself to seem less than in control. Jeremy was tender that evening at Oak Farm, attentive and solicitous, and Ann Eaton couldn't help but think of him the way he had been with her on several occasions over the previous year.

It had begun in September 1984, when Jeremy had – uncharacteristically – sent her a card for her thirty-fifth birthday. Ann had telephoned him to say thanks, and he had chuckled and said, 'Oh well, I am your favourite cousin, aren't I, Ann?' and Ann had wondered exactly what to make of the remark. As she recalled it, Jeremy had spent the following months buttering her up. The old coldness between them had melted, and Jeremy never seemed to miss an opportunity to treat her with kindness and to behave in a pleasant manner whenever their paths crossed. In the past, Jeremy had prickled and sulked when Ann had made suggestions about the running of the caravan site. Now, his response was invariably 'Good idea!' What was more, he had taken to issuing repeated invitations to Ann to visit him at his cottage and to use his sunbed. The joke was, Ann remembered uneasily, that there was no lock on the door of the room where the sunbed was kept.

Now, as they exchanged words of comfort, Ann wondered what such solicitude was leading to.

When Ann arrived at White House Farm shortly before lunch the following day, Wednesday, 14 August, she found Jeremy on the landing. He was discussing a family portrait with Basil Cock and a valuer from Sotheby's who was dictating notes to a woman assistant. The house seemed crowded with strangers milling about, so Ann retreated downstairs to make some sandwiches in the kitchen.

Ann Eaton could hear Jeremy's voice drifting down from the landing as she busied herself with the sandwiches. Suddenly a large blue car, a Citroën Pallas, swept into the farmyard and pulled up right outside the kitchen window. Ann Eaton recognized the car as having belonged to Nevill Bamber. In the passenger seat sat Julie Mugford, who saw Ann's puzzled expression and smiled. The young man who was driving got out of the car and walked into the kitchen with Julie. He shot a smile at Ann Eaton and made some comment about her cutting sandwiches. He spoke with a New Zealand accent and was deeply suntanned. He introduced himself as Brett Collins.

Collins explained that he was a friend of Jeremy's, who had spent three months with him in New Zealand when Brett had a catering business there. The business had since been sold, Brett Collins added, and he'd been on holiday for most of the summer, spending several weeks with Jeremy at Goldhanger. He'd been on a trip to Greece when he heard about the tragedy at White House Farm. He'd taken the first available flight to London. Ann Eaton was struck by the easy familiarity that existed between this newcomer and Julie Mugford. Brett Collins relaxed expansively in one of the period kitchen chairs, admiring its quality and telling Ann Eaton that he knew a lot about antiques. Indeed, he announced, he had a house full of them.

After lunch, Jeremy produced some of the family jewellery. Ann noted that the professionals from Sotheby's seemed unsure about the various pieces, but that Brett

Collins spoke knowledgeably and with assurance about their values. Jeremy seemed to watch appreciatively as Brett carefully examined his mother's rings one by one. Later, when the pair from Sotheby's had set off back to London, Jeremy found Ann alone in the kitchen. 'Come upstairs,' he said.

In his parents' bedroom, Jeremy had set out the family silver in two separate sections. The finest porcelain crockery stood stacked in piles behind, and paintings had been propped up on the bed. Pride of place in this cornucopia of valuable heirlooms went to Granny Bamber's Meissen porcelain clock. Ann's first thought was for the security of these family treasures, and she asked Jeremy if he was going to put everything away. He smiled and shook his head. 'When I come into this room, I want to see nice things,' he said. Before leaving the house with Jeremy that evening, Ann had to persuade him to close the bedroom curtains.

While Jeremy was showing Ann his heirlooms, his uncle, Robert Boutflour, was asking questions at Osea Road Caravan Site. In conversation with the site manager, Jim Carr, Boutflour was astonished to learn that Carr's son Robbie, an officer in the Metropolitan Police, had some information about Jeremy which he intended to pass on to detectives in Essex. Robbie Carr wanted to know if the family objected. Robert Boutflour told Jim Carr to encourage his son to tell the police as much as he knew. At the same time, Boutflour confided his suspicions of Jeremy to Jim Carr.

Jim Carr listened intently. When Boutflour had finished, Carr announced that it was now his turn to share a confidence. It concerned a registered letter, sent to 9 Head Street, Goldhanger, but addressed to someone called Foakes. A Mrs Foakes and her grandson had recently moved out of the cottage in Head Street so that Jeremy could move in. The postman, knowing this, had taken it to Mrs Foakes instead of delivering the registered letter to Jeremy. When her grandson had opened it, the letter was found to contain £100 in cash and a note saying 'I trust this is to your satisfaction'. The Foakes family were baffled. They knew nothing of the sender of the letter, or of its contents. But the mystery was solved when Jeremy Bamber called on Mrs Foakes and claimed the letter and the cash, angrily blaming young Foakes for opening it. Later, the boy's grandmother had remonstrated with Jeremy, but he had replied: 'You needn't bother about that any more. The man who sent it is behind bars.' No one had been able to find out who had sent the letter, Jim Carr added, just that it had come from an address in Scotland. But people were saying, claimed Carr, that Jeremy Bamber was dealing in drugs.

NINE

SEVEN days in, and nothing. The press had all but closed the story down, leaving Tolleshunt D'Arcy to its dead and promising to return only for the funeral and the appearance of the grief-stricken son. Even the local weekly, the *Maldon and Burnham Standard*, had relegated the massacre to an inside page, lamenting the killing of what it labelled 'the nicest family in the village'. As for the police, the head of Essex CID, Taff Jones, having spent the Saturday following the murders playing in a charity golf tournament, had taken a couple of days off, leaving the daily routine to Detective Inspector Bob Miller from Braintree.

It was Miller who gave evidence when the inquest into the five deaths opened at Braintree that morning. He told the deputy Essex coroner, Geoffrey Tompkins, that post-mortem examinations had confirmed that all five members of the family had died from gunshot wounds. 'In the case of Sheila,' Miller told the court, 'the wound had been inflicted by her own hand.'

Later, in the CID office at Witham, just as Stan Jones was telling Miller that he felt like getting Jeremy Bamber in and having a go at him, Detective Inspector Ron Cook, the careworn scene-of-crime officer, arrived carrying a big folder of A4 glossy colour photographs of the massacre scene. Stan Jones took the folder and idly began flicking through the prints. Suddenly he glanced up at Cook, as though something inside him had just clicked. 'Ron,' he whispered, 'give me a photograph of the kitchen, quick!' Cook drew a picture from the folder.

'There it is!' said Stan Jones.

'There *what* is?'

'That Aga with the reddy-coloured surround. I bet that bloody paint on the end of that silencer is the same as round that Aga.'

It was the moment to try another ruse. Stan Jones called Jeremy at Head Street and asked him to come over to Witham as soon as he could, giving as a reason that he needed Jeremy's written permission to return to White House Farm to measure some rooms for the coroner. He lied. About an hour later, Jeremy Bamber walked into Witham Police Station with his friend Brett Collins. Would it be all right for Collins to be present when he saw Sergeant Jones? No, he was told, it would not be all right. Collins was sent to sit outside in the car, and Jeremy was ushered into Stan Jones's office. Bob Miller, the inspector, and Ron Cook, the scene-of-crime man, greeted him with handshakes. There was some desultory conversation about the forthcoming funerals, and about Sheila and her taste for the London high life. Then Stan Jones doubled his lie, and said again that he needed Jeremy's permission to go back to the farm to get some measurements for the inquests. He added that he would go with Ann Eaton since she had a key. That will be all right, Jeremy told him, provided that nothing gets stolen.

Stan Jones flashed him his dirtiest look. 'Don't talk like that, Jeremy,' he snapped. 'I don't like it.'

Jeremy smiled slowly. 'Only joking,' he replied.

As soon as Jeremy had driven off with Brett Collins, Jones called Ann Eaton, asking her to meet him at White House Farm. He wanted the house opened up that same night, so that officers could carry out some more investigations. Officially, Jones explained, they wanted to take some more measurements. Unofficially, he confided, they wanted to examine the mantelpiece surrounding the Aga cooker in the kitchen. But if anyone asked – especially Jeremy – she was to stick to the official story. Ann Eaton drove back to White House Farm, where Jones was waiting with Detective Inspectors Miller and Cook.

Ann unlocked the kitchen door, switched off the newly installed burglar alarm, and invited the detectives inside.

They seemed interested in the clothes hanging in the wardrobes, and asked Ann to point out what had belonged to June Bamber and what had belonged to Sheila. They also asked about the dozens of pairs of women's shoes stored in the various bedrooms, and took away two pairs that had belonged to Sheila. Someone had mentioned the letter that Jeremy had tossed into the kitchen bin, but although Bob Miller made an extensive search, this letter couldn't be found. Ron Cook took a sample of red paint from the heavy wooden mantelpiece over the Aga, using his penknife to scrape a few flakes into a small plastic bag. Although he said nothing to the others, Stan Jones was looking carefully at two deep gouge marks in the paintwork, on the underside of the mantelpiece. He knew these marks were more than ordinary wear and tear, that they were two definite, heavy, recent blows.

Still later that Wednesday evening, Detectives Miller and Jones paid another visit to the Eatons at Oak Farm. The officers explained that the uncovering of the rifle silencer certainly seemed to raise new doubts, but that they remained unconvinced that the scene at the farm represented anything other than four murders and a tragic suicide. Ann and Peter Eaton repeated their misgivings; in particular, Ann stressed that the murderer could easily have broken silently into the house through one of the windows. Their grief was now becoming tempered by resentment, frustration and deepening suspicion of their cousin Jeremy. It was clear that the family accepted the view of the villager in Tolleshunt D'Arcy who had reportedly taken Jim Carr to one side and hissed: 'That evil little bugger isn't going to be allowed to get away with this, is he?'

TEN

As ANN EATON drove over to White House Farm the following morning, Thursday, 15 August, she found her thoughts pre-occupied by the whereabouts of the bicycle that used to belong to June Bamber. Ann could not find it anywhere around the farm.

The farm secretary, Barbara Wilson, was already at work in the office when Ann arrived. Mrs Wilson, checking her files, was able to tell Ann Eaton that June Bamber had bought the bicycle from a man in Maldon in mid-July. It was an old 'sit up and beg'-style machine with silver mudguards. June Bamber had given £40 for it. Once again, Ann checked around the farm and outbuildings, but she found nothing.

If the search for the missing bicycle proved fruitless, Ann Eaton fared better in the hunt for the missing letter. This was the envelope that Jeremy had taken from the pile on the kitchen shelf the previous Monday and thrown into the bin, saying it was for someone using White House Farm as a convenience address. Earlier searches of the farm's rubbish bins had drawn a blank; now, Ann Eaton found herself rummaging through the garbage for a second time. Her persistence was rewarded: she found the elusive letter in the bin by the scullery. It was addressed to 'A. J. Barker c/o White House Farm, Tolleshunt D'Arcy', but it contained nothing more than a circular. Ann Eaton was unsure whether it would be of interest to the police, but placed it in her handbag for safe keeping. Ann then loaded a box of June Bamber's best china into her car – it would be needed for the funeral reception – and drove to Goldhanger. At Jeremy's cottage, Julie Mugford answered the door and helped Ann to stack the borrowed cups and saucers on the sideboard near the microwave.

Julie told Ann that she and Jeremy were going to Colchester later with Brett and Liz. The main purpose of the trip was to buy some suitable clothes for the funerals.

That afternoon the four called at White House Farm to pick up provisions for the following day. While the women packed food and drink into the car, Jeremy hunted in the office upstairs, searching for a stash of money which he kept insisting must have been hidden by his father 'somewhere in the house'. He found nothing.

Jeremy now seemed restless. Later, at Bourtree Cottage, he suggested that the four of them – himself, Julie, Brett and Liz Rimington – should go out for dinner. Over the meal the talk was mainly of money, about the type of new car Jeremy planned to buy and how he wanted a jet ski. With the money he would inherit, he could buy a bar or a restaurant that the four of them could run. The conversation continued along these lines when they arrived back at the cottage. With the funerals to face the following day, Julie excused herself and went to bed; Brett Collins, too, went up, leaving Jeremy and Liz Rimington talking in the sitting room. Both were feeling mellow from the meal, and Jeremy was rambling about his parents having wanted him to marry Julie. Had they not been murdered, he mused, he would have probably married her and lived in Goldhanger for the rest of his life. Now they were dead, his life would be very different. Liz murmured that the deaths of his parents shouldn't make any difference as far as Julie was concerned; either you marry someone or you don't, she said.

'Perhaps, in time,' Jeremy replied. 'I don't know.'

The talk turned to the killings. Liz Rimington asked

Jeremy about Sheila's mental state, and he told her about the plans to have the children fostered. 'The family all thought she was just going back to London,' Jeremy explained, 'but I'm the only one who knew she was going in the nut house.' Liz Rimington thought that Jeremy was simply trying to over-dramatize the situation; she knew that Sheila had suffered mental breakdowns in the past, but no one had suggested she was due to return to hospital. In any case, it was late. She rose and said she was going up to bed. Then Jeremy looked up at her with an expression of blank inscrutability. 'Anyway,' he added, 'I'm the only person who really knows what happened that night.'

ELEVEN

FRIDAY was a sombre day. It was the day of the Bamber funerals; Nevill, June and Sheila were mourned by the villagers of Tolleshunt D'Arcy at a service in the fourteenth-century church of St Nicholas, where both parents had worshipped and served as churchwardens. The funerals were scheduled for early afternoon. In the course of the morning, Jeremy and Brett Collins were seen in Goldhanger carrying a large tea urn from the direction of the village hall, laughing and joking. Brett himself recalled that Jeremy spent the morning 'in reasonably good spirits', and Julie remembered seeing him swallow several tranquillizers, knocked back with a stiff drink or two. Liz Rimington, still staying at the cottage to keep Julie company, reported a 'jovial' Jeremy taking Valium tablets 'like they were going out of fashion'. The others confined themselves to one tablet each. Brett suggested that Jeremy accentuate his grief by wearing white powder on his face. It was, the New Zealander declared later, 'purely a joke'.

Virtually the entire village turned out for the funerals. Those unable to cram into the church stood in hushed, respectful groups around the gate or milled in the road with the waiting journalists and photographers. When the cortège arrived from Goldhanger, men bared their heads. Many of the women sobbed quietly into handkerchiefs. Leading the mourners and weeping uncontrollably, Jeremy Bamber walked slowly behind the coffins carrying the bodies of his parents and adopted sister. He leaned heavily on Julie Mugford, hatted and veiled in black.

Colin Caffell, with his parents and sister, followed. Then the Eatons and the Boutflours. The vicar of D'Arcy, the Rev. Bernard Robson, said prayers for Nevill Bamber, his 'sweet-natured' wife and Sheila 'for her caring as a mother'. The congregation sang Psalm 23 and one of June Bamber's favourite hymns, 'Lord of All Hopefulness'. Jeremy sat at the front with Julie, just feet from the three coffins lined up abreast on the steps of the medieval chancel. The vicar, in his address, spoke of the village's sense of shock and loss, and reminded the mourners of the Bambers' close involvement in many aspects of the life of D'Arcy. Of June Bamber, Mr Robson reminded the mourners that she had expressed her religious faith openly, often to the embarrassment of others. Nevill Bamber, quieter, had worshipped regularly. Sheila Caffell knew the Gospel too.

Members of the family, led by Jeremy and his girl-friend, went on to the crematorium at Colchester for a private cremation. By the time they returned to Gold-hanger for coffee and sandwiches, Jeremy had regained his composure and seemed devoid of emotion. Avoiding members of his family as far as he could, he stayed in a corner with Julie and a group of his friends.

Jeremy went upstairs to change. When he returned in his casual gear, it was a signal that the reception was over. People finished up their drinks, exchanged condolences, mumbled goodbyes. Most of the surviving relatives had been invited to join Ann and Peter Eaton for supper at Oak Farm. Later, a group of them drove over to White House Farm to take a look at the house. This was the first time that most of the relatives had been there since the murders, and the occasion was a muted one. The gathering returned to Oak Farm and spent the rest of the evening in a lengthy family conference.

Jeremy, meanwhile, was in party mood. As well as

Julie, Brett Collins and Liz Rimington, two friends from London, Andy and Karen Bishop, had stayed behind, and it was Andy Bishop who suggested going out for a meal. Everyone thought it was an excellent idea except for Julie who complained that she wasn't in the mood to go out. But Jeremy insisted. He told Julie that he was glad the funerals were over and that the events of the day hadn't bothered him too much. Now it was time to relax. His idea was to have a meal at a small, expensive restaurant on the main street in Burnham-on-Crouch called the Caribbean Cottage. All six piled into the big blue Citroën that had belonged to Nevill Bamber, and which Brett Collins was now using.

They began with cocktails at the bar, then moved to their table. The meal was excellent. They drank champagne, then wine, then more champagne. Julie sulked, so Jeremy wandered tipsily around the restaurant talking to the other customers, while Brett consoled himself by chatting up two young men he met at the bar. Everyone got very drunk. At the end of the evening, Brett Collins took one of the strangers back to the cottage at Goldhanger where they spent the night in his room.

Before leaving for the restaurant, Jeremy had spent some time setting the video-recorder to tape both main television news bulletins. But when the revellers returned, Jeremy found that the machine had failed to work properly. He angrily rewound the tape, blaming the gadget and his own ineptitude for missing the bulletins. He had set great store by the television coverage of the funerals; after all, he had announced to his friends, as he fiddled with the controls of the video recorder, he hoped the cameras would show his best side.

The next morning was Saturday. Jeremy and his friends had planned a weekend at the seaside, but his first concern was to buy a set of national newspapers to see how the funerals had been reported. He spread them out on a table and gazed approvingly. Jeremy remarked to Andy Bishop that he was glad that both Julie and Brett were anxious to establish a long-term relationship with him, and pleased that he was at the centre of a 'tug-of-love' tangle.

The weekend destination was Pevensey, just outside Eastbourne, where Andy Bishop's parents had a seafront house. The four of them drove down in two cars. On the way, Julie and Jeremy had a row. So after lunch in a roadside pub outside Sevenoaks, Julie swapped places with Andy Bishop and was driven the rest of the way by his wife, Karen. Jeremy and Andy drove on ahead and chatted about Jeremy's future plans. Jeremy said he wanted to sort out the farm, the wills and the death duties and then go away on holiday. Andy Bishop asked if he planned to keep the tenancy of the farm, but Jeremy said he doubted whether he could do so. If he had to quit, Jeremy added, he would like to buy either a small farm of his own or a flat in London and open a wine bar with Julie.

As for his surviving relatives, Jeremy told Bishop he was upset with them for taking things from the farmhouse and asking for things that rightfully belonged to him. He was also annoyed with Brett Collins and Liz Rimington. They'd taken advantage of his new wealth, he said, and now they expected him to pay for everything.

The following Monday the twins, Nicholas and Daniel Caffell, were buried at Highgate Cemetery in north London. Jeremy and Julie attended; David Boutflour, his mother and sister were also among the mourners. It rained heavily all morning. The family gathered at Colin Caffell's flat in Maygrove Road, Kilburn, at noon. During the service at St James's Church, Hampstead, Jeremy seemed composed, but Julie wept copiously.

At Highgate Cemetery, the rain grew even heavier, and after the burial the mourners dashed for the black funeral cars, drawn up outside the cemetery chapel. Ann Eaton, her mother and brother were sharing one of the cars. It was just about to move off when a woman knocked on the window, opened the door and climbed in. It was Ina Pargeter, the wife of Jeremy's cousin, Anthony Pargeter. She was in tears. The others thought she was distressed because of the funeral, but Ina Pargeter shook her head. She explained that running through the rain, she had dashed for the car containing Jeremy Bamber. 'You're not coming in here,' Jeremy had hissed, pointing in the direction of the Boutflour car. 'Go with that lot.'

TWELVE

THE POLICE investigation seemed to be getting nowhere. On Tuesday afternoon, Robert Boutflour and Ann drove over to Witham Police Station. They learned that Stan Jones was on leave, and saw only Detective Constable Barlow. He listened as they itemized the points they felt warranted further investigation: the registered letter from Scotland containing £100; a receipt, apparently for the supply of drugs; and the disappearance of the bicycle June Bamber had bought for £40 in the middle of July. And there was a curious aspect of June Bamber's character that everyone in the family agreed might prove significant: June, unlike Nevill, had been a very light sleeper. Often she imagined she heard noises downstairs and would wake her husband to ask him to investigate. Had June been woken by the sound of Jeremy stealing in through a downstairs window? Had Nevill been sent creeping down the stairs, only to confront his son in the kitchen, armed with the loaded Anschutz rifle? Detective Constable Barlow made a note. It would be considered as a possibility.

When Ann arrived home, Peter Eaton was waiting with news. He had seen Jeremy, who had announced that he was taking Julie and Brett to Amsterdam for a couple of days. In his absence, Peter had been officially appointed farm manager-designate by Basil Cock. Jeremy told Peter that his first task would be to gather in the harvest at White House Farm, but to do nothing else with regard to autumn cultivation. Instead he was to concentrate on Vaulty Manor.

With Jeremy away, Ann Eaton seized the chance to do some further sleuthing. On Thursday morning, 22 August, she drove over to Goldhanger and checked that Bourtree Cottage was empty. She walked up the path at the back of the house. To her amazement, leaning against the fence by the back door, Ann saw a lady's red 'sit-up-and-beg'-style bicycle with silver mudguards. The wheels were bright chrome, and Ann saw that the tyres and wheel-rims were covered in a yellowish mud. She jumped back into her car and drove home to telephone Detective Constable Barlow at Witham with the news of her discovery. Yes, he said. He'd seen it himself the day before when he, too, had gone calling on Jeremy at Goldhanger. Jeremy, however, had already left for Holland.

With Julie and Brett, Jeremy had driven to Harwich, parked the Astra at the docks, and boarded the overnight ferry to Amsterdam. The trio travelled first class, because the trip was part holiday and part business. Jeremy and Brett wanted to buy cannabis. Brett, who had a brother living in Amsterdam, knew of a bar where cannabis was traded, and they made their purchases at lunchtime the following day, much to Julie's disdainful irritation. At the five-star Hôtel de l'Europe, Brett and Jeremy packed the cannabis into drinking straws which were then slipped into jumbo-sized tubes of toothpaste. Jeremy had spent nearly £100 on the drug and there was so much of it that he couldn't fit it all in, so he commandeered a bottle of Julie's cocoa-butter skin lotion. That night, the three enjoyed a de luxe dinner in one of Amsterdam's most exclusive restaurants.

The journey home started badly. At the Hook of Holland ferry terminal, Jeremy discovered he had lost their return tickets. He promptly bought three more first-class tickets and tickets for a cabin in which, for the entire duration of the crossing, all three smoked cannabis.

Still more was smoked that evening at Jeremy's cottage. A friend of Jeremy, Charles Marsden, called round, and someone suggested going out for dinner. Once again, the venue was the Caribbean Cottage at Burnham, although for some reason the party didn't eat. They just drank.

Jeremy telephoned Ann Eaton early the following Saturday morning, to say he had plans for the weekend. He wanted to go to London on Sunday to see the Notting Hill Carnival. On Monday he would be in Colchester for Julie's twenty-first birthday party. After that, he added, he'd be in the cottage on his own. Julie was moving into a new flat in London. Jeremy told Ann that he'd like to come over one evening in the week to see her.

Nettled by what she saw as entirely self-centred plans, she snapped that he ought to do something about sorting out his grandmother's jewellery. She had been dead nearly four years, and although Anthony Pargeter and Jackie Wood had been given a few small treasures, nothing had been properly settled regarding the division between the various cousins of Betty Bamber's valuables and heirlooms. Surely all this should be sorted out so that the family could then concentrate on how best to administer the estates of Nevill and June?

Jeremy, not surprisingly, was furious. Ann was not even related to Betty Bamber – and anyway everything had been willed to Nevill Bamber. It was only out of the goodness of his father's heart that the Pargeters had been given a few knick-knacks. If they wanted to complain, they would have to do so before the granting of probate. Ann then asked what Jeremy intended to do about the contents of White House Farm, the furniture and a number of valuable paintings. Simple, Jeremy replied. Everything would be sold. Everything, that is, apart from a few items of furniture which he was going to keep for himself.

Ann reported this conversation to her father. Boutflour was becoming increasingly impatient for action, and next day – although a Sunday – he telephoned Detective Constable Barlow at Witham Police Station. Boutflour couldn't understand why Jeremy hadn't been detained for questioning, and why his cottage hadn't been searched by forensic scientists. Once again, Barlow listened patiently to the catalogue of suspicions. All he could say was that tests on the silencer were under way, but that they would take three weeks to complete.

Next day, Robert Boutflour and Ann drove over to White House Farm. In the kitchen, father and daughter tried an experiment. Ann opened the fanlight window over the kitchen unit that looked out over the back yard. She then went outside, set the catch and closed the window, tapping it in a way that caused the catch to fall into the 'locked' position. This secured the window, and made it impossible for it to be opened again from the outside. Boutflour and his daughter agreed that someone could slither through this open window if they wanted to leave the house without using the door. Ann Eaton telephoned Witham Police there and then to tell them about the window experiment. Meanwhile, Robert Boutflour stood and contemplated the fanlight. This was the window where Ann had found drops of bloodstained water on the sill when the police had allowed her in to the house to tidy up three days after the murder. Boutflour saw that there was still an unaccountable smudge on the glass immediately below the fanlight. Dirty, dried-up drip marks could still be seen on the cross-piece of the window frame, as if someone had wiped it down in a hurry.

On his way home, Robert Boutflour called in at the Osea Road Caravan Site and spoke to the manager, Jim Carr. Carr was proving a highly productive source of local gossip, and Boutflour was anxious to keep abreast of it. Today, Carr had news of the enigmatic Brett Collins. It appeared that the 'catering business' that Collins had boasted of selling back in New Zealand was no more than a snack bar on the beach at Auckland. Boutflour asked Jim Carr to contact some friends in New Zealand for a rundown on Collins.

The following afternoon, Robert Boutflour again visited the police at Witham. Had they heard anything more about the history of Brett Collins? Detective Constable Barlow said he had heard from the police liaison officer at New Zealand House in London: it seemed that Collins had no criminal record, and that he had been in England for some time. His stay in the UK had been interrupted only by a trip to Greece for a holiday. But Barlow had more important news: initial results from the forensic laboratory on the rifle silencer found in the gun cupboard at White House Farm indicated that there was definitely blood on it. But at this stage, no one could say whether this was human or animal blood. The results of further tests would be through in about another week. They might even prove, said Barlow, whether the silencer had been fitted to the rifle when some or all of the fatal shots were fired.

This was the best news that Robert Boutflour had heard since the investigation began. He was more convinced than ever that his adopted nephew had slaughtered the family and that he had done so wearing either a tracksuit or a wetsuit. Boutflour passed this theory on to Detective Constable Barlow at Witham, along with another snippet of information that had come his way. According to Stewart Sinclair, the man running the shop at Osea Road Caravan Site, Jeremy was planning to go to Spain in early September for a holiday.

When Ann Eaton arrived at White House Farm on

Wednesday morning, 28 August, she found the house-keeper, Jean Bouttell, working in the kitchen. She said that Brett Collins was upstairs, looking through some old coins. Ann asked where Jeremy was, and Mrs Bouttell said he was in his father's den. On her way through, something on the shelf caught Ann's eye. It was an ordinary-looking box about eighteen inches wide, but it struck her that it had been placed on the exact spot where she had seen a spare back-door key only a few days before. Out of curiosity she undid the lid and was riffling through the papers and stamps inside the box when Jeremy called out from the den, 'Don't look in there, Ann, it's private.' Ann apologized. Clearly Jeremy was unhappy about his cousin poking her nose in at White House Farm. Any doubt was dispelled later that morning when Jeremy asked Ann to hand over her back-door key. He explained that Barbara Wilson, the farm secretary, would need it to let herself in the following Friday.

The following morning when Robert Boutflour drove up to White House Farm and parked his car, the Astra was backed up to the kitchen door. Jeremy was loading ornaments, pictures and other family treasures into the boot of the car. He told his uncle that he was taking everything to Sotheby's to have them valued, cleaned and catalogued with a view to selling them as soon as probate had been granted. Basil Cock, as executor, knew all about it. Boutflour said nothing, but turned and stumped off, making a mental note to tell the police of what he had seen. Boutflour had already telephoned the CID at Witham that morning to tell them that he thought the discarded tampon might have been used to clean the silencer; to his annoyance, he'd been told that the only officer who appeared to be on the case, Detective Constable Barlow, had been called to London on urgent business. Boutflour determined to mention Jeremy's visit to Sotheby's on Barlow's return the following day.

This left time to do some further investigating of his own. He crunched down the back drive and on to the track that led from Pages Lane to the neighbouring Brook House Farm. Boutflour was looking for cycle tracks, the sort of tracks that could have been left by Jeremy as he rode his mother's bicycle back to Goldhanger in the middle of the night after carrying out the murders at the farm. The narrow track leading to Brook House was seldom used by through traffic, and the only signs of activity that Boutflour could make out were the marks of tractor wheels.

THIRTEEN

THE WEEK of her twenty-first birthday, which should have been one of the happiest of Julie Mugford's life, turned into a thoroughly miserable one, thanks to Jeremy and his constant companion Brett Collins.

Suffering from the after-effects of an asthma attack, Julie had spent a wretched Saturday moping at Jeremy's cottage. On the Sunday morning, the three drove to London, calling to pick up Liz Rimington on the way. They spent the day at the annual Notting Hill Carnival and returned to Essex in the late afternoon. On the way home, Liz invited the others in for coffee. In her flat, Julie witnessed a strange incident. Jeremy and Brett were sitting together on the sofa, and as if it were the most natural thing in the world, Brett laid his head on Jeremy's lap, and Jeremy began stroking his hair. It was perhaps at that moment that Julie Mugford realized the impossibility of her position.

Julie's birthday fell on the Monday, the late summer Bank Holiday A small family celebration had been arranged for that evening, with Jeremy and Brett joining Julie and her parents for a dinner party at a restaurant near Colchester. The evening was not a success. Brett Collins proposed a toast, and surprised everyone by raising his glass not just to Julie's future happiness but to 'the engaged couple'. Jeremy was beside himself with rage and refused to respond, saying that they had absolutely no plans for getting engaged. It was, he observed much later, very embarrassing for everyone.

For Julie herself, it was the final straw. Later that

night, at the cottage, she told Jeremy she would be returning to London in the morning. She still loved him, she explained, but the situation with Brett had got to the point where she felt totally excluded. She wanted to continue seeing Jeremy, but she could no longer share his house with Brett about.

The next night, in London, however, Julie Mugford gave a very different reason for leaving Jeremy.

She had arrived back at her digs in Caterham Road, Lewisham, exhausted and depressed. Everyone was away apart from her friend Susan Battersby. Julie suggested going out for a meal, so in the evening the two women walked into the centre of Lewisham. Susan thought that Julie seemed nervy and on edge. Crossing the High Street, they were talking about Jeremy when Julie blurted out something that shocked Susan Battersby and caused her to stop in her tracks. 'You don't know how evil Jeremy is,' Julie said.

Susan Battersby followed Julie across the street and put a hand on her arm. 'Jeremy did it, didn't he?' she asked.

Julie's eyes were brimming. 'No,' she replied, 'not Jeremy. He didn't do it. He paid somebody else.'

They went into the Pizza Hut and sat at a table. By now, Julie Mugford was visibly shaking. Over the meal, Susan Battersby pressed her friend to tell her what she knew. Julie demurred at first. 'Expect the worst,' was all she would say. But Susan Battersby insisted. Julie, distressed, pushed her plate aside and dabbed her eyes with her napkin. First, she made her friend promise not to tell another living soul, and then confided that Jeremy had hired a mercenary to murder his entire family.

Piece by piece, her story emerged. The mercenary was the lover of a woman who knew Jeremy's former mistress, Sue Ford. Julie had met him, and disliked him. Jeremy had decided that in order to inherit his parents' money in time to enjoy it, he would have to get rid of them. He and the mercenary struck a deal: Jeremy would pay him £2,000 for the killing contract. After the murders, according to Julie, the mercenary had fled abroad, waiting for things to cool down.

Jeremy had even worked out a way to disguise his complicity in the murder plot. On being told the news of his family's murder, he would promptly be sick by thinking of his favourite dog, Bramble, which had been killed by a car. This, Julie added, was how Jeremy was able to give a convincing performance on the morning after the murders when he walked into one of the farm fields alone and appeared to vomit.

She couldn't go to the police, Julie explained, because she still loved Jeremy and couldn't bear the thought of him in prison. It was hard to explain, but although she disliked him as a person, she still loved him.

The revelations distressed Susan Battersby. Looking at her friend, nervously glancing at the faces of the early-evening diners, she felt unutterably sad that Julie should have become tangled up in such an evil enterprise. Susan's thoughts turned back to the day she first met Jeremy. It was on the first day of the spring term when he brought Julie back to college and took both girls out for a meal. He had been charming and attentive. During that term he would visit most weekends and at least once in the week, always bringing Julie flowers or gifts and whisking her out to restaurants. And yet there was something disturbing about this dark, good-looking young farmer from Essex that troubled Susan Battersby.

Susan considered Julie Mugford to be her best friend, and she now realized that the reason she disliked Jeremy was that he seemed to exert a malevolent influence over Julie. Susan knew that Jeremy grew cannabis to smoke and to sell, and that Julie had been involved in small-time dealing in and around college. Susan Battersby had disapproved, and had warned Julie against bringing cannabis into their digs at Caterham Road. This got back to Jeremy, who had taken delight in teasing Susan for what he considered to be her killjoy attitude to a harmless habit. If Jeremy was at the house and someone knocked at the door, Jeremy would gleefully announce that the drug squad had arrived to arrest her. Susan Battersby remembered that Jeremy had been smoking cannabis heavily in the weeks leading up to Christmas 1984. He smoked it in the house at Lewisham, in pubs and in his car. Julie had been upset and tried to persuade Jeremy to give the habit up. It seemed to Susan Battersby that Jeremy liked to smoke and deal in cannabis for effect. It brought him friends and popularity. He didn't seem to make much money out of it. She felt he was trying to ensnare Julie in his flashy lifestyle: that way, she wouldn't be able to betray or break with him.

Susan Battersby never bothered to disguise her antipathy towards Jeremy Bamber. Jeremy himself cordially reciprocated. Matters came to a head between them two days after the Pizza Hut disclosures when Jeremy and Brett Collins turned up at Caterham Road for another celebration of Julie's twenty-first birthday. The idea was to throw a party for all her student friends, and most of those present were either drunk or high. Music was blaring in the sitting room and a crowd had gathered in the kitchen to watch the finishing touches being put to Julie's birthday cake. Jeremy was squeezing some cream on to the cake when Susan Battersby, in a foolish fit of horseplay, grabbed the aerosol container and brandished it at Jeremy, threatening to squeeze the cream down his neck. In an instant, Jeremy's mood changed to a thunderous rage, and he picked up the cake and rammed it into

Susan's face. The startled girl screamed. 'Why did you do that?' she cried, as the other partygoers drunkenly urged her to retaliate.

'You're such a child, Susan,' Jeremy snapped, licking bits of cake and cream from his fingers.

Susan Battersby flung the aerosol aside, fled upstairs, locked herself in her room and burst into tears.

FOURTEEN

WITH the laughing figure of Brett Collins sprawled in the passenger seat of the silver Astra hatchback, Jeremy sped north along the A12. It was still only a few minutes after 8 a.m. when they took the exit slip at Hatfield Peverel and turned the car along the back road towards Maldon. Jeremy glanced at his fuel gauge, and told Brett that he needed petrol. A perk of his work at White House Farm, he explained, was the free use of his family's own petrol pump at Vaulty Manor. It was 8.15 when Jeremy pulled up behind his grandmother's farmhouse and switched off the engine. Robert Boutflour saw the car pass the kitchen window and went out to speak to Jeremy. Filling up the car, he explained that he and Brett were on their way back from London, having left a carload of pictures and other heirlooms at Sotheby's to be valued. Brett flashed one of his increasingly irritating smiles. 'See you later,' he said.

He did. Robert Boutflour had arranged to go to White House Farm later that morning to collect two farm forks which David Boutflour had negotiated to buy from Jeremy. When he arrived, Boutflour found that a tractor and trailer had been backed up to the kitchen door. His daughter Ann, who was with him, went into the kitchen to demand to know what was going on. Jean Bouttell, the housekeeper, told her that Jeremy and Brett were having a clear-out. Jeremy had gone into Maldon to see the bank manager, leaving Brett in charge of the operation. Father and daughter were dismayed, and Ann took Jean Bouttell aside to ask her not to throw anything of sentimental value away. Robert Boutflour went up to the office to ask Barbara Wilson to issue him with a receipt for the forks. Back in the kitchen, Jean Bouttell made the visitors some coffee. Brett Collins was there. By way of a conversation piece, he produced one of the Bamber family's oldest treasures, a magnificent seventeenth-century gentleman's dress coat in plum velvet, trimmed with gold braid, sequins and lace cuffs. Remembering Brett Collins's self-proclaimed expertise on antiques, Robert Boutflour ventured to ask his opinion of the coat. Before he knew it, Collins had sprung to his feet and put it on himself, exclaiming, 'Very collectable items these, much sought after.' Boutflour could scarcely credit that anyone, least of all a stranger, could be so disrespectful.

Robert Boutflour turned the talk away from the coat and towards Brett Collins's world tour. Brett said he planned to return to London and to Paris before moving on. Boutflour pressed him for some information about his family background. Collins mentioned that his grandfather had been an engineer who had designed armaments and munitions before emigrating to New Zealand towards the end of the nineteenth century to begin a new life as a farmer.

Having listened politely to the history of the Collins family, Robert Boutflour asked to be excused, since he was expected home for lunch. He collected the forks, for which he had paid Jeremy £50, while Ann took with her some of June Bamber's favourite biscuit tins which Jean Bouttell had managed to salvage from the general clear-out. (That evening, Jeremy telephoned Ann at Oak Farm, complaining that she'd taken the tins without his permission. Ann indignantly pointed out that Jean Bouttell had given her the tins, and Jeremy relented, asking that he and Ann should remain friends.)

At Witham that afternoon, Robert Boutflour called on

Detective Constable Barlow to share his theory about the tampon possibly being used to clean the silencer. He urged the detective to order tests to check the silencer for fibres. He also passed on his suspicions that Jeremy might have used one of the footpaths or farm tracks to steal to and from White House Farm on his murderous mission. Boutflour's experiments had taken him along every single path and track between the farm and Jeremy's cottage at Goldhanger. He wanted to discover which was the shortest and easiest route to take without running the risk of being seen. Boutflour had concluded that Jeremy might have used one of three possibilities: one was a direct route across fields (three miles); the second also crossed fields but via tracks and footpaths that added another half mile to the journey; and a third route was four miles long and followed the sea wall along the saltings that fringed Goldhanger Creek. At least two of these routes, Boutflour reminded Detective Constable Barlow, could be used by someone either on foot or on a bicycle.

Barlow, who had been making notes, now put down his pencil and regarded Boutflour across the table. There were aspects of the case, Barlow agreed, that didn't seem to add up. Boutflour seemed a man of discretion, someone who could be trusted. For that reason, Barlow explained, he was going to take him into his confidence.

First, Sheila the suicidal, homicidal maniac. There was no evidence, Barlow revealed, that she had been suffering from any drug-induced psychosis. Also, according to her boyfriend, Freddie Emami, Sheila had lost all muscle coordination in her last weeks. If she wanted to drink from a glass, she would need to use both hands and her movements in bringing the glass to her mouth would be very erratic. If she wanted to put out her left arm, the right arm moved out involuntarily to balance it.

Second, Jeremy the bereaved innocent. Police had been checking the timings described by Jeremy in his statements. They did not tally with the timings fixed by other witnesses. What was more, Barlow added, every detective at Witham was convinced that Jeremy Bamber was guilty of murdering his family.

On Friday one of Jeremy's old girlfriends, Virginia Greaves, made a chance reappearance. Virginia, a twenty-three-year-old personal assistant, had been a member of the Frog and Beans' drinking set for about three years; she had been a girlfriend of Michael Deckers at one time, and had had an affair with Jeremy in the days before Sue Ford arrived on the scene. At the time of the Bamber killings, she hadn't seen him for over a year. She had sent him a condolence card, but had received no response. Then, through Michael Deckers, she had heard that Jeremy was trying to find someone to rent Sheila's old flat in Maida Vale and to act as landlady when Jeremy himself wasn't there. The prospect appealed to Virginia Greaves, and she telephoned Jeremy at his cottage. He was out, so she left a message on his answering machine. On Friday afternoon, Jeremy returned her call.

After some conversation about the Maida Vale flat, Jeremy invited Virginia Greaves out to dinner with himself and Brett Collins. Julie was still in London. Virginia agreed, and that evening, Jeremy arrived at her family's cottage near Colchester to pick her up. In the car, Jeremy complained about the behaviour of his surviving relations, saying they were for ever in and out of White House Farm and helping themselves to its contents. He told Virginia Greaves that he was getting no support from his family and that they only seemed interested in what they could get. On the way to dinner, Jeremy stopped off at Bourtree Cottage where he telephoned Ann Eaton. 'I don't mind you having things,' was the gist of his message, 'but I'd rather you did it while I'm at the house.'

The three of them dined at the Caribbean Cottage. At the end of the evening, they returned to Goldhanger. Virginia Greaves spent the night in bed with Jeremy. The seduction was pivotal, in that it rekindled an affair which had apparently fizzled out years before. At the time, it seemed nothing more than the comforting of a bereaved and bewildered young man by a solicitous and affectionate former girlfriend. But it was to sow a seed of jealousy in the troubled heart of Julie Mugford.

Jeremy had arranged to visit Julie in London on the Saturday morning, so he called her with an excuse and said he'd be there later. Then he drove Virginia home. Her mother was pleased to see him again, offered her condolences over the tragedy and invited him to stay for lunch. Despite his promise to Julie, Jeremy accepted the invitation, and sat out in the garden on his own while Virginia and Mrs Greaves prepared lunch in the kitchen. When Virginia wandered back outside, Jeremy took her hand and told her how much he still cared for her, even though their affair had ended years before. Jeremy added that he wanted to be around people who cared for him, rather than with his grasping relations. After lunch, the pair returned to Goldhanger. In the car, Virginia turned to Jeremy. 'Do you want me to be sympathetic,' she asked, 'or would you rather I didn't mention what's happened?'

'No,' Jeremy replied, 'I just want to be around happy people. And I don't want to be alone.'

It was turned three o'clock in the afternoon by the time he and Virginia arrived at Goldhanger, so he telephoned Julie again to make another excuse and to say he'd be late. In fact it was 5.30 p.m. before Jeremy, Brett and Virginia Greaves left the cottage to drive to London.

They called for petrol at Vaulty Manor. Pamela Boutflour came out while Jeremy was filling up and told him that she had broken the news to Jeremy's Granny Speakman about the deaths at White House Farm. The old woman had been told that Sheila had done it, and she seemed to have taken it quite well. Jeremy's aunt added that, with the accountant's permission, she had been to the White House and taken some of her sister's jewellery. She had done this partly to ensure its safekeeping, since some of the items had been in the Speakman family for generations. She mentioned particularly a locket that had belonged to her own grandmother, a piece Mrs Boutflour treasured especially. Jeremy was displeased. 'Remember, Aunty Pammie,' he replied, 'it's my family too.'

Pamela Boutflour checked herself. 'Well,' she said, 'you'd look very silly wearing a locket, wouldn't you, Jem?'

Jeremy finished fuelling the car. Perhaps, he suggested, the two of them could go through the jewellery together. Mrs Boutflour nodded and said he could come any time. As he jumped back into the Astra and fired the engine, he wound down the window and smiled at his aunt. 'I'm interested in the teeth,' he said. Then, putting the car into gear, he revved up and drove off down the drive towards the main road, leaving Pamela Boutflour puzzling over this strange parting remark – an ironic reference to a small box of children's milk teeth belonging to Jeremy and Sheila, which had been kept by June Bamber as a memento.

Speeding south on the A12, Jeremy complained bitterly about his interfering relatives. Telling his grandmother about the deaths of the Bambers was not a good idea, he said, because the shock of it could kill her. And it was silly to keep valuables for purely sentimental reasons because money was needed to meet legal fees.

By the time Jeremy had dropped Virginia at her sister's house in London and left Brett at Sheila's old flat in Maida Vale, he was running very late indeed. Julie was seething by the time he arrived at Caterham Road just after 8 p.m.

What happened that evening, and what Julie and Jeremy said to one another, would be described by both of them later in sharply contrasting statements, but there is no doubt that Julie Mugford spent most of the following day in floods of tears. She called round to see Liz Rimington and told her that Jeremy had finished their affair. Liz Rimington said that as far as she was concerned, Julie was better off without him. She wasn't prepared for Julie's response. 'You don't know the half of it,' Julie said.

Liz Rimington pressed her to explain. At first, Julie said she simply couldn't, that she didn't dare, and that in any case, what had happened was so incredible that she doubted whether anyone else would believe her. Piece by piece, Liz Rimington teased out the story. Since Christmas, Julie explained, Jeremy had been planning to murder his entire family.

'Did he do it?' Liz Rimington asked.

'No.'

'Who did, then?'

'A friend of his.'

It was Matthew McDonald, Julie said at length. He'd done it for £2,000. Liz Rimington's reaction to this was to advise her friend to go straight to the police. Otherwise, she added, not just Julie but the people around her could be in danger. But Julie said that going to the police was out of the question.

On the Monday morning, she telephoned her former schoolfriend Karen Bishop in Stockwell. She sounded very upset and depressed, and said she was totally confused about her relationship with Jeremy. Karen Bishop went round to Caterham Road, took one look at Julie and told her to pack a bag. She could stay with her and Andy until she'd sorted herself out. Julie accepted the offer with gratitude. That evening, over supper with the Bishops, she gave them an edited version of what she had told Liz. Jeremy, she explained, had a mental problem. He was a psychopath. He felt no sadness about the deaths of his family and his view of what had happened was totally devoid of emotion. Without being explicit, Julie explained there were things Jeremy had done which were so terrible that she couldn't bring herself to talk about them.

Julie told her story to the Bishops in a series of conversations during the first week in September. Some of what she said they knew already: for example, that Jeremy used and grew cannabis at his cottage, and that he was promiscuous and attracted to partners of both sexes. But most of her story was new. They listened in stunned amazement.

Julie said she'd stumbled on a letter which Jeremy had kept stuffed in the tape compartment of his car. It had been written by his mother, to be read in the event of her death. In it, June Bamber apologized for the way in which she'd sometimes treated him. Jeremy had just laughed at this letter, and declared that he was glad she was dead. Then there was Jeremy's obsession with money and material possessions. Julie had tried to persuade him that money wasn't everything, but over the summer Jeremy's obsession had grown even worse. This struck a response in Karen Bishop, who had noticed that Jeremy never missed an opportunity to talk about money, especially in the presence of his friend Brett Collins.

Collins, they agreed, exercised an unwholesome influence over Jeremy. His arrival in Britain in June had prompted a heightened interest by Jeremy in the acquisition of material wealth. Since the massacre, the pair of them had spoken only of liquidating as many of the contents of White House Farm as they could, selling the family silver – literally – not just through Sotheby's, but in dribs and drabs through local antique dealers in exchange for ready cash.

And yet Julie still said nothing to the Bishops about Jeremy hiring a mercenary to murder his family, nor of her own suspicions about Jeremy's true role in the tragedy. Instead she continued to hint at hidden depths to Jeremy's wickedness that she was simply not prepared or able to confront. All she would say over and over as she chain-smoked cigarettes and sipped nervously at a glass of wine was that since the murders, Jeremy had acted very strangely. She also told the Bishops that she had arranged to meet Jeremy on Wednesday afternoon at Sheila's flat in Maida Vale, and that she realized the relationship would have to end.

Wednesday found Julie Mugford sitting disconsolately on the step outside Sheila's flat at Morshead Mansions, Maida Vale, waiting for Jeremy. This was the moment she had been dreading, the confrontation she knew was now inevitable. Typically, Jeremy was late.

When he finally drove up, it was – inevitably – with Brett Collins. Julie demanded to see Jeremy alone, and they crossed the road to a café and sat down.

A few minutes later, Brett Collins came in to find them talking about moving some of Julie's furniture from Caterham Road to her new flat in south-east London. Brett said Jeremy was wanted at the flat. A local dealer had arrived to price some silver. In the flat, the telephone rang. Jeremy picked up the receiver. It was Virginia Greaves.

Virginia had received a message to call Jeremy that afternoon, but it was obvious that someone else was in the room. 'Is Brett there?' she asked.

Jeremy smiled. 'No, it's Julie,' he said.

Julie asked who was on the phone. Jeremy said, 'It's Virginia, and I'm asking her out.' Julie went wild.

Hearing the commotion, Virginia asked, 'What's the matter?'

'It's Julie being angry.'

Julie lunged across and slammed her hand on to the telephone receiver buttons. The line went dead.

'What happened?' asked Virginia Greaves when she called back a moment or two later.

'Julie was asking who was on the phone.'

There was some conversation about Virginia Greaves moving into the flat when Julie ran into the bedroom, picked up a wooden Chinese box belonging to Jeremy and hurled it at the dressing-table mirror. The mirror smashed.

Virginia: 'What's that?'

Jeremy: 'Oh, Julie just smashing some plates up.'

Another crash.

Virginia: 'What's that?'

Jeremy: 'Julie's just put her wrists through the window.'

Virginia: 'I don't want anything to do with that. I'll speak to you sometime.'

'Goodbye, then.'

Jeremy threw down the portable phone. Julie was shaking with rage. Jeremy glanced at the broken mirror. 'Why did you do that?' he asked. Julie said she thought Jeremy had been cruel to ask another woman out while she was still there. She stood staring tearfully out of the window. Jeremy sat on the dressing-table. They spoke briefly about Virginia Greaves; Jeremy said he felt he had

147

every right to ask her out now that his relationship with Julie was at an end. Julie wheeled round and slapped him hard across the face. Jeremy leaped up, seized her right arm and twisted it up behind her back, pushed her roughly down on to the bed and raised his arm as if to strike her. 'Go on then!' she shouted. 'Hit me! And if you do I'll go straight to the Essex Police.'

At that moment, the Essex Police certainly seemed in need of help – or so Robert Boutflour thought, for it was on that day that he telephoned Stan Jones at Witham CID to complain about the lack of action. Jones, on his first day back after his holiday, had to admit to Boutflour that it was slow going. The detective explained that it was a matter of priority; since the case was still being treated as four murders and a suicide, it was classed as non-urgent. Robert Boutflour angrily demanded action. What did he have to do to convince the police that they were being hoodwinked? Stan Jones was sympathetic but explained that a lowly sergeant was in no position to accelerate the inquiry single-handedly. Jones suggested to Boutflour that if he wasn't satisfied with the direction and pace of the investigation, he should write to the chief constable. Boutflour decided to go one better. Thanking Stan Jones for the suggestion, he immediately telephoned Essex Police headquarters at Chelmsford.

Experience of bureaucracies as a young farmer working for the War Agricultural Advisory Service nearly forty years before had taught Boutflour how to short-circuit the usual channels. Within a few minutes he was speaking personally to Essex's Assistant Chief Constable (Crime), Peter Simpson. Boutflour was polite but insistent. The police were fouling up on the Bamber case. What was Simpson going to do about it?

Peter Simpson listened as Boutflour outlined his suspicions. It was a compelling story: a weak and uncoordinated young woman overpowering a strong, well-built farmer in his own kitchen? Shooting her own children and her parents before putting the rifle to her own neck? Jeremy apparently unmoved by the loss of his family, and already preparing to sell off most of the contents of the farm? Simpson jotted some notes on a pad as Boutflour poured out his story. He told the assistant chief constable that he was convinced that Jeremy was responsible for the murders. Finally, Simpson had heard enough. He told Boutflour that he would appoint a senior detective to reinvestigate the case from the very beginning to see where – if anywhere – things had gone wrong.

FIFTEEN

WHEN Stan Jones got back to his office after lunch, he was surprised to find two visitors from headquarters waiting for him. One was Taff Jones, who still clung to his initial reading of the scene at White House Farm and who was convinced that Sheila had murdered everyone in it before shooting herself. The second man was Jim Kineally, a detective superintendent from the Chelmsford HQ with a reputation of being a stickler for detail. Stan Jones's first reaction was to wonder whether, during his three weeks away, something had happened that warranted so heavy a turnout of top CID brass. He and Kineally shook hands. They were old friends, having served together as young constables, but there was no reminiscing as the three men sat down. Kineally explained that he'd been detailed by the chief constable to review the progress of the Bamber case, to see what the officers had established and to learn what had been done with that information. Stan Jones was relieved. It had been a tough time for him. He knew that Taff Jones had been about to move him off the case, and word had come back that Taff thought he'd actually flipped over the Bamber business. At last. Stan Jones thought, something's moving.

The three detectives spent the rest of the afternoon going through the case, analysing what was known, scrutinizing the evidence from the farmhouse, reviewing the suspicions of Robert Boutflour and the other relatives.

In Stockwell, Julie Mugford was telling Karen Bishop

that her affair with Jeremy Bamber was over. Julie showed her friend a cheque for £400 which Jeremy had given her, drawn on the farm account. Julie said she'd been paid off; Jeremy had told her to use the money to take herself and Liz Rimington on holiday. Jeremy said it was his wages cheque for the month, and that Julie should look on it as a twenty-first birthday present. This, Julie said, was the second cheque that Jeremy had given her since the killings. The first, also for £400, was drawn on Jeremy's personal account. He'd described the money as 'expenses', compensation for Julie being unable to keep up her part-time playleader's job in the weeks following the murders.

On Friday morning, two days after the split with Jeremy, Julie broke down completely. She and Karen had been talking about Julie's feelings for the murdered Bambers. Julie said she still couldn't believe they were dead. She was desolate with grief, especially for the twins, and explained that she had been much closer to them than Jeremy ever was. Jeremy himself was evil. The Devil incarnate. Julie admitted that she no longer loved him, but pitied him.

When Julie had regained her composure, she telephoned Jeremy at Goldhanger. She wanted to hold him to his promise to help her move her belongings from Lewisham to her new digs in Hither Green. Jeremy arrived after lunch with Brett Collins, loaded up Julie's things at Caterham Road and drove over to her new flat. On the way, Jeremy asked her if she had been watching the film *Fatal Vision* that had been screened on TV over two nights in the course of the week. Julie said she'd seen part of one episode. It was the story of an American army officer accused of the massacre of his family. Jeremy told her he couldn't bear to watch it, because 'it freaked me out'. They parted on what Julie later reckoned to be 'reasonably amicable' terms. In fact, this was to be the last time the couple saw each other.

On this, the day of her move to Hither Green, Julie had thanked Karen and Andy Bishop for seeing her through a difficult week and had told them that she was planning to get away for a week's holiday with Liz Rimington before the start of the new college term. But the final split with Jeremy seems to have caused her to change her plan, and to review events in a new and different light. She telephoned Liz Rimington at her London flat. Once again, Liz urged Julie to go to the police with her story, but she insisted she couldn't do it. Julie stayed the night at Liz's flat, and on Saturday morning the two women discussed Julie's plight at length. Eventually she agreed to seek the advice of Liz Rimington's former boyfriend, Malcolm Waters, the co-owner of the Frog and Beans in Colchester. Liz called him there and then. 'Come up,' he said, 'and I'll meet you at the station.'

Malcolm Waters knew who Julie was, but they'd never mixed socially, even though she'd worked for him over the Christmas holiday eighteen months before. He knew that she had just split from Jeremy, but he was quite unprepared for her emotional outburst on their arrival at his house. Julie burst into tears. 'I don't know how to put this,' she cried, 'but I'm sure Jeremy was involved in those murders!'

Waters was shocked, but wondered at first if he wasn't merely listening to the anguish of a jilted woman. He questioned her closely to establish if she really had any inside information about the case or whether she had simply been reading the newspapers. Once again, Julie named Matthew McDonald as the man Jeremy had paid to murder the family. Malcolm Waters knew McDonald, but only as a customer. Julie said Jeremy had agreed to pay him £2,000, and was now selling things from the farm to raise the cash. She explained that Jeremy had planned it all for months and now he was boasting about having got away with it. Jeremy, she added, had threatened her with reprisals if she confided in anyone else. What was she to do? Waters's advice was brief: go straight to the police.

Stan Jones was planning an evening out with his wife Helene when the telephone rang. It was someone at Witham Police Station saying that Liz Rimington wanted to speak to him urgently.

'I bet this is Julie coming forward,' Jones murmured to his wife as he dialled the number. 'Guarantee it.' The phone was answered almost at once. The conversation was extremely brief.

'Liz? Stan Jones.'

'Hello.'

'Have you got Julie with you?'

'Yes.'

'Is it about the Bamber case?'

'Yes.'

'Is she making allegations?'

'Yes.'

'Right,' Stan Jones said. 'I'll be right over.'

With a hurried excuse to his wife, Stan Jones jumped into his Citroën Dyane, still wearing his jeans and white trainers. The journey to Colchester up the A12 took less than an hour. As he drove, the detective's mind was racing ahead to the prospect of arresting Jeremy Bamber, the man he'd always said had been responsible for the White House Farm killings. It was as if all the weight of the misbegotten investigation had been lifted from his shoulders. He thought of the senior officers, his 'Guv'nor' Taff Jones, and all the sarcastic remarks he'd endured at the office. Now he knew he would be proved right after all.

At Malcolm Waters's house in Colchester, Stan Jones asked Julie point-blank: 'Did Jeremy do it?'

'Yes.' She could hardly bear to look at the detective after all the deception, all the half-truths. But Stan Jones smiled a reassuring smile.

'Right,' he said. 'Come on, let's go.'

In the car to Witham, Julie explained that she just couldn't live with Jeremy's secret any more. She had tried to deny the truth to herself by trying to believe Jeremy's story about hiring a hit man. But it didn't work. She couldn't sleep, it was preying on her mind, and now she just wanted the truth to come out.

At Witham Police Station, Julie was cool and calm, but mostly relieved. The local CID inspector, Bob Miller, was called in from home, and Julie repeated her allegations to him. Next to arrive was Detective Superintendent Mick Ainsley, the senior CID officer on duty. Stan Jones spoke to him briefly and told him the gist of what Julie Mugford was saying. Ainsley immediately decided the situation warranted a call to the head of Essex CID, Taff Jones, who was spending the evening at an official dinner. 'While we're all waiting for the boss,' Ainsley told Stan Jones, 'you'd better make a start on her statement.' Ainsley added that he personally would make arrangements to pick up Jeremy. Stan Jones led Julie into his office.

'I nearly told you on that second day after the murders,' she said quietly.

'Yes,' said Stan, 'I know. I should have pushed you a bit more.'

SIXTEEN

AT SEVEN O'CLOCK the following morning, Sunday, 8 September, Detective Chief Inspector Taff Jones rang the doorbell of Sheila's flat in Morshead Mansions, Maida Vale. It was some minutes before a dishevelled Jeremy Bamber came to the door. He looked blearily at the small group of detectives gathered on the front step. Taff Jones told him he was being arrested on suspicion of murdering his family. Inside the flat, they found Brett Collins sleeping naked in one of the beds. He was woken and told to get up. He was going back to Essex with his friend.

Jeremy dressed in a green shirt and jeans, and laced up his favourite white baseball boots. The waiting detectives told them they were being taken to Chelmsford for questioning. Jeremy grabbed a canvas bag and packed quickly: a blue jumper, blue shirt, some socks and underwear were stowed with a spare pair of shoes.

By nine, they were in Chelmsford. At police headquarters, Jeremy was told to turn out all his personal belongings. These included a wooden box containing £1,460 in notes, a cheque for £589, some small foreign coins, a building society passbook and three cheque-books. At 9.35, Taff Jones walked him to the detention room. Bamber was given a cup of tea and some breakfast. At 11 a.m., he was taken up to the interview room. DCI Jones showed him a chair and formally cautioned him.

'What was your relationship like with your mother?'

'Rough and smooth.'

'Did you antagonize your mother by speaking to her about religion?'

'It's not really fair, the way you angle your question. About eighteen months ago, we'd have had heated arguments which was through a lack of understanding for each other's views, and due in part to Mother's strong character and (to some extent) my immaturity, but over the last couple of years, eighteen months, we've found much more common ground, due somewhat to mature discussion and all of us giving a little and trying to be more understanding.'

'Was your relationship, then, over the last six months quite amicable?'

'Yes, it was quite amicable. But every now and again we would have our moments. But in general things were more loving towards each other.'

The interview moved on to the events of the murder night. 'At one stage during the evening, I believe you took the .22 rifle out to shoot a rabbit. Where did you get it from?'

'The gun? Out of the study, I think.'

'Was the silencer on it?'

'No, I don't think so.'

'Did you put the silencer or telescopic sights on the gun?'

'No.'

'Do you know where they are kept in the house?'

'No. In the study, I should think.'

'Did you use the gun?'

'Did I fire a shot?'

'Yes.'

'No.'

'What did you do with the gun when you returned home?'

'I put it down by the seat thing [the bench], unclipped the magazine, and put it down by the side.'

'Who was in the house at that time, when you returned?'

'Everybody. Mother, Father, Sheila and the twins. I think the twins, the last time I came in the house, were in bed.'

'What conversation did you have with Sheila and your parents?'

'We talked about what I was doing on the farm, talked about general things and about things we were going to do in the future. We talked about Sheila and the twins and their future. They [Nevill and June] spoke with regards to her coming down to Essex, having the twins fostered, paying someone to look after them, and Sheila working on the caravan site. Just general things that could happen.'

'Who took part in the conversation?'

'All of us. Mother, Father, Sheila and me.'

'Did Sheila react to the conversation of someone else looking after the kids?'

'She didn't really. Although I wasn't paying much attention to the conversation. She didn't really express any reaction . . .'

'. . . When you spoke to Julie on the phone, did you not say to her words to the effect of "Tonight's the night"?'

'No.'

'Are you sure?'

'Certain.'

'Have you not planned over a number of months to get rid of your parents, Sheila and the children?'

'No.'

'Did you go back to the farmhouse and shoot all five of them?'

'No.'

At 1.30 p.m., Bamber was taken back to his cell and given a meal. Then he took a catnap.

*

Stan Jones was furious when he learned about this first interview with his prime suspect. He was already angry that he'd not been allowed to arrest Jeremy personally, that he'd been left at the margin of events taking down Julie Mugford's statement. He couldn't understand why he'd been denied his big chance. He consoled himself with the idea that the bosses had considered he was getting on so well with Julie Mugford that they couldn't risk sending him to London in case she changed her mind while he was away. Anyway, Stan Jones reasoned, arresting Jeremy Bamber was just a formality. It was also the one chance Taff Jones might get to restore some of his lost credibility, to cover himself in some much-needed glory. But then word came out of the big set piece interview that Jeremy was denying everything. Despite all that Julie had said, Taff was getting nowhere.

Julie Mugford, for the moment Essex Police's most valuable property, had spent the night in a room at the cadet hostel at Police Headquarters at Chelmsford, with Liz Rimington sharing the room to keep her company. On Sunday morning, both women were driven back to Witham in a police car. Neither had brought her overnight things, and they had no toothbrushes or toothpaste. Stan Jones, with his characteristic bluntness, immediately nicknamed Julie 'Dogbreath'. 'Bloody hell,' he said, 'you stink. You'd better have some of these.' He offered his tube of Polo mints. Liz Rimington was dispatched to organize overnight bags. Taking her statement – an extended history of her affair with Jeremy and his role in the murders – was going to be a long job.

Stan Jones sat Julie down and gave her a cigarette. He told her that in giving her statement, everything – everything – would have to come out. Anything and everything that had ever happened between her and Jeremy Bamber.

It would have to come out and be included in the statement. Everything. Nothing at all could be held back. There were to be no skeletons left in any cupboards.

'In that case,' said Julie, blowing a stream of smoke at the ceiling, 'I'd better tell you about the burglary.'

Julie briefly explained that Jeremy had burgled the office at Osea Road Caravan Site earlier in the year and had stolen nearly £1,000 from the safe. She had gone with him, she admitted, to act as lookout.

'You're saying you were involved?' Stan Jones asked. Julie nodded. She also admitted getting involved in Jeremy's cannabis deals.

'Right,' said Stan Jones, putting on his glasses and taking a pad of statement forms from a drawer in his desk. He flashed her one of his smiles. 'Let's begin at the beginning.'

The interview with Jeremy Bamber resumed at Chelmsford police headquarters at 4 p.m. Taff Jones and Detective Constable Mick Barlow were the questioners:

'... On the night of 23 or 24 March this year, a burglary occurred at the Osea Bay [sic] Caravan Site where £980 in cash was stolen. Was [sic] you involved in that burglary?'

'Yes ... Julie and I went down there. Broke in, as she has said ... I knew I'd be number one suspect, but that they couldn't prove it. The money would come in handy buying drinks and things for the house ...'

'Why did you do it?'

'To bring home to the other directors and people involved in the caravan site that we were too lackadaisical, and the reasons why we were always getting done. It was to prove a point.'

'At the time of your arrest this morning, in the small brown box which contained your money there was a

small plastic bank bag which appeared to contain cannabis. What is it?'

'Grass. Marijuana.'

'Where did you get it from?'

'Holland. Amsterdam.'

'Is that for your own use?'

'Yes. Julie's and mine. We were the only ones who
smoked it.'

'There was also a pipe in that box. Is that yours?'

'No. Well, it is now. It belonged to Sheila. And when I
went to her flat I found it.'

'Do you deal in drugs?'

'No.'

'Have you ever dealt in drugs?'

'No, not in the last twelve months, but [there were] a
couple of deals to a guy in Scotland who I met hitchhiking
near Birmingham. I sold him three lots, although he
didn't pay me for the last. These transactions were done
through the post.'

'Now. With regards to the deaths of your parents,
sister and her kids – and bearing in mind Julie is telling
us the truth about these things – what Julie says you said
to her on the night in question is something to the effect
of "Tonight's the night". Did you say that?'

'No.'

'You received a phone call from your father some time
after three?'

'Yes. I can't remember the exact time now, but I put it
in my original statement.'

'When the phone was cut off, did you ring back
immediately?'

'Yes, twenty or thirty seconds later.'

'And you tried a couple of times?'

'Yes, my phone has a memory redial. I normally use it
when a number I try is engaged.'

'Did you *then* phone your girlfriend?'

'Yes.'

'And how long were you on the phone to her?'

'A minute, two minutes. Not very long as I had to ring the police.'

'Did you *then* ring the Chelmsford police?'

'Yes.'

'Did you know the number?'

'No, I had to look it up.'

'Approximately how long would it have taken you to find the number and get through?'

'Ten minutes at the outside.'

'And then you've got another ten minutes when you were on hold to the police.'

'About five minutes. It seemed like ages. Times are approximate.'

'Were all these phone calls made to give the appearance it was not you involved in the shooting of your parents?'

'No.'

'Sure about that?'

'Yes.'

'Have you discussed with your girlfriend getting rid of your parents?'

'No.'

Taff Jones strode back to his office and telephoned Stan Jones at Witham. He came straight to the point. He was getting nothing out of Jeremy Bamber. The girl – Julie Mugford – must be neurotic, he declared. She's telling lies, making everything up.

'Hang on, she can't be telling all lies,' Stan Jones replied. 'She's coughed the burglary. And she's coughed the drugs. That's all true, isn't it?'

Taff Jones agreed that Jeremy had admitted the burglary.

'Well then,' Stan Jones replied, 'she's telling the truth, isn't she?'

That evening, in the detention room at Essex Police headquarters, Jeremy Bamber was served a takeaway meal of fried chicken and chips. By 9 p.m. he was asleep. At Witham, where there was no police canteen on a Sunday, Stan Jones sent out to a local hotel and shared coffee and sandwiches with Julie Mugford, served on a silver tray. During the meal break, the telephone rang. Jeremy's cottage had been searched, Stan Jones was told, and a load of equipment for growing marijuana seized. There was also a lady's red bicycle leaning against the kitchen wall. The scene-of-crime people had decided to bring that in as well. It was going well at Witham, Stan thought to himself as he drove home. But how long was it going to take Taff Jones to get a confession out of Jeremy Bamber?

SEVENTEEN

MONDAY morning began with a case conference at Essex Police headquarters. Peter Simpson, the Assistant Chief Constable (Crime), took the chair. All the CID top brass sat round a big table in one of the conference rooms. Stan Jones and a couple of detective constables joined them. Simpson went round the table, asking everyone for their views on the case, and an opinion on the role of Jeremy Bamber. When it came to Stan Jones's turn, he couldn't resist glancing at Taff Jones, glaring at him from across the table. 'I think Bamber's our man,' said Stan Jones, 'and I've thought so from the word go. Can I tell you why I think it's down to Bamber?'

He itemized the points one by one: the fact that Sheila's feet and legs were clean, while the kitchen had resembled a bloodbath; the fact that Jeremy had behaved throughout with a remarkable nonchalance and without genuine remorse or distress; and the fact that according to his girlfriend Julie Mugford, Jeremy Bamber had been plotting the slaughter of his family for the best part of a year. Stan shot a second glance at Taff Jones, who was shaking his head silently. The room was quiet. Then George Harris, the divisional superintendent who had turned out at the farm on the morning of the massacre, spoke. After listening to Sergeant Jones, Harris told the meeting, he, too, was persuaded that Jeremy Bamber was responsible. People around the table who'd been non-committal until this point now began nodding sagely. Stan Jones looked across at Taff Jones. It was a perfect opportunity for the head of the CID to give in gracefully and to admit that he may have been wrong. Instead, Taff Jones cleared his throat and said, 'No. My original theory still stands.'

All eyes now turned to Peter Simpson, the officer in overall command of the investigation. 'I've listened to every word that's been said,' he murmured, 'and I must go along with Sergeant Jones.'

At 11.26 a.m., Jeremy Bamber was formally charged by the police with burglary at the Osea Road Caravan Site. An hour later, he was back in the interview room. Now Taff Jones asked the questions.

'On the day of the funeral, it's been alleged that prior to the funeral and after it you were in a very happy mood. Is that so?'

'"Happy" is the wrong word.'

'How would you describe it?'

'Manic depression.'

'Was Brett [Collins] not joking with you about your feelings and the way you looked?'

'He may have been joking to raise my spirits. He made me laugh. He wasn't there to make me sad.'

'Did he suggest that you should put some white powder on your face and some black under your eyes to make you look sadder?'

'Jokingly. Because of the knowledge that my photo would be in the paper. And that morning I'd been made to laugh on a few occasions, it may have been said. But as it happens, by the time I arrived at the church my mood had changed to awful pain, tears, etcetera. I'd been harassed by the press.'

Later that afternoon, Jeremy was served a meal of salad, bread and biscuits, and allowed a shower. His fingerprints were taken, and he was seen by his solicitor, Bruce Bowler. At 6.45 p.m., Jeremy Bamber was led from the detention room to the magistrates' court. He was again charged with burglary at the Osea Road Caravan Site, and remanded in custody for four days. Back in the detention room, Jeremy asked for a meal to be sent in at his expense, along with a six-pack of Pepsi. After a short walk in the exercise yard and a second shower, he was locked up for the night shortly before 10 p.m. In less than an hour, he was fast asleep.

Shortly before 9 a.m. the following morning, Jeremy was served breakfast and took a twenty-minute walk around the exercise yard. In the detention room, he was allowed a can of Pepsi, which he drank from a plastic cup. At 11.45 a.m. Stan Jones arrived and led Jeremy Bamber upstairs to the first-floor interview room.

Stan Jones had spent two days on Julie Mugford's statement. Now he had the job he really wanted – interviewing Jeremy Bamber. Detective Constable Clark sat in. So did Bruce Bowler.

Jones began the interview by reminding Bamber that he was still under caution. Then, the core question: 'Did you murder five members of your family?'

'No,' Jeremy Bamber replied.

The first session of what turned out to be a marathon interview lasting three days was concerned mainly with Bamber's relationship with Julie Mugford. He described their first meeting towards the end of 1983 at Sloppy Joe's, and the couple's first date on Boxing Day of that year. To Jones's suggestion that Jeremy became a boy-friend of Julie, Bamber insisted that '*she* became *my* girlfriend'. He agreed that his mother had disapproved of the fact that by Easter 1984 Julie was living with him during her college holidays at the cottage in Goldhanger. Jeremy had just moved in, and the place needed decorat-ing and furnishing. Julie, who had an eye for such things, helped plan the decor and pick out the carpets and the furniture. Jeremy was more interested in equipping the cottage with luxuries such as a sunbed, a television set with teletext, and other electrical gadgets. He told the detectives that he had bought it all with £3,000 of his own savings, plus a bank loan of £1,000. He denied ever complaining that his parents hadn't done enough for him, like buying the carpets and furniture for him. As Bamber himself put it, 'Why should they?' He was comfortably off on his own account. He was drawing a salary and a bonus from the farm, a fee from the caravan site, lived in a rent-free house and drove a free car with unlimited free petrol. Bamber himself reckoned the package was worth between £18,000 and £20,000 a year.

The two detectives questioned Jeremy about his parents' legacy.

'What would you gain if your parents were dead?' asked Jones.

Bamber: 'Nothing.'

'Surely, if your mum and dad died, you'd be left something?'

'True.'

'What would you be left?'

'You can see the wills. Look at the wills.'

'Would you and Sheila be left half shares, basically?'

'Yes.'

'What about the twins?'

'I don't remember if they are mentioned in the wills. I think they are, but I'm not sure. But certainly not in name.'

'So if Sheila and your parents died, you'd basically get everything?'

'Understandably so.'

'What would you have got?'

'Most of it. Everything.'

After the lunch break, the questions about Julie continued. Bamber repeatedly denied discussing with her any plan or plot to murder his family, despite Julie's assertion that for well over a year, Bamber had often spoken of killing them. So why, the detectives asked, should Julie tell lies?

'I think there are many reasons,' said Bamber.

'Tell me the reasons,' said Detective Sergeant Jones.

'Jilted love being the main one.'

'If she was jilted,' said Jones, 'and accused you of murder, and you were charged, she'd have lost you anyway. So how can you say "jilted"?'

'Yes,' Bamber replied, 'she has lost me. And if she could put me behind bars, then no one else could have me either.'

'She still loves you, and keeps wishing this was a dream,' the detective went on. 'Why would she try and get you into trouble?'

'That's her opinion.'

'She states that some time last year, you told her that you'd like to kill all the family, which included Sheila and the twins. Do you remember that?'

'I never said anything of the sort.'

'She states that she said to you: "I can understand you talking like that about your parents, but why kill Sheila and the twins? They've done nothing to you." Do you remember saying that?'

'It was never spoken about. Ever.'

'She says that you told her that Sheila was crazy and had done nothing on the farm, so she didn't deserve anything. Did you say that?'

'No.'

'She states that by killing her it would be getting her out of her misery. Did you say that?'

'No.'

'She says you also said it would be doing the twins a favour as well if they were killed, as they would grow up disturbed because of the way they were being brought up. Did you say that?'

'No.'

'She says that from July 1984 . . . you were paranoid about killing the whole family. Did you say that at any time?'

'No.'

'She said that you stated you would like to commit the perfect murder. Did you say that?'

'No.'

'She also states that you said you'd go to the house for supper in the evening when they were all there, and put something in their drinks to make them sleep well. You said that your father would be in the lounge having a drink and a cigarette. You'd use gin and vodka on the floor, set fire to the house, and the police would believe that [your father] had accidentally set the house on fire with the cigarette end when he'd fallen asleep in the chair. The fire would destroy all the evidence. Did you say all that to her?'

'No,' replied Jeremy Bamber.

EIGHTEEN

WHILE Jeremy Bamber was giving an account of himself, the police were also talking to two other men about their role in the events leading up to the massacre at White House Farm. The first was Brett Collins, who had been arrested along with Jeremy and driven to Chelmsford.

In his statement Collins said he and Jeremy had first met in Auckland in the autumn of 1981 when he had been introduced by a mutual friend. Jeremy had stayed at Collins's house for about three months before moving on to Australia. The two had next met in June 1985 when Collins flew to London from Hawaii. Jeremy drove Collins up to Goldhanger where they had spent part of the summer. Brett Collins said he found Jeremy's parents pleasant enough, but considered Nevill Bamber 'a bit reserved and standoffish' and had been told that June Bamber had been mentally disturbed. He never met Sheila, but had come to know Julie Mugford quite well. 'They seemed to be close,' he reported, but 'more on Julie's side than on Jeremy's. He seemed to want more of a friendship but she was obviously thinking of marriage.' Collins added that Jeremy had been two-timing Julie by going out with other women.

Brett Collins explained that he had flown to the Greek island of Mykonos for a holiday on 20 July. Seeing the White House Farm murders reported in the English newspapers in early August, he had caught the first available flight back to London 'specifically to be with Jeremy and to help out'. Over lunch on his first day back, Brett Collins found Jeremy 'vacant and not seeming like the person I left a month ago'. Collins claimed to have avoided the subject of the murders, saying he didn't want to push Jeremy on the subject. Julie filled him in on the details. But as the weeks passed, Collins had been emboldened to discuss with Jeremy the subject of his inheritance. According to Brett Collins, Jeremy expected to get his mother's share of the Osea Road Caravan Site, which would give him a 50 per cent stake in it. Some of the land at White House Farm was owned – rather than tenanted – by the family, and this would be left to him. So would some shares in the house in Guildford formerly owned by Nevill Bamber's mother.

The police questioned Brett Collins about Bamber's behaviour on the day of his parents' funeral. Collins recalled that in the morning, Jeremy had been in reasonably good spirits, mainly because he was surrounded by his friends. By way of a joke, Collins himself suggested that Jeremy coat his face with white powder to make it look as if he had been grieving for weeks. This was purely a joke, Collins insisted. In the days leading up to the funeral, Jeremy had been 'very upset, shocked and cold to us all'. His family had advised him to look to the future and to put the tragedy behind him. Brett Collins himself was eliminated as a suspect after he gave police full details of his holiday itinerary.

On Monday evening, 9 September, two armed police officers arrested Matthew McDonald as he arrived at the home of one of his mistresses in the Prettygate district of Colchester. McDonald was the 41-year-old self-employed plumber and central heating engineer whom Julie claimed Jeremy had hired to massacre his family for a fee of £2,000. At Witham Police Station, McDonald was told he was suspected of the Bamber murders. In fact, he was quickly able to establish an impregnable alibi by referring detectives to another woman with whom he said he had spent the murder night. This woman, a part-time secretary whom McDonald had met at a nightclub in Colchester, confirmed that it was her custom to sleep with him at her home once a week, on either a Tuesday or a Wednesday, and that on the night of the killings at White House Farm, McDonald had been with her from 8.30 in the evening until 5.30 the following morning when he left for work.

Having satisfied the police on the question of his whereabouts on the murder night, Matthew McDonald proceeded to tell them his story. He confessed that he was a married man whose wife was a nurse, but that he enjoyed a freewheeling life in the bars and clubs of Colchester, usually in the company of other women. McDonald clearly remembered where and when he'd first encountered Jeremy Bamber. It was on 5 November 1981 at the Frog and Beans wine bar. Jeremy's appearance was memorable too. He wore full make-up and a pair of very bright red skintight jeans. Both men were on their own, and struck up a conversation over a drink. Visiting the Frog and Beans ten days later, McDonald ran into Jeremy for a second time. Jeremy was with his girlfriend, Suzette Ford, and her friend Christine Bacon, whose marriage was about to end in divorce. He called McDonald over, and the foursome was complete. McDonald and Christine Bacon soon began an affair. And at some point, Matthew McDonald also slept with Suzette Ford. When Jeremy found out, he was furious. Shortly after this, McDonald left the country to work on a building contract in Libya. When he returned to Britain two months later, the nights out as a foursome were less frequent.

But in the early summer of 1983, Jeremy contacted McDonald again, asking if he could supply him with some cannabis seeds. Like Jeremy, McDonald used to smoke grass [marijuana], and the couple did a deal involving McDonald supplying Jeremy with some seeds in return for a bag of marijuana. Another transaction the following winter involved McDonald paying Jeremy £5 for a 3-gram piece of cannabis resin. Jeremy said he'd obtained it from Freddie Emami, Sheila's boyfriend.

Matthew McDonald's dealings with Jeremy Bamber in the months that followed were based exclusively on drugs. In the spring of 1984, McDonald visited Jeremy's cottage in Goldhanger and saw that he was growing cannabis plants on his window sill. On this and on subsequent visits to Bourtree Cottage, McDonald and Jeremy smoked grass together. McDonald told the police that he hadn't seen Jeremy since December 1984, nine months before the murders. Jeremy called round to Christine Bacon's house and gave her two ducks for Christmas, telling her he'd shot them with his new rifle.

Later, asked about the stories of fighting-abroad as a mercenary soldier, Matthew McDonald said he'd never even been in the forces. There was a story about him being a mercenary when he went out to Libya, he explained, and although it was pure fabrication he kept it going because 'it made people think I was somebody'. In fact it was all totally untrue. As for the claim that Jeremy Bamber had offered him £2,000 to murder his family, this too was a pack of lies.

Detectives checked out McDonald's story with the two women with whom he'd admitted conducting concurrent affairs. Christine Bacon, now divorced, said that because Matthew was self-employed and carried out subcontracts for other firms, 'I never know where he works or exactly what type of work he does.' And although Matthew was the father of her baby son, they had never lived together as man and wife. Matthew supported the child by making regular maintenance payments to her in cash. Mrs Bacon told police that she thought Matthew McDonald was divorced, and that although she didn't know his address or telephone number, she believed he lived somewhere in Colchester. 'The reason for this,' she explained, 'is that he often says he has to go home and feed his dog. He's normally only gone about five or ten minutes.'

McDonald's other mistress, Mary Southgate, another divorcee, was also under the impression that Matthew was divorced. She told police that he visited her from time to time, normally on a Tuesday or a Wednesday evening, when he would stay the night and leave at about five in the morning. He explained that he had a dog to walk, or that he was meeting his work partner. McDonald had told her that he made a living as a plumber, and that he used to be in the Army. The subject was never discussed in any detail, but according to Mary Southgate, McDonald had never claimed to be a mercenary soldier.

Taff Jones read Matthew McDonald's statement. The self-employed plumber might have been guilty of two-timing his wife and mistresses, but not of murdering five members of the Bamber family. He picked up the telephone on his desk and dialled a number. Matthew McDonald was free to go.

The detectives were intrigued by the tale told by another of Jeremy Bamber's friends, the sales manager for a computer firm, called Charles Marsden. Marsden was also the boyfriend of Liz Rimington. He described how he'd become part of Jeremy's set at the Frog and Beans wine bar in Colchester. He explained that in a crowd that included women, Jeremy would splash out with money to the extent that he could be called 'flash'. 'He was impressed by money,' Marsden added. 'He was impressed by people who spend a lot and the things that money could buy, such as expensive cars.' Although he worked for a modest wage on his father's farm, Jeremy had boasted that one day he would be a wealthy man. Marsden took this to mean that one day Jeremy expected to inherit his parents' money.

In December 1984, Jeremy had announced that his entire family were getting together to celebrate Christmas. This was unusual. During a drinking session at a wine bar in Maldon, Jeremy had confided to Charles Marsden that if the farmhouse were to burn down over Christmas, everything would be his. 'I thought at the time that this was a strange thing to say,' Marsden reported, 'but didn't particularly take any notice.'

At teatime on the day following the White House Farm massacre, Jeremy Bamber had appeared at Charles Marsden's office in Colchester. Marsden knew nothing of what had happened, and Jeremy poured out the story that Marsden later read in the newspapers. The two men drove to a little pub outside Colchester and talked for about half an hour. 'I thought it strange that Jeremy had come to see me with this news,' Marsden admitted, 'but I thought he was probably in shock.' What struck Charles Marsden most forcibly was that in speaking of Sheila – the sister he said had murdered his entire family and then shot herself – Jeremy showed neither emotion nor anger towards her.

Marsden said that he had visited Jeremy at his cottage the previous Thursday night. Brett Collins had cooked them a chicken dinner and the three had then repaired to the Caribbean Cottage at Burnham for drinks. Jeremy had announced that he and Julie had split up the previous weekend. While he didn't give a specific reason, Marsden had the impression that Julie had disliked Brett Collins. In any case, Jeremy added, he now had a new girlfriend, Virginia Greaves, who used to go out with Mike Deckers of the Frog and Beans. Jeremy also told Charles Marsden that he and Brett were going to sell Bourtree Cottage and move to Sheila's flat in Maida Vale. Virginia would move in too, Jeremy added.

The detectives seemed anxious to probe Jeremy Bamber's sexual habits and preferences. They learned from Charles Marsden that Jeremy possessed an animal magnetism for women. Marsden said that while he knew of only two serious girlfriends, Suzette Ford and Julie Mugford, Jeremy had had many one-night stands. He enjoyed going to clubs, such as Stringfellows in London, pulling women. Marsden recalled an evening before the murders when he and Jeremy had gone drinking at Jeremy's local, the Chequers at Goldhanger. They had picked up a couple of girls, one of whom had agreed to return with them to Jeremy's cottage. Marsden, very drunk, had crashed out in Jeremy's bed. Some time later, he'd been awoken by movement in the bed. Lying there half asleep, Marsden realized that Jeremy had brought the girl upstairs and that the couple were having sex. The idea of three-in-a-bed sex excited the detectives' curiosity still further. But Charles Marsden was at pains to insist that he hadn't taken part in the sex session. And when Jeremy returned from walking the girl home, Marsden himself had got up and driven home.

Stan Jones was nettled by all these stories about Jeremy's strange lifestyle. To him, Jeremy's behaviour since the killings seemed incompatible with the behaviour of a bereaved innocent. Yet Jones had failed to find a fingerhold, a chink in Bamber's story that could be exploited and whittled at. The detective's anger and frustration only boiled over once in his mental chess game with Bamber, and that was on Tuesday morning as they walked from his cell to the interview room.

'You did it, didn't you?' Stan Jones growled. 'I knew

you did it from the second day. You won't get away with it. You're sick, you need help.'

Jeremy made no reply.

NINETEEN

STAN JONES was sure he was going to wring a confession from Jeremy Bamber. 'I had a strange feeling we were going to get a cough,' he recalled. 'A gut feeling.' Had procedures been different, he thought, had the detectives been allowed to tape-record the interview, Jeremy Bamber might have confessed. The Police and Criminal Evidence Act (PACE) was just around the corner, heralding changes to the rules governing the interviewing of suspects, but these changes came too late to be applied in the case of Jeremy Bamber. 'He got into so many corners,' Stan Jones remembered, 'but he had time to think while we were writing the questions and answers down. It was all going so slowly. He'd answer one question, then he'd have time to consider the next question even before you'd asked it! He was ahead. And to me, the only person who could do that was the murderer.'

On Tuesday afternoon, 10 September, Stan Jones and Mick Clark were still interviewing Jeremy Bamber in the presence of his Chelmsford solicitor, Bruce Bowler. They were discussing the ways of getting in to White House Farm without a door key. Julie had said that Jeremy told her he had found a way to get in and out without anyone knowing. Stan Jones asked if that was true.

Jeremy said, 'That is untrue.'

'Do you know a way in and out of White House which anyone wouldn't discover?'

'No.'

'Only, you see, Julie states that there was a window in the house with a catch on it. You can open the window and close it, bang on the frame from the outside and the catch will close, giving the appearance that the window is secure — and is, in fact, secure. Furthermore, she states that you told her of such a window. Did you tell her?'

'I don't think so.'

Surely,' said Stan Jones, 'the answer should be "No", shouldn't it? Because you've just said you don't know of such a window at the White House.'

"I don't think so" is another way of saying "No".'

'So you couldn't have told her about such a window?'

'No.'

'You see, in the White House, there is one window which can do exactly what she says you told her. What have you to say about that?'

'There may be such windows, but I don't know about them.'

'How would she know of such a window if you hadn't told her?'

'She's been to the house. She might have spotted that type of window.'

'Are you telling me that she's in your parents' house and she's going round trying to find a way in and out without anyone knowing?'

'She might do, to make her story look better.'

'What story?'

'The allegations against me having involvement in my family's death.'

'When are you saying she's done this, then?'

'I'm not suggesting she has or hasn't, but she's had opportunity in the last six weeks.'

'The opportunity to do what?'

'To look round the house.'

'For what reason?'

'To look for this particular window that you and her say exists.'

'I can't see what you're getting at, to be quite honest.'

'I'm not getting at anything.'

'I believe that in fact you told her about this window, and what she says is true, there is such a window and I believe you told her about it. Is that correct?'

'No.'

The detectives moved on to another claim made by Julie Mugford, that Jeremy experimented with her tranquillizer pills, to see if they could be dissolved in drink without leaving a taste. 'She states,' said Stan Jones, 'that when she came down to see you a few days later, [you said] the pills were useless and didn't have the desired effect. Did you say that?'

'No.'

'But she did bring the pills down?'

'They were her medication that she brought with her.'

'Is it true she brought them down?'

'They were her medication and she brought them with her,' repeated Jeremy Bamber.

'So she is telling the truth when she says that she brought pills down to your house when she was doing her teaching practice last year?'

'She needed the tranquillizers so she brought them with her.'

'So,' said the detective sergeant, 'she is telling the truth about the pills, that she brought them down to Goldhanger?'

'She brought her medication down with her, yes.'

'Yes what?'

'Yes, she brought her medication down to Goldhanger.'

Stan Jones looked at Bruce Bowler, then at Jeremy Bamber. 'You don't like to tell me that Julie tells the truth when she says she brought the pills down to Goldhanger. She says she did and you confirmed it. That is the truth which you try to deny. It's obviously true what she said. And I feel the reason you won't admit she's telling the truth is because I might believe her when she says you told her the story of trying the pills out to use them for murder. What do you say to that?'

'She did bring her medication down to Goldhanger for her tension or whatever, and not for me.'

'If she is telling the truth about bringing the pills down, why has she made up the story about the other part?'

'Ask her,' said Jeremy Bamber.

The interview moved to the night of the killings. Jeremy said he watched television that night and telephoned Julie. Then he went to bed, and slept 'like a log'. In the middle of the night, he was woken by a telephone call from his father. The call was cut short, and when Jeremy tried to call his father back, he got the engaged tone.

'You then phoned Chelmsford Police Station and told them what had happened. Is that right?'

'No,' said Bamber, 'I think I phoned Julie before them, first.'

Stan Jones asked, 'Why phone Julie before phoning the police?'

'I don't remember my reasons.'

Stan Jones pulled some papers from a folder. 'In your first statement,' he said, peering over his glasses, 'you stated verbally and in writing that you first of all phoned the police and then Julie. Why have you changed your story?'

'I don't remember the sequence of events.'

'But you have just said here that you phoned Julie before the police, and you don't remember the reasons why you did so. So why are you now saying you don't remember the sequence of events?'

'Because I had forgotten the times and the sequence.'

Stan Jones reminded Jeremy Bamber that he had been

asked by several police officers about his actions that night, and that he had said he phoned the police before calling Julie. So what *was* the correct order?

'I don't remember,' said Jeremy, 'but my first statement was done at the time and must be correct.'

(In his statement on 8 August, Jeremy Bamber claimed that he called Chelmsford Police 'immediately' after getting the engaged tone. He timed his father's call at about 3.10 a.m. According to this first statement, it was 'about 3.25 a.m.' when he telephoned Julie to tell her something seemed to be wrong.)

'So you are saying that you phoned the police before phoning Julie?'

'That must be the case.'

'So why – today – have you said you phoned Julie before the police?'

'Mistake.'

'Are you sure it's a mistake,' murmured Sergeant Jones, 'and not a lie?'

'Yes.'

Jones was setting a trap. 'Tell me again who you phoned first, the police or Julie?'

'I don't remember, it's in my statement.'

'You are saying that your first statement is correct?'

'Yes.'

'Do you remember speaking to Detective Chief Inspector [Taff] Jones on Sunday?'

'Yes,' said Bamber, 'and making the same mistake.'

'What do you mean by that?' asked Stan Jones.

'I think I was muddled,' said Jeremy Bamber. 'He asked me [about] the same sequence of phone calls and I wasn't sure of them either.'

Stan Jones reminded Jeremy that he had told Taff Jones on the previous Sunday that he had tried a couple of times to call his father back. Then, he had told the detective chief inspector, he had telephoned Julie. Not the police. He had spoken to Julie for only a minute or two – 'not very long' – because he had to telephone the police. 'Do you remember saying that?' asked Stan Jones.

'I think so,' Jeremy said slowly. 'It just shows how easily one can forget the sequence of events.'

Taff Jones's next question had been: 'Did you then ring the Chelmsford Police?' To which Jeremy had replied, 'Yes.' Did Jeremy agree?

'I think that is what I said.'

'Let's get this straight,' said Stan Jones. 'On the day in question, you say you phoned the police *then* Julie. On Sunday you tell DCI Jones you phoned Julie first *then* the police. Today you first of all tell us you phoned Julie first and *then* the police (agreeing with what you told DCI Jones) and now you've gone back to phoning the police first and *then* Julie. Do you agree this is what you have said?'

'I could remember my conversation with DCI Jones and so it was said the same today but my first statement is the true one. And it shows how easy it is to muddle events, the sequence of events, after two months . . . seven weeks.' [In fact, five weeks.]

Stan Jones looked at his watch. It was 5.30 p.m. 'To finalize this, your first statement states you phoned the police first and *then* Julie. Is that the correct and honest version?'

'Yes,' said Jeremy Bamber.

At 9 p.m. Jeremy was taken back to the detention room for the night. The interview had lasted about nine hours with a meal break of ninety minutes. Stan Jones and Mick Clark drove over to police headquarters where Mick Barlow was still taking down the closing pages of Julie Mugford's statement. She had been telling the detective about Jeremy's liking for drugs, his desire to be a big

182

spender and his sexual preferences. Stan Jones sat down and read through the sheaf of typewritten sheets.

According to Julie, Jeremy's penchant for cannabis had grown into a cottage industry. He'd grown it for his own use, and to sell in London. Seeds had been planted and propagated inside and outside Bourtree Cottage, in the garden, on the kitchen window sill, even in the airing cupboard. The plants were subsequently harvested and dried out over a clothes horse and in the microwave oven. The dried leaves were then minced in a herb grinder and stored in jars under the stairs. Julie had admitted selling some of the cannabis at Goldsmiths' College, while Jeremy had established a postal market in Scotland with a man from the Stirling area whom he knew as Hamish McTavish. The success of this business had encouraged Jeremy to buy a bigger propagator, and to plant another batch of cannabis seedlings between two of the barns at White House Farm. To his fury, the plants at the farm had been eaten by rats. But those growing in his back garden beneath a home-made cloche flourished to such an extent that an officer from the Essex drugs squad had called round to examine them. This was Jeremy's cue to destroy the entire crop.

According to Julie Mugford, Jeremy needed to smoke cannabis and became very moody without it. When Brett Collins arrived in June, Jeremy's consumption of grass had increased. Julie estimated Jeremy's income from drugs dealing at between £800 and £900 a year. His monthly salary from the farm amounted to about £400, and he received about £1,000 a year from the Osea Road Caravan Site. As a result he enjoyed a very good lifestyle, always buying the best and splashing out when entertaining his friends. Julie said Jeremy would think nothing of paying expensive entrance fees at nightclubs and ordering drinks from a waitress rather than queuing at the bar. 'Jeremy wasn't a rich man,' Julie said, 'but he had very expensive tastes. He was forever moaning that his father didn't pay him enough money and that his share in the caravan site should have been more. It also upset him that Sheila should receive so much money and do nothing for it.'

It was in the course of giving her statement on the evening of Tuesday 10 September that Julie Mugford made two admissions concerning her complicity in two criminal acts. The first elaborated on her role as accomplice in Jeremy's burgling of the Osea Road Caravan Site office in March 1985. She described how they'd walked to the site hand-in-hand along the seafront, and how Jeremy had thrust his hand through the letter-box for the key which hung on a piece of string. Posting Julie as a lookout, he had opened the safe and strewn papers from the safe all over the office to make it look as though it had been ransacked. After closing the office door behind him, and posting the key back through the letter-box, Jeremy had grabbed hold of her hand and the couple had run back to the sea wall and had then walked along it to the Mill Beach pub for a drink and a game of pool. Later, at Bourtree Cottage, he'd spread the money all over the floor to look at, before stashing it all in his little Chinese trick box and calling Charles and Liz to arrange an expensive night out. The following evening the foursome dined out at Fifi's in Colchester and drank pink and white champagne all evening. The bill came to £125.

Julie's second criminal admission concerned a cheque fraud. She and her flatmate, Susan Battersby, had done it almost on the spur of the moment, taking a train to the West End of London and falsely reporting Susan's handbag containing her cheque-book and credit card as having been stolen. The two women then visited several shops in Oxford Street, with Julie signing Susan's cheques in exchange for clothes and shoes for themselves and a pair of jeans and an expensive coffee machine for Jeremy. In all they 'spent' about £800. Jeremy seemed pleased with his presents, and admonished the girls jovially, saying they'd been naughty. Julie shamefacedly admitted that she had done wrong but, being an impoverished student, had merely done it 'to prove something'.

Stan Jones closed the file and glanced at his watch. It was turned midnight. It was time to go home.

TWENTY

AT 11 A.M. next morning, Wednesday, 11 September, Detective Sergeant Jones resumed his interview with Jeremy Bamber. Detective Constable Clark took the notes. Jones was increasingly vexed by Jeremy's attitude. He sat slouched in the chair in his jeans and white sweater, staring hard at him and replying to questions in a sing-song 'Y-e-e-s' or 'N-o-o-o'. He seemed always to be on his guard, evasive, ambiguous.

Jones asked him about the murder weapon, the .22 Anschutz rifle. 'When was the last time you shot anything with that rifle?'

'Fired? Or hit and killed?'

'Both.'

'A week, maybe a fortnight. Are we taking as a reference point the date of my parents' death or today?'

'I thought it would be quite obvious we're talking about before your parents' death. So please answer that question.'

'Just checking.'

'When was the last time you fired that gun before your parents death?'

'A week to a fortnight before.'

Sergeant Jones asked Jeremy about his mother's bicycle, which had been found propped up against the wall behind Bourtree Cottage. Jeremy had said earlier that he had left the bike there some time prior to 6 August, the last day of his mother's life. Was that right?

'I didn't say "prior to the 6th". I said it's been there six to eight weeks.'

'Are you saying six to eight weeks before the murders?'

'No.'

'What *are* you saying?'

'That the bicycle has been at my house six to eight weeks.'

'You're avoiding the question,' said Stan Jones. 'How many weeks, days, months was the cycle at your house before the murders?'

'I can't say whether the bike was there before the murders,' Jeremy replied. There was a pause. 'But if it was,' he added, 'a few days.'

'. . . You told me yesterday the bike was there a few days or a week before the deaths.'

'Correct.'

'And you took it over in the car.'

'Correct.'

'Are you now saying the cycle wasn't there until after the deaths?'

'No.'

'When did the cycle arrive at your house, before or after the deaths?'

'It arrived six to eight weeks ago. I think a few days before the murder.'

'So why have you this last five minutes been evading the answering of a simple question?'

'I answer the questions truthfully and to the best of my ability to make sure that my statement is 100 per cent honest,' said Jeremy Bamber.

Stan Jones leafed through a sheaf of typewritten papers on the table in front of him. 'So,' he said, 'you know Charles Marsden?'

Jeremy said he did. 'He and I were very close a few years ago, and not so close now as I don't really see him that often.'

The detective continued to look through his papers.

'Do you remember me yesterday putting to you that Julie had said that you intended to drug the family and burn the farm down when they were all in it?'

Bamber said he remembered, and that Julie was telling lies.

'You see' said Stan Jones, running a finger down one of the statements, 'Charles Marsden also says the same thing. He says that around Christmas time last year, when all the family, your parents, Sheila and twins were there, you told him that if you burned the house down with all them in it, you'd get everything. Is he telling lies as well?'

Jeremy said he didn't remember discussing the matter with Marsden, and that he concluded that his friend was lying. Stan Jones put the statement down on the table. 'Julie's telling lies,' he said, recapping, 'and he is telling lies. For what reason?'

'No comment.'

Oddly it was not until this afternoon session on the third full day of questioning that Jeremy was challenged with the story that he had paid Matthew McDonald £2,000 to murder his family. He said it wasn't true, and that he would let the police check his bank statements to confirm that no such payment had been made.

Jones then switched the subject to the morning after the murders, and the arrival of Julie Mugford at Bourtree Cottage. Jones reminded Bamber that he had allowed the couple a few moments alone together in the dining room. Julie Mugford now claimed that during their embrace, Jeremy had whispered in her ear, 'I should have been an actor,' and chuckled. Stan Jones himself had heard 'either a cough or a chuckle' as he opened the door to find Bamber breaking away from the embrace with Julie. 'I believe that what she's saying is the truth,' said the detective, 'and that you are, in fact, an actor.'

'I don't think I can act,' Bamber replied, 'and the rest is untrue. I probably did kiss and cuddle her.'

'Are you saying I'm mistaken when I heard a chuckle?'

'You also said "a cough".'

'Do you think I'm mistaken if I heard a cough or a chuckle?'

'I can't say,' said Jeremy, 'because I can't remember every cough, sigh, breath or whatever from two months ago.'

The third day of the interview ended shortly after 8.30 p.m, after one last exchange.

'Was Sheila a good shot with a rifle?' asked Stan Jones.

'Don't know,' Jeremy replied. 'I hadn't been with her shooting targets.'

'Have you ever seen her shoot?'

'Can't remember.'

'I'll tell you that no one I've spoken to has ever seen her fire a gun. You say you can't remember, so it could well be she's never fired a gun in her life. Would you agree?'

'No.'

'You say you can't remember her ever firing a gun. Why say "No" to my question?'

'Because she might have.'

'I'll tell you this,' said Stan Jones, lowering his voice and fixing Bamber with an unwavering gaze. 'Over twenty bullets were fired into the bodies of your family. I won't tell you the exact amount, but I *will* tell you every one, apart from one, hit the target.'

For the first time in three days, Jeremy Bamber visibly flinched. 'You're a hard bastard,' he murmured. 'I don't want to know about things like that.'

Stan Jones gathered his papers together and squared them up. 'Would you agree it would take a very good shot to achieve that?'

'No comment,' said Jeremy Bamber, choking back the tears.

Jeremy had now been questioned for a total of some twenty hours over a period of three days, and he'd continued to deny any complicity in the killings at White House Farm. But for Stan Jones, the feeling that Jeremy was concealing his guilt was growing stronger by the hour. The timing of the telephone call to Julie Mugford in the middle of the murder night still nagged him. The call to Chelmsford Police had been logged at 3.26 a.m. If he could get a definite fix on the call to Julie, proving that Jeremy had phoned her *before* calling the police for help, it would be compelling evidence against Bamber. So far, the clearest evidence about the timing had come from Julie Mugford's flatmate, Susan Battersby, the twenty-one-year-old student teacher with whom Julie had undertaken the West End shopping spree using the 'stolen' cheque-book. Susan Battersby's recollection was of waking in the middle of the night to the sound of the telephone ringing on the landing outside her bedroom. She was about to get up to answer it when she heard Julie's voice on the landing. 'I looked at my clock radio next to my bed,' she reported, 'and noticed that it was 3.15 a.m. This might not have been the exact time,' she added, 'as sometimes I set the clock ten minutes fast so I can stay in bed that little bit longer in the mornings. What I can say is that the time would not have been later than 3.15 a.m. I heard Julie say the name Jeremy a couple of times, but I didn't hear any other conversation. Her voice sounded worried. I then went back to sleep . . .'

'. . . *the time would not have been later than 3.15 a.m.* . . .' If Susan Battersby was correct, it proved that Jeremy Bamber had called Julie Mugford in Lewisham at least eleven minutes before summoning help from the police at Chelmsford. Could it be checked? Stan Jones jotted down a list of people who had slept the night at Caterham Road. As well as Julie Mugford and Susan Battersby, there was Douglas Dale and a friend of Julie's from Manchester, Helen Eaton. She'd been staying for a few days while looking for digs in London. Helen Eaton remembered being woken by the telephone at 'about 3 a.m.'. She heard Julie get up and answer it, but thinking it was just 'a dirty phone call' Helen had gone back to sleep.

Could Julie Mugford's story be tested in other respects? Jeremy had insisted throughout his interview that Julie had lied about every point that damaged him. But what about other points that might not, in themselves, prove incriminating? What did Jeremy Bamber have to say about them? Stan Jones ventured to find out. If Bamber accepted at least part of Julie's statement as the truth, it would go some way towards showing that her story wasn't some fantastic invention, cooked up in the death throes of an unhappy love affair. Sergeant Jones asked Bamber about the call he made to Julie on his return to Bourtree Cottage at about 10 p.m. on the night of the killings. Did he remember that?

'No comment.'

According to Julie, Bamber had blamed the lateness of the call on the fact that he had only just got home from work after having supper with his parents and Sheila. 'No,' said Bamber, you're inferring that I was late phoning because of the meal, and not because of work.'

'Did you say to [Julie] you'd had supper with your parents and Sheila, and had seen the twins?'

'I don't remember.'

'What she has said must be true, mustn't it, because you *did* have supper, *did* see your parents, *did* see Sheila and *did* see the twins, didn't you?'

'That's your opinion.'

'Mr Bamber, that's not my opinion. You, a short while ago, told me just that.'

'I did see my parents, Sheila and the twins, as I've already said. But when you say "What she's said must be true", it's your opinion.'

'Julie is telling lies, is she?'

'Julie is telling a lot of lies.'

'Not once during any interview I've had with you (as far as I can remember) have you admitted that she's telling the truth. Is that right?'

'I can't comment because I can't remember everything in 117 pages.'

'. . . You don't like to admit that Julie is capable of telling the truth, do you?'

'Julie is just as capable to [sic] tell lies as truth,' said Jeremy Bamber, 'and in your questions you hardly ever give me one where she is telling the truth.'

Stan Jones was wearying of the game of cat and mouse. 'You phoned [Julie] at 10 o'clock that night. Truth or not? Please answer: Truth or not?'

'Truth.'

'You phoned her at 3.30 time, around 3.30 time, according to you. Please answer: Truth or not.'

'Truth.'

'You phoned her about 6 o'clock time. Please answer: Truth or not?'

'Truth,' said Bamber.

'. . . What was the point in phoning her up?'

'There were probably many reasons.'

'Again you avoid answering the question,' declared Stan Jones. 'What was the main reason for phoning her up?'

'I could guess now, but couldn't be sure of all the reasons I had then.'

'The main reason you rang?'

'You want me to guess?'

'It's not a matter of guessing,' said the detective. 'You know why you phoned her up, don't you?'

'To tell her what was going on.'

'What *was* going on?'

'My father had phoned me, I phoned the police and I don't really need to expand any more as you know the contents already.'

'Again, you avoid the question. What did you tell her, in your own words?'

'Try as I might to explain to you that I don't remember the contents of that phone call from nearly two months ago, you keep asking me the very same question.'

'Do you remember your father phoning you? And answer yes or no.'

'Yes.'

'Remember phoning the police station? Answer yes or no.'

'Yes.'

'Remember phoning Julie 3.30 a.m. time? Yes or no.'

'How can I say "Yes" to a question when you slip in a time I'm not sure about? But yes, I did phone her around 3.30. Not exactly.'

'You phoned her about 6 a.m.? Answer yes or no.'

'Yes.'

'Do you remember the contents of your father's call? Yes or no.'

'Exactly, no. But pretty much, and there were only a few words.'

'Remember the contents of the phone call to the police station?'

'No.'

'You don't?'

'No.'

'Do you know the *rough* contents of the phone call to the police station?'

'No, not really. I can remember a few points, but not much.'

'Can you remember the rough contents of the phone call to Julie at around 3.30 that morning?'

'No.'

'Do you know the rough contents of the phone call about 6 a.m. that morning?'

'No, not really. But the main point was: Don't go to work.'

Stan Jones leaned back, removed his glasses, closed his eyes and rubbed them with a gesture of weary resignation. 'It appears to me, Mr Bamber,' he said quietly, 'that you're avoiding at all costs answering my questions which I think are very simple. And I must assume by that, you are doing it for some reason. Are you an actor and also a liar? Because I consider that's the way it comes over to me.'

'No,' said Jeremy Bamber.

Sergeant Jones shifted back to the evening of the murders, and Jeremy's story that he had taken the .22 rifle from the house in order to shoot some rabbits. Had Jeremy worn gloves?

'No, I don't think so. You went over this yesterday, when I explained.'

'You explained in rough words that you weren't wearing gloves. Is that right?'

'No comment.'

'You see, that gun has been examined, and there are none of your fingerprints on it. One would have thought that, having picked it up, loaded it, gone outside, back indoors, unloaded it, put it down, there should be some of your fingermarks on it. Do you agree?'

'I can't really comment, but one would imagine so. I'm no print expert,' said Bamber.

Detective Sergeant Jones now raised the stakes. 'I will also tell you this,' he went on, replacing his glasses and reading from a forensic report on the table in front of him. 'At this moment in time, there's only one fingerprint on the stock or butt of that gun, and that is one mark of Sheila's.' He glanced up at Jeremy. 'I will go further. I have told you that Julie has told us you've been planning the murders for some time. She's told us how you did the shootings. And she's told us the only thing you were worried about in committing your perfect crime was the fingerprinting of the gun. She told us you were worried in case Sheila's fingerprints didn't come out on the gun properly. In fact, what she said you told her is perfectly true, as there is only one fingerprint mark on the butt of that gun.'

Jones removed his glasses once more. What did Jeremy have to say about that?

'I can't really make any comment, other than I had nothing to do with the murders. And that fingerprint is your department.' Jeremy Bamber stared straight at Sergeant Jones.

When the interview resumed after the evening meal break, Bamber continued to stare directly at Stan Jones. The sergeant found this so disconcerting that, at one point, he asked Mick Clark specifically to note it in the record of the interview. The questioning turned back to Jeremy's story of hiring Matthew McDonald to murder his family. Sergeant Jones reviewed the position. According to Julie, when she found herself alone with Jeremy on the evening after the murders, he had claimed that McDonald had acted as a hired assassin. In a phone call from the farm, McDonald had told Jeremy that the job had been completed, and that for a man of his age,

Nevill Bamber had put up a terrific fight for his life. According to Julie, McDonald had told Jeremy that he'd had 'a mental blank' and had fired seven shots into him. Julie, said Stan Jones, had been 'spot on' about Nevill Bamber putting up a fierce struggle. And since this fact was never publicized, the police knew that what Julie said was the truth.

Stan Jones pointed out that the only person who could possibly know such facts must be either the murderer himself or someone acting for him. Jeremy had denied telling Julie the story of the hit man.

'She's telling lies, you say?'

'It looks that way.'

'How would she know about the violent struggle? The only ones who did know were the police and the murderer or his accomplice in the crime.'

'I can't comment on something I know nothing about.'

'She goes on to say even more. She says you told her that the twins had been killed in their sleep,' said Sergeant Jones. 'I know for a fact that one of the twins died with his thumb in his mouth, and it appears the other twin was also asleep. What Julie says you told her about that is a fact. How could she make that up if you, or someone, hadn't told her?'

'I don't think I'd even mentioned anything about that,' said Bamber. 'You're trying to tell me that I told her, when in fact *you* did. And I can prove it.'

'Precisely, Mr Bamber, but she couldn't have made up the bit about your father putting up a fierce struggle because no one knew, only the murderer or an accomplice . . .'

'Or the police,' Bamber interrupted, 'as you've already said.'

'I've told you,' said Stan Jones, 'that no mention of a violent struggle has been mentioned anywhere. What do you say to that?'

'That's your opinion,' replied Jeremy Bamber. 'The police to me, at the time, were like open books.'

Stan Jones moved on. 'Julie also states that you told her that Matthew [McDonald] made Sheila lie down and shoot herself. You went on to say that a Bible was then placed on her chest. It's a fact that she was shot twice, and that a Bible *was* placed alongside her. Did you tell her all this?'

'No.'

'Is she making it up?'

'I can't say.'

'When you received that alleged phone call from your father, why didn't you phone 999?'

'Don't know.'

'You thought there was trouble sufficiently enough to phone the police after looking up the telephone number. Why not phone 999?'

'Don't know.'

'You're intelligent. Why not 999?'

'Don't know.'

'When you phoned Julie and told her the trouble, why phone her at all?'

A pause. 'No comment.'

'Why not phone a nearby relative?'

'No comment.'

'I suggest, Mr Bamber, that you are an actor. Or don't you agree?'

'That's your opinion. I don't.'

Another change of tack. Jones reminded Bamber that his father had been violently attacked, and received other wounds apart from gunshots. Some of those injuries were thought to have been inflicted upstairs, and some downstairs. The police didn't believe Jeremy's story that his father had telephoned him for help. When they broke into the house they found the telephone in the kitchen was off the hook. Stan Jones showed Jeremy a photograph of the telephone, with a box of loose ammunition alongside. 'That phone, if we're to believe you,' said Stan Jones, 'should have been handled by your father. There is no sign of any blood on it. Which is remarkable, considering your dad was injured upstairs and eventually killed downstairs.

'I suggest that you killed your father and lifted the phone off the hook to substantiate your astonishing story about not being able to phone him back. Did you?'

'No,' replied Jeremy.

Another switch, this time to Julie's claim that Jeremy could get in and out of White House Farm through various downstairs windows. This was no secret, he said. Indeed, it was such an everyday occurrence that, in Jeremy Bamber's own words, 'in the last six months I can't say how many times I've done it.' Now he was shown another photograph. It showed the window of the downstairs toilet. Jeremy agreed that he had in the past used a knife to open the catch and climb through into the house. Stan Jones suggested to Bamber that on the night of the massacre, he'd climbed through that window, closed and latched it behind him, committed the murders and got out through the window in the kitchen, the catch of which could be made to fall into place from the outside with a sharp tap. 'Is this, in fact, what you did when you killed your family?'

'No,' said Bamber, 'I did not kill my family.'

It was turned 9.30 p.m. Bamber's solicitor, Bruce Bowler, was glancing at his watch. Stan Jones knew that he would have to wind up the interview within the hour. He moved the questioning on to Jeremy and Sheila in the rape field on the last afternoon of her life.

'You told us she was with the twins, and you had a ten-minute chat. Surely you must remember part of the conversation?'

'No,' said Jeremy Bamber.

'Are you sure you don't remember what you said?'

'No comment.'

Stan Jones shrugged. 'Seems strange to me that you only remember things when it is to your own advantage, but make no comments when you are put on the spot. Any comment?'

'No comment.'

'I believe you didn't like Sheila, and it's possible she said something to you, possibly on that Tuesday, as there's an entry in her diary saying words to the effect: I didn't mean to be horrible to Jeremy. Did you have an argument with her that Tuesday?'

'No,' Jeremy replied, 'not even a cross word.'

'I put it to you that over a period of time, you were obsessed with the idea of killing your family so you could have the benefits of what your parents had worked for. I believe that you murdered your whole family, made it look as if Sheila had done it and then committed suicide. Julie has said this, and some of the things she said you told her have in fact been true. Did you kill the members of your family?' asked Detective Sergeant Stan Jones.

'No,' said Jeremy Bamber, 'I did not, and I didn't have any plans to do so, or any involvement in their deaths.'

Next morning, Friday, 13 September, Jeremy Bamber was driven to the magistrates' court in Chelmsford, emerging from the police van before a battery of cameras handcuffed and with a thick sweater pulled over his head. In court, he was charged with the theft of £980 from Osea Road Caravan Site. As he had no previous convictions and was being accused of only a minor offence, the police knew that the magistrates would have to grant him bail.

The police were right. He was released on unconditional bail and remanded to appear again on 16 October. He emerged from the court with his head again covered by his pullover, and stepped into the van without replying to any of the questions thrown at him from the milling crowd of reporters.

Stan Jones watched as Jeremy was driven back to the police station to pick up his personal belongings. 'After eighteen hours of questioning,' he recalled, 'we hadn't got a cough. But we'd got Julie Mugford's statement. It was one against the other. And we were still waiting for a full set of reports from the forensic labs.' All the detectives on the case felt sick about Jeremy Bamber walking free from court. Even Taff Jones confessed to being upset.

As the van carrying Jeremy disappeared into the Chelmsford traffic, reporters gathered round his solicitor, Bruce Bowler. The lawyer confirmed that Bamber had spent three days of 'intense questioning' about the White House Farm massacre, but he had 'vehemently denied' being involved in any way.

TWENTY-ONE

WHEN Julie Mugford telephoned her friend Karen Bishop late on Friday evening, it was Karen's husband Andrew who answered the phone. Andrew Bishop thought that Julie had gone on holiday to Malta the previous weekend, and was shocked to learn that in fact she was in protective police custody, having denounced Jeremy over the murders of his family. Julie told him that although she and Liz Rimington had planned a holiday in the sun, she'd been unable to go because of what she knew about Jeremy's role in the White House Farm affair. Andrew Bishop asked her what she meant. 'Isn't it obvious?' cried Julie. 'I'm amazed that Karen didn't realize what I was trying to tell her last week. Jeremy was involved in murdering his family.'

Jeremy himself had driven to London on his release from court to spend the weekend with Brett Collins, Virginia Greaves and her sister Anji at Sheila's flat. The four spent the evening drinking in the West End. Some time after midnight Jeremy telephoned his old friend Michael Deckers in Colchester. 'He sounded very drunk,' Deckers reported. Jeremy had spent five days in custody and had hit the town in a big way as soon as he had the chance. He told Deckers that he'd been grilled for twelve hours a day 'because the police think that I've committed murder'. In fact, Deckers already knew that Jeremy had spent the week being questioned. Anji Greaves had called him, saying that Jeremy's arrest in London was splashed all over the papers. Charles Marsden had also called to say that he'd been interviewed by detectives no fewer than three times.

Jeremy told Michael Deckers that he'd admitted burgling the caravan site office. Deckers said he couldn't understand how the police could have kept him locked up all week just to be questioned about stealing some money. Jeremy explained that the police were quizzing him about the murders of his family, not just about a minor burglary. He insisted to Deckers that he was innocent, and said there was no evidence. Jeremy also expressed amazement at the number of people who were telling lies about him. Jeremy rang off saying he would call on Deckers in Colchester the following Monday, when he was due to pay another visit to his accountant and his solicitor.

The press, meanwhile, had scented dynamite. They knew that Jeremy was now considered a possible suspect in the White House Farm case, but it was plain that the case against him remained feeble and fragmentary. There were some half-hearted attempts to smother the dither and delay with a blanket of disinformation. Unofficial sources within the CID leaked a wholly spurious theory about Sheila being massively indebted to a London drugs ring, and rekindled the 'hit man' story to lend credence to it. On 15 September, two days after Jeremy's release on bail, the *Sunday Times* reported a prediction from the assistant chief constable of Essex, Peter Simpson, that the reopened inquiry would take several weeks to complete. Simpson denied that the investigation had been hampered by the initial assumption that no outside person was involved, but admitted that the original assumption – that Sheila had been responsible – might have been mistaken.

Officially, however, Sheila remained the chief suspect. Her former husband, the sculptor Colin Caffell, had returned from a fortnight's holiday at the beginning of September to find that Jeremy and his friend Brett

Collins had emptied Sheila's flat and had sold most of the items of value. Caffell felt angry and upset, and demanded to know why Jeremy had stripped the flat before he'd been given a chance to buy anything himself for sentimental reasons. Jeremy replied that he needed money for death duties. Anyway, he added, he was hard up himself.

In a statement to the police two days after Jeremy's arrest, Colin Caffell had said he had the impression that the whole family were ganging up on Jeremy because he'd been left with a controlling interest in the family caravan site. Jeremy had told him that his relatives had offered to buy some of his shares to wrest control from him. One of them had sent him a solicitor's letter demanding three valuable paintings from White House Farm, and threatening him with proceedings if Jeremy didn't comply. Jeremy himself told Colin that the paintings were the most valuable items in the house, and that he planned to ignore the demand.

Colin Caffell's girlfriend, 31-year-old Heather Amos, remembered Jeremy talking about his greedy relatives. He had said that after death duties and capital gains tax, he estimated he would end up with about a third of the total value of his parents' estate, and that his grasping family didn't realize how little would be left. Jeremy had told Heather Amos that he'd had Sheila's flat professionally cleaned, and that although he and Brett planned to live there, he was going to let out one of the rooms. He said he had thrown nothing away, and that Colin Caffell could have anything he wanted. But when Colin and Heather called at the flat to see Jeremy on the evening of Saturday, 7 September – the night before his arrest – they were appalled to find that the place had been cleared out. 'Both Colin and I were very shocked and upset,' Heather Amos told detectives, 'because everything to do with Sheila and the boys had been moved out and stored in carrier bags and the like in a cupboard.' Two paintings stood in the hall, apparently awaiting valuation. The artistic Colin recognized one of these pictures as a Bamber family heirloom and told Jeremy that in his opinion it should be kept for sentimental reasons. But what upset Heather Amos as much as the talk of selling off the contents of the farm and the flat was Jeremy's hard-faced attitude to Julie. Having explained that he had finished with her, he added that he planned to seduce a girl whom he'd invited in as a lodger. Since he fancied her, Jeremy said he would only charge her £35 a week rent including bills.

Five days in a police cell had given Jeremy an appetite for more than just a night out in London: he and Brett Collins agreed that a holiday was in order. They decided to take a car down to the south of France, to spend a few days eating, drinking and just lazing in the Mediterranean sun. On Monday, 16 September, Jeremy visited his solicitor and told him he was going abroad, but would be back to appear in court in mid-October on the burglary charge. On his way back to London, Jeremy (accompanied by Brett Collins) called in at White House Farm to pick up some documentation which he needed to take his car abroad. The farm was locked and empty; Jeremy easily managed to get inside by slipping the catch on the window of the downstairs toilet and clambering through.

A few miles away, at Vaulty Manor Farm, Jeremy's aunt, Pamela Boutflour, was talking to a detective on the inquiry team who was writing down her statement. Her husband, Robert Boutflour, listened as she recalled the events of the previous few weeks. One of the aspects of the affair that had puzzled her was Jeremy's uncharacteristic behaviour since the tragedy. Previously he had made a point of calling in on his grandmother, Mabel Speakman, whenever he drove out to Vaulty to fill up his car from the farm's own petrol pump. Since the shootings he hadn't done so, always arriving to fill up in the company of his friend, Brett Collins, and making no effort to call on either his grandmother or the Boutflours, who had moved in to look after the old lady. Pamela Boutflour thought this was odd. Every time she told her nephew that he ought to go up to see his grandmother, Jeremy simply shrugged and said, 'I will.' Mrs Boutflour was also puzzled that Jeremy had made no effort to come over to sort out his mother's jewellery. Pamela Boutflour's daughter, Ann Eaton, had collected it from the White House, with the executor's permission. But despite repeated requests, Jeremy had fobbed her off, saying he would go over some time and sort it out. Mrs Boutflour thought it very strange that since the massacre, Jeremy had never asked her to help him sort out his mother's belongings. Neither had he asked the family for any help. 'In view of the fact that Jeremy now inherits everything of Nevill, June and Sheila,' Mrs Boutflour told the detective in her statement, 'I find it very disturbing that he's not asked my husband and me for any advice or help.'

Pamela Boutflour said that she and her husband had discussed the tragedy at great length, and had discussed it with their daughter, Ann. 'None of us are happy with the explanation that we have been given for the cause of this tragedy,' she declared. 'Sheila was supposed to have gone berserk with a gun, and shot the whole family, including the twins. This shook me very much, because Sheila wasn't a violent person, and I don't believe she did this. I know she had never used a gun and wouldn't know *how* to use a gun.

'I know that Sheila would never harm the twins. She was devoted to them. Although she wasn't well, and was suffering from depression, she would never have harmed her children. I have never even heard her speak to them severely.' Furthermore, Mrs Boutflour added, there was now this mysterious talk of Sheila being involved with drugs. June had never mentioned anything about either Sheila or Jeremy being involved with drugs. 'This is all new to me,' said Pamela Boutflour. 'I know nothing of drugs.'

JEREMY BAMBER had felt under pressure from the newspapers from the outset. Reporters had been calling him from the first morning of the inquiry, asking for quotes, digging for background, curious about the lifestyle of the debonair young farmer who now stood to inherit a fortune as a result of the tragedy at White House Farm. But no sooner had he achieved front-page notoriety as the 'Bambi brother' arrested at his sister's London flat than the newspapers refocused the story on the well-worn 'hit man' theory. WHO KILLED BAMBI? screamed the *Mirror* on Thursday 12 September. MERCENARY IS HELD IN HIT MAN PROBE. The story claimed that the 'dramatic theory' of a hired assassin having gunned down the Bambers was a 'new twist' in the investigation as detectives began questioning a former mercenary. In fact, Matthew McDonald, who'd been no nearer the thick of battle than a Libyan building site, had already been released without charge, and, on the day the *Mirror* bruited his detention, was telling a detective constable about Jeremy's duck-shooting exploits as they sipped tea at the home of one of McDonald's mistresses.

On the following Monday, as Jeremy and Brett Collins prepared to leave for their holiday in France, the *Mirror* splashed the news that the silencer had been found in the farmhouse, renewing pressure on Essex Police and raising, in the words of reporter Peter Kane, 'grave doubts about their handling of the case'. The paper also reported another discovery, that of a curious pattern of torches and flashlights beamed at the sky 'and possibly forming a dropping zone for a light plane carrying drugs'. The report failed to mention that the silencer had actually been found not 'by police hours after the gruesome massacre' but by members of the Bamber family three days later. Neither did it produce any evidence to support the dropping-zone story. But it hardly mattered. What was important was that it pitched the White House Farm murders back on to the front pages and into the public consciousness for the second time in less than six weeks. Next day, under the heading 'THE BAMBI BLOODBATH – MURDER OR SUICIDE?, the paper reported that Sheila took hard drugs and owed two notorious drug barons £40,000. Apart from Sheila's problems, the *Mirror* added, detectives hadn't ruled out other lines of inquiry linked to drugs. Villagers in Tolleshunt D'Arcy had reported receiving envelopes containing as much as £100 in cash addressed to 'a member of the Bamber family' but posted to the wrong house. Police evidently believed the money represented a pay-off for the supply of drugs, deliberately misdirected to bamboozle them. Readers with a passing knowledge of the case could not have doubted that this money was destined for Jeremy.

The reaction of Essex Police to these disclosures was one of ill-disguised panic. When the local newspaper, the Colchester *Evening Gazette*, posed the question that must have occurred to its readers many times since the arrest, questioning and subsequent return of Jeremy Bamber – 'When will police make up their minds?' – the question so nettled the senior officers on the case that, in spite of growing public concern, they ordered what the paper called 'a virtual wall of silence' around the case. The paper recalled the remark of the assistant chief constable, Peter Simpson, that he had no regrets over the way the police had handled matters. 'Yet,' it added with almost heroic understatement, 'some rank-and-file officers are known to be seriously embarrassed by the way the inquiry has progressed.' To underline the point, the paper reported the launch the week before of house-to-house inquiries in D'Arcy and Goldhanger, a step usually taken during the first days of a major inquiry. The *Gazette* interviewed a woman who'd been questioned by police as though they were conducting a census rather than a murder inquiry. 'They asked me how many people there were in the household,' she reported, 'and the date of birth of all the family including the children. They wanted to know where we were all born, and my maiden name.'

Meanwhile the newspapers were stoking up the 'hit man' story. The *Evening Gazette* reported 'the latest twist in the mystery', the revelation that Nevill Bamber may have been savagely beaten before being murdered. The paper said Mr Bamber's body bore massive bruises on his arms and shoulders, suggesting he may have been brutally clubbed with a gun butt before being shot. The story placed a huge question mark over the idea that the killings were the work of slightly built Sheila Caffell. So did a second revelation – that the murder weapon was reloaded.

In the face of this public clamour, the police were forced to respond. Peter Simpson sought to stifle speculation by insisting that it could be several more weeks before police knew for sure what had really happened on the murder night. He pointed out that they were still awaiting reports on the forensic, ballistic and pathological aspects of the massacre. In the meantime, Simpson added, the police still had 'an open mind' on the question of whether it was murder or suicide. Simpson dismissed his critics who had claimed the inquiry had been bungled. Declaring himself satisfied with the progress of the investigation, he admitted that new information had forced them to widen the scope of the inquiry. But he rejected the 'wild speculation' spread about by certain newspapers. He ruled out reports that the killings were connected with international drug smuggling, and discounted talk of a hired hit man.

Far from snuffing out newspaper speculation, Peter Simpson's constabularian denials merely served to rekindle it. Next day, the London *Standard* ran a full-page article analysing the case with the kind of clarity that seemed to have hitherto eluded the professional investigators. Reporter Yvonne Roberts visited one of the village's three pubs, the Thatcher's Arms, to find out what the villagers thought about this case. 'What upsets us,' one unnamed customer told her, 'is that the whole family's life has been reduced to a series of newspaper headlines. And none of them has got it right. The day after it happened, a lot of people in the village knew the police had it wrong,' he added. 'We knew for one reason only: common sense.'

No one would subscribe to the notion that the killings were the handiwork of a drug-crazed London model. The villagers were anxious, as they put it, to dress Sheila Caffell in her rightful clothes. She hadn't modelled seriously for five years. She was a single parent, a part-time cleaner. Her only 'glamour', for the locals of Tolleshunt D'Arcy, came from having a London address.

The *Daily Mail* joined the guessing game the next morning, with another full-page feature headed FIND THE KILLER!. 'In Tolleshunt D'Arcy,' wrote reporter John Passmore, 'almost everyone has become an amateur detective.' Less whimsical was another report on the same page pointing to the existence of two vital scientific reports on the forensic and ballistic aspects of the killings. The *Daily Mail* had pressed Assistant Chief Constable Peter Simpson to qualify his official open-mindedness by accepting the possibility that the Bambers were, indeed, all murdered. But the question would only be settled when the detailed dossiers arrived from the forensic science laboratory at Huntingdon.

For the detectives, the week seemed endless. There were so many statements to be organized and taken that Stan Jones had to set up a makeshift system of monitoring the blizzard of paper to make certain that everything was codified and cross-referenced. In the incident room at Witham, some fifteen detectives, working in shifts, gathered the statements together. In the five weeks between the killings and Julie Mugford's denunciation of Jeremy, the police had taken about thirty statements, including several from the armed officers who'd stormed the farmhouse. But Julie's statement implicating Jeremy in the killings unleashed a flood; in the ten days that followed detectives took at least 100 more, including one from Ann Eaton that ran to nearly 150 pages of typescript. Stan Jones read every statement that landed on his desk, marking up anything he thought should be answered by Jeremy Bamber on his return to Britain. By the time Jones and his colleagues had finished, the list covered ten sheets of foolscap. In addition, there were meetings several times a day with Taff Jones, who remained sullenly convinced that the investigation had taken a turn down a blind alley, and who found himself trapped unhappily between a sergeant who had never wavered in his belief that Jeremy Bamber had massacred his own family and an assistant chief constable, Peter Simpson, who was inclined to agree. On an overcast morning in the last week of September, all three men were driven to London in Simpson's official chauffeured car. At the Whitehall office of the Director of Public Prosecutions, the officers presented the deputy DPP with the police case against Jeremy Bamber.

Before the establishment of the Crown Prosecution

Service, it was the DPP's department that decided whether to proceed with a prosecution in serious criminal cases. The department needed to satisfy itself that a *prima facie* case against the suspect existed, and that there was sufficient evidence on which to charge him. Stan Jones was still not convinced that the police had enough evidence against Bamber that would survive the rigours of a full scale criminal trial. He had bought with him the lengthy list of questions that he'd compiled while reading through the dozens of statements from Bamber's family and friends. He need not have bothered. The sober-suited official at his desk read through the file, asked some questions, made some notes, then, gathering the papers together and smoothing them down, announced that in his opinion, the police had amassed enough evidence to charge Bamber with murder. Stan Jones wondered if it wouldn't be a good idea to tax Bamber on his other points first, but the deputy DPP held up his hand. No, he said, there's enough there already. In law, once a suspect has been formally charged with an offence, the questioning stops.

Driving back to Chelmsford along the A12, Stan Jones knew that his next task was not to charge Jeremy Bamber but to find him. Police had kept him under surveillance ever since his arrest at Sheila's flat on 8 September, but now that Jeremy had gone abroad, the police had to all intents and purposes lost him. Back at his office in Witham, Stan Jones telephoned Julie Mugford and told her the problem. Julie remembered that Jeremy always booked his holidays through a particular travel agency, but inquiries there drew a blank. So Stan Jones called on another travel agency he knew in Maldon and asked if they'd had a recent booking in the name of either Jeremy Bamber or Brett Collins. They had. Collins had booked ferry tickets for himself and Jeremy, but although there was a complete record of their outward itinerary, the tickets were open-ended and there was no knowing when the pair were due to return to the UK. Taff Jones telephoned the Special Branch office at Dover and explained who they were looking for. Special Branch agreed to watch the passenger lists and to alert the police in Essex when the names Bamber and Collins appeared together.

The call came the following Sunday, 29 September. Stan Jones, enjoying a day off at home, answered the telephone to hear a young constable on duty at Witham with a message from Special Branch: 'Get down to Dover as quick as you can. Bamber's nicked.' It was true. Jeremy and Brett Collins had arrived on a ferry from France shortly after lunch. Special Branch had signalled their interest to customs officers who'd detained the two men for questioning in the customs car hall. While Jeremy and Brett sat in one of the interview rooms expecting to be questioned about their duty-free allowances, Detective Sergeant Harry Hutchison hurried from the Kent police office at the Eastern Dock building together with a detective constable. Told he was being detained on suspicion of murder, Bamber was cautioned and replied simply: 'OK.'

While his quarry was sitting in one of the police offices having his documentation checked, Stan Jones was hunched in the back seat of a police Ford Escort as it hurtled down the M20 towards Dover. Detective Constable Mick Clark was at the wheel, with Detective Inspector Bob Miller in the passenger seat, urging Clark to drive faster, despite the heavy Sunday afternoon traffic. 'Mick drove like a maniac,' Stan Jones remembers, 'while I was sitting in the back, my brain going round and round at thirty thousand revs.' Just outside Dover, the Escort hit another car being driven by a French holidaymaker. No one was hurt, but the officers spent several minutes brandishing their warrant cards, and trying to explain to the bewildered tourist in schoolboy French that they were in a hurry to arrest an important murder suspect. With Gallic scepticism, the Frenchman waved them on their way. The detectives finally arrived at the docks at 5.45 p.m. Jeremy Bamber was sitting on his own in one of the police offices, seemingly unperturbed. Brett Collins had disappeared. Stan Jones marched down the corridor, Miller and Clark following in his wake. They'd agreed that this should be Stan's collar. Stan remembers thinking that this was where the charade had to end. All the old familiarity with Jeremy, the tragically stricken young man he'd first met less than two months before, had to be abandoned. There was no 'Hello, Jeremy', no 'Hello, Stan'. The detective just walked straight in through the door, put his hand on Jeremy's shoulder and told him he was being arrested for the murders of five members of his family. He'd be taken back to Essex to be charged. Stan Jones read out the formal caution and waited for some response. But all Jeremy Bamber did was to close his eyes, lean back in his chair as if he was about to take a nap, and murmur: 'OK.'

Jeremy stretched and half opened his eyes. Stan Jones asked him if he wanted a cup of tea. 'Yes,' said Bamber. 'Two sugars.' Later, sitting drinking his tea, Jeremy turned to Mick Clark.

'Was it your day off today, Mick?'

'No,' said Detective Constable Clark,

'When do I get to see a solicitor?'

'We'll arrange one when we get to Chelmsford,' Stan Jones replied.

'Are you telling me the truth?'

But Stan Jones wasn't going to be goaded. He took another sip of tea and looked at Bamber over the rim of his mug. He looked fit and tanned after a fortnight in the

Mediterranean sun. In his expensive V-neck jumper, jeans and white baseball boots, Jeremy Bamber looked every inch the relaxed British tourist looking forward to getting home and telling friends and family about his holiday. He started to hum, as if waiting for something to happen. Then he began pulling bits of fluff out of his maroon jumper, teasing out single threads of wool which he'd chew, wrap around his tongue and use to clean between his teeth. As Stan Jones observed, he might just as well have been on a picnic. 'It was the most disappointing arrest, really. Innocent people protest their innocence at a moment like that. All Jeremy talked about was his holiday.'

According to Jeremy, the trip hadn't been entirely successful. He complained that he'd driven hundreds of miles to and from St Tropez, and that he'd been stricken by food poisoning after eating at an expensive restaurant there. Jeremy said he'd been prescribed some medicine which he needed from his car. DI Miller took his car keys and fetched it for him.

Stan Jones and the other officers spent nearly an hour on the phone to Essex, arranging for charge sheets to be typed up to await their arrival, and making other administrative calls. It was 7.20 p.m. before Stan Jones returned to the office where Jeremy was waiting, handcuffed him and led him outside to the waiting car. The trip to Essex took just over two hours. Jeremy seemed to have little to say for himself, other than to remark on how lovely St Tropez had been, and that the roads in France had been less congested than in Britain. The congestion inside the Ford Escort also bothered him. Bamber sat in the back, handcuffed to Stan Jones. Bob Miller, the detective inspector, sat in the front and Mick Clark drove.

'I thought you'd have sent a better car than this to pick me up,' Jeremy said.

'It's the best we could do,' Miller replied.

'I suppose it's what's inside that counts.'

'Yes,' said Bob Miller, 'precisely.'

At the entrance to the Dartford Tunnel, Clark pulled over and went with Miller to telephone to Chelmsford, leaving Bamber cuffed to Stan Jones in the back of the Escort. 'We were sitting there for about five minutes,' Jones reported, 'before I realized that Bamber was staring at me. When you know someone's looking at you like that, you can't resist looking back, can you? So I said I didn't know why he was staring at me like that but that if it made him feel better, well, carry on. But it really bugged me, that stare.' They arrived back at Essex Police headquarters in Chelmsford at just after 9.30 p.m. Bamber's solicitor, Bruce Bowler, arrived shortly afterwards. At 10.15 p.m., Jeremy Bamber was formally charged on five counts of murder. He made no reply.

TWENTY-THREE

WORD of Jeremy Bamber's arrest at Dover took only a matter of hours to trickle down to Fleet Street. Several of the tabloids remade their later editions to splash the story on the front page, illustrating it with pictures of Bamber at his parents' funeral. When he appeared at Maldon magistrates' court next morning charged with the murders of five members of his family, the hack pack was out in force. Bamber said almost nothing during the course of the ten-minute hearing. He simply acknowledged his name, age and address and, when asked if he understood the charges, he replied quietly: 'Yes.' His solicitor, Bruce Bowler, made no application for bail. He said Bamber had been interviewed at great length about the murders and had 'consistently and vehemently' denied any involvement. 'He stands before you today as an innocent man,' Bowler added. When Bamber was remanded in custody for nine days, he was led handcuffed from the court to a waiting white police van, past a gaggle of photographers and cameramen. Then he was driven off to Norwich Jail.

From the moment he was arrested and charged on five counts of murder, Jeremy went to great lengths to see that his defence was as highly tuned as possible. He took the view that a local firm of solicitors, unused to assembling and running the defence in a high-profile murder trial, simply would not do. 'Because of the seriousness of the charges,' he wrote in a letter to Bruce Bowler, 'the unusual – if not bizarre – circumstances surrounding this case and the fact of my entire innocence, I require a solicitor of immense skill and experience of complicated cases, and the backing of a very substantial team to support him, to secure my freedom.' Bamber wanted a major player. He wanted Sir David Napley. In 1985, Sir David was probably the best-known solicitor in London, with a reputation for tackling tough defences. In 1979, he prepared the defence for the former Liberal Party leader, Jeremy Thorpe, when he was accused of conspiracy to murder. Jeremy Bamber approached Sir David two days after his first remand appearance, through his new girl-friend, Anji Greaves, sister of Virginia.

According to Anji Greaves, Bamber had taken up with her two days after his parents' funeral. They had been friends for years, but never lovers. But when Jeremy called at her London flat to ask her advice on getting rid of Julie Mugford, the couple ended up in bed. 'I thought the poor guy needed affection, comfort and cuddles,' Miss Greaves explained after the case in an interview with the *Sun*. The 'twenty-five days of passion' that followed, according to the newspaper, aroused jealous hatred in Bamber's scorned former girlfriend, Julie Mug-ford. Anji described Julie as childish, possessive and a gold-digger. 'I was giving him the love in bed she should have been giving him,' she told the paper. 'She was just giving him mouth.'

Anji Greaves appeared at Sir David Napley's office in Covent Garden a few days after Bamber's first remand appearance. Sir David received her with courtesy, but explained that he was personally unable to take the case on a legal aid basis. However, he did introduce her to one of his partners, a young solicitor called Paul Terzeon. Sir David explained that Terzeon would take the case on the firm's behalf, and that he personally would review the papers before the proceedings to commit Jeremy Bamber for trial.

In the meantime, Bruce Bowler continued to act for

Jeremy Bamber. It was Bowler who presented Bamber's application for bail when he appeared in court for the second time on Wednesday, 9 October. The magistrates refused the application, ignoring an offer from Bamber's friend Michael Deckers to put up a surety of £1,000. As for Jeremy's application to change his lawyers, the chairman of the magistrates, George Ginn, was equally dismissive. 'It's not your right,' Mr Ginn told Bamber at one point. But on 1 November, after considering the application further, the bench agreed that Sir David Napley's firm should take over Bamber's defence. Bruce Bowler had argued it was right that in such a serious case the defendant should be allowed to have a solicitor of his own choice to defend him.

Paul Terzeon visited his new client in Norwich Jail. The lawyer was impressed. He found Bamber an attractive and sociable young man, not unintelligent and easy to talk to. But when the prosecution papers were served some weeks later, Terzeon realized just how difficult the case would be to win. Julie Mugford, the most dangerous witness of all, had given several separate statements to the police; Terzeon and his staff spent days combing through them, noting what had been said in which, and comparing each statement with the information that had appeared in the newspapers. Terzeon had to admit that Julie Mugford's story did have what lawyers call 'the ring of truth' about it. The solicitor spent a week in Norwich going through all the papers with Jeremy. There were sheaves of statements, depositions, notes, letters, plans and photographs. Jeremy stuck to his story. He hadn't murdered his family. Only once did he betray any emotion to Paul Terzeon. Terzeon had gone through all the statements of the prosecution witnesses, noting Jeremy's comments on each one, discussing the contents, gauging his reaction, but there came a moment when it was relevant to show him the photographs of the scenes of crime. Terzeon showed Jeremy a photograph of his murdered father, slumped on his chair beside the Aga in the kitchen at White House Farm. That was when (for the first and last time) Jeremy wept in front of his lawyer.

Like most defendants protesting their innocence on a serious charge, Jeremy wanted his lawyer to stand up in front of the magistrates and to argue that the police simply did not have a case. But Terzeon and Napley knew that this would never work. So after discussing the case at length, they agreed on a 'paper committal', a procedure whereby Bamber was sent for trial without the evidence being exposed and tested in front of the magistrates. The alternative was fraught with hazards. For example, Terzeon could have challenged the prosecution to call Julie Mugford to testify at the committal stage, and tested her story under cross-examination. If the defence had done so, and if Bamber had been sent for trial nonetheless, the prosecution would have then had time to repair any holes in Julie Mugford's testimony. Terzeon and Napley decided that in Bamber's case that would have been too risky.

During his interviews with Paul Terzeon at Norwich, Jeremy never wavered in his protestations of innocence. So if he was not the killer, who was? Terzeon commissioned an eminent forensic pathologist, Professor Bernard Knight of the University of Wales, to test the possibility that Sheila was responsible. Knight was virtually certain she could not have been. 'You can never totally discount anything,' observed Paul Terzeon after the case, 'but looking at it from a jury's point of view, we could see there were difficulties there.' So if not Sheila, who? Jeremy told Terzeon he didn't know.

This vacuum left Paul Terzeon with a very difficult case. Quite aside from the forensic intricacies, there was also the question of whom to brief for the defence. Jeremy's first choice was George Carman QC, the best-known defence barrister in the country, hailed as the greatest jury lawyer of his day, the best examiner of witnesses and certainly the most expensive. It was not an inappropriate choice. Carman had come to national prominence in 1979 when he was briefed in the Jeremy Thorpe case by Sir David Napley, Thorpe's solicitor. Carman famously demolished the prosecution witness Peter Bessell and clinched Thorpe's acquittal by keeping his client out of the witness box, so robbing the prosecution of the chance to cross-examine him. It was a bold stroke. Indeed, it is Carman's audacity that draws the admiration of other barristers. 'He's got terrific balls,' said one. 'He will take risks that his opponents would never consider.' George Carman was duly offered the brief to defend Jeremy Bamber. But to Jeremy's dismay, Carman turned it down. He was just too busy.

It was a setback, but a short-lived one. Napley unhesitatingly sent the brief to another northern barrister, Geoffrey Rivlin QC. Rivlin, a small, watchful and fastidious man, had been instructed by Napley's firm in several big fraud cases. But he had also appeared in many murder trials, chiefly as prosecutor. Paul Terzeon knew of his talent for getting to grips with cases in which there was a massive amount of documentation. In the Bamber case, Terzeon estimated that there were some 1,200 statements, each of which had to be minutely examined. This was a case calling for an acute, analytical mind rather than Rumpolean bluster. What was needed was a clinical dissection of the evidence to demonstrate to the jury the deep and possibly fatal flaws in the police investigation. Geoffrey Rivlin was the ideal choice.

Rivlin accepted with alacrity. It was a matter of pride to Geoffrey Rivlin that he had never turned down a brief to defend a man accused of murder. Besides, the case was certain to represent a landmark in any lawyer's career, such was the sensational nature of the killings, the personality of the accused man and the high-octane coverage accorded the story by the British media. He knew the case was not only important and interesting in its own right, but also one of maximum gravity and seemingly maximum difficulty. More important, though, Geoffrey Rivlin refused to believe it was unwinnable.

At first, reading carefully through all the statements and case notes, he was assailed by the sheer scale of the labyrinthine difficulties and doubts presented by the evidence. But re-reading the files and thinking matters over, Rivlin realized that there was a way through the maze. Rivlin saw that the route to an acquittal lay not through launching swingeing attacks on the police but through hard, circuit-board logic. It was a case calling for a scalpel rather than a bludgeon.

In a major murder trial, leading counsel on either side is shadowed by a junior barrister whose role is to help run the case, to support the leader, marshal witnesses, see that the right documents are available at the right time and occasionally take over in court to examine or cross-examine some of the minor witnesses. Paul Terzeon, as Bamber's instructing solicitor, gave some thought to who should be briefed as Geoffrey Rivlin's junior, given Rivlin's phlegmatic and taciturn nature. Terzeon's choice was a young barrister named Edmund Lawson, an extrovert, clubbable lawyer with a reputation as a workaholic who fuelled himself on all-night brainstorming sessions and a seemingly endless stream of cigarettes. Terzeon had reckoned on Jeremy taking to Lawson more than Geoffrey Rivlin and he was right. The three lawyers meshed well together. And Jeremy Bamber seemed reassured by the wide range of legal personalities working on his behalf.

This was not a defence devised amid the cloistered hush of barristers' chambers. Bamber's lawyers mobilized themselves. Terzeon visited him regularly in Norwich and later, as the trial approached, at Brixton Prison in south London. Rivlin and Lawson both paid visits to White House Farm, learning the internal geography, travelling the route to and from Goldhanger, familiarizing themselves with Tolleshunt D'Arcy and the villagers. The team of forensic experts retained by the defence spent a day at the farm and held a conference in the dining room. They inspected the cache of exhibits stored at Essex Police headquarters, and travelled to the forensic laboratories at Huntingdon where the defence's firearms expert, Lieutenant-Colonel Peter Mead, examined the murder rifle, test-fired it repeatedly into a big lump of beeswax, and stripped down the silencer. Another forensic expert, Dr Patrick J. Lincoln, who advised the defence on blood characteristics (and who later went to Australia to give evidence in the so-called dingo baby case), also examined the bloodstained silencer. Dr Lincoln was able to confirm that the results of tests conducted at Huntingdon showed that the blood which had blown back into the silencer was specific to Sheila Caffell. This was depressing news for the defence team. It indicated that Sheila had been shot while the silencer was fitted to the rifle. Since the rifle had been found without the silencer (which was downstairs in the gun cupboard) Dr Lincoln's evidence seemed to exonerate Sheila, and to indicate that she, like the others, had been murdered.

But Jeremy Bamber continued to protest his innocence.

By late summer the problems facing Geoffrey Rivlin and the Bamber defence team had been sharply crystallized. One of the lawyers characterized the difficulties as three separate but parallel tightropes which Rivlin would have to walk, in front of the watching jury at Bamber's trial.

1. The killer was either Jeremy Bamber, or his sister Sheila. *On Bamber's own evidence* it was either him or her. The key was the phone call. Jeremy had telephoned the police and reported his father as saying that Sheila had gone crazy with the gun. *Sheila. No one else.* So it was either Sheila or Jeremy. The defence were stuck with that fact. Their case then had to be that Sheila *was* the killer. Unfortunately, although there had been a ferocious fight in the kitchen between Nevill Bamber and his killer, leaving blood all over the smashed-up kitchen, there was scarcely a mark on Sheila, whose fingernails were unbroken and perfectly manicured. There were other difficulties with the suggestion that Sheila was responsible for the murders. People said Sheila adored the twins.

2. Was Jeremy telling the truth or was Julie Mugford? The dilemma here was that there were two ways the defence could approach Julie Mugford's evidence: they could attack her character, or they could attack her story.

As far as her character was concerned, Julie and Jeremy had seemed all of a piece in the months leading up to the murders. They had played Bonnie and Clyde in the burglary at the caravan site office and there had been talk of the couple getting engaged. So any effective attack on her character would have to be based on the way she behaved *after* the killings. By all accounts, Julie joined in all the jauntings, but so did Jeremy. This required special care on the part of the defence lawyers. After all, Julie could turn round and say: 'Well, what about Jeremy?'

As for her story, the fact was that all her statements appeared remarkably consistent. The lawyers set two people to work, going over all her statements line by line. Geoffrey Rivlin repeated the process personally, looking for the smallest loose brick that might be dislodged to bring the whole story crashing down. But all her statements meshed convincingly, and her story undeniably resounded with 'the ring of truth'. So the defence lawyers changed tack. Instead of looking for inconsistencies *between* Julie Mugford's various statements, they decided to exploit the differences between her story and the evidence of other prosecution witnesses.

3. The third tightrope was the silencer. The defence were faced with a double-bind over this. The first was that it was found at the opposite end of the house (and on a different floor) from where Sheila lay dead. The second was that it apparently contained Sheila's blood. If Sheila had killed herself, the silencer couldn't have been on the gun. Her arms weren't long enough to allow her to jam the silencer under her chin and pull the trigger. In any case, the defence reasoned, no crazy person would have bothered with a silencer. So was the blood found inside it *necessarily specific* to Sheila? The defence lawyers asked every surviving member of the Bamber family if they would submit to a blood test. They all agreed. The result was that the blood of Jeremy's uncle, Bobby Boutflour, was found to be of the same grouping as that inside the silencer. The defence were therefore able to cast doubt on the specificity of the silencer blood.

The police investigation had been such a shambles that it was tempting for the defence to concentrate on this aspect of the case and to demolish the police's credibility altogether. But Rivlin determined not to do so. Rubbishing the police, he maintained, could be counterproductive. After all, the defence were concerned to keep open the option that Sheila was the White House Farm killer. And that – the jury would recall – was the first theory of the police themselves. Dr Peter Vanezis had put the killings down to Sheila on day two of the inquiry, and the police had closed the case down. So the defence lawyers were concerned to strike a fine balance between portraying the police as efficient on the one hand and downright incompetent on the other.

Staying aloft on all three tightropes – and concentrating on damage limitation – underpinned the defence team's entire strategy. But there were some more positive aspects to the case. The most encouraging, from the defence viewpoint, was that Sheila Caffell was without a doubt a very disturbed young woman. According to her psychiatrist, Dr Hugh Ferguson, Sheila could have been capable of such a frenzied attack. Furthermore, Sheila's own wounds were located beneath her chin, so suicide was a possibility. It was vital to the defence that such a possibility was not excluded. If those wounds beneath Sheila's chin had not been self-inflicted, then it followed that she must have been killed by someone else. Such a person would have had to have committed four murders and simulated Sheila's suicide. The defence's expert in forensic pathology, Professor Bernard Knight, was deeply sceptical. His emphatic view was that it would have been extremely difficult for an assailant to have set up such a elaborate scenario. So when all the possibilities had been considered, theories tested and likelihoods looked at, Jeremy Bamber's defence team was brought to the conclusion that perhaps Sheila really might have been capable of such unimaginable slaughter after all.

TWENTY-FOUR

SHEILA had gone crazy before. Shrieking, fist-beating crazy, to the point where even a grown man like Freddie Emami, her Iranian friend, became terrified for his own safety.

Emami, 41 and separated from his English wife, told police he considered himself to be more of a confidant to Sheila than a boyfriend. Freddie had met Sheila at a party in 1981. What struck him was that she seemed slow, unable to grasp simple concepts, and appeared to be 'the sort of person who relied on others to make decisions'. Freddie counted himself among Sheila's decision-making friends. 'She would bring her problems to me,' he told detectives, 'and we would discuss them. These problems were mainly family or money worries.'

When Freddie met Sheila, she was living in a flat in Hampstead with her twin sons. She was finding it difficult to cope. The flat was a mess, and – worse – it was damp. Nevill and June visited her there, despaired of the conditions and asked Freddie if he could help find Sheila a new flat. Freddie obliged by suggesting a pleasant ground-floor flat in a Victorian block in Maida Vale called Morshead Mansions. Both Freddie and Colin Caffell (whom Freddie knew) helped with the move. Sheila and the children all seemed very happy in their new home. But Colin expressed concern that Sheila might not be able to afford to pay all the household bills.

Freddie found that Sheila worried over the smallest of problems. Following at least one miscarriage in her teens, one source of great anxiety had been Sheila's fear that she would never have children. 'She was petrified,' Freddie said. But after the birth of the twins in the summer of 1979, she seemed to have focused her fears on her adoptive mother. Freddie reported that Sheila disliked her deeply for constantly quoting religion at her. This would upset Sheila and annoy her. 'I would say that Sheila had a very quick and violent temper,' he went on, 'which she would lose over the simplest of things.' However, Freddie also added that he had never seen Sheila use physical violence on anyone.

In the autumn of 1984, Sheila changed. 'She became extremely depressed,' Freddie reported, 'and withdrew into herself.' Such was this withdrawal that Sheila ceased to share her troubles with Freddie, although he noticed that every time she visited White House Farm, she returned more depressed than ever because of her mother. She told Freddie that June would preach to her about boyfriends, that she was wrong to sleep with them, and that she should always remember God. Sheila gradually deteriorated, Freddie said, until the day on which Nick fell out of a London taxi on the way home from a visit to White House Farm. The child wasn't seriously hurt but Sheila was nonetheless horrified. She blamed herself for the accident, and told friends that instead of concentrating on what the children were doing, she'd been preoccupied with her mother's religious ravings. The accident was the last straw for Sheila; three weeks later she went into hospital suffering from her first mental breakdown.

Freddie didn't visit Sheila during her stay at Dr Ferguson's clinic in Northampton. Shortly before she was allowed home, Sheila telephoned Freddie and said that while she counted him as a good friend, she thought it best that she tried to sort out her problems alone. Freddie agreed. But a few weeks later, with Sheila back in Maida Vale, she telephoned again to tell Freddie that she was broke. Freddie called round a day or two later and gave her some money. 'She appeared well in herself,' he observed, 'although you could see she wasn't completely recovered.'

The relationship between Sheila and Freddie – whatever its true nature – seemed to fizzle and drift. Freddie bumped into her on a couple of occasions in London nightclubs, but Sheila was always with others and apart from saying hello the couple hardly spoke. Then, in the early summer of 1985, at Sheila's suggestion, Freddie Emami called at her flat. Freddie found her 'jumpy, uptight and panicky' although he didn't know why. While he was there, Sheila telephoned a close friend called Tara. Freddie heard her apologizing to Tara about a religious book that June Bamber had dropped off at Tara's house a couple of days before. During the call, the phone went dead. Suddenly Sheila became hysterical, mumbling something about the phone being bugged. Freddie described what happened next in a statement to detectives: 'She became like someone possessed, ranting and raving. She was striking herself and beating the wall with her fists. I tried to calm her but she didn't seem to hear me. I became extremely frightened, not only for her but for myself.'

Sheila kept talking about the Devil and God, saying that God was sitting opposite her. Contrary to what her mother was telling her, God loved her. With Freddie looking on helplessly, Sheila picked up the telephone and called her former mother-in-law, Dorothy Brencher, but asking to speak to Dr Ferguson. Freddie took the receiver from Sheila and explained to Mrs Brencher that Sheila was ill again. Sheila promptly began hitting herself harder than ever and shouting abuse. Hearing children's voices in the background, Mrs Brencher told Freddie she would be over straight away. When she arrived at Morshead

Mansions, Sheila announced she was hearing voices, some-times from God. She said she had to put the world to rights, and began gabbling about things that were troubling her. She kept getting up and walking quickly round the flat, hyperactive. Mrs Brencher told Freddie to call a doctor. Sheila's own GP, Dr Angeloglou, was on holiday and a locum was alerted. By the time he arrived, Sheila had calmed down and was sitting very quietly looking sad and forlorn. 'When I caught her eye,' Mrs Brencher remembered, 'she would give me a very quick, bright smile, but it would go immediately.' Sheila told the locum about hearing voices. The doctor said he would give her an injection but Sheila refused. He prescribed some pills instead, and Freddie was dispatched to the chemist while Mrs Brencher arranged for her ex-husband, Reg Caffell, to collect the twins. Meanwhile, Tara's hus-band called to pick up his daughter who was staying with Sheila. Freddie had alerted him, fearing that 'something nasty' might happen. 'I was extremely concerned for everyone's safety,' he recalled. 'I felt Sheila may use violence towards someone.' Arriving back with Sheila's pills, Freddie met Mrs Brencher at the front door. Mrs Brencher announced that she was leaving. Sheila, she said, had kicked her out.

Inside the flat, Freddie found Sheila ranting once more. He tried to calm her down but couldn't. She was flailing her arms about, beating herself with her fists, crying and shouting. Freddie was frightened and again telephoned for a doctor. This time, one of Dr Angeloglou's partners arrived. Sheila refused to let him examine her, shouting that she was being poisoned. 'By this time,' Freddie Emami recalled, 'she had become completely irrational. The doctor eventually left without being able to do anything.' Freddie called a third doctor. But he, too, was unable to get near Sheila. Instead the doctor scribbled a short note to Dr Angeloglou, which he handed to Freddie, together with a prescription for a stronger drug. Freddie glanced at his watch. It was late. Looking at Sheila, Freddie decided he would have to stay the night.

Sheila was clearly still in the grip of an inexplicable frenzy. Freddie took the precaution of telephoning Nevill Bamber at White House Farm to tell him that his daughter seemed to be out of control. Nevill apparently told him that he would drive to London first thing in the morning to collect her. Despite Freddie's pleading, Nevill insisted he couldn't come any sooner. 'It eventually got to the stage where I could no longer handle the situation,' Freddie reported in his lengthy statement to police after the massacre. 'Sheila was behaving like a person possessed, rambling about the Devil and God.' In what seems to have been the grip of mounting panic, Freddie fetched Sheila's next-door neighbour to try to help calm her down. Sheila sat quietly combing her hair, her expression a blank mask as she stared vacantly into space. Then, for no apparent reason, the tumult began again as she erupted into a violent spasm of ranting and raving. All night Sheila sat, now calmly combing her hair, now seized by uncontrollable fits, until the sound of the door-bell at dawn announced the arrival from Tolleshunt D'Arcy of Nevill Bamber. 'When her father walked into the flat,' Freddie recalled, 'Sheila became a different person. She spoke to [him] in a calm and collected manner. I couldn't believe the change in the girl.'

Her night of psychotic madness was just five months before her death and the slaughter of her family. When Sheila was discharged from St Andrew's at the end of March, her friend Tara told Freddie that Sheila was better but 'not the same person'.

In fact Sheila was behaving very oddly. A distant cousin, a 14–year-old schoolgirl called Helen Grimster, meeting Sheila for only the second time in her life, found her not only strange but frightening. Finding herself alone with Sheila in the lounge at White House Farm, Helen Grimster had to endure an hour-long diatribe about drugs, religion, witchcraft and suicide. Sheila had asked her about school, and said she remembered being bullied which was why she hadn't enjoyed her own schooldays. As Sheila spoke she began to roll a joint. 'When she lit the cigarette, it smelt a bit strange,' Helen Grimster explained. Sheila offered Helen a smoke, but the young girl turned the offer down. Sheila wondered if Helen had ever tried taking drugs. Helen shook her head. Sheila said she thought everyone should at least try. As Sheila sat smoking, the talk turned to suicide.

'She asked me if I'd ever thought of killing myself,' Helen Grimster recalled, 'and she said that she contemplated suicide on more than one occasion.' Then, what Helen considered to be this 'singularly peculiar' conversation took another unexpected turn. Sheila announced that she thought she was a white witch. She explained that she had to get rid of the evil in the world. Helen listened, terrified. According to Sheila, June Bamber had told her she had lost her soul, and urged Sheila to be more religious.

At about this time, Sheila seems to have expanded her social horizons, going out most evenings with a string of different boyfriends. The twins were living with their father, Colin Caffell, for most of the time, and Sheila had more free time to go out and enjoy herself. Freddie's attitude to Sheila's gallivanting isn't entirely clear. In a statement to detectives investigating the shootings, he gave the impression of being wounded by Sheila's decision to start seeing other men. Nevertheless he said he continued to call on her ('on about ten occasions since she came out of hospital') but found that she had com-

Young Jeremy, the farmer's boy.

At school.

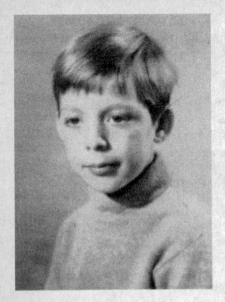

At home.

With a favourite pet.

Nevill Bamber at White House Farm.

The kitchen at White House Farm. Nevill Bamber's chair (centre) beneath the mantel-piece where police found tell-tale scratch marks.

Detectives examine Nevill Bamber's blue Citroën outside Jeremy's cottage. (Photo © Syndication International)

June Bamber's bicycle outside the kitchen at White House Farm. The open window was Jeremy's way of entering the house without a key.

Remanded in custody. (Photo © Syndication International)

Arriving for committal proceedings. (Photo © Syndication International)

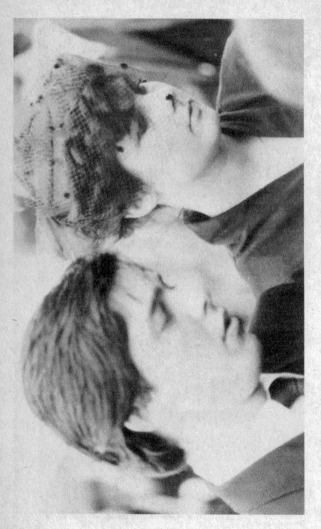

Jeremy and Julie Mugford at his parents' funeral.

PC Chris Widdon with the murder weapon, a .22 Anschutz rifle and silencer. (Photo © Syndication International)

Nevill Bamber on his wedding day in 1949.

The twins, Daniel and Nicholas Caffell. This photograph was found torn into pieces at Sheila's flat in London after Jeremy's arrest.

June Bamber (left) and her niece, Ann Eaton.

Nevill and June Bamber at White House Farm.

Nicholas and Daniel Caffell. (Photo © Syndication International)

IN LOVING MEMORY
OF
R. NEVILL & JUNE
BAMBER
BOTH AGED 61 YEARS
TRAGICALLY TAKEN FROM US
7TH AUGUST 1985
FOR EVER WITH THE LORD

The Bamber Grave at Tolleshunt D'Arcy.

Sheila Caffell, the girl next door.

Sheila Caffell, the model girl 'Bambi'.

The gun cupboard (and inset) in Nevill Bamber's den.

pletely changed, having become very slow and deliberate in the way she spoke and a difficult woman to talk to. Freddie said he saw her socially only once. That was on the Friday before she died, 2 August, when he bumped into her at a nightclub. A group of revellers, including Sheila and Freddie, went back to Morshead Mansions where a party was under way in one of the flats. In the course of the party, Sheila mentioned she was going to another party the following night with her ex-husband Colin, and that she was going to White House Farm with the twins on the Sunday. Sheila asked Freddie to keep an eye on her flat while she was away: she was worried about burglars.

The first Freddie knew of the tragedy was when he called at Morshead Mansions on the day after the killings to check that Sheila's flat was secure. A group of waiting newspaper reporters broke the news to him. Freddie was shocked and incredulous. 'Had it just been [June] Bamber who had been killed, I could accept it,' he explained, 'as [Sheila] disliked her intensely. But to think she's killed her father and children is difficult to comprehend.'

As a close friend of Sheila, Freddie Emami was questioned at some length by detectives on the White House Farm case. He was driven to Essex and interviewed for several hours, completing his initial statement at 11.30 p.m. on the Thursday after the killings. Police were entirely satisfied that Freddie the babysitter had nothing to do with the tragedy. But one of the many aspects of his statement that intrigued Jeremy Bamber's defence lawyers as they prepared their case was the possibility that Sheila just might have been seized by another fit of psychosis, and – in a blind and frenzied rage – might have seized the gun that Jeremy had carelessly left lying around. For there was evidence that on the night in March, five months before, when Sheila had gone crazy in the flat in London, she had lost all hold on reason and reality. When Freddie spoke to her about that fearful night when she had beaten on the walls with her fists, lashed out at him and called him the very Devil, Sheila said she could remember nothing about it. Freddie realized that Sheila believed he had made the story up. He also remembered that she hadn't recognized anyone who'd called at the flat that night – and that Sheila had got it into her head that everyone she knew and everyone who'd called to help was either trying to hurt her or to murder her.

TWENTY-FIVE

OTHERS knew Sheila as well as Freddie did, and some knew her better, but she doesn't seem to have had a best friend as such, and there's evidence that some women were intimidated by Sheila's melting good looks and her ability to hold men spellbound.

Sandra Elston, who had known her for most of her adult life, thought Sheila was a beautiful-looking woman but that she exhibited at least two fatal flaws: lack of confidence and gullibility. 'She needed to be constantly reassured that she looked good,' said Mrs Elston, 'and liked to talk about herself.' Sheila would talk about everything and anything, but people who thought Sheila was stupid were mistaken. She was not.

Sandra Elston remembered thinking that Sheila often teetered on the edge of paranoid schizophrenia, such as the night (in May 1985, a couple of months after the psychotic seizure in her flat) when she told Sandra that she was convinced that her friend Freddie was the Devil. But recalling this conversation later, Sheila had laughed about it and said what a fool she'd been. On another occasion, she told her friend Sandra that she was convinced the CIA were following her. 'She used to get a lot of ideas into her head,' Sandra Elston remembered, 'but never followed them through. I think she wanted to make a success of something, no matter what it was. She always wanted things to be nice and rosy all the time.' Sandra Elston thought the best word to describe Sheila would be 'insecure'.

What brought the two women together was the fact

that both had known and loved Colin Caffell. In 1971 when she was 19, Sandra Elston became his fiancée; the engagement had lasted nearly three years but the couple broke it off early in 1974 and parted amicably. In 1976, returning to London after graduating at Liverpool University, she occasionally saw him socially and began to form a friendship with his new girlfriend, the pretty, long-legged model they called Bambi. Theirs was the kind of friendship that survives long periods without contact; it also endured with neither knowing every intimate detail about the other. Sandra knew comparatively little about Sheila's adoptive family in Essex, only that 'she liked her Dad' but felt that her mother was 'rather interfering'. They had spoken of Jeremy only once: according to Sheila, her brother had 'got a lot better' since meeting his girlfriend, Julie Mugford. Sandra Elston said that Sheila always gave her the impression that she and Jeremy weren't particularly close.

Sandra saw Sheila regularly in the last three months of her life. She seemed concerned about her latest breakdown, and afraid that she might have 'one of her silly fits' in front of the twins. Dan and Nick were living with Colin for most of the time, visiting their mother on odd days and sometimes staying the night. Even though the arrangement minimized the chance of the boys seeing their mother in the throes of a seizure, the fact remained that Sheila missed having them around. 'I knew,' Sandra Elston reported, 'she really wanted them.'

In late July, for the first time in about two years, Colin Caffell telephoned Sandra Elston. He invited her to a party, and a few days later, Sandra called round to Colin's flat in Kilburn for a meal with him and the twins. They spoke about Sheila, and Colin admitted he was worried about her health. But when Sandra saw Sheila a day or two later, it wasn't her health that preoccupied her but her hair. Sheila said she'd just spent a lot of money on having it cut, and that it looked awful. Sandra suggested that she went back to the hairdresser to complain. The good news was that Sheila had been offered a job. But she was concerned that she was coming down with a cold. This, her terrible haircut and her perennial worries over money seemed to be Sheila's only preoccupations.

Sandra found it hard to believe that Sheila could have shot her family in another crazy rage, but thinking about her recent breakdown and her 'silly fits', her friend agreed it might have been possible. But, she added, Sheila could not have slaughtered in cold blood; she would only have gone on such a rampage in the course of a fit. Then again, Sandra told the police, Sheila was terrified of losing contact with her twins sons. Sandra remembered something that Colin had said over the meal at his flat, about Sheila, in the grip of madness, being unfit to look after Dan and Nick. That wasn't Colin Caffell's own opinion, she explained. He was quoting June Bamber.

And yet, looking at the official records of Sheila's years of motherhood, she seems to have taken every care with the two golden-haired little boys. The twins were only two when the family came to the attention of the authorities. Four days before Christmas 1979, Sheila referred herself to the social services department of Camden Council in north London, saying she was having problems with her marriage. Interviewed by a social worker, Sheila admitted having temper tantrums, and to having deliberately injured herself by punching her hand through a window. She had also deliberately provoked her husband Colin. Sheila's notes also recorded the fact that she had hallucinations and feelings of paranoia. Sheila asked to be referred to a psychoanalyst.

The marriage broke up in July 1980. In November,

because Sheila – a single parent with two children – was having problems, the case was referred to another social worker, a recently qualified young woman called Barbara Babic. She learned that since June, the twins had been looked after under a day-fostering arrangement. This meant that they were cared for every morning so that Sheila could spend time looking for work. After the split with Colin, he and Sheila shared custody of the twins, an arrangement that Barbara Babic reported worked well. In the summer of 1981, Dan was admitted to hospital with an ear infection, and the social worker expressed some concern that Sheila was slow to take her children to the doctor unless prompted by someone else. At about the same time, Dan was noted as having a scald, but at a case conference held on 4 August it was felt that this was accidental and that neither he nor his twin brother was considered to be at risk. Her social workers also felt that Sheila's reluctance to take the children to the doctor's fell short of deliberate neglect.

Barbara Babic formed the opinion that Sheila had a low self-image. Her GP had referred her to a plastic surgeon for a silicone-implant operation on her breasts, on the grounds that this would improve her chances of getting work as a model. This operation took place in the late summer of 1981. But Sheila's self-esteem was also influenced by other, more powerful feelings about relationships between mother and children. She spoke to Barbara Babic about how her own experiences as an adopted daughter had spurred her to have children of her own. She gave Barbara Babic the impression that she was fond of her adoptive father Nevill Bamber but that she had 'some difficulty' (Barbara Babic's phrase) with her adoptive mother June. This was one reason, Mrs Babic reported, that Sheila thought it important to trace her own natural mother.

She set about this in the autumn of 1981, writing first to the Church of England Children's Society who had placed her in the adoptive care of the Bambers in early 1958. The formalities of tracing natural parents involved Sheila in much form-filling and heart-searching, but the following year, at Heathrow Airport, she was able to greet her real mother when she stepped off a plane from Canada on a special visit to see the daughter she had never really known. The reunion seems to have been a source of great joy to Sheila. 'She didn't appear to have changed as a result of it,' Barbara Babic noted. And although the procedure of tracing her mother, making contact and setting up the meeting had been a mental and physical strain, Sheila seemed 'no more stressed than I would have expected'. Barbara Babic lost contact with Sheila at about this time, when Sheila moved to Maida Vale and became the responsibility of Westminster City Council. At the time of her transfer, Sheila was attending group therapy for mood swings, but while Mrs Babic noted Sheila's 'ups and downs', she could see no evidence of any mental instability. Sheila, she reported, lacked confidence, but she was attractive and always looking for outside interests. Friendly but scatty, there was no malice in her, and while she was a disorganized young woman, she loved her small twin boys. But although Sheila strove to be a good mother, she was not a natural one. She wanted Colin to share the responsibility of raising the twins, because she was overwhelmed by the idea of doing it on her own.

A week before her death, on Wednesday 31 July, Sheila telephoned a friend living nearby in Maida Vale, Jane Robinson, complaining of feeling fed up and lonely. Jane asked her over to join a small houseful of friends and their children. It was a fine summer's afternoon and the women sat out on the verandah, drinking wine and talking. One of Jane's guests, a nurse from Nottingham called Caroline Heath, who had never met Sheila before, saw her arrive and thought she looked a mess. Her make-up might have been slapped on anyhow, her hair was greasy, she looked very pale and seemed to be hiding behind a pair of very dark sunglasses that she never took off. 'Throughout the afternoon,' said Caroline Heath, '[Sheila] appeared to be fidgety and on edge.' At times she stared blankly into space. She drank a couple of glasses of wine and smoked her way through a whole packet of twenty cigarettes. Sheila spoke only in fits and starts, and when she did speak it was mainly about herself. Caroline Heath gathered that Sheila was lonely after her divorce. She had men friends but she didn't feel that they cared for her.

When Sheila spoke about her family, it was to explain baldly that they lived in a farmhouse in Essex and it struck Caroline Heath that there was no hint of family intimacy. Sheila said she liked the peace and tranquillity down there – a curious remark since the family knew she actually disliked the country atmosphere and complained about being woken at White House Farm by the sound of birdsong at dawn. She told the listening women about her career as a model and that she had worked in Japan. Caroline Heath sensed that Sheila thought no one believed this, and remembered thinking Sheila seemed insecure. Sheila explained she hadn't worked for a few months 'because she felt down', but was now looking for work again. 'The impression I got,' said Caroline Heath, 'was that she seemed desperate to find work, as she even mentioned looking for work as a housekeeper or domestic.' To Caroline Heath, Sheila confided about her mental breakdowns, saying the most recent had been triggered by her divorce and the fact that a number of things (she didn't say *what* things) had been getting on top of her. But Sheila added that she was looking forward to visiting her parents over the coming weekend with the twins. She felt it was some time since she'd been really close to the boys.

At one point in the conversation, Sheila mentioned to Jane Robinson some injections she was having. Being a trained nurse, Caroline Heath surmised from this and from her general manner that Sheila was a schizophrenic. 'The impression I got of her that afternoon was that she appeared very frightened and paranoid. She never really opened up at any stage, and seemed to be always on the defensive.'

Caroline Heath saw Sheila again the following afternoon, when Jane Robinson held a barbecue party at her house and invited round a group of friends including Colin Caffell, Sheila and the twins. The transformation was astonishing. Sheila looked radiant. She had had her hair done, her make-up was straight, she was dressed for a party and she looked pretty. Far from the withdrawn depressive of the day before, Sheila was talkative and in good spirits. Busy helping to serve food and drink at the barbecue, Caroline Heath saw Sheila only occasionally in the course of the party, but she noticed that Sheila stuck closely to her ex-husband Colin, and seemed to ignore the twins who were left to their own devices. She neither offered to help with the refreshments nor did she want to play with the children like the other parents. She drank little but smoked a lot. 'Underneath,' Caroline Heath reported, 'I sensed that all was not well with Bambi. She seemed to be trying to make a good show of it, but at times she seemed to have a vacant look about her, as though she was deep in thought about other things.' Six days later, hearing of the massacre at White House Farm, Caroline Heath felt sickened. But looking back on the two sunlit afternoons she had spent in Sheila's company in the last week of her troubled life, she said, 'I can't say it was completely unexpected.'

TWENTY-SIX

MOST of this information about Sheila and her moments of madness had been scooped up by the police in the days immediately following the tragedy at White House Farm. Sheila's Iranian friend, Freddie Emami, for example, had described her psychotic night of tortured incoherence in a lengthy statement made at Witham Police Station on the day after the massacre. It seems to have been pivotal in helping to incline the police towards Jeremy's theory that she had seized the loaded gun in the course of a brainstorm. The problem facing the defence was that although Sheila was clearly a dangerously unbalanced young woman, there was no real evidence to show that she possessed a propensity for *violence*. The prosecution might well have made rather more of this than they did, but preferred to keep the spotlight firmly on Jeremy and his own wilful and wayward personality.

Jeremy's own lawyers canvassed several psychiatrists for an opinion. Would the clinical diagnosis recorded in Sheila's files support a suggestion that she had the potential to erupt into such murderous violence? The answer was no, it would not. This left the lawyers with a huge problem: Jeremy's defence would have to hinge on the suggestion that Sheila was the killer, but there was nothing to support this notion, either in her clinical history or in her known experience with guns. Although the unexplained problem of the silencer remained, the defence gambled on being able to convince a jury that Sheila was the most likely culprit. 'After all,' as one of the lawyers put it, 'she was undoubtedly somewhat potty.'

But there was another, more dangerous, road to follow. Jeremy's lawyers decided they would at least have to float the notion that malice may have inspired the surviving relations to fit up Jeremy. The danger of this explosive approach was obvious: it might detonate without warning and backfire on Jeremy himself. So rather than launch a full frontal attack on the surviving family, the lawyers decided simply to canvass the idea. Certainly Geoffrey Rivlin faced an uphill task in trying to persuade any jury that the family could be so venal as to incriminate Jeremy falsely in such carnage.

On the face of it, Rivlin, with his softly spoken, understated Yorkshire manner, was not considered an aggressive advocate. Yet the Bamber case disclosed a hidden steeliness. 'Rivlin in fact is very tough,' said a barrister who'd been led by him in other cases. 'Tough as old boots. Very thorough, very diligent. And the fact that it's all done in a quiet North Country voice makes the whole thing rather effective.'

Jeremy was sceptical. He wanted a showdown in court – a full-frontal assault on the police evidence. He seemed neither crushed nor daunted by his forthcoming ordeal. Far from it. Jeremy always exhibited an enthusiasm for the trial and exuded total confidence that it would result in his acquittal. 'He rather relished his own role in it,' said one who saw him during the run-up to the trial. 'He received a lot of fan mail, and to some extent he did enjoy the notoriety.' Jeremy's lawyers visited him and listened to his theories about what might have happened on the night his family died. Patiently, the lawyers insisted that their strategy of picking at unexplained anomalies and teasing out the stray threads in the prosecution case was the best way to cast doubt in the minds of the jury.

The defence lawyers were bullish in Jeremy's presence, but in private there were moments of deep gloom. The worst came the week before the trial opened, when the defence team held a case conference at Geoffrey Rivlin's chambers in the Temple. An eminent psychiatrist expressed his opinion that Jeremy exhibited several classic symptoms of the psychopath: chief among these was the genuine belief that he was completely innocent of any crime. With the passage of time, he said, memory drifts to the back of the mind and eventually falls off, so that the original image – and the memory of it – is forgotten. The doctor believed that Jeremy Bamber had killed his family, and that the awfulness of what he'd done had been pushed to the back of his mind and now it had dropped off. In short, the psychiatrist concluded, if ever there was a psychopath, it was Jeremy Bamber.

It was a depressing moment. Lights flared in the late September dusk. The lawyers stared glumly at each other. The psychiatrist gathered up his papers, wished everyone a pleasant weekend, and left to catch his train. Edmund Lawson disappeared for a few moments and returned with a bottle of gin and some glasses. Drinks were dispensed. Rivlin sat at his desk and regarded the others through his glinting gold spectacles. He acknowledged their raised glasses and their good wishes for a successful outcome in court. 'One thing I have to say to all of you,' he murmured, his deadpan Yorkshire vowels hanging on the smoky air. 'Let's not get depressed.'

The spell was broken. Rivlin's words shattered the mood like hot coals thrown on to ice. 'The way he said it just cracked us all up,' one of those present recalled, 'and we all just burst out laughing.'

TWENTY-SEVEN

CHELMSFORD CROWN COURT is a modern, massively ugly building, squat and forbidding in chocolate-coloured stone. Court Number One is the biggest of six, and like the building itself, has a depressing air of unavailing optimism, akin to that of a small provincial airport. It is a very large and windowless box, with a low ceiling, white lighting and cream walls. The institutionalized brightness is relieved by copious fitments of light oak, a grey and red carpet and seats covered in a synthetic material the colour of dried blood. Empty, the room fills with the hum of air-conditioning that stifles the acoustics; full – completely full – as it was on the opening morning of Jeremy Bamber's trial, the air is so deadened that anyone outside the central well of the court can scarcely hear a word that is being said. So when leading Crown counsel Anthony Arlidge QC rose to open the case on Thursday 2 October 1986, everyone – jury, family, press and public – strained to hear.

Arlidge told the jury that Jeremy Bamber stood to inherit £436,000 from his parents if the entire estate went to him in the event of his sister's death. There was no evidence that he had seen his parents' correct, legally drawn-up wills, but it was clear that he'd seen a rough draft. Asked by the police if he knew he would inherit if Sheila and his parents died, Bamber had replied: 'Understandably so.'

Bamber claimed to the police that on the evening before the murders he had loaded the rifle in order to shoot rabbits, but hadn't fired a shot. He had unloaded the rifle and left it. When he phoned the police early the following morning to tell them of the emergency at the farm, he described receiving a frantic phone call from his father which was suddenly cut short by a click followed by silence, as though someone had put their finger on the button to cut the call off. When the line went dead, Jeremy Bamber said, he tried to ring back but got no reply. The police asked the operator to test the line at White House Farm and found that it was open with the phone off the hook. They could hear the sound of a dog barking. Bamber told them that Sheila had a psychiatric history, 'would go mad at anything', and had gone mad before. His father, Bamber added, had a collection of guns. The police told Bamber to meet them at the farm. They overtook him on the way, and realized that he wasn't driving fast to the scene.

Police broke into the locked house by forcing a scullery door and found a scene of disarray in the kitchen where the body of Nevill Bamber lay. The phone was off the hook, the mantelpiece scarred, probably by a rifle butt, a lampshade lay broken on the floor and the dead man's watch was found underneath the rug. It appeared that Nevill Bamber had been injured by the rifle butt. Seven gunshot wounds were found in him, including two to the right side of the head and two close together on the forehead. Prosecuting counsel claimed Jeremy Bamber had wounded, beaten and then finished him off. Upstairs, Daniel lay in bed with five gunshot wounds in the head, and Nicholas with three. In another bedroom, June Bamber had seven gunshot wounds, including one between the eyes and one to the right side of the head. She had apparently staggered around the room before being finished off. Sheila was lying dead on the far side of the room with two gunshot wounds to the neck.

Afterwards, Bamber left his mother's blue-covered

Bible beside his sister's body and the rifle across her chest. Then he returned home to Goldhanger to phone the police. In a statement, Bamber described Sheila as a paranoid schizophrenic with debts, a drug problem and a history of violence towards her children. His sister was 'a nutter' who claimed to be the Virgin Mary and Joan of Arc.

The jury of seven men and five women were shown thick albums of photographs showing the scenes that had confronted police when they broke into White House Farm on that August morning fourteen months before. The murder weapon was also shown to the jury. Arlidge pointed out that Bamber had proved himself an accurate shot during a shooting competition with one of his cousins, Anthony Pargeter.

Days after the funerals, with police believing that Sheila had committed suicide after the murders, Bamber started to spend money, staying at de luxe hotels in Eastbourne and Amsterdam with his girlfriend. But their relationship deteriorated and eventually, on 7 September, a month after the killings, Julie Mugford went to the police. 'It is no exaggeration to say she was besotted with him,' said Arlidge. 'But on 7 September she told police that Jeremy Bamber had confided his responsibility for the deaths.'

Bamber was arrested and interviewed for three days, but denied responsibility. But it was apparent, Arlidge went on, that he was being very careful about committing himself on simple matters of fact. Bamber's demeanour when interviewed was also unusual; he stared fixedly at one of the detectives and occasionally answered questions in a sing-song tone.

Although Bamber was released on bail, it was becoming clear that all was not as it had first appeared. This impression increased and became overwhelming as the investigators uncovered various pieces of new evidence.

First, there was the history and character of Bamber's adopted sister, Sheila, the woman who was supposed to have shot dead her own sons as they slept. The evidence showed that she was a loving mother. She knew virtually nothing about guns, and had no aptitude for shooting. She was nothing like as strong as her adoptive father, Nevill, whom she was supposed to have overpowered. Her feet were clean, her hands well manicured with the nails unbroken. 'Anyone loading at least twice, and firing that gun,' said Anthony Arlidge, 'would be expected to have considerable traces of lead on their hands. Swabs from her hands showed only a very low level of lead which could have come from the atmosphere in which the bullets were fired.' Moreover, had Sheila loaded the gun, one would have expected to find traces of oil and lead on her nightdress. There were none.

Anthony Arlidge moved to the question of how Bamber may have got into the locked farmhouse and out again. The window of the ground-floor bathroom was shut, he explained, but the catch was not secured. The net curtain had been found covering some toiletries on the sill. When the window was painted earlier in the summer, the painter noticed that the catch could easily be slipped. When a forensic expert examined the catch, he found scratch marks which had been made since the painting. In October, a hacksaw blade had been found on the ground outside the window. 'The scratches on the catch matched the spacing of the teeth on the hacksaw blade,' Arlidge told the jury. 'Deposits of paint and brass on the blade matched the window.' The expert's conclusion was that the hacksaw blade had been used to force the catch open. In an interview, Bamber himself admitted there had been times when he had got into the house by manipulating the catch on that window. As for Bamber's exit route, Anthony Arlidge drew the jury's attention to a fanlight above one of the windows in the kitchen. The family's housekeeper, on being shown a photograph of the scene the police found, noted that several items around the sink had been moved, including a bottle of Fairy liquid, a sink tidy and a sponge.

Three days after the killings, Jeremy Bamber's cousins, Ann Eaton, and her brother, David Boutflour, had found the silencer in the gun cupboard beneath the stairs. Traces of red paint found on the end of the silencer matched the paint on the underside of the kitchen mantelpiece: each sample was nine layers thick. A blob of blood on the end of the silencer was analysed and found to be the same grouping as Sheila's. Neither Jeremy Bamber's blood, nor the blood of any of the four other victims, matched this blob.

Asking the jury to consider the significance of the silencer, Anthony Arlidge pointed out that given the length of Sheila Caffell's arms, 'it would be extremely unlikely, if not impossible' for Sheila to have shot herself with the silencer on.

There was a further mystery. The telephones at the farm had been switched round shortly before the killings. Lightning from summer storms in June 1985 had knocked out the entire system, and two of the phones had been replaced. But after the massacre, the dial-type phone found off the hook in the kitchen was the one that normally stood on Nevill Bamber's bedside table. The phone that should have been in the kitchen – a modern, digital type – had disappeared. It eventually turned up under a pile of old magazines, and was in perfect working order.

Moving on from the telephones, Arlidge touched on the question of the timing of Bamber's phone calls in the middle of the murder night. After the call from his father, Bamber claimed to have dialled first the police (looking up the number of Police Headquarters at Chelmsford rather than dialling 999), then his girlfriend, Julie Mugford. But another girl at Julie's flat in London who heard the phone ringing said her bedside radio clock, which she normally kept ten minutes fast, read 3.15 a.m. A third girl in the flat also heard the phone ringing, looked at her clock and noted that the hour digit read 2. So, said Arlidge, if Bamber called the police at 3.26, and telephoned Julie between 2.55 and 3.05, it was clear that he had not only lied about the order of the calls, but had left 'an extraordinary gap' between calling Julie and ringing the police for help.

The jury heard how Jeremy Bamber and Julie met in November 1983. The following April, Julie began to spend much of her time at the cottage in Goldhanger. June Bamber, a strongly religious woman who served as a local churchwarden, disapproved and called Julie a harlot. Bamber told Julie how he hated his parents and wanted to get rid of them. But when Julie suggested that he 'cleared out' he replied that he had too much to lose. At Easter 1985 he told Julie's mother, Mary Mugford, that he had heard his own mother was thinking of changing her will in favour of the twins.

From the beginning Bamber was trying, according to Miss Mugford, to commit the perfect murder, a murder that would not be discovered. After disregarding a plan to sedate his parents, shoot them and set fire to the house, because the insurance cover was too low, he devised a second plan. This was to stage the killings himself, and make it look as if his sister had committed the crime because she was mad. He told Julie that he had found a way to get in and out of the house without trace, leaving through a kitchen window which would appear to have been shut from the inside due to the design of the catch. 'On the evening before the murders,' Arlidge said, 'he phoned his girlfriend in Lewisham and said he had been thinking of the murders and decided it would be tonight or never. She told him not to be so stupid.'

Julie was allowed to join Bamber at his cottage, hours after the murders had been committed. There, said Arlidge, they embraced in private. According to Julie, 'he chuckled and said, "I should have been an actor."' Later that day, when Julie questioned him further, Bamber pretended that he had hired a friend called Matthew McDonald to carry out the murders for him for £2,000. 'As days passed,' Arlidge continued, 'her loyalty became strained and at one point in a restaurant he said he had no feelings about the killings and agreed there must be something wrong with him.' After the couple continued to argue on different occasions, Bamber went to France and was arrested after returning from St Tropez on 29 September to be charged with the murders.

Arlidge sat down. His opening speech had started low-key and, if anything, had ended lower still. The catalogue of cataclysmic events that had driven Jeremy Bamber to the dock a few feet behind this mild-mannered, bespectacled lawyer had been outlined with all the passion of one of the duller catechisms. Even Bamber himself, crisp and alert in his hand-finished blue suit, had slumped back in his seat as the speech went on and now seemed bored and preoccupied, like a cinema-goer impatient for the main feature.

The prosecution began to call witnesses. One of the police officers at the scene of the crime, PC Stephen Myall, said Bamber's attitude as they waited for armed reinforcements 'seemed remarkably calm' considering the information relayed to the police. Myall spoke to him about a number of matters as the night wore on, but his demeanour did not change. Bamber demonstrated no impatience of any sort. Myall said his talk with Bamber turned to cars. Bamber told him that he hoped his family's caravan park, where he worked, would 'stand him a Porsche' later in the year. This point was picked up by Rivlin in cross-examination. Myall agreed that cars were just one of many topics he and Bamber discussed 'to keep his mind as far away from the house . . . as possible', to try to keep him calm. And while it was Bamber's mention of a Porsche that made the headlines the next morning, there was little to support the notion of his harping on the subject, knowing that his family were lying dead in the house nearby.

Inspector Douglas Adams (promoted from sergeant since the killings) told the jury of a conversation with Bamber in which a means of establishing a rapport with Sheila was discussed in the event of the police trying to lift a siege in which she was involved. Adams testified: 'Mr Bamber said that she might want to speak to a Dr Ferguson from Harley Street who had treated her, and that she liked to be told she was pretty.' Cross-examined, Inspector Adams agreed with Rivlin that at one stage Bamber had asked, 'What if anything has happened in there? They're all the family I've got.'

Dr Ian Craig told of the terrible scene inside the house as he was led from room to room by Chief Superintendent George Harris. Craig, a police surgeon for twenty-seven of the thirty-one years he had been in general practice, said establishing a time of death was very difficult. From what he saw, 'it could have been any time during that night'.

Dr Craig told Rivlin how he had suggested taking Jeremy Bamber for a walk because he was in a state of shock. Dr Craig said Bamber asked, 'Why can't my father come?' to which Craig replied, 'Because he has been killed.' At this, Bamber broke down and cried. Dr Craig gave him some whisky from a flask in his car.

Later, he appeared to vomit. While they were walking, they discussed what had happened at the farmhouse the previous night. Jeremy Bamber said they had discussed the possibility of fostering the children because the family were concerned that his sister had been guilty of 'non-accidental injury' to the twins. That, Dr Craig explained to the court, meant 'physical child abuse'. Dr Craig said he asked Bamber if he had reported this to the police or social services, but Bamber said he had not done so.

Farm labourer Leonard Foakes said he had worked for the Bambers for a total of thirty-six years, and lived in a tied cottage at White House Farm. He had been harvesting oil-seed rape the day before the shooting. Returning home for lunch, he had met Sheila Caffell and one of the twins 'and she looked happy enough to me'. In the afternoon, he returned to harvesting and noticed nothing unusual in Jeremy Bamber's manner.

Leonard Foakes said that when Bamber first started work on the farm four or five years before, he had talked about his future. 'At the time, we were putting in some new barn equipment and he said if anything happened to his parents, he would just sell the whole lot and pack up.' But, cross-examined, Foakes agreed that in recent years Jeremy Bamber had developed an interest in the farm and appeared to become keen. 'He settled down quite well,' said Foakes. His wife, Dorothy Foakes, who also worked on the farm, recalled an incident when they were potato riddling in the autumn of 1984, a year before the killings. Jeremy Bamber said he did not get on with his sister 'and wouldn't share his money with her'. On the night of the murders, Mrs Foakes heard his car speeding away from the farmhouse about 9.30 p.m. She added he always drove away fast.

It was left to Detective Inspector Ronald Cook, the senior scene-of-crime officer at White House Farm on the morning after the massacre, to explain the series of shortcomings during the early stages of the investigation. He admitted that a grey hair found stuck to the blood-stained silencer belonging to the murder weapon had been lost and that the silencer itself had only been found three days after the murders by relatives of the victims and handed to the police. Detective Inspector Cook said the laboratory had not been warned of the hair, which went missing in transit. The judge told Cook: 'They should have been told, shouldn't they? You know they should.'

The jury heard about other omissions. Cook said that several weeks after the murders he found two fingerprints on the .22 semi-automatic Anschutz rifle. On 23 October he identified one belonging to Jeremy Bamber (his right forefinger on the butt). He also found a print of Sheila's right-hand ring finger. Under cross-examination, Cook admitted that despite his nineteen years' experience as a fingerprint expert, the weapon had been handled by officers who had omitted to wear protective gloves. He agreed also that photographs of Sheila's body showed that the gun found across her chest had been moved by officers. But this was done, Cook explained, to allow him to examine marks on her wrist, and photographs were taken throughout. A Bible belonging to June Bamber, found at Sheila's side, was not tested for fingerprints.

When Cook finally emerged from his ordeal in the witness box, the colour had drained from his face and there were tears in his eyes.

TWENTY-EIGHT

ON THE FIRST Saturday of the trial the Bambers' farm secretary, Barbara Wilson, went missing. Her husband Keith telephoned the police at Witham to say she had walked out of the house saying she was going because she could stand it no longer. She was due to give evidence on the Monday.

Stan Jones tracked her to a friend's house and arranged to meet her at the village hall in D'Arcy. His greeting was characteristically jovial: 'What the bloody hell do you think you're playing at?' Barbara Wilson smiled sheepishly and said she'd drive him home. The detective thought she seemed strange, 'a bit blank, a bit vacant'. He offered to drive her car, but she insisted. On the way over to Maldon, she drove so fast that Jones spent the journey clinging to the passenger-door handle, thinking that she might be suicidal. As they sped through Goldhanger, Stan Jones was asking her where she'd been, why she'd just taken off like that. Barbara Wilson explained she'd simply blown her top. To her, it was natural, her own way of solving a problem. She was sorry that Keith had overreacted. The police response had been an embarrassing overkill, but Stan Jones, thinking that an important witness was wobbling, was taking no chances. What was more, he had a suspicion that Barbara Wilson might know more than she was telling.

Two plain-clothes police officers knocked on Mrs Wilson's door on the Sunday morning and stayed with her all day. The detectives had been ordered there for two reasons: to make sure that she didn't wander off again; and to see if there was anything further she wanted to say about the murders at White House Farm. Barbara Wilson sensed that they were trying to prise something out of her, and considered her position. Feelings of guilt were welling up inside her that she had known of Nevill Bamber's forebodings but had failed to act on them. Had she done the right thing? Or should she now, at this late stage, confide in the investigators about the day Mr Bamber had sat in the farm office and foretold his own violent death? Perhaps, she felt, it was time to tell. (In the event she did, but Barbara Wilson's statement amounted technically to 'hearsay evidence', and the lawyers told the police that it was inadmissible.)

Next day in the witness box, Barbara Wilson described Jeremy's behaviour in the weeks following the killings, when he took over the running of the farm. Mrs Wilson had spoken to Jeremy about the contents of the house. He had asked her to sort out the insurance and to increase the cover because the contents were under-insured. Jeremy mentioned some particularly valuable items: a clock, some pictures and antique furniture.

Mrs Wilson also recalled the day Jeremy appeared in the farm office and told her to clear everything out. He told her he didn't want anything left that reminded him of his father. She described his manner as 'a bit arrogant a bit nasty. He wasn't saying it as if he was upset.' Rivlin challenged her in cross-examination, suggesting that she had misinterpreted Jeremy's manner. But Mrs Wilson was in no doubt as to Jeremy's feelings. 'When someone comes upstairs, sits in a chair with his feet on the desk and swivels round and tells me in the manner that he told me to clear things out,' she retorted, 'I am not mistaken.'

Jean Bouttell, the housekeeper at White House Farm, told the jury that she had worked there for some twenty years. In all that time she had never heard Jeremy Bamber say anything nasty about his family. Neither had she seen him show any violence towards them.

The first member of the surviving family to give evidence, Pamela Boutflour, June Bamber's sister, described how she'd telephoned White House Farm at about 10 p.m. on the murder night. Mrs Boutflour, a grey-haired woman in her sixties, said she knew her sister had been worried about Sheila. And when Mrs Boutflour herself spoke to the young woman the night before she died, she had seemed quiet. 'Sheila didn't say much,' Mrs Boutflour recalled. 'I seemed to do most of the talking. She didn't chat like she generally did. She was quieter.'

Mrs Boutflour was followed into the witness box by her son, David Boutflour. Boutflour described how he found the silencer while searching Nevill Bamber's gun cupboard three days after the massacre. Later, at Peter and Ann Eaton's house, he had noticed that some small pieces of 'blue' had been knocked off the silencer. Bluing, he explained, was a protective coloration on the surface of the metal. The silencer had been knocked about so badly that pieces of blue had been removed, 'and for a gun only some few months old to be knocked about in that way was quite surprising'. Boutflour added that the silencer would have had to have been hit with a force similar to that applied by a hammer.

Boutflour went on to tell the jury how he noticed 'a considerable amount' of red paint on the knurled end of the silencer. As he tried to unscrew the knurled end to examine the baffles inside, he saw 'a red blob'. He grabbed a plastic bag and wrapped the silencer in it to prevent any further contact. The police were notified and the silencer was picked up. A few days later, David Boutflour went on, he returned to the kitchen of White House Farm and saw the damaged paintwork on the mantelshelf surrounding the Aga cooker. He also saw a mark closely resembling the knurled texture of the silencer.

David Boutflour's sister, Ann Eaton, recalled that in July 1985, the month before the murders, Jeremy had appeared at the Eatons' home, Oak Farm, and announced: 'Ann, I want to buy a gun.' Ann explained that her husband, Peter, was a gun-dealer as well as a farmer. Jeremy said he wanted to buy a five-shot automatic 12-bore shotgun.

'What do you want that for?' Ann had exclaimed. 'You don't shoot.'

'Oh,' Jeremy had replied, 'I rather fancy myself as the country squire and I thought I might get into shooting.' Ann Eaton and her husband had explained that using such a weapon on a pheasant shoot wasn't considered sporting. The matter had been dropped.

She was then questioned about Sheila Caffell. Ann Eaton described Sheila as a very pretty girl but not at all practical. She said she had never seen Sheila with a gun of any sort. Nor had she ever seen her shoot. When the police told her of their theory that Sheila had been responsible for the shootings at White House Farm, Ann Eaton said she wanted to look for herself. 'I did not believe the story that was going around,' she explained. 'I just wanted to look for clues.' The subsequent search resulted in her brother David finding the silencer in the gun cupboard. Later, he and Ann's husband, Peter, examined the silencer as they sat around the kitchen table at the Eatons' farm. Ann said she saw something 'jam-like' on the end of the silencer, 'sort of coagulated blood, I suppose'. She added that, at the time, she didn't know whether it was rabbit blood. Geoffrey Rivlin seized on this remark at the start of his cross-examination. Having established that Mrs Eaton had shot for several years, he asked, 'How could you imagine that the blood on the end of the silencer might be a rabbit's blood?'

Ann Eaton wasn't prepared for the question. 'I don't know,' she replied.

Rivlin pressed her. 'That is what you told the court. How could you imagine that it might be a rabbit's blood?'

'Jeremy said he had been shooting rabbits the night before.'

Rivlin blinked. 'Had you ever seen rabbit's blood or any animal blood at the end of a silencer?' he asked.

'No,' said Mrs Eaton, 'I had never seen one of these guns before.'

'Or at the end of a gun?'

'No.'

'So why,' Rivlin repeated, 'did it stick in your mind that it might be rabbit's blood?'

Ann Eaton was rattled. 'I really don't know,' she snapped. 'Because Jeremy said he'd been shooting rabbits the night before.'

Rivlin left it at that.

In the course of the next hour or so, Rivlin drew from Ann Eaton her feelings, first for Sheila and then for Jeremy. It seemed that the Bambers had been at pains to conceal the fact that Sheila had suffered a mental illness. Ann Eaton told the court that despite this, Sheila had written to her from hospital in Northampton in March 1985 to say that she was there 'because of general stress' and because she hadn't been taking care of herself.

Sheila had been an occasional visitor to the Eatons' home. Sheila, she explained, wanted to talk a lot, about her life in London, about the twins and about their father Colin. This was all very well in the evenings, Ann added, but with a household to run and lunch to get ready, 'I haven't a lot of patience to sit in the morning.'

As for Jeremy, sitting feet away in the dock, Ann Eaton was just as dismissive. She described a row they'd had over the future of the Speakman farm, Vaulty Manor at Goldhanger. The Eatons had been interested in buying the farm. But Jeremy had confided to Ann that his father was planning to buy Vaulty Manor himself. Ann had flown into a rage, and had torn down all the wallpaper in one of the lavatories at Oak Farm. Indeed, the relationship between Ann and Jeremy was always a volatile one. In 1984, however, Jeremy had sent her a birthday card, something he did not usually do. 'Jeremy was very, very pleasant to me in the last year,' Ann testified. The birthday card was followed by repeated invitations to Ann to use the sunbed at his cottage. Ann had cracked a joke about there being no key on the other side of the door. She told the jury that Jeremy seemed to have been buttering her up. Even old rivalries in the running of the caravan site were forgotten. Jeremy greeted all Ann's suggestions with an enthusiastic 'Good idea!'

But Ann Eaton was not to be fooled. She was used to Jeremy's wind-ups and teasings. Once, he'd announced that he'd won some money on the Premium Bonds. Ann was completely taken in until she asked June Bamber, who said, 'Of course he hasn't!' And there was the time he'd posed as a director of the caravan site to a potential client before he had been appointed to the board. 'That man was completely taken in by you,' Ann had said. 'Oh, Ann,' Jeremy had retorted. 'If you say something convincingly enough, you can convince anybody of anything.'

Another of Jeremy's telling phrases was recalled by his uncle, Robert Boutflour. Mr Boutflour said he and Jeremy had been discussing security problems at the Osea Road Caravan Site in the winter of 1984–5. They had debated whether the police should be called in to deal with intruders at the site, or whether the company should set up its own vigilante group. 'I told [Jeremy] that if you shoot to wound, you are setting yourself up as a target for the rest of your life. If you shoot to kill, you would be committing a crime which your conscience would not permit you to live with,' Robert Boutflour testified. He added that he was deeply shocked when his nephew replied, 'Oh no, Uncle Bobby, I could kill anybody. I could even kill my parents.'

Rivlin cross-examined Mr Boutflour on this point. 'I suggest that Jeremy didn't say anything at all about killing his parents,' said Rivlin.

'You can suggest it,' Boutflour replied, 'but I was there and I heard it.'

A further witness on the fourth day of the trial was Anthony Pargeter. He described how he and his cousin Jeremy staged an informal shooting competition behind a barn at White House Farm in 1984. They set up a brick and took it in turns to fire at it from a range of 20–25 yards until it was blown to smithereens. Mr Pargeter, who had shot in competitions at the National Rifle Association range at Bisley, told the court there was 'very little difference' between them in terms of marksmanship. Spending a weekend at the farm ten days before the killings, Mr Pargeter said he opened Nevill Bamber's gun cupboard and saw a new-looking .22 Anschutz rifle fitted with a telescopic sight and silencer. Later, Jeremy took the Anschutz down to one of the fields to inspect the borage crop with his father.

But if Jeremy was familiar and competent with firearms, his sister Sheila was portrayed as a total novice. Her former husband, Colin Caffell, who was married to her for two years, testified that he had only ever seen Sheila with a gun once. That was on a modelling assignment when she used it as a prop. Nor did she have a violent disposition. 'She had a very hot Latin temper,' said Colin Caffell, 'but any violence was usually towards inanimate objects.' He said he recalled one occasion when the couple had rowed and Sheila put her hand through a window. But the most violent she ever became was when she slapped him on the face. 'She was always very kind to the twins,' he added, 'and very gentle.'

Colin Caffell admitted that he and Sheila had split up shortly after the birth of the twins in 1979. But he added that he none the less spent a lot of time with the boys. He said Sheila had two spells in hospital suffering from nervous breakdowns. During and after her second hospital stay in March 1985, the boys lived with him at his flat in London. The role reversal, he explained, was to take pressure off her.

Reviewing the case as they travelled back to London, Rivlin and Lawson felt the first four days of the trial had gone well. So far, the police testimony had been plodding and inept. The jury had heard no direct evidence linking Jeremy Bamber with the killings; indeed, they had heard little more than a set of theories from a hostile and suspicious family circle struggling to come to terms with the most unimaginable nightmare. Jeremy Bamber himself was emerging as a young man with a deeply unattractive side to his personality. But that in itself was not enough. The prosecution had to prove he was a five-times murderer.

Jeremy himself had appeared confident and cool, sitting attentively in the dock and returning the admiring glances of the women who had queued for seats in the public gallery. Edmund Lawson wondered what they were making of the case. Then he wondered whether they were really following it at all.

But it would be for the jury to decide. As the Crown case unfolded, it became clear that the silencer was the crucial clue. But what if the defence could show that the police may have unwittingly contaminated the silencer themselves, finding it lying amidst the carnage complete with blood traces and the single grey hair? Was it possible that one of the forty or so officers who swarmed through the house that day might have found it and replaced it in the gun cupboard, not realizing its significance? Lawson knew that the theory seemed laughable at first blush. But was it? After all, the police who discovered the bodies in the Bambers' bedroom had admitted moving the murder weapon and Sheila's hand even before the arrival of a photographer.

More persuasive, perhaps, was the suggestion that Jeremy himself, far from being the killer, had been framed by his adoptive family. Already, in cross-examining some of the surviving relatives, Rivlin had explored the notion, particularly with David Boutflour who had found the silencer. It was obvious to most observers in court that there was no love lost between Boutflour and Jeremy Bamber. But it was clear that the defence still had an uphill task in persuading the jury that the malice the relatives bore towards Jeremy was so poisonous as to drive them deliberately to incriminate him in such a devastating crime. What was more, the prosecution was about to present its star witness, the young woman who single-handedly threatened to dispel any lingering doubts.

TWENTY-NINE

IN A BREEZILY PATTERNED but demure blouse and pleated skirt, a white leather bag slung over one shoulder, Julie Mugford took the oath with none of the self-assurance that might be expected of a newly qualified teacher of twenty-two. Quietly, and hesitantly at first, she told the jury how, while a student at Goldsmiths' College in London, she took a holiday job as a restaurant waitress at Sloppy Joe's Pizza Palace in the High Street, Colchester. It was November 1983, and Jeremy Bamber was working there as a cocktail barman. On Boxing Day that year, she and Jeremy went as a couple to a party at the home of the restaurant owners in Lexden, Colchester. The following day, Jeremy took her over to meet his parents at White House Farm.

She continued to see him most weekends, and sometimes in the week when Jeremy drove down to London and stayed overnight. Just before Easter 1984, he moved into his cottage in Head Street, Goldhanger. Julie explained that the cottage belonged to the farm, and Jeremy lived there rent-free. But Jeremy decorated and furnished it at his own expense, and took out a bank loan to buy furniture. Julie spent most of the Easter holidays helping to decorate, stripping wallpaper, painting and helping Jeremy choose the furniture.

The one cloud on the horizon was Jeremy's mother. She plainly disapproved of Julie staying at the cottage and said so to her face. Mrs Bamber said she couldn't understand how Julie's mother could allow it to go on. 'She thought, basically, our relationship was just a sexual one,' Julie said in evidence, 'and thought that I was a loose woman or harlot. I was upset and offended, and I proceeded to tell her we were very good friends, and that came first before sexual matters.' But June Bamber was not persuaded. She made Julie Mugford an offer. Rather than live at the cottage with Jeremy 'because of what the neighbours would think', June Bamber would provide her with a flat in London or Colchester. Julie angrily turned the offer down flat.

In the summer of 1984, Julie took a three-week holiday in France, returning to live with Jeremy at his Goldhanger cottage and working for a time at North Maldon Growers nearby. Christmas 1984 and Easter 1985 were both spent at Goldhanger. During the college term Julie was now living in digs, sharing a house in Caterham Road, Lewisham, with her best friend Susan Battersby and two young men, Jim Richards and Charles Thaloway. Jeremy Bamber was a regular and frequent visitor. From time to time, he and Julie talked about his parents. According to Julie, Jeremy said he resented the fact that they wanted to run his life, telling him what to do and complaining that he wasn't working hard enough on the farm. They also tried to tell him whom he could and couldn't see. Jeremy, she added, didn't like it.

Then there was Sheila. Julie said she first met her when she came calling at Jeremy's cottage at Easter 1984. Thereafter, when Sheila was staying at White House Farm, she often came over to Goldhanger in the evenings for a drink. Despite the surface cosiness, Jeremy confided in Julie that the birth of the twins had sent his sister crazy. According to Jeremy, Sheila 'had done some horrible things to him when they were younger' and now he didn't get on with her at all. Julie Mugford said he wouldn't expand on what these 'horrible things' were. But what made Jeremy angry was that Sheila was then living in a very expensive flat at Maida Vale in London, with everything – including bills – paid for by his parents. Jeremy felt this was unfair, since Sheila did nothing to earn such treatment, while he was working on the farm. But Julie had been unsympathetic. 'I said, for somebody of his age, he ought to be appreciative of what he had,' she told the court. 'And I said if he hated it so much, why didn't he just get out and leave it? He replied by saying he had too much to lose.'

In the summer and autumn of 1984, Jeremy's comments on his family became more bitter. 'He used to tell me that his parents were really getting down his throat,' said Julie Mugford, 'and he said often he wished he could get rid of them all [including Sheila and the twins] and they were dead. Just so that he could live his own life and get on with doing things he wanted to do.'

Jeremy, she said, had explained why he wished his family dead. He felt that his father was getting old and couldn't handle things. His mother was mad, and he'd be putting her out of her misery. Sheila was mad too, unhappy and with nothing to live for. The twins, because of their upbringing, were emotionally disturbed and unbalanced. Moreover, they were a weight round their father's neck. Colin Caffell, according to Jeremy, couldn't get any proper work because the boys were living with him all the time. Jeremy felt he'd be doing Colin a favour by releasing him from such a burden.

Julie Mugford told the court of her reaction to these revelations. 'I just disregarded them as idle chit-chat,' she explained, 'because on occasions I have been angry and said I wished I could be rid of somebody. I just construed it as that, that he was angry. But as they got more frequent, they worried me a little, but I still disregarded them. I thought he was just over reacting.'

Between October and December 1984, Jeremy's threats

to kill his entire family became more specific. He outlined alternative ways of doing it.

Method 1: His original idea was to drug the family over supper by slipping tranquillizers into their drinks. He would then leave, go home to Goldhanger, then return to White House Farm on foot or by bicycle, pour alcohol on to the carpets and set a match to it. It was Nevill Bamber's custom to sit up late in the living room with a gin and tonic. The scene would have been staged in such a way as to suggest that he had nodded off, and that a dropped cigarette or a falling log from the grate had started the fire. Julie said Jeremy had given much thought to how he would get into the house undetected, because his father always locked all the doors last thing at night.

Julie's reaction to this plan was to dismiss it as 'vile' and 'horrible'. She added it was ridiculous to try to burn the house down because it was too beautiful to burn and that it would be difficult to torch because it was so big. Eventually, Jeremy agreed; the house would be difficult to burn and the place was so big that any fire would be seen from a distance. So he had changed his mind. In any case, there were valuable things in the house that weren't insured. These included a Meissen clock, which was stored in a suitcase underneath Mr and Mrs Bamber's bed. Such were the practical problems that made Jeremy change his mind about the way in which he would murder his family. At Easter 1985, his thoughts turned to gunfire.

Method 2: This would involve shooting everyone in the house. Jeremy devised a way of getting in and out through one of the downstairs windows undetected, and planned to pin the blame on a deranged Sheila. Jeremy's plan was to make Sheila the scapegoat by staging the massacre to make it look as though she had shot everyone before committing suicide. He told Julie that he'd killed some rats on the farm with his bare hands to see if he had the courage to kill his family.

Julie's reaction to this second plan was one of disbelief. 'I got really upset,' she recalled, 'and I told him that I'd rather he didn't mention it . . . I didn't believe he meant it.'

On Saturday, 3 August 1985, Julie told the court, she travelled from London to Goldhanger to spend the weekend with Jeremy at the cottage. When she arrived, she was surprised to see a lady's bicycle outside the back door of his cottage. Jeremy said it belonged to his mother, and that he had brought it over for Julie to use. But she recalled Jeremy telling her that part of his murder plan was to leave his car outside the cottage and to make his way to White House Farm through the back fields and along the sea wall, avoiding the main roads.

Jeremy telephoned Julie at about 9.50 p.m. the following Tuesday. She had been trying to reach him all evening, but he explained that he'd only just arrived home after having supper with the family at the farm. Julie said she was in a good mood, having had 'a really nice day' at work. Jeremy, on the other hand, sounded depressed. She told him he sounded 'pissed off' and he replied; 'I *am* pissed off.' He explained he had spent the whole day on the tractor, thinking about killing his family. He added that it was going to be 'tonight or never'. Julie replied, 'Don't be so ridiculous.' Jeremy said she would probably hear from him later. 'Oh, sure,' was her sarcastic reply.

In the small hours of the following morning, Jeremy telephoned her again. 'Everything is going well,' he announced. 'Something is wrong at the farm. I haven't had any sleep all night. 'Bye, honey. I love you lots.'

Blearily, Julie replied, 'Go to bed. Everything will be OK in the morning.'

At 5.40 a.m., the phone rang for a third time. It was Jeremy. He said Sheila had gone mad. He explained he had only one 10p coin and couldn't speak for long. But he told Julie not to go to work, and that a police car would collect her and take her to Goldhanger where he would explain everything. In the dining room of Jeremy's cottage, the couple embraced. Jeremy muttered, 'I should have been an actor,' and just laughed. Later that night, when the police had gone, Julie asked Jeremy if he had done it. He said he hadn't, but that he had hired a local plumber, Matthew McDonald, to carry out the killings.

At this point in her evidence, Julie Mugford, whose voice had seemed tremulous and husky, seemed to falter. Anthony Arlidge, leading her through the examination, asked if she was all right standing up. The judge leaned forward and said she could sit down if she wanted. Julie asked for a seat, and a chair was lifted into the witness box. She went on to describe what Jeremy had told her about Matthew McDonald and the killings. She said Jeremy had briefed McDonald about who slept where. He specifically instructed the hit man to telephone him at Goldhanger using the portable phone. The point of this, Julie explained, was that the portable had a memory re-dial button. If anyone checked later, it could be shown that a call was indeed made from the farm to Jeremy's cottage. Matthew McDonald had telephoned accordingly to say that everything had been done. He'd had 'a bit of a struggle' with Jeremy's father. For an old man, he'd been very strong and had put up a fight. According to Jeremy's story, Matthew had been so angry at meeting such unexpected resistance that he had had a mental blank and had shot seven bullets into Nevill Bamber. Having accomplished his mission, McDonald had fled the country. Jeremy had arranged to pay him £2,000.

Why, asked Arlidge, had Julie Mugford not gone to the police with this story?

'Initially I didn't want to believe what I thought I was thinking,' Julie replied, 'and I wanted to ask Jeremy about it first. I 'was scared myself to believe it, and Jeremy said that if anything happened it would also happen to me, because I knew about it.' Julie Mugford choked on the words.

'Just take it steadily,' Arlidge murmured. The whole court strained to hear.

'He said that if I ever said anything that I could be implicated in the crime as well as he could,' she explained, 'because I knew about it.'

Arlidge reminded Julie of the statement she made to the police on the day following the killings, in which she had made no mention of Jeremy's story. She explained that at the time, 'I didn't really know what to believe.' On the Thursday evening, she and Jeremy went over to her parents' house in Colchester, partly to escape from newspaper reporters. Still upset, she had told Jeremy that she needed to talk to him. They went for a walk round the block, during which Julie went through everything she had said in her statement to the police. Jeremy must have been greatly relieved. 'He said that was fine, because in the phone calls he said certain things, and he said I could repeat them because he said if I said as near to the truth as possible I couldn't be picked up on it.'

Their pact came under pressure during the course of the following weekend, when the couple stayed with Colin Caffell at his flat in Kilburn. Knowing what she knew, Julie was sickened by Jeremy's grotesque behaviour. 'I couldn't handle the fact that Colin was being so nice and genuine towards him,' she explained, 'and all the time Jeremy was just conning him.' Julie confronted him. 'I asked him how he could carry on living,' she said.

To get herself through the weekend, she asked if they could go out on the Saturday evening. They did. They shared a Chinese meal with Colin Caffell and some of his friends, and went to the Band Aid concert at Wembley stadium. Next morning, Julie and Jeremy returned to Essex.

For much of the following week, they lived it up. Brett Collins and Liz Rimington came to stay, and the four ate out every night. There were visits to a French restaurant in Maldon and to Fifi's in Colchester. On the Thursday, all four went into Colchester to buy clothes for the funerals. Jeremy seemed 'very happy', according to Julie. He bought her a black dress from Miss Selfridge in Keddies department store for £32.99. With himself, he was more lavish. He spent £198 on a Hugo Boss designer suit, and £30 on a tie. Back at Goldhanger, Jeremy asked Julie if she thought he was behaving properly, particularly in public. Julie said she thought he was being far too happy. They joined Brett Collins and Liz Rimington in the lounge. Brett Collins remarked that Jeremy looked too healthy. He joked that for the funeral of his parents the following day, Jeremy ought to put white on his face and black on his eyes to make himself look mournful.

Before the funeral, all four swallowed Valium tablets. Jeremy braced himself with a couple of stiff drinks. That evening, they were joined by two of Julie's friends, Karen and Andrew Bishop, who had helped out with the funeral arrangements. The six of them drove over to Burnham-on-Crouch for dinner at the Caribbean Cottage restaurant. In the event, no one ate very much, but everyone was drinking. There were cocktails and there was champagne. 'We were really quite drunk,' Julie recalled.

Nursing hangovers, Jeremy, Julie and the Bishops drove down to Sussex the following morning. On the way, Julie and Jeremy argued. 'I kept on asking him how he could be behaving like that,' she told the court, 'and I kept on repeating, "Two thousand pounds for five lives . . ."' She said she couldn't understand how, if Jeremy *had* hired a hit man, the assassin had agreed not to be paid until afterwards. It didn't make sense. Jeremy's reaction was simply to tell her not to worry, that everything would be all right. Julie sank into silence. When they stopped for lunch, it was suggested that they swapped cars, and Julie drove the rest of the way with Karen Bishop. The row continued at Pevensey. Walking on the beach, Julie told Jeremy that she wasn't returning to Goldhanger 'because he didn't need me there any more, because Brett [Collins] was there'. Jeremy protested. 'He said that wasn't true and he loved me and needed me to be there. And he said, "Please come back." So I did.'

Julie and Jeremy were together on the last Thursday in August, at a party to celebrate her birthday at the house in Lewisham. Thoroughly confused and upset by now, she confessed that she didn't really want Jeremy to come. But he did, having telephoned to say he'd be late, and eventually arriving with a bootful of drink from White House Farm. Jeremy was back in London on the Saturday evening, when he took Julie to Blazer's restaurant in Blackheath. Driving there from Lewisham, they argued again, this time over plans for another holiday. Jeremy had dithered over making a booking, and this had annoyed Julie, who said she thought they'd end up going nowhere. 'Don't be so stupid,' Jeremy had retorted, 'we're definitely going away somewhere.' But now he announced that he couldn't take time off from the farm. However, by way of a birthday present, Jeremy said he would pay for her to go on holiday with Liz Rimington. Julie was furious. 'Do you love me or not?' she cried. Jeremy said he didn't know. He didn't know what he felt any more.

Over dinner, they talked about the murders. Tearfully,

Julie told him she didn't know how he could have done it. She said she couldn't cope with the fact that Jeremy was being so normal and living a charade. Why had he told her? Why was he doing this to her? Jeremy replied that he didn't know why he had told her. But he said she had nothing to worry about. Julie explained that she was feeling guilt for both of them, and wanted Jeremy to feel what it was like. Jeremy said there was nothing to feel guilty about. Anyway, he pointed out, there was nothing she could do about it. Julie warned Jeremy that she didn't know what she was going to do or say. He pleaded with her not to do anything stupid, but Julie couldn't promise anything 'because I didn't know what I thought any more'. Jeremy paid for the meal, and the couple drove back to Lewisham.

At Caterham Road, the others were still up, so Jeremy and Julie went upstairs. In Julie's room, she again asked him why he'd murdered his family, and accused him of ruining her whole life. Jeremy denied this, pointing out that she still had her friends and a job. Julie Mugford now described to the court the series of events that were to culminate in her denunciation of him a week later. She confronted him with a photograph of herself, taken before the murders 'when I used to be happy'. She also showed him a love poem she had written in the early stages of their relationship. Jeremy's eyes filled with tears as he read the lines. Looking up at Julie, he said he hoped she was satisfied 'now that I had a pound of flesh'. Then he broke down. Later, as the couple got ready for bed, Julie surreptitiously took his car keys and hid them under the bed 'so that he wouldn't leave me in the house on my own'. They lay down together. Jeremy was just nodding off when Julie placed a pillow over his head and whispered that he would be better off dead. 'If you were dead,' she murmured in his ear, 'you would always be with me.'

A few days later, Julie Mugford told the court, she again spoke to Jeremy in private. The setting was a café across the road from Sheila's old flat in Maida Vale where Jeremy was staying with Brett Collins. Julie was still upset, angry and confused about what was going on between her and Jeremy. As for his part in the murders, she couldn't understand how Jeremy could be so selfish. 'You're giving me an ultimatum,' he replied. 'I either confess or carry on a relationship with you.' He explained that he wanted to be able to do what he wanted to do. And as far as Julie knew, 'that did not include me'. 'He just wanted to be my friend,' she added in a voice no louder than a whisper. Then she bowed her head and sobbed quietly. The court adjourned for a few moments.

On the resumption, Arlidge asked Julie to keep her voice up as much as possible so that everyone could hear. She now described returning to the flat with Jeremy, and his receiving a telephone call from his former girlfriend Virginia Greaves. In a fury, Julie shouted something down the phone, then cut the call off by pressing the receiver button with her finger. When Virginia rang again a few moments later, Julie picked up an ornamental Chinese box and flung it into the bedroom mirror, smashing it to pieces. Jeremy appeared in the doorway, thinking Julie might have put her hand through the window. But when he saw the smashed mirror, he flew into a rage, accusing her of breaking the only mirror in the house. How dare she speak to a friend of his like that? Julie slapped him round the face. Jeremy seized her right arm and twisted it up behind her back and looked as if he was going to hit her. 'Go on, then,' Julie cried, 'and I will go straight to the Essex Police!'

Jeremy immediately released Julie's arm and lay down on the bed. He was very quiet. Julie, remorseful, said she was really sorry and that she wouldn't do anything to hurt him. She would never do anything like that. He could trust her. On the way home in the car, Julie kept apologizing for saying such awful things to Jeremy, and for threatening him when he trusted her. Four days later, she went to Essex Police and told them the whole story.

THIRTY

Jeremy Bamber said that he had jilted Julie Mugford, and now Geoffrey Rivlin needed to prove it to the jury. At the start of his cross-examination, he drew from Julie the admission that she had been in love with Jeremy Bamber, and that she had wanted very much to marry him. There was some doubt over whether Jeremy could father children, she said, but throughout the first flush of the romance, marriage remained a serious possibility. However, she added, at the time of the killings at White House Farm in August 1985, she was unhappy with Jeremy. 'I was either extremely upset with him, or happy with him,' Julie explained. 'It was very erratic.' Even after she had denounced Jeremy to the police, she remained in love with him. As she put it: 'I loved him, but I didn't know whether I could live with him or be with him. But my emotion towards him didn't change, apart from the fact that I found it difficult to be physically close to him. There was a terror that now had been created. I still loved him.'

Rivlin turned to the episode when Jeremy received a telephone call from Virginia Greaves some three weeks after the murders. 'When you threw that box at the mirror,' Rivlin suggested, 'that was because you were jealous, was it not?'

'It was because I was hurt,' Julie Mugford replied.

'You were jealous?'

'No,' she insisted, 'I was hurt.'

Julie agreed with Rivlin that the affair with Jeremy was cooling at that point. But she added that such a cooling was mutual.

'You knew by that time that, really, a future relation-ship with him was unlikely?'

'It was unlikely because I couldn't get close to him.'

'You knew that he, at that time, didn't want a future relationship with you, did you not?'

'He wanted me to still be there,' Julie replied, 'but he wanted the relationship terms to change.'

'He didn't want you still to be his girlfriend, did he? That is, his full-time girlfriend?'

'No.'

The question seemed simple enough, and the answer simpler still. But the judge now interrupted. 'I'm not sure what you mean,' said Mr Justice Drake to Julie Mugford, 'when you simply say "No". Put the question again, Mr Rivlin.'

Geoffrey Rivlin did so, drawing from Julie Mugford a concession that at the time of the Virginia Greaves tele-phone call, she (Julie) was not included in Jeremy's plans for the immediate future. Moreover, Julie went on, it was very unlikely that she would ever marry Jeremy.

'That is why you went to the police, was it not?'

'No, that's not why I went to the police at all. That was not my reason.'

Rivlin pressed on. 'You had been desperately badly jilted?'

'No,' Julie Mugford replied firmly. 'I did not go to the police because I was jilted by Jeremy.'

Rivlin moved on. What about her statement to the police the day after the murders, which had contained no mention of Jeremy's confession to the killings? Julie ex-plained that she had 'omitted a few points' in order to protect Jeremy. Why? Because she loved him.

'You were trying to protect him after – according to you – he had planned the killing of five people, including two small children?' asked Rivlin with studied incredulity.

'Yes,' Julie replied, her voice trembling again. 'I didn't know what else to do. I didn't want to believe it. I didn't know whether I could believe it.' That was why she'd asked to identify the bodies. She wanted to ask the advice of Sheila and her mother.

The court fell completely silent.

Rivlin blinked at her through his gold-rimmed spectacles. 'When you say "the advice of Sheila and her mother", you are talking about the dead Sheila and the dead mother?'

'Yes, that's correct,' said Julie defiantly, 'but I believe in the spiritual world. I believe you can talk to people and help them reason out. I believe there is a God. I had no other option. They would know what happened. Nobody else would.'

Leaving it at that, Geoffrey Rivlin moved on to a detailed examination of the statement Julie Mugford made on the afternoon of Thursday, 8 August, shortly after her return from the mortuary. This was the first statement she gave to the police, in which she reported the contents of Jeremy's three phone calls to Lewisham, but made no mention of his complicity in the murders. Julie now added that in the course of the first conversation, shortly before 10 p.m. on the Tuesday evening, Jeremy had told her, 'It's tonight or never.' Rivlin challenged this. 'He did not say, did he, "It's tonight or never"?'

'Yes,' said Julie, 'he did say that.'

Rivlin picked up her statement, three typewritten sheets stapled together. 'And what you have put in this statement is the truth, is it not?'

Julie flushed. 'It is the truth, but I am not a liar.' Again, her voice broke with emotion and she clasped her hands together nervously. 'He said, "It's tonight or never," and it's as simple as that.'

She glanced quickly at Jeremy Bamber, gazing at her from the dock. 'He told me, and I didn't say it to the police initially because I was scared.' She glared down at Rivlin. 'Is that OK? Is it excusable for somebody to be scared?' Again, Julie choked on the words, and covered her eyes to hide the tears. 'I'm sorry, my lord,' she sobbed.

Rivlin paused a moment as Julie dabbed her eyes with a tissue and composed herself. Then he moved to the second telephone call made by Jeremy Bamber at about 3.30 a.m. This was the call in which she had reported Jeremy as saying there was 'something wrong' at White House Farm and that he didn't know what to do. The call had ended with the words ''Bye, honey. I love you lots', and Julie had gone back to bed. 'I didn't, however, go back to sleep,' she told Rivlin. 'It was after I put the receiver down that the information sank in a bit more. I didn't know what to say or what to do, and I had no way of phoning Jeremy back because I only had incoming calls on my telephone.' Julie explained that Lewisham was not the sort of place in which to wander in the middle of the night in search of a telephone box, 'so therefore I just had to sit and think and fret over it. I didn't want to believe what I'd heard, but I had no choice. I wanted to talk.' In fact, she had gone back to bed, eventually dropping off to sleep. At about 5.40 a.m. she'd been woken by the third telephone call. It was Jeremy, ringing from a public call box, saying words to the effect that 'Sheila's gone wild'.

Julie Mugford's first statement had ended with her identifying the bodies at Chelmsford mortuary. Rivlin went back to her motives in volunteering for such an unpleasant task. Julie testified that she had offered to do it partly because she couldn't believe what was happening, and partly because Jeremy had quite categorically refused to do it. The rest of the family had said they couldn't bear to look at the bodies, so Julie, being non-family, had offered to do it to help them all.

'Why did you not tell [Jeremy] to go and do his own dirty work if he had been responsible for all of this?' asked Geoffrey Rivlin.

'Because when somebody you love tells you something like that, you don't want to believe it, and I didn't know what the truth was. I wanted to ask him,' Julie added. 'It was too horrific to believe. My subconscious believed it, but I didn't want to believe that anyone could do that, let alone anyone close to me. It's something beyond my powers of reasoning. I didn't want to, but at the same time I did.'

The defence needed to test Julie Mugford's state of mind leading up to the moment on 7 September when she told the police that Jeremy had confessed to murdering his family. 'I could not live with that knowledge,' she told Rivlin. 'I didn't want to think it, but my subconscious told me it was true and I couldn't cope with it.' This, she insisted, was the only reason she went to the police.

But Rivlin was scornful. Bluntly, he suggested that she had conceived the notion of Jeremy planning and executing the murders only after she'd been jilted by him. Julie flatly denied this. She pointed out that she confided in her best friend, Susan Battersby, in London on 27 August, before Jeremy told her that their affair was over. Indeed, it was Julie who felt that the relationship was in trouble, even before the killings. She had wanted to spend the summer of 1985 in London, but Jeremy hadn't wanted her to go.

As for Jeremy's story that he had hired Matthew McDonald to carry out the murders, Julie Mugford admitted to having been dumb-struck. The whole situation was 'so beyond belief' that she didn't know what to think. Jeremy's account was that Matthew McDonald had made Sheila shoot herself. 'He said it was no problem,' Julie told Rivlin. 'Sheila just lay there and did it voluntarily.' That, at least, was what Jeremy had told her. Matthew had been told how to get into the locked house through a window in the kitchen which could be opened and closed from the outside. Once inside the house, he had reported fighting with Nevill Bamber and had fired seven shots into him.

Rivlin sought to show that this detail, among others, could have been picked up from newspaper accounts of the massacre. He pointed out that the fact that Nevill Bamber had been shot seven times had been plastered over the newspapers. 'I was unaware of that,' Julie replied. 'As far as I knew, that was printed after I had given my statement. I wasn't looking and scouring the papers every single day. I had a look, yes, but I wasn't looking in there to make up a story.'

Then there was Julie's revelation that she had sought to contact the murdered Bambers through the spirit world. Questioned by Rivlin, Julie explained she wanted to know the truth. 'I wanted to talk to Sheila, but I didn't know how I could talk to her. I just wanted her to be able to communicate with me. However, I suppose I prayed a lot and I was asking God for things, but they didn't say anything back. I just knew I had to tell somebody what I knew.'

Rivlin asked if she was in a very confused state of mind at that point. Julie replied that she was in two minds. She believed one thing and didn't want to believe it. 'If that can be described as confused,' she said, 'so maybe I was.'

Geoffrey Rivlin paused. 'You say you were in two

minds. Will you tell the court what were the two minds you were in?'

Her reply confused everyone. 'In my subconscious I believed something, because I could not believe it . . . everything was there . . . and in my consciousness I didn't want to believe what my subconscious was telling me. I didn't want to believe it, but I did at the same count. I didn't know what to do about it.' Rivlin tried to clarify matters. 'Does it all boil down to this: in your subconscious you say you believed that Jeremy was involved, but in your consciousness you did not?'

'That is incorrect,' Julie replied. 'What I said was my subconscious was telling me something that my consciousness didn't want to believe. But, however, I had no option. That is what I said. Not wanting to believe something and believing it are different.'

Julie admitted under cross-examination that from the Wednesday night following the murders to the day she went to the police a month later, she and Jeremy had never discussed the details of the massacre at White House Farm. She explained that this was because he had told her previously how it would be done. However, she did question him about the way he felt emotionally about what he'd done. How could he cope? How could he carry on living a normal, happy life with that on his mind? 'He said he confirmed it to himself,' Julie reported, 'although he did miss his old man occasionally. That was the only regret he had.'

In the weeks that followed the killings, Julie had spent a lot of time with Jeremy and his friends, eating and drinking, and knowing all the time that he had murdered his family. She admitted to Rivlin that she didn't cope with the knowledge very well at all. On one occasion she cried. Jeremy told her that was enough; she was allowed one outburst, but that was all. Another time, as Jeremy sat talking to Liz Rimington at his cottage, Julie sat upstairs and became so upset that it triggered some sort of asthma attack. Eventually she was seen by a doctor and prescribed antibiotics. A couple of nights after the murders, she confided in Liz Rimington that she thought Jeremy was the Devil incarnate.

'I didn't know who would believe me,' Julie recalled. 'The police were convinced. Why should they believe me? I didn't know what to do. I was scared – just scared – what Jeremy might do to me, or what his friend Matthew might do to me, and whether people would think I was going mad. That was my own fear, but I couldn't live with it any longer.'

But how, Rivlin asked, was she able to cope with remaining in Jeremy's company, going out to dinner with him, sleeping with him? 'I didn't know what else to do,' she explained. 'Jeremy knew what I knew. I was scared for him. I was scared for me. The only person I could be with who knew why I was behaving in a neurotic way – something I am not – was Jeremy. I had no option. But I couldn't handle it anyway.'

Rivlin returned to his theme of jilted betrayal. 'What upset you, apart from this terrible tragedy, was that it was apparent to you that you were losing Jeremy Bamber.' Julie shook her head. 'And that is why, I suggest, you became neurotic.'

'No, I wasn't neurotic,' cried Julie, 'and I didn't think that.' Her voice rose querulously. 'The reason why I went to the police was that I couldn't cope with the guilt that I felt for Jeremy. That's the only reason I went to the police. Not because I felt he was slipping away from me, but because I couldn't cope with such a hideous thing.'

'You had coped with it for quite some time,' Rivlin remarked.

'I was sorting out in my mind what to do,' Julie

replied. 'I didn't know what to do. I didn't want to believe it. I thought maybe it was a nightmare which would go away. It didn't go away, so as soon as I could, I got out of Jeremy's company and I left. He asked me to stay, but I didn't say I wanted to. He asked me. Maybe he was the one who was scared as well. He asked me to stay in his company and I left. And as soon as I was away from Jeremy I could say something.'

'He told you he wanted time to sort himself out?'

'Not before I left. Not before I told Susan Battersby how I felt. No, he didn't. He told me that after he came to see me.'

'In fact,' said Rivlin, 'the whole thing blew up and you went to the police when you realized you had lost the man.'

'No!' wailed Julie Mugford.

'The man who had asked you to marry him, and the man whom you hoped to marry?'

'No!' she cried. 'I've told you – and the rest of the court – that it was me that left originally. On the Tuesday. On the weekend before I said I couldn't cope, I didn't know what to say or do. He said, "No, please stay with me. I need you here." *He* said that. Not me. So therefore, on returning to London, I said something to somebody else, not because I thought I was losing him. I had left. I had gone. I packed everything I had to pack in my bags and left.'

'Miss Mugford, are you an honest person?' The question was asked without pause.

'Yes, I am an honest person.'

'Really?'

'Yes, really.'

'Completely?'

Julie Mugford had walked into Rivlin's trap. 'What do you mean by "completely" honest?'

'You know of one or two incidents in the past, do you not?' Rivlin fixed his gaze on the young woman. She looked away.

'Yes, I do,' she admitted, 'but everyone in their lives makes mistakes.' After a moment's thought, she added, 'Honesty is doing something about them, realizing where you've done wrong. If you make a mistake, you correct it, and from that you can become a more honest person.'

Geoffrey Rivlin proceeded to remind the court of the incidents from Julie Mugford's past in which she had been less than 'completely honest'. There was the burglary with Jeremy at the office of the Osea Road Caravan Site in March 1985. And there was the cheque-book fraud committed in 1984 with her friend Susan Battersby, in which they had bought some £800 worth of goods. Julie admitted her role in the fraud, but stressed that her conscience had driven her to confess what had happened to the bank manager and she had repaid the money.

Rivlin reminded the court that it was not until October 1985 – the month after telling the police of Jeremy's role in the murders – that Julie finally went to the bank with her explanation. Having admitted the fraud to the police, Julie received a caution for it.

'And each time you were involved in one of those cheque offences, you were telling lies, were you not?'

'Yes.'

'And you are pretty good at it, are you not, Miss Mugford? You can do it all right, can you not?'

'No, I am not.' Julie shook her head once more. 'I am not good at telling lies. I made one mistake. That was my biggest mistake. I've done my best to get over it. Just because I did that doesn't mean that I lie about everything else, because I don't. As far as I'm concerned, I'm more honest than a lot of people I know because I had the courage to admit that I'd done that. I didn't have to.'

THIRTY-ONE

WHEN JULIE MUGFORD stepped into the witness box to continue her evidence on the sixth day of the trial, she found that a small bundle of papers had been placed on the ledge in front of her. These were photostats of various press reports relating to the White House Farm murders, most of them taken from the national tabloid press, dated 8 August 1985.

Geoffrey Rivlin reminded Julie of her evidence the previous day. Asked what she had learned, if anything, from the newspapers on the day following the massacre, she had replied that she had learned nothing at that early stage. Jeremy had bought the newspapers that morning, but because the police were with her most of the time, Julie said she didn't have an opportunity to read the papers at that stage. What was more, she explained to Rivlin, she didn't particularly want to look at them. 'They were there because Jeremy bought them,' she explained. 'He wanted to look at them, not me.' Jeremy sat down and read them at the dining-room table in his cottage. From time to time he pointed things out to Julie, such as a reference to the value of White House Farm. But she stressed again that she did not sit and read the papers herself.

'Miss Mugford, are you really sure that it is right that you did not?' asked Rivlin.

'I'm absolutely positive that is right,' said Julie Mugford.

'I'm not suggesting you spent an hour by the fireside newspaper-reading,' Rivlin explained, 'but what I am suggesting is this was all information that was available to almost everyone in the land at the time.'

Julie agreed, but pointed out that on the day the articles appeared, she was giving statements to the police and attending the mortuary. When would she have read them?

Rivlin was seeking to show that information Julie gave in her statements to the police could have been gleaned from press reports of what had happened, rather than from Jeremy Bamber sharing his guilty secret with her. But after quoting at length from several such reports, it seemed that Julie Mugford was immovable. She was sticking to her story that, while Jeremy may have devoured the press coverage of the killings, she had scarcely given it a passing glance.

'I was aware that the press had printed things but, however, I wasn't sitting down reading them. [. . .] Jeremy read them, not me. I know what I know because of him.'

Rivlin ventured to test this assertion. Did she not, from reading newspaper reports, get the general gist that Nevill Bamber had been shot seven times?

'No,' said Julie Mugford.

'Are you saying you got that from Jeremy?'

'I *know* I got that from Jeremy.'

She was not to be shaken. But neither did Rivlin retreat. After quoting at length from other press reports, he placed the bundle of cuttings back on the table in front of him and put the point for a last time. 'You knew, did you not, from what you read in one or other newspaper, a great deal about what had happened or what was said to have happened in the house that night?'

'No, I did not,' Julie insisted. 'I re-emphasize the fact that I got my information from Jeremy. He told me.'

Geoffrey Rivlin had rather more success with Julie Mugford when he returned to her story that Jeremy had tested his courage by killing rats with his bare hands. Cross-examined, she now revealed that to Jeremy's amusement, the rats had eaten some of his home-grown marijuana, and the drug had slowed them down. Mention of marijuana had presented Rivlin with a golden opportunity.

'Miss Mugford,' he murmured, 'I wasn't going to ask you about marijuana at all.'

Julie glanced nervously at Jeremy Bamber. As if to fill the silence, she began to fluster. 'I feel it's of relevance,' she explained, 'because Jeremy was saying that the rats had slowed down because of it. That may have been how he caught them. He didn't tell me.'

'But why did you mention that? Was that in an effort to make life more difficult for Jeremy?'

'No, it was not.'

'Did you smoke marijuana?'

'I smoked Jeremy's marijuana, yes.'

'You smoked Jeremy's marijuana?'

'Yes, that is correct.'

'He did smoke occasionally, and you did occasionally?'

'No,' said Julie. 'Jeremy smoked frequently. I smoked occasionally. Jeremy will verify that himself.'

Rivlin glanced at the jury, then adjusted his spectacles. 'Miss Mugford, you are, of course, a bright, intelligent young lady. You don't wish to miss any opportunity whatsoever, do you, to make your evidence sound as black as possible for Jeremy?'

'No. Again, I'd like to correct you there. I'm telling you only what he's told me. The evidence is black without me adding anything. He knows that, and I know that. But he knows that he can't admit that. He has told me. I believed him. I don't need to add anything.'

'Do you not?'

'No, I do not. I have no intention of adding anything. I

don't like saying any of it. I hate it. He told me. I am telling you.' Again, emotion appeared to well up inside her. Rivlin paused. He was nearly finished with her. Just a few more questions.

Rivlin wanted to impress on the jury how Julie had rallied to Jeremy's support in the days and weeks following the murders, and how she had spent many hours trying to comfort him. She agreed that she had comforted and supported him, even to the extent of being at his side at the funerals, despite having begged him not to make her go. But all the time, she had questioned him about why he had done the murders. 'You ask him how affectionate I was,' she said, indicating Jeremy in the dock. 'I didn't even like him to touch me.' For much of the time, Brett Collins was there. She was so distraught by the time she and Jeremy drove to Pevensey with the Bishops that she had told him she wanted to leave. Jeremy had begged her to go back with him. The memory of it again appeared to distress Julie as she stood gripping the rail of the witness box.

'It was apparent to you, was it not, at that time, that you were breaking up and he was going to go his way?' asked Rivlin.

Julie, close to tears, swallowed and said, 'No, it was not apparent. That is totally incorrect. If somebody begs you to go back with them, that doesn't make the point apparent that he doesn't want you there any more. It does quite the converse.'

She wiped her eyes with a tissue. Rivlin looked at his notes, then at Julie. 'I am not going to – and I know how upset you are – continue to go through all of these days day by day, but I suggest that you spent a great deal of time together?'

'We were together, yes, but the majority of the time, again, I re-emphasize, Brett was there.'

'Finally, I suggest to you that you have painted an untrue picture?'

'I have painted a picture only by what Jeremy has said to me. I don't like doing it. I've never wanted to do it. But do you not understand what it's like to know something like that and not know what to do? He knew what it was doing to me.'

A tear appeared to course down Julie's face.

'An untrue picture?'

'No, it's not untrue.' She said this so quietly that it was almost lost. She seemed close to breaking down.

Rivlin checked his notes again. 'If you just listen to me, please, because this is the last question I hope that I will have to ask you: an untrue picture of your feelings and the way that you were behaving, in contrast to his feelings and the way that he was behaving?'

She shook her head in despair.

'No,' whispered Julie Mugford, 'that is untrue.'

As Geoffrey Rivlin sat down, Anthony Arlidge rose to re-examine. There were only a few more questions. Just a few loose ends to tidy up. They took less than ten minutes. Then Julie Rayner Mugford stepped down from the witness box. Her ordeal had lasted a day and a half. Throughout her evidence she had broken down and sobbed. Her departure from the witness box seemed to signal a release of tension. Spectators in the public gallery whispered among themselves; counsel sorted through their papers amidst a relieved outbreak of coughing and shuffling of feet.

Julie Mugford's mother, Mrs Mary Mugford, followed her daughter into the witness box. She told the jury about the relationship between Jeremy, Sheila and their adoptive mother, June Bamber. She said Jeremy hated his mother and blamed her for turning Sheila mad. And he resented her for loving the twins more than him. 'Jeremy disliked his mother intensely,' she declared, 'and I felt he was more affectionate to me. He used to call me "Mummy" all the time. He offered me his mother's small car which had been bought that Christmas. This was just after the shooting. A list had been drawn up and he was going to keep no mementoes, which I thought very strange. He said he wanted to sell everything, and that it was a pity I had just bought a car.'

Jeremy resented his mother because she sent him away to boarding school. 'And he never, ever forgave her for that,' added Mrs Mugford. 'Apparently, she was a religious maniac, and he always blamed her for making Sheila mad.' A few months before the murders, Mrs Mugford said Jeremy had told her his mother was thinking of changing her will in favour of her grandsons, the twins on whom she doted. Jeremy, she went on, never spoke to his mother and his mother never showed any affection to him. He often spoke of this.

Next into the witness box came a tall, erect man wearing glasses and a sharp grey suit. This was Matthew McDonald, the Colchester plumber named by Julie Mugford as the man who'd murdered the family after being offered £2,000 by Bamber to do it.

Anthony Arlidge QC swiftly disposed of Matthew McDonald's evidence. 'Did [Bamber] ever offer you £2,000 to kill five members of his family?' he asked.

'No,' was McDonald's firm reply.

The jury heard that Matthew McDonald had been with a woman friend on the night of the massacre. He explained how the story of his being a mercenary had gained some currency in the Colchester area, as he'd once worked as a site manager for a construction firm in Libya and had travelled to Malaysia. It was after this that the rumours had started.

Two friends of Julie Mugford also gave evidence.

Susan Battersby confirmed that Julie had confided to her what Jeremy had said about hiring Matthew McDonald to kill his family.

Elizabeth Rimington testified that on the day of his parents' funeral, Jeremy had taken Valium 'as if it was going out of fashion'. That evening, he had been 'very cheerful' when they all went to the Caribbean Cottage restaurant for dinner. She knew that Jeremy was keen to buy a Porsche, and added that after the murders, she had seen he had lots of brochures relating to cars.

The last witness on day six was Detective Sergeant Neil Davidson, one of four scene-of-crime officers on the case, and the man who, on 1 October, found a small, rusty hacksaw blade lying on the ground outside the downstairs shower room at White House Farm. Cross-examined by Geoffrey Rivlin when the trial resumed next morning, Davidson explained that he almost literally stumbled across the blade while checking scratch marks on the window frame. Questioned by the judge, the sergeant agreed that as soon as he arrived at the farm shortly after 9 a.m. on the morning of the massacre, senior officers – up to chief superintendent – were telling him that this was a case of four murders and one suicide. Davidson also agreed that the murder-plus-suicide theory coloured his initial examination of the scene. As many as twenty-five officers examined the farmhouse, but they didn't carry out a full scene-of-crime search. Davidson admitted opening the door of the gun cupboard where David Boutflour later found the silencer, but did not inspect the carpet for bloodstains. He also failed thoroughly to check work surfaces in the kitchen where Nevill Bamber's body was found. Rivlin extracted from him the admission that the police stuck to the theory that Sheila was the killer, not just after the initial 'search' of the house, but following the post-mortems and beyond.

As the trial moved into its seventh day, the jury heard from a student friend of Julie Mugford, an Army officer called James Richards who rented a room at her digs in Lewisham. He remembered having a conversation with Jeremy in the summer of 1985 when Jeremy said, 'I hate my fucking parents.'

'He expressed that view two or three times,' he said. Cross-examined, Richards added, 'It really did sound like hate.'

THIRTY-TWO

As JEREMY BAMBER'S trial moved towards the end of its first full week, the principal figure still seemed curiously detached from the drama unfolding around him. Throughout the evidence, Jeremy had sat quietly, as though no more than an interested spectator at someone else's show, listening intently to the evidence but showing no emotion, even as the grisly details were adduced to the jury, occasionally passing a scribbled note to his counsel as a point occurred to him. But now, on the seventh day of the hearing, the emotional temperature began imperceptibly to rise.

Into the witness box stepped the balding, formally suited figure of the Bambers' family accountant, Basil Cock. As executor of the estates of Nevill and June Bamber, he had combed through their private papers and taken home for safe keeping the contents of a drawer which he had found in the main bedroom at White House Farm three days after the murders. Among the documents in this drawer was an envelope addressed in Mrs Bamber's handwriting to her husband and her sister, Pamela Boutflour. It was marked 'Not to be opened until my death'. Mr Cock said it had nevertheless been opened. When he read it, he found it suggested small mementoes to be given to her godchildren and others. The message, undated, was addressed to her 'darling' husband, daughter Sheila and Jem, the family nickname for Jeremy. It read:

My darlings ... Should anything happen to me and I

have to leave you, I write this to tell you of my love for
you and to thank you for all you have given me. All I ask
is that God will love and protect you through the years
ahead, and that some day, God willing, we may meet
again. My love always, my darlings. Mums.

The poignancy of this farewell letter from his mother drew the first sign of emotion from Jeremy since the start of the trial. He closed his eyes, fought back tears and swallowed hard before burying his head in his hands. Basil Cock, the family's accountant for seventeen years, told the court he thought the letter had been written a considerable time before the killings. But when he handed the letter to Jeremy Bamber, he looked at it and said he thought it was more recent. When Jeremy's emotions welled up, Mr Cock had left him to his private grief.

Although Mary Mugford had testified to hearing Jeremy speak of his mother's plans to change her will in favour of the twins, Basil Cock said he'd never been notified of any intention to change the will. But he did reveal a hitherto undisclosed dispute within the Bamber family concerning some land. Mr Cock told the court that late in 1984, Nevill Bamber had given Jeremy a small farm, so that he could continue working on the land if the tenancy at White House Farm was ever lost. But the deal had given rise to a dispute over who actually owned this smaller farm. Mr Cock said it had been left to Nevill Bamber by his mother when she died in 1981. But Nevill Bamber's nephew, Anthony Pargeter, was claiming it as his by right. One other small insight into the Bambers' financial affairs came with Basil Cock's disclosure that following the massacre, more than £2,000 in cash was found in White House Farm, most of it in the farm safe. He also revealed that he had raised the insurance cover on the contents of the farmhouse from about £17,000 to

£50,000. But after the killings, Jeremy had trebled the cover to £150,000.

The crown's bloodstain expert, John Hayward, showed the jury Sheila Caffell's bloodied turquoise nightdress. He said it indicated that she had initially been shot in a reclining position and not while lying down. Jeremy Bamber remained impassive as the frilly nightdress was exhibited. Nor did he react when his father's torn and bloody blue pyjama top was shown to the jury. Mr Hayward, in evidence, said that when he examined some of Jeremy Bamber's clothing several weeks after the killings, he had found spots of blood on the sleeve of one of his jackets and also on a bathrobe. Blood was also found on the passenger seat of Bamber's car. Although he'd carried out tests, Mr Hayward said he was only able to establish that the blood on the clothing was human.

More crucial, however, was Mr Hayward's evidence regarding blood on and in the silencer. He testified that one inch of blood found inside one of the chambers of the silencer belonged to Sheila. He conceded that there was 'a very remote possibility' that the blood inside the silencer could have been a mixture of that of June and Nevill Bamber. Blood had also been found smeared on the outside of the silencer, but not in sufficient quantity to find out to whom it belonged.

The evidence of the next expert witness, pathologist Dr Peter Vanezis, continued to cast the court into a mood of sombre gloom. Dr Vanezis told the jury that Sheila Caffell suffered two point-blank gunshot wounds to the neck. The first would have stunned her and caused a lot of bleeding. Sheila would have been disabled 'by the mere shock of the injury and the pain' of this first bullet. The point was not lost on the jury. If Sheila had used the silencer to fire this first bullet into her own neck, she must then have packed it away. Then she would have needed to walk upstairs and shoot herself again. Dr Vanezis told the court that it would not have been possible for Sheila to walk up and down stairs suffering from the injury of the first bullet. Furthermore, there was no evidence that Sheila had been involved in any fight or scuffle.

Dr Vanezis returned to the witness box at the start of the second full week of the trial to tell the jury about how he believed the other victims were shot. He said Nevill Bamber had put up a fierce fight for survival before dying under a hail of blows and bullets. During this death struggle, he received two black eyes, and his face and head were badly cut and bruised. The 61-year-old farmer's body was a mass of cuts and bruises, and his scalp had been badly fractured – injuries, Dr Vanezis testified, that were consistent with an assault from a rifle butt. He said that Mr Bamber – six foot four inches tall – was shot a total of seven times. He was probably fighting for his life until the first of four head wounds killed him. 'In my opinion,' the pathologist told the jury, 'he was no longer struggling when the four shots to his head were fired but with all the other wounds he obviously was.'

During this evidence, Jeremy Bamber sat in the dock looking pale and tired. Often he closed his eyes and bowed his head as the injuries were catalogued to the court. Dr Vanezis moved on to deal with those of Mrs June Bamber, who had died with seven gunshot wounds to her body. Like her husband, she had put up a desperate fight for life. Dr Vanezis said there had been a trail of blood leading from her body – found on the floor by the bedroom door – to the opposite side of the bed. She had probably used her arms and legs in an automatically defensive way to ward off the shots fired at her. A stream of blood down her body showed that she had been standing up during some stage of the attack, Dr Vanezis said. Mrs Bamber was wounded in the neck, right arm, right knee, and twice in the chest. Despite her injuries, she had managed to struggle across the bedroom floor before being shot twice in the head. Those two shots, said Dr Vanezis, had proved quickly fatal.

And the twins. The killer had pumped five bullets into the back of Daniel Caffell's head. The shots appeared to have been fired in quick succession. Four bullets were found at the base of the little boy's skull. A fifth had been blasted into his head above the ear. His twin brother Nicholas also died quickly as he lay sleeping, shot three times in the head.

Dr Vanezis agreed under cross-examination that there was nothing to suggest that Sheila Caffell, like the two other adult victims, had tried to fight off her attacker. 'From the pathological evidence alone,' he conceded, 'I would not be certain one way or another whether she had taken her own life or whether somebody else had done it.' Geoffrey Rivlin suggested that the two bullet wounds found in Sheila's neck and under her chin were in a place typical of suicide victims. But, Dr Vanezis replied, 'One should never be surprised by the sites of suicide injuries.'

The court heard next from Malcolm Fletcher, a ballistics officer from the Home Office forensic science laboratory at Huntingdon. He had established a series of experiments with the silencer fitted to the .22 rifle. Three women volunteers, all of whom were roughly Sheila's height (5 feet $7\frac{1}{2}$ inches), tried to see if they could re-enact a way in which Sheila could have shot herself. 'Getting the rifle in position wasn't a great problem,' Fletcher explained, 'although it was awkward to handle.' But on the few occasions they could reach the trigger, the women 'found it physically impossible to press the trigger because of things like the length of nails'. Even so, he conceded that there was 'a remote possibility' that Sheila's wounds could have been self-inflicted if the silencer had been fitted.

Malcolm Fletcher explained the blood would have been forced into the silencer as the rifle was pressed right up against flesh and fired. This was the jury's introduction to the phenomenon known as 'backspatter'. 'My opinion is that the blood in the sound moderator was due to a contact shot to the neck of Sheila Caffell,' he said. 'In my opinion, the sound moderator was fitted to the gun at the time the two shots were fired into Sheila Caffell's chin.'

Elsewhere in his evidence, Fletcher said there were no telltale signs on Sheila's nightdress to suggest that she was the murderer. He explained why he would have expected to find traces of oil and soot on the killer's clothes; the bullets would have been coated in lubricant and the gun, when fired, would have given off a residue which would have left marks on skin or clothing. 'After twenty-five shots from the gun, I would think there was a good chance of there being some marks on her,' he said. But he added, 'I couldn't find anything on Sheila Caffell's nightdress.' Moreover, Sheila's hands were clean and free from oil. In fact, said Malcolm Fletcher, Sheila's nails looked as though she had just had a manicure. Furthermore, the gun used in the massacre was prone to sticking. During laboratory tests, the weapon's magazine release mechanism kept jamming, and on one occasion Fletcher had broken a thumbnail trying to clear the magazine after firing it. But he agreed that once the person firing the rifle had the knack, it was 'very easy'.

Malcolm Fletcher testified that twenty-five cartridges found at White House Farm had been fired from the .22 semi-automatic Anschutz rifle. He added that the where-abouts of the cartridges showed that the weapon had been loaded twice with the magazine in the course of the killings. Fletcher demonstrated how the magazine, which could hold ten bullets, could be loaded into the rifle, and explained that pushing the bullets could become difficult as it filled up. Asked if a feeble and unpractised Sheila could have managed the rifle herself, Fletcher agreed that any adult or a teenager could fire it, and that there was no significant recoil.

Continuing his evidence as the trial went into its ninth day, Malcolm Fletcher said that by studying scene-of-crime photographs and reading a pathologist's report, he had been able to guess how close the rifle had been when the shots were fired. Under cross-examination, however, by junior defence lawyer Edmund Lawson, Fletcher admitted that some gun experts did not believe in the theory of backspattering. Moreover, the .22 rifle used at White House Farm was the gun least likely to cause such a phenomenon. Lawson also questioned Fletcher about why the blood of Nicholas Caffell was not found in the silencer even though the sleeping child had been shot twice with the weapon pressed right up against his head. (The experts were divided on the number of contact wounds. Only Sheila appears to have definitely suffered such a wound; others – to Nicholas, for example – may have been inflicted at very close, but not contact, range.) 'There's no forensic scientific evidence to suggest that anything attributable to the body of young Nicholas was found in the moderator or in or on the gun,' Edmund Lawson declared. Malcolm Fletcher replied that the two shots might have been fired after a fatal wound had been inflicted on Nicholas. This could have stopped blood pumping around the young boy's body.

Another expert, forensic scientist Brian Elliott, said that tests showed that Sheila had only a tiny amount of lead – a millionth part of one gram – on her hands.

However, volunteers who loaded eighteen bullets into the same rifle in a laboratory had much higher levels of lead on their hands. The implication, Elliott concluded, was that Sheila had not carried out such a process.

Sheila's GP, Dr Ann Wilkinson, gave evidence about medication. She said Sheila was receiving monthly doses of a powerful tranquillizer, Haloperidol, designed to control schizophrenia. A month before the massacre, Sheila had consulted Dr Wilkinson and asked for a cut in the prescribed dosage. Sheila had explained the drug was making her drowsy and slowing her down. Dr Wilkinson agreed that Haloperidol had the side effect of sedating some patients. Accordingly, she decided to halve Sheila's monthly dose from 200 mg to 100 mg.

A detective constable, David Hammersley, suffered the unhappiest ordeal of the day when he gave evidence about the police investigation at White House Farm. Hammersley, with five years' experience as a scene-of-crime officer, was one of four such officers sent to the farm on the morning of the massacre. He spent three days there, but had to admit, under cross-examination from Geoffrey Rivlin, that he failed to search the gun cupboard where the bloodstained silencer was subsequently found. Hammersley said he didn't even know of the cupboard's existence until 'some weeks afterwards'.

Rivlin drew from Hammersley a series of damaging admissions concerning the shortcomings of the initial police investigation at the farm. No swabs were taken from Sheila's hands, feet or legs. The plastic bags encasing her hands and feet had never been forensically tested. And when he was sent to Maida Vale in London to check for fingerprints at 2 Morshead Mansions, he didn't realize that the flat had been the home of Sheila Caffell. In fact, he thought it was where Jeremy Bamber lived when he was in London.

Another police officer, PC Peter Woodcock, giving evidence on day ten, also admitted failing to spot the bloodstained silencer, even after kneeling down and peering into Nevill Bamber's gun cupboard. 'If you *had* seen a sound moderator anywhere in the house, you wouldn't have been interested, would you?' Rivlin asked.

'No, my lord.'

'Why not?'

'At that stage of the initial search,' Woodcock explained, 'all I was concerned in was looking for people who were armed. The secondary consideration was if we came across any weapon.'

Woodcock, who at the time of the killings was a firearms instructor with ten years' experience, did not agree with Rivlin that a silencer would have stuck out like a sore thumb.

Other detectives told their stories. The jury heard how, on the day of the killings, Jeremy Bamber authorized the police to remove and destroy bloodstained items found in the farmhouse. They heard how, two days later, he asked if the police could tell the sequence in which his family died because – according to legal advice – this could affect his parents' wills. And they heard how, in lengthy interviews with the police, Jeremy had called Julie Mugford 'a persistent liar'. Asked to give a reason why he thought Julie might have lied, Jeremy was said to have replied: 'Jilted love was the main one. She's lost me and if she could put me behind bars, nobody else could have me either.' Nevertheless, the court also heard about a note Jeremy tried to send her when questioned by police the day after Julie denounced him. The note read:

Hi, darling. Hope this gets to you from Stalag 13. Thinking about you. Sorry we're splitting up. I love you. Stinker.

The prosecution case was nearly complete. The last

police witness was Detective Constable Mick Clark, who had been with Jeremy in the hours following the discovery of his murdered family. Clark said he and his police colleagues were surprised how calm he was, and that he seemed more concerned about the harvest than about his dead family. Clark said that after being told what had happened, Jeremy had told him: 'Sheila ought to be in a nut house for what she's done. The officer said police were concerned that Jeremy had failed to appreciate what had happened. When another detective – Stan Jones – spelled it out to him, Jeremy had called him 'a hard bastard'.

Detective Constable Clark said that Jeremy was very calm as he tried to arrange for one of the farm-hands to carry on with the harvest. Indeed, the search for one of the men to help out with the crops occupied Jeremy for much of the morning of the massacre. The detective spent much of the rest of the day taking Jeremy's statement. Meanwhile friends and relatives streamed into the cottage to offer their condolences. Clark said, 'He was in a bit of a jovial mood. He would laugh at things then.' One of Clark's concerns was that Jeremy was being harassed by the press. Reporters were calling on the phone and knocking at the door. 'We discussed ways to cure it,' Clark recalled. But when he returned to Jeremy's cottage the next day, he found that Jeremy had bought all the newspapers it was possible to buy and had spread them out along the sofa.

At the conclusion of the Crown case, Jeremy Bamber's defence lawyers were due to open their case. But it was already well into the afternoon. Given that Bamber himself would be the first defence witness, the judge gave the jury the option of ending the sitting for the day and to begin hearing his testimony the next morning. The jury agreed, and the court rose for the day.

THIRTY-THREE

BEFORE Jeremy Bamber began his evidence, Geoffrey Rivlin outlined the defence case to the jury. 'The defence is that Jeremy Bamber did not commit these killings,' he began. 'It is for the prosecution to prove that he is the guilty party, and they need to do that with good and relevant evidence.' Sheila Caffell's mental state the night her family was massacred was a major consideration for the jury, Rivlin added, but it was not up to the defence to prove that she, or anyone else, did the killings. Sheila was a loving and devoted mother within the limits of her illness, but she was in fact 'a very sick girl', suffering from 'overt psychotic symptoms' which triggered frightening hallucinations. She thought she was a white witch and had delusions about killing her twin sons and her mother, June Bamber.

'Sheila increasingly thought she was being taken over by the Devil,' Rivlin went on. 'She had become involved in a complex of ideas with regard to her children. She had visions of having sex with them and suffering violence at their hands. These were little titches of six. She expressed certain morbid thoughts that she was capable of murdering the boys. She had fears that they were able to become evil and murderers themselves.'

He said it was very difficult for people with no experience of what someone like Sheila was suffering to imagine what might be going on in her mind. Psychiatric tests showed that Sheila should have had the assistance of a community psychiatric nurse. As far as was known, Rivlin told the jury, she had not had that help. In August 1985

Sheila was not diagnosed as being violent, but the illness was potentially very dangerous. Sheila had a tendency to relapse without any external influence. Something might have happened to have made her relapse into a state of psychotic behaviour. Sheila was on a course of tablets and had been warned not to touch any drugs like cannabis, yet traces of cannabis had been found in her blood. Rivlin regarded the jury. 'You have to decide,' he continued, 'whether anything did happen to trigger off that catastrophe.'

The defence would show that the evidence of Julie Mugford, who had told police that Jeremy Bamber, her then boyfriend, had carried out the killings, was 'badly flawed'. Rivlin said it would be shown that her evidence was 'demonstrably unreliable and unacceptable'. He would produce witnesses who would paint a picture of Jeremy Bamber different from the one which had been presented by the prosecution.

With that, Jeremy Bamber was led from the dock and walked the few yards to the witness box. After some formal preliminaries, Rivlin asked Jeremy point-blank if he had murdered five members of his family.

'No,' he replied.

Rivlin asked Jeremy about his knowledge of weapons. Jeremy agreed that he had some experience of guns, and had no difficulty with the rifle that had been used to kill his family. He said that Sheila had limited experience of handling guns, but added that she had been out walking with people in shooting parties.

On the night before the massacre, Jeremy said, the family had talked of taking Sheila's six-year-old twins away from her. Sheila sat silently at the table while her parents debated the adoption idea. 'Fostering was mentioned as a means of helping her with her children, whom she found very difficult,' Jeremy told the jury. 'It was a broad discussion about what we could do to help Sheila in relation to her problems. Her mental illness was causing us worry because of the lack of interest in herself, lack of interest in really anything.' Jeremy said Sheila sat quietly throughout the conversation. 'She didn't seem to react to anything that evening. It was as if she was just not concentrating. She was just sitting there, and occasionally she would just say something like "I want to stay in London", or a few words. But she didn't really seem to be paying much attention.'

Jeremy denied he had cycled to White House Farm on his mother's bike, slaughtered his family with a rifle, then cycled back to his cottage in Goldhanger. He told the court he had a 'very loving' relationship with his mother and father. But he conceded he did have some problems with his mother because of her obsession with religion. 'There was,' he agreed, 'a lack of understanding on both sides.'

As for Sheila, Jeremy described her as a paranoid schizophrenic who had contemplated suicide several times and was physically violent towards the twins. 'She wanted to be with God,' he added. 'She wanted to go to heaven. She wanted to take people with her and she wanted to save the world.' Jeremy said there was no animosity between him and his sister, but he found it difficult to cope with her bizarre behaviour in which she said alternately that she was Joan of Arc, God and the Virgin Mary. She also said she wanted to lead the Campaign for Nuclear Disarmament.

When Rivlin turned to events on the night of the massacre, Jeremy Bamber seemed less composed. Tears welled in his eyes as he described his father's last desperate telephone call for help. The call woke him in the early hours. 'It was Dad,' he said quietly. 'He said something like "Come quickly, Sheila's gone crazy, she's got a gun."

It ended and there was no more. I didn't get a chance to say a single word. The phone had gone dead.' Jeremy said he tried two or three times to phone his father back but the line was engaged. Then he telephoned the police.

Only towards the end of the five-minute call did the officer seem to take him seriously, Jeremy continued. His next call was to his girlfriend, Julie Mugford. 'I needed a friendly ear,' he explained. 'I told her there was trouble on the farm. She told me to go back to bed, as if she thought the whole thing was a practical joke.' Jeremy said he then drove from his cottage in Head Street, Goldhanger, to White House Farm. On the way he was overtaken by a police car. He told the jury that he drove slowly because he didn't want to get to the farm before the police. When he got there, he told them about the phone call and the gun, and tried to explain that Sheila was mentally ill. 'I was frightened, wanting to know what had gone on. I was scared.' While he and the police were searching the grounds, a sergeant said he had seen shadows and had seen a curtain move. 'We thought we saw something and we ducked down behind the hedge,' said Jeremy Bamber. 'I was trying to explain. I didn't think the police understood the nature of Sheila's illness. I was trying to convince them that she was very unpredictable.

'They asked me if she had used a gun before, and I said there were lots of guns in the house and she could have used any of them.' The police eventually entered the building. Asked why he hadn't gone in after them, Jeremy replied, 'That's where Mum and Dad died.'

He said that the following evening, two detectives, Mick Clark and Stan Jones, had been taking a statement from him at his cottage and had joined him for a drink before they left. Jeremy said the officers drank a previously unopened one-litre bottle of whisky, and Jones got drunk.

Jeremy admitted that he had got in and out of White House Farm many times using ground-floor windows, but denied doing so on the night of the killings. Asked about Sheila's behaviour, he said that she had punched one of the twins in the face during an argument in Nevill Bamber's car. Another time, she had spent an entire night on the telephone talking to her father about her problems. As for Julie Mugford, Jeremy said she'd been 'really jealous' when another former girlfriend, Virginia Greaves, rang him up. Julie had banged the phone down. When Virginia rang back, Jeremy heard breaking glass and found that Julie had thrown an ornamental box at a mirror. 'She was really angry,' he said, 'and slapped me across the face. I grabbed her arms and pushed her on the bed. She mentioned going to the police because she thought I was going to hit her.' Jeremy added that he did not hit her.

Anthony Arlidge rose to cross-examine. Courteous, unhurried and understated, the conversational tone of his questioning masked a deadly intent. Jeremy admitted burgling the family caravan park office at Osea Road of £980 to demonstrate how insecure it was. He agreed with Arlidge that he could have made the point without actually stealing the money, but added that the money was important to him.

'Why was the money important to you?' asked Arlidge.

'Greed,' replied Jeremy Bamber.

Arlidge asked him about his family. Jeremy said he got on well with his father, but conceded that his mother's religious attitudes were sometimes difficult to live with. His relationship with her had been 'a standard loving, normal, caring relationship'. However, there were times when they used to antagonize each other, particularly over Jeremy's girlfriends. On one occasion, Jeremy and his mother hadn't spoken for about a fortnight because of some disagreement. He agreed that he had told Mrs Mary Mugford that his mother had been 'a contributory factor' in Sheila's madness. As for Sheila herself, apart from one or two trivial incidents, there was nothing particularly antagonistic between them. But he had found her very difficult to understand for the last two years of her life.

He was asked about the conversation with the farm secretary, Barbara Wilson, about clearing out the office following the killings.

'Is it right,' Anthony Arlidge inquired, 'that you came up the stairs, sat in the chair, swivelled round and put your feet on the desk?'

'No,' Jeremy replied. 'That isn't specifically correct . . . I was . . . at the time I put my feet on this sort of little gargoyle at the front, and I rested one foot on there while I was on the telephone to someone.'

'You didn't put your feet up on the desk at all?'

'No, I didn't. I mean, it could give that assumption. There are gargoyles on the front and I rested one foot on the front.'

Arlidge moved on to the evidence of the soldier, James Richards, who shared digs with Julie Mugford and had given evidence about Jeremy saying he hated his parents. Jeremy denied saying this, but agreed it was the sort of thing that young people might say when complaining about their parents. Jeremy's voice had now dropped to a whisper, and both the judge and Geoffrey Rivlin had to ask him to speak up so that the jury could hear. The judge was particularly anxious to hear more from Jeremy on the subject. Why should James Richards come to court and swear that Jeremy had said, with vehemence, 'I hate my fucking parents'?

The judge's intervention seemed to silence Jeremy Bamber.

'He said that you said it two or three times,' the judge reminded him.

'That is what he said,' Jeremy agreed.

Mr Justice Drake was not satisfied. 'Can you explain to the jury why you think that man should come along and give that evidence to this court if it is not true?'

Jeremy paused. 'I can only surmise, my lord, that people's recollections of such events have been changed because of the way I have been portrayed in the newspapers, because he is a friend of Julie's, and he doesn't know me that well. Really, I don't know the reasons why people do this. I wish I did,' he added.

In fact, Jeremy agreed with Anthony Arlidge that everyone who had been asked about him had lied.

Questioned further, Jeremy admitted to liking the good things in life, and said he owned a sunbed, a colour television with teletext, and had often spoken of buying a kit car which could be passed off as a Porsche. He also admitted reading his parents' draft wills when he found them in the farm safe four or five years before. Arlidge quoted one of the provisions in Nevill Bamber's will.

> If my son, Jeremy Nevill Bamber, is, in the opinion of my trustees, farming with me at the date of my death, or the date of the death of my wife, whichever is the later, and are reasonably satisfied that he intends to carry on farming thereafter, can then [sic], subject to a legacy of £10,000 to my daughter Sheila, the remainder of my residuary estate should go to my son.

Jeremy agreed that the will effectively tied him to the farm in order to inherit. The clause had come as something of a surprise. 'I didn't know it existed until I read it just now,' he said.

The court rose earlier than usual that afternoon. The judge told the jury he was conscious that Jeremy Bamber had been in the witness box all day, and it was right to finish early. Mr Justice Drake also announced that the jury had asked to see the murder weapon being loaded and fired. Arrangements would be made for a demonstration to be held the following Monday.

THIRTY-FOUR

DAY TWELVE of the trial began with an empty jury box. Anthony Arlidge said he was concerned about one of the jurors. Once or twice during the course of the evidence, the man had shut his eyes and it seemed to some that he was actually asleep. Arlidge conceded that he may simply have been listening closely to the evidence with his eyes closed. Mr Justice Drake said he hadn't seen the sleeping juror, but if he had indeed nodded off, the judge could discharge him. The jury filed in, and heard a short lecture from the judge on the need to appear to be listening to all the evidence. Then Jeremy Bamber returned to the witness box.

Arlidge picked up the point that, throughout his evidence, Jeremy had indicated that certain witnesses were lying about their conversations with him, or their recollections of those conversations. Speaking of his uncle, Robert Boutflour, Jeremy said it was 'very dangerous' to guess at why he might not be telling the truth. As for James Richards, and the conversation about hating his parents, he was simply mistaken. The conversation had happened long before, and Richards had been influenced by the charges against him and the adverse publicity.

The judge tried to short-circuit the point. 'You think that the allegations and publicity against you have affected them?'

'Well, I'm sure it has,' Jeremy replied.

The judge asked if he had any comment on the other witnesses. Jeremy said he thought there were only two people who were actually lying: Julie Mugford – who had just made up her story – and Robert Boutflour.

With that, Anthony Arlidge proceeded with his questions. At length he came to the night of the murders, and the episode in which Jeremy had taken the loaded .22 Anschutz to shoot some rabbits. On his return, and not having fired a shot, he left it in the kitchen. A dangerous thing to do? suggested Arlidge. Yes, Jeremy agreed, and he now wished he hadn't done it.

'Just think about it for a minute. How long do you think it would have taken you to carry that gun and that magazine and put them in the den and gone out the back door?'

'Yes,' Jeremy replied quietly, 'I wish I had done it now.'

'How long would it have taken you?'

'Well, minutes really. Seconds. Not very long, minutes.'

'Seconds?'

'Well.'

Arlidge sensed his quarry tiring. 'Thirty seconds, you could have done it, couldn't you?'

The answer was little more than a mumble. 'Maybe I could have done it, yes.' Then a pause. 'I was being lackadaisical,' he added, as if to himself.

'Pardon?' said Arlidge, 'You were being lackadaisical?'

Silence. 'You are whispering now,' observed the judge.

'Sorry,' murmured Jeremy Bamber. 'Everything plays on . . . hangs on every word, my lord.'

'You were reducing your answer to a whisper,' the judge repeated.

'It was something to myself, my lord.'

Arlidge pressed home. 'You said, "I was being lackadaisical," didn't you?'

No answer.

'Didn't you?'

'That is what I said to myself, yes.'

But Jeremy's original explanation for leaving the loaded gun lying around was that he was in a hurry to get back to the field for the combine. Jeremy agreed he was in a hurry, adding that he still should have put the weapon back in the gun cupboard. 'But I didn't know what was going to happen, did I?'

'You are not telling the truth about it, are you?'

'That,' Jeremy Bamber replied softly, 'is what you have got to try and establish.'

Later in cross-examination, Jeremy and Arlidge clashed a second time. Arlidge was trying to pin Jeremy down to an exact form of words he had used in evidence the day before. 'Well, if I said that yesterday,' Jeremy said, 'I can't be sure they were the exact words I used. No, I can't. I may have said it yesterday when you were pressurizing me, but I can't say that my recollection is any clearer.'

Anthony Arlidge said, 'Did you feel you were being pressurized yesterday?'

'You pressurized me all the time, yes.'

'Did I?'

'Yes.'

The pressure was piling up again. Jeremy's answers were becoming increasingly evasive and negative.

When he telephoned the police for help, did he remember he had left a loaded gun in the house?

'I don't know.'

When had he first thought of it?

'I can't pin myself down on that.'

Before arriving at the farm, had he thought of it?

'You are asking a question that I can't answer. I am sorry.'

Had he connected his father's reported cry, 'She's got the gun', with the gun Jeremy had left standing in the kitchen?

'I don't know, I don't know.'

Twice in half an hour, Jeremy asked for a glass of water. Shortly after midday, the jury were given a short break. While they were out of court, Geoffrey Rivlin made an application to the judge about the presence, during Jeremy's cross-examination, of three of his relatives. Rivlin said they had been deliberately placed out of Jeremy's eyeline, but the problem was that, from time to time, they'd been seen to be talking and reacting to Jeremy's evidence. The jury had seen and noted their reactions. 'This is a very, very important stage,' Rivlin remarked, 'and it is undesirable that there should be any distraction of that nature.' The judge agreed that the relatives should leave.

Jeremy Bamber was reinstalled in the witness box. Why, asked Anthony Arlidge, had he not summoned the police to White House Farm by dialling 999? Jeremy explained that it didn't enter his head.

'Was the reason you didn't dial 999 because you didn't think there was much urgency or much danger?' Arlidge asked.

'It didn't enter my mind to do so,' Jeremy reiterated. 'If it had done then I would have rung 999. I agree, I would have done . . .'

Arlidge suggested that from what Jeremy had told them, the police had assumed that Sheila had recently had experience of target shooting, that she had used all the guns before, and that loaded guns were left lying around White House Farm as a matter of course. 'That isn't the information they were furnished with,' Jeremy insisted.

Arlidge moved on to talk about Julie. Jeremy said the affair had been cooling since Christmas 1984 when he began losing interest. 'I didn't use to go and visit her in the week like I used to before,' he said, 'and I didn't do

316

as much for her as I did before.' Jeremy said Julie knew of one occasion when he had been unfaithful to her; there had been others. In turning to her on the morning of the murders, 'I was being unfair and using her for emotional support because I needed it.' On August Bank Holiday Monday, nearly three weeks later, there had been the embarrassing moment when Jeremy had to deny any 'engagement' in front of everyone. The following Saturday, at another restaurant in south London, Jeremy said he ended the relationship completely.

Julie had never challenged him about living a façade. She had never asked, 'Why are you doing it?' There had been no talk of her 'feeling the guilt for both of us'. Nothing about feeding marijuana to rats.

Jeremy did agree that he had spent freely after the murder of his parents, eating in restaurants and staying in expensive hotels. He also conceded that on the night of his parents' funerals, having spent £228 on clothes, he enjoyed a champagne evening at the Caribbean Cottage restaurant at Burnham-on-Crouch.

Arlidge had nearly done with him. The questions had continued in a steady, unhurried flow, as matter-of-fact as a holiday check-list. Now, Arlidge placed his papers on the table in front of him, fingering his black silk robe and gazing directly at Jeremy Bamber, defiant in the witness box.

'You see,' said Arlidge with an air of restrained exasperation, like a bank manager dealing with a wayward client, 'the truth of the matter is, is it not, that you did kill five members of your family.'

'No, that is untrue.'

'And you used Sheila's madness to cover for it.'

'That is untrue.'

'And you did get in through that window that night, didn't you?'

'No, that is untrue.'

'The downstairs toilet?'

'No, that is untrue.'

'And out through the kitchen window?'

'No, that is untrue also.'

'And used that bicycle to get back over the sea wall?'

'No, that is untrue.'

'And you did shoot the first four people with a silencer on?'

'That is not so.'

'And you shot Sheila with the silencer on, didn't you?'

'That is untrue.'

'And then, when you came to fake her suicide, you realized that it wasn't possible for her to shoot herself with the silencer on.'

'That isn't true also.'

'And that is when you had to hastily change your plans and take it downstairs.'

'That's not so.'

'You killed them all, didn't you?'

'No,' replied Jeremy Bamber. 'I did not.'

THIRTY-FIVE

HIS MARATHON eight-hour ordeal in the witness box at an end, Jeremy Bamber returned to the dock and sat down. It was now down to others. A series of character witnesses now testified.

Paul Osborne, who ran a Colchester snooker club called Qs, said in a written statement that he knew Jeremy as a pleasant, polite and straightforward person. Osborne added that he seemed to work hard, and enjoyed a good relationship with his family. After the killings, Jeremy had seemed very tired and upset. Earlier, Jeremy had told him how disappointed the family were that Sheila had given up a promising modelling career to get married. Jeremy and his parents had been worried in case Sheila had a nervous breakdown.

Charles Lapridge, who sold the Bambers some machinery for the farm, described them in a written statement as a typical Essex farming family. Jeremy had been easy to deal with, and seemed to get on very well with his father. There never seemed to be any disputes between the family when he visited the farm.

A Colchester chartered surveyor, Richard Buck, said he considered Jeremy to be an ally to him when it came to business matters concerning the Osea Road Caravan Site. 'He was a straightforward sort of person. Out of his family, I found it most easy to deal with him.'

In another statement, farmer Thomas Howie from Chapel Farm, Little Totham, said that although he'd known June and Nevill Bamber all his life, he had never got close to Jeremy and Sheila. 'I got the impression that

Nevill and June had difficulties with their children,' he stated, 'although I may have got that impression from my parents. I believe Sheila and Jeremy never fitted into the family as Nevill and June had wanted them to.'

The landlord of Jeremy's local pub, Trevor Jones of the Chequers in Goldhanger, described Jeremy as a model customer, very pleasant, polite and charming. Jones, a keen pigeon shooter, said he once invited Jeremy to go shooting with him. But Jeremy had replied; 'I couldn't hit the side of a barn.' After the massacre of his family, Jones saw him briefly and said he looked haggard and upset. Edmund Lawson asked him if Jeremy was splashing money about. Jones replied that he was not.

Evidence on day thirteen of the trial focused on the character and mental problems of Sheila Caffell. Her boyfriend at the time of her death, Iranian restaurant manager Freddie Emami, said in a statement read to the jury that he feared Sheila would 'do something nasty' months before the killings at the farm. Emami said Sheila had a 'deep and intense dislike' for June Bamber. 'Her mother would preach to her about her boyfriends and said it was wrong to make love with them,' he reported. According to Emami, June Bamber also told Sheila she had lost her soul. After June's lengthy moral sermons, Sheila would ramble on about God and the Devil. After hearing of the massacre, Emami said, 'If it had just been her mother, it would be understandable, as she disliked her intensely.' But he added that he couldn't believe she had slaughtered her father and twin sons as well. He said Sheila fantasized about having sex with her sons. She also fantasized about violence with them.

Sheila's consultant psychiatrist, Dr Hugh Ferguson, said that when she was admitted to St Andrew's Hospital, Northampton, in August 1983, she mentioned suicide.

'She said she had to have some kind of exorcism and that if there was no hope of that, she would want to die,' he told the jury. After treatment with drugs, Sheila's paranoid schizophrenia became 'more manageable' but she then suffered what Dr Ferguson called 'a natural relapse'. He added: 'She wanted to be in touch with God and she wanted to be by Jesus's side, but she was very demented and incoherent. I did not regard her as actively seeking to die or as suicidal.' Dr Ferguson said that Sheila's concept of evil had emanated from her adoptive mother. 'At the age of seventeen, her mother found her in a rather sexually provoking incident and called her the Devil's child. This concept of the Devil's child had lingered to some extent,' he said. Asked by Geoffrey Rivlin for his reaction on hearing news of the killings, Dr Ferguson replied, 'I felt shock and horror. I did not feel she was someone who could be violent to her children or to her father, but I was aware that she was a badly disturbed woman.' Rivlin asked if Ferguson had experience of cases where people had killed members of their family and themselves. Dr Ferguson said he had.

'Are you aware of whether harm is always the motive, or the reverse?'

'I have to agree,' replied Dr Ferguson, 'that in many tragic cases, the motive is opposite to harm.'

Ferguson told the court about Sheila's drug habit. He said he didn't think her problems were drug-induced; rather, they were down to ongoing schizophrenia. Early in Sheila's treatment, Dr Ferguson had warned her about taking cannabis. Despite this, and warnings that illicit drugs could make her more vulnerable to relapse, Sheila had also taken cocaine. She was prone to changes in her mood which could be brought on rapidly.

The psychiatrist's testimony brought the morning's proceedings to an end. Jeremy Bamber was taken down to the cells and driven back to prison. The trial was now on the move. Arrangements had been made to meet the wish of the jury to hear the murder weapon fired. Accordingly, a motley motorcade was drawn up at the doors of the court: a coach for the jury, another for the lawyers, a black limousine for the judge. The press contingent followed in their Fords and Vauxhalls. Their destination: the Fingringhoe Ranges on the Essex marshes, some twenty-five miles from Chelmsford. As one reporter observed, the convoy was the fastest thing on wheels in Essex. At speeds touching 80 m.p.h., flanked by police outriders with flashing blue lights, it sped north along the A12 and through the centre of Colchester. Police held up the lunchtime traffic as the high-speed motorcade was waved through busy road junctions. At the ranges, a few miles south of Colchester, firearms expert Malcolm Fletcher gave the jury their first close-range view of the .22 Anschutz rifle. Fletcher shot several rounds into a large block of soap while the jurors strained against the October wind to hear for themselves the difference the silencer made to the sound of the rifle as it was fired.

Bamber's junior counsel, Edmund Lawson, had elected not to travel with the other lawyers on the Bar coach, but to make his own way to Fingringhoe by car. He managed to get lost in the maze of back roads leading out on to the remote marshes, and by the time he arrived the demonstration was over. But Andrew Munday, junior Crown counsel, had travelled with the others and managed to make a small but telling point on behalf of the prosecution. One of the minor mysteries was that a shell had been found at a point where no shot had been fired. Fletcher's own theory was that the rifle had jammed, and his own tests at the laboratory in Huntington supported the idea. Munday asked Fletcher in the course of his demonstration about the likelihood of the weapon jamming. To Munday's astonishment (and, he admitted later, as if 'heaven sent') the rifle promptly jammed.

In court next day, a consultant psychiatrist hired by the defence, Dr John Bradley, gave evidence about Sheila Caffell's mental condition. He made it clear that he had never met or treated Sheila but said he had experience of disturbed women killing their families because they thought it was the best thing for them. They could do it, Dr Bradley said, because they feared the children would be hurt by outside forces, or because they felt they were inadequate mothers and that their children deserved better. Sheila's psychiatric case history showed that she was obsessed with evil, and that for two years before her death she was preoccupied with the theme of possession by the Devil. Sheila believed that the Devil had given her power. She also believed that her children would grow up to be evil, and that her mother, June, was possessed by demons and needed to be exorcized.

Dr Bradley said disturbed mothers were also prone to overkill. He had come across cases where women had used more than one means to kill their children. One of his patients had gassed her children, then strangled them, he said. Dr Bradley said that using a gun to commit killings and then attempting suicide was a common pattern of behaviour in such cases. He said the reduced dose of Haloperidol given to Sheila was very small at 100 mg, but none of the drugs used to combat a patient's split personality could provide an insurance policy against relapse into illness. Dr Bradley added that schizophrenics could collapse after incidents of 'high expressed emotion', like demands made by children or spouses, or by too much love being lavished on the patient by people near to them.

Defence pathologist Professor Bernard Knight told the court that he'd known many cases of women killing their children, then committing suicide. A Bible, he said, was part of the ritualistic scenario of suicide. It was also known, he went on, for killers to tidy up after committing murder before turning the gun on themselves. Professor Knight said Sheila Caffell had been upright – probably sitting on a bed or leaning against it while sitting on the floor – when the gun was fired. As there was so much blood on her nightdress, there must have been some delay – up to a few minutes – between the two wounds.

THIRTY-SIX

THE DEFENCE finished presenting its case on the four-
teenth day of the trial. All that remained were the closing
speeches from leading counsel, followed by the jury's
deliberations. But first, there were two matters to deal
with. There was a query from the jury, passed in a note
to Mr Justice Drake, concerning Jeremy Bamber's uncle,
Robert Boutflour. They wanted to know if Boutflour
might be lying about his adopted nephew because he
would inherit money himself from the wills of Nevill and
June Bamber. Anthony Arlidge told the jury that if Jeremy
was convicted of murder he would not inherit his parents'
fortune. In that event, civil proceedings might be necessary
to determine how the estate should be split up. Boutflour
himself would not be a beneficiary, but his wife Pamela
might be entitled to a substantial part of the £436,000
estate.

The other matter exercising the jury at this stage of the
trial concerned the loading mechanism of the murder
weapon. They had heard from the prosecution that the
magazine was difficult to load, and that the bullets left
traces of oil and other residues. But Sheila Caffell was
found with clean hands and undamaged fingernails after
the shootings. Accordingly, the jury were allowed to
retire to their room to practise loading live bullets into a
.22 Anschutz magazine. On their return to court, Anthony
Arlidge stood to deliver his closing speech.

The murders, he said, could only have been committed
by Jeremy Bamber or his sister Sheila. Jeremy himself
had made it a 'two-horse race' by telling police that his

father had telephoned him for help during the massacre, saying Sheila had gone berserk with a gun. That, said Anthony Arlidge, was Jeremy Bamber's 'fatal mistake'.

He added: 'It cannot be someone completely outside those two because of the telephone call. It meant that it was Sheila who was running amok with the gun if Nevill made that telephone call. If, on the other hand, Bamber did not get that telephone call, if that is a lie – and I am going to suggest it is – there can only be one reason for his lying and that is it was he, Jeremy Bamber, who had done it and was trying to cover it up. The defence is therefore tied to the one suggestion that it was not Bamber because it was Sheila.'

A famous American defence lawyer had once attributed his success to the strategy of trying everyone but the defendant. That was true in this case, insofar as the defence had analysed both Sheila and the police officers involved. Arlidge accepted that Sheila Caffell was mentally ill, and said that her listlessness at the time of the murders may have been due partly to the drugs she was prescribed.

She was also obsessed with religion, but the Bible found by her side was part of the attempt by Jeremy Bamber to fake her suicide. Arlidge asked the jury whether Sheila – 'a slip of a girl' – could have bludgeoned her well-built father into submission, and said that she showed no signs of having suffered any violence, and may have decided to offer no resistance to Jeremy Bamber.

Arlidge turned to the role of the police, and admitted that they should have done their job better. It would, he agreed, have been better had they looked more closely at the gun cupboard. It would have been better, too, if the police hadn't assumed automatically that Sheila killed her family before committing suicide. But he added, 'It's not for me to praise or to defend the police. It's not part of my job in this case.' It wasn't important how the case was approached initially. 'Maybe there could have been other tests that could have been done,' he said. 'But you have to try the case on the evidence that you have and not the evidence that you don't have.'

The evidence of Julie Mugford lay at the heart of this case. 'Somebody in the case is lying, and lying their head off,' said Anthony Arlidge. 'Either Julie Mugford is lying, or Bamber is lying. It is something you have got to face.' The question for the jury was: 'Which one do you believe?' Arlidge urged them to remember the way in which the couple had given their evidence. 'Julie Mugford was full of emotion and spoke freely and fluently. Jeremy Bamber's evidence was, in the main, very carefully calculated. He was thinking all the time: "Where's he going next? I mustn't let myself get pinned down too much to this, or too much to that."' Julie spoke of how she'd cried and shaken after being told by Bamber he had killed his family. She was still shaking in the witness box. Arlidge said Bamber had trusted Julie to keep quiet after they'd burgled the Osea Road Caravan Site office. He thought he could trust her when he talked about the murders. 'If you've got a girlfriend you think you can trust, what better than to whisper it in her ear?'

Julie, he said, had needed great courage in facing police interrogation and going through a court appearance in which she had to admit she'd been involved with Jeremy Bamber in a burglary, in forging cheques, and in smoking cannabis with him. Arlidge contrasted Julie's heroic ordeal with that of Jeremy Bamber, painting him as a cool, calculating killer.

The circumstantial evidence was stacked against Bamber, declared Anthony Arlidge.

- Sheila's blood on the silencer meant she was shot with the silencer fitted on the rifle. Therefore it would have been impossible for her to have done it herself.
- Sheila's physical size and lack of bruising didn't square with the fight that had obviously taken place in the kitchen with her six-foot four-inch father.
- Sheila had no interest in or ability with guns. Bamber had recently shown interest and had noticeable ability.
- The paint on the silencer, which matched that of the mantelshelf in the kitchen, indicated the silencer had been fitted during the shootings.

Arlidge said the blood in the silencer was the 'giveaway, damning evidence' that Sheila could not have killed herself. 'Sheila can't have taken off the silencer because she would have been dead after the second shot. It's far more likely that someone had shot everyone with the silencer on, then, when he tried to fake the suicide by placing the rifle on the body, realized she could not have shot herself. So, he removed it, because there is only a small amount of blood on the outside, the size of a pinhead. He wouldn't have appreciated the giveaway, damning piece of evidence inside.'

Dealing with Bamber's reaction to his father's telephone call for help, Arlidge scorned his explanation for not dialling 999. 'What reaction would anybody have receiving that telephone call?' he asked the jury. 'Most people would think: Emergency! Danger!' But not Jeremy Bamber, who said it had not crossed his mind to dial 999. Instead, he had telephoned Chelmsford Police Station. 'This is an explanation that can't stand up in a month of Sundays,' Arlidge declared. But he added that Bamber had been very concerned that the police should come and pick him up, so it would be 'absolutely apparent' he wasn't at the farm.

Arlidge told the jury that Bamber's call to Julie Mugford before he called the police was also suspect. 'If you realize your family is in danger, what are you doing ringing up your girlfriend in Lewisham in the middle of the night for some moral support?' he wondered.

According to Anthony Arlidge, a number of Jeremy Bamber's explanations failed to stand up. For example, there was the evidence of Ann Eaton, who said that a month before the massacre, Bamber had asked about buying a five-shot gun. He had told her husband that he wanted to become a country squire. But according to Bamber's own evidence, he only wanted it for pigeon-shooting. Then he had said that he had removed the telescopic sight in order to clean the rifle. Arlidge pointed out that it was unnecessary to take it off to do so. Moreover, putting it on again was time-consuming. 'Of course, you would want to bother if you were thinking of shooting people at close quarters because it would get in the way,' said Arlidge.

From detail, Arlidge moved to consider the wider questions posed by the case. He maintained that for members of the Bamber family and people who knew Jeremy Bamber to have lied or to have given evidence they were unsure of would be 'pretty incredible'. 'Can it be,' he asked the jury, 'they all got it wrong?' Even if they had a motive, he went on, 'you would have to be very, very nasty people to do that. It would be a pretty incredible thing to do.'

He reminded the jury that Bamber had told one of the farmhands that he didn't get on with his sister and wouldn't share his money with her. James Richards had reported Bamber telling him vehemently, 'I hate my fucking parents.' His uncle, Robert Boutflour, had told of a conversation in which Jeremy said he could easily kill his parents. Arlidge said if Jeremy Bamber had not told him that, Boutflour must be an extremely malicious man indeed. 'Can it be that all this string of people have got it wrong?' he asked.

THIRTY-SEVEN

IN THE DAYS of capital punishment, the closing defence speech at a murder trial was apt to be likened to a fight for the life of the man in the dock. The metaphor encouraged the best and the worst in defence advocates as they appealed for the last time for the hearts and minds of the jury. These were the men and women who would decide the fate of the defendant; and the lawyer battling to save his client from the gallows was often tempted to dramatic heights of persuasion. It was the last throw of the dice.

Times, however, have changed, and Geoffrey Rivlin, preparing to draw together the strands of Bamber's defence, knew that Jeremy's fate couldn't be allowed to turn on any reckless appeal to the jury's emotions. As the evidence drew to a close, Rivlin had already drafted a closing speech. This was refined in second and third drafts, revised in response to points raised by Arlidge in his own speech to the jury. It would be a fastidious, cool and finely argued defence to the end.

Rivlin began with a word of reassurance to the jury. The case wasn't lacking in human drama, he declared, but it was lacking in proof. He stressed that they should only convict Bamber if they were sure he was guilty. Many of the prosecution's points were merely theories. Then there was Julie Mugford, who had cried throughout her cross-examination and who'd continued to cry and to protest, letting slip 'droplets of poison' into the case. 'Julie Mugford is a very intelligent young lady,' Rivlin declared. She must have known that in those circumstances it was almost impossible to cross-examine her. But 'as if by magic' she had stopped crying when the prosecution had questioned her. Jeremy Bamber, on the other hand, couldn't win. If he showed emotion, it was crocodile tears. If not, he was calm and cold-blooded. Rivlin reminded the jury that Julie's evidence about bodies and bullets could have been gleaned from the newspapers and not from Jeremy Bamber, as she had claimed. Julie's evidence, Rivlin added, was demonstrably unreliable and unacceptable. She could hardly have been a more forceful witness, but, Rivlin asked the jury, were they dealing with a consummate actor (in Jeremy Bamber) or a consummate actress (in Julie Mugford)?

When the court reassembled on Thursday morning, the sixteenth day of the trial, Geoffrey Rivlin turned his attention to Essex Police, and the way in which they'd handled the aftermath of the massacre. He invited the jury to consider the fact that a succession of police officers had looked inside the gun cupboard in Nevill Bamber's downstairs den, but had managed not to see the silencer. Rivlin described the situation regarding the silencer as a 'desperately dangerous' one. 'Four police officers, three of them highly experienced, went to that gun cupboard, which is tiny, and didn't notice the silencer propped up against a box. If the silencer was in the cupboard, how did so many police officers appear to have missed it?' Rivlin asked, glancing at the jury.

Rivlin reminded the jury that between twenty and forty police had gone to White House Farm on the day of the massacre. But only eleven had been called to give evidence at the trial. Some, including the most senior officers at the scene, Superintendent George Harris and Inspector Bob Miller, had not given evidence. Why not? Rivlin asked. 'It isn't just a grouse or a grumble to ask you why we haven't heard all these important witnesses,' he went on. 'It's an extremely important and serious matter.'

Geoffrey Rivlin moved on to deal with the forensic evidence. It would be extremely dangerous, he added, to place any more reliance on it other than 'reliance of a low level'. There'd not been a single scrap of forensic scientific evidence to link Bamber with the killings, while the silencer evidence, for example, was, in Rivlin's submission, very unsatisfactory. Blood found on the silencer could have been a mixture of Nevill's and June's, or it could have been Sheila's blood.

There was nothing sinister, he went on, in Bamber leaving the gun lying around. 'Don't people leave things lying around?' he wondered. 'What's all the fuss about? It's just one of those airy-fairy points – one of many – that's said to build up a case against this man. It wouldn't be good enough in a shoplifting case, and it's certainly not good enough when we're considering the case of a man charged with five murders.'

And what of Sheila? Could she really have done this terrible deed? Yes, in Geoffrey Rivlin's submission, she could. If Sheila had been seized by one of her fits, she'd have been quite capable of killing her father. Rivlin said the court was dealing with a mad girl who might be thinking at that time that her father was 'anybody'. The Crown had asked how Sheila – 'a slip of a girl' – could have bludgeoned her six-foot four-inch father to death. But Rivlin invited the jury to picture Sheila in the grip of her madness. 'If you had seen her when she was having one of her fits, would you have said: "Just a slip of a girl, just a chit of a girl"?' he asked.

Rivlin mapped out for the jury a possible countdown that might have led to Sheila embarking on the killings. He added he wasn't just talking of some fanciful possibility, a 'pigs-might-fly' possibility, but a serious possibility that Sheila did it. He said the court had heard that Sheila, a schizophrenic, had left hospital on 29 March 1985 even though she needed 'proper psychiatric care' The next day, she was talking about suicide and ridding the world of evil. On 31 July, Rivlin went on, Sheila 'looked a mess, was fidgety and appeared frightened and paranoid'. On 1 August she was at a barbecue party where she reportedly ignored the twins and wore a vacant look as if deep in thought. Two days later, at another party, she was vacant and seemed 'very far away'. Rivlin claimed it all added up to Sheila having a relapse and that 'things were building up.' On other days, there had been nothing strange about Sheila's behaviour.

On the night of the massacre, June Bamber, a deeply religious woman, had not attended her usual Bible class. Jeremy, meanwhile, was still out working in the fields. When Sheila spoke to her aunt, Pamela Boutflour, on the telephone at about 10 p.m., she didn't say much and didn't say goodbye. 'What,' Rivlin asked the jury, 'is going on in Sheila's mind?'

'All the evidence reveals that Sheila that very night would be heading for – if she was already not in – a state of schizophrenic relapse,' Geoffrey Rivlin told the jury. What he described as the 'overkill' of the twin boys was consistent with that of an altruistic killing: each boy had received several bullets to the head.

An expert had told the jury that it would have been very difficult for a third party to have shot Sheila in the position in which she'd been found. Unlike the other victims, the two shots to Sheila hadn't been 'bang, bang'. This pointed towards Sheila having done it herself. And as for the prosecution's assertion that there were no traces of Sheila having fired the gun, Rivlin said he disagreed: traces of iron, copper and lead had been found on her hands.

Sheila could have washed the blood off her hands after the other killings. Rivlin reminded the jury of Professor Knight's evidence that people in such circumstances did perform mundane tasks.

Rounding up the evidence concerning Sheila, Geoffrey Rivlin said her mental history in the years leading up to the murders had been one of gradual deterioration. She had been obsessed with the Devil and evil; she was paranoid and the victim of hallucinations. It was no coincidence, as the prosecution had claimed, that she'd had a schizophrenic relapse on the night Jeremy Bamber had left the gun lying about. 'What really would be a coincidence is this,' Rivlin declared. 'If she'd had a serious relapse on the very night that Jeremy Bamber had decided to kill everybody off. Now that really would be an amazing coincidence: two of them going absolutely mad in the house on the same night.'

If Jeremy had murdered his family, he would have acted very differently, Geoffrey Rivlin told the jury. He would not have told the police that his father had phoned him. Because this would then have fixed a time on the murders. Jeremy Bamber had no way of knowing when the police would burst into the house. The police could have gone straight in immediately Bamber called them. And if Bamber had killed his family a lot earlier, it would have been discovered by the warmth of their bodies.

If Jeremy had told Julie Mugford all the things she said he had, why would he ask the police to collect her? 'If he had murdered those five people that night, would he have dared to have asked the police to go round and pick her up?' Rivlin asked. 'How was he to know when she was met with the catastrophic news that five people had been killed in a house, including two children, that she's not going to immediately break down, break up and say: "My God, he's done it"?

'How was he to know she's not going to go up to him and beat him with her fists on his chest and say: "You murderer, you murderer! What on earth have you done this for, you madman?"

Geoffrey Rivlin regarded the jury, listening intently through the insistent hum of the air conditioning. Throughout the trial, he had resisted the temptation to lapse into theatrical gestures, to let his voice rise much above conversation pitch. And now, reaching at last his final few moments with the jury, he still kept his cool. There would be no big finish, no final flourish, merely the plainest of thoughts that had run through the case from the very first day like a single snagged thread.

'It just doesn't add up,' said Geoffrey Rivlin.

THIRTY-EIGHT

MR JUSTICE DRAKE, a wartime RAF veteran and holder of the Distinguished Flying Cross, enjoyed a reputation among lawyers as a sound and sensible judge with a sense of humour. As he smoothed down his papers and gathered himself to begin summing up the case to the jury, he may well have reflected, if only for a moment, that he would need all the soundness and sense he could muster to strip the case down to its central issues, and to discard the loose ends and ragged edges before turning it over to the jury. His sense of humour, on the other hand, was unlikely to be exercised in a case that arose from an act of such unspeakable horror. The judge crystallized matters straight away with the plainest of plain questions. 'Quite simply,' he asked the listening jurors, 'do you believe Jeremy Bamber or do you believe Julie Mugford? If you are sure that Julie Mugford told you the truth, then it means you are sure that the defendant told her that he had planned the killings and had, in fact, carried them out.' Dismissing the idea that Matthew McDonald had been engaged as a hired assassin, the judge added: 'If [Bamber] did say that, it can only have been a form of cover-up because he did not wish to say to Julie that he had killed his family by his own hands. But if you are sure that Julie was telling the truth, it follows that the defendant has told you lies, and it follows that the defendant is guilty.'

There was a second question for the jury to consider. Were they sure that Sheila had not murdered four members of her own family and then committed suicide? The evidence, he declared, showed that either Jeremy or Sheila was the killer ('We are not concerned with any fanciful imaginations of some mysterious third party having appeared on the scene . . .').

Did Sheila do it? The question, the judge argued, involved a number of issues of which one was paramount: was the sound moderator on the gun when the second and fatal shot entered her body? If so, he added, since the evidence was that she would have become instantly unconscious after that second shot, it followed that she could not have removed the moderator afterwards. It followed equally that someone else did, and that could only have been Jeremy Bamber.

The third question concerned the mysterious telephone call in the middle of the night. Was there ever such a call? If so, the jury could not be certain that Sheila was not the killer, and Bamber would be not guilty. 'But if you are convinced on the evidence that there was no such call, then does it not inevitably undermine the whole of this story? For what conceivable reason could he invent a story that his father telephoned him and said that Sheila had gone berserk and had got the gun unless he was aware, in fact, that the family were dead, and dead by his own hands?'

Mr Justice Drake warned the jury against pinning too much importance to inconclusive evidence, such as that concerning the kitchen window or June Bamber's bicycle, or being deflected by minor issues such as the grey hair found on the sound moderator ('Is that really a matter of any importance in this case at all?').

Mr Justice Drake reminded the jury that he was there to give direction on matters of law and to provide assistance on matters of fact. He stressed that it was for the prosecution to prove its case by convincing the jury that Jeremy Bamber was guilty of murder. 'Murder is the unlawful killing of one person by another who, at the time of the killing, intends either to kill or to cause really serious harm to the victim,' said the judge. 'In this case, if Jeremy Bamber fired the gun, then it is clear that he intended to kill each of the victims. The issue in this case is . . . not whether murder was committed, but whether or not [Bamber] committed it.' Legally, the jury had to answer a single, straightforward question: Had the prosecution satisfied them so that they were sure that it was Jeremy Bamber who killed those five people?

The judge turned briefly to the involvement of Sheila, reminding the jury that Bamber's defence was that it was she who fired the gun, killing first her adoptive parents and twin sons before taking her own life. But it was not for the defence to prove that it was Sheila. It was for the prosecution to prove that it was not.

Now the judge issued advice to the jury on how to approach the evidence itself, and warned them against paying attention to reports of the trial on radio, television and in the press. He also pointed out that in weighing the value of the evidence, every witness started as an equal: police officers, expert witnesses – and the defendant. 'He starts equally with everyone else,' the judge observed.

But there was special mention at this point for Julie Mugford, and her admission that in 1984 (with Sue Battersby) she had passed dud cheques totalling some £800. Bamber, the judge recalled, was claiming that Julie's evidence against him was fabricated and that she was a brazen, blatant liar. 'Of course,' the judge continued, 'the fact that a person has committed some offence, or has at some time lied in the past, in no way proves that they can never again tell the truth . . . It does not prove that at all.'

In Julie Mugford's defence, the judge pointed out that she had volunteered her dishonesty to the bank and repaid the money. As for her involvement with Jeremy in the burglary at the Osea Road Caravan Site, Julie had merely been asked to keep watch while Jeremy himself stole the money. That was how the jury had come to learn of Jeremy's previous dishonesty. 'But what I must stress to you,' the judge continued, 'is that the sole reason you have heard about the matter is so that you may have it in your mind in weighing his evidence, and it in no way at all – *absolutely no way at all* – indicates that he must have killed his family at the White House Farm on August 7.' What the burglary demonstrated, however, was the degree to which Jeremy trusted Julie. The prosecution were saying that the incident threw light on the fact that Jeremy was willing to confide in Julie his plan to kill his parents and his involvement in the actual killing.

The judge dealt further with Julie Mugford's evidence. '[Bamber] says that she has told a pack of lies about him – vindictive, poisonous lies – because he jilted her, and that ever since he made it plain to her that she was not to have him as either a husband or a continuing boyfriend and lover, she has lied out of vindictiveness . . . Whether or not you think that she may have fabricated all that detailed evidence and stayed in the witness box, sticking to her story for some two days, because he had ceased to be her boyfriend is – like everything else in the case on the evidence – a matter for you to decide.' The jury listened as Mr Justice Drake expanded on the likely motivation of a scorned woman. '. . . The person feeling jilted may, in order to hurt the other, tell some lies about them, and for that reason I have not the slightest doubt that without any warning from me whatsoever you would approach the evidence of Julie Mugford with a great degree of caution. And my advice to you is simply to do just that.'

The advice from the judge went further. 'First, consider her evidence and consider what you made of her. Do you think that her evidence generally had the ring of truth about it? Well, if not, then you reject her evidence and that is the end of it. But if you do think that she appeared to you to be truthful, if you think that her story – told and maintained over a couple of days in the witness box – did appear to you to be truthful, then bear in mind the possible motive she might have to tell lies, and look to see whether there is in this case any other evidence, entirely independent of hers, which would lead you to the conclusion – to point to the fact – that [Bamber] was guilty of these murders. If so, that would tend to support the fact that her evidence is true.' But the judge added a note of caution, advising the jury against convicting Bamber on Julie Mugford's evidence alone, while rejecting the rest of the prosecution's case. The jury needed to look for evidence to support her story. For example, if they found that there was no middle-of-the-night phone call from Nevill Bamber to Jeremy, that would be convincing support for Julie's evidence.

Having dealt in some detail with the crucial evidence of Julie Mugford, Mr Justice Drake now led the jury back to the central issues of the case, and the essential components of the evidence advanced by both sides. Jeremy Bamber's defence was that he was never in the White House Farm on the night of the massacre, and that the murderer must have been Sheila Caffell. Accordingly, he had produced evidence to show she was mentally ill, and had argued that her conduct in killing her family was entirely consistent with that illness. The prosecution, on the other hand, said there was an overwhelming case to prove Bamber guilty: his admission of guilt to Julie Mugford, the evidence to show that he never received a phone call from his father, and the overwhelming evidence to show that Sheila did not commit suicide, and that after her death, someone else removed the silencer from the gun. That 'someone' could only have been Jeremy Bamber.

The judge grasped the vital issue of whether or not the silencer was on the gun when Sheila died. According to the prosecution, it was absolutely clear that the silencer was fitted when Nevill Bamber was attacked in the kitchen. The red paint on the knurled end and the mark on the mantelpiece showed that, on that fact alone, the silencer was on the gun during the fight in the kitchen. According to the prosecution, for Sheila to have been the killer and then to have committed suicide, the scenario would have been as follows:

During the night, she took the gun – left (according to Bamber) without its silencer – and somehow, from somewhere, at some time, she went and fetched the silencer from wherever it was and screwed it on to the gun before starting the killings. 'If so,' asked the judge, 'why? What did she know about the silencer, and if she knew enough to think that it did moderate the sound far more than it in fact does, why on earth should she take the trouble to go and fetch a silencer and put it on before she started the killings?

'The mother and father were presumably in bed. Why go and get the silencer before shooting them? If she put it on in the middle of the killings, in the middle of what went on, or in the middle of the shootings, then is it really conceivable for one moment that she would have done so: start the shootings and then after perhaps someone was already injured and the father was up, then go out to wherever the silencer was (possibly in the cupboard) get it and screw it on in the middle of the fighting? Inconceivable, is it not? As the defence say, it just does not add up.

'And then, since the silencer was on the gun when she was fighting her father in the kitchen, why on earth should she have taken it off afterwards and then put it in the cupboard where, on the evidence, it was found on 10 August? Why? If she had killed everyone and was about to commit suicide and put the gun to her neck and found that she could not reach it, is it seriously to be suggested that anyone, whether mentally upset or not, would then unscrew the silencer, go back to the cupboard, put it in the box and then return upstairs to the bedroom before taking her life by two shots – with some interval between one and the other?'

The judge moved on to discuss the blood in the moderator, reminding the jury of the prosecution's contention that the overwhelming likelihood was that it was Sheila's blood. It had come, he went on, from a contact wound in Sheila's neck 'which because of the length of the gun with the silencer could not have been her own shooting' and was, therefore, a wound caused by Bamber. Arlidge, in his closing speech, had boasted that the case for the prosecution was so strong that even without the sound moderator the jury would be justified in feeling sure that Bamber was the killer. 'You can throw the sound moderator out of the window,' Arlidge had declared, 'and still the prosecution say they have an overwhelming case.' Mr Justice Drake was concerned that the jury may have misinterpreted Arlidge's remark. He was not saying: 'Forget the sound moderator.' He *was* saying: 'There are so many facets to the prosecution case that [the jury] can lay aside any individual part, including the sound moderator, and the case remains overwhelming. As if to leave no doubt as to where he stood on the matter, the judge added: 'I must say to you that he is right, that it is possible for you to find the defendant guilty on a number of different approaches from the prosecution evidence.'

The fact that the police had leapt to the conclusion that Sheila had killed her family and then taken her own life was of very limited relevance. It did, however, explain why so much of the evidence was obtained so late in the day; it was clear that the police search of the farm in the immediate aftermath of the massacre lacked the care and thoroughness that should have been used had the police not believed that it was Sheila who had killed and then committed suicide. The gun cupboard had not been properly searched until three days after the killings – even then, not by the police, but by a relative. So the original opinion of the police, the judge repeated, was wholly irrelevant. (Later in his summing-up, the judge modified this assertion, pointing out the prosecution's claim that the police had been led to their original conclusion by Bamber himself, as part of his murderous scheme. 'The conclusion they jumped to was precisely that planned by the defendant,' the judge added. 'To that extent, the conclusion of the police *is* a matter for you to bear in mind.')

The jury were given a warning at this point. Mr Justice Drake counselled against trying to build theories, based on the evidence, about exactly what had happened at White House Farm on the murder night. 'What you can, and indeed what you should do, is look at the facts – the hard facts.' For example, Nevill Bamber appeared to have fought in the kitchen with the killer who'd hit him with the rifle as well as shot him with it. There was the fact – what the judge suggested might be the single most vital in this case – that the silencer scored a mark on the mantelpiece. 'Does that not demonstrate beyond any doubt that the silencer was on the gun at the time that the fight was on in the kitchen?' he asked the jury. Other facts were fairly certain: that June Bamber had been shot first while in bed, and that Nevill Bamber had been shot and wounded in the bedroom before going down to the kitchen.

Turning to the question of motive, Mr Justice Drake reminded the jury that it was not necessary for the prosecution in a murder trial to prove any motive at all. However, in this case, the Crown's contention was that Bamber had been motivated by greed; he wanted his parents' money, or as much of it as he could get from their estates when all the rest of the family were dead. Provisional valuations put the combined estates of Nevill and June Bamber in the region of £436,000, although, as the judge pointed out, the true value was probably rather higher. The relevant question, he added, was to do not with the actual worth of the estates, but with what Jeremy Bamber *believed* them to be worth, and how he would benefit on the death of his parents. Bamber appeared to have examined some draft wills and had some idea of where the money might go. But what mattered was not the value of the estates but his belief that he might have benefited that counted in considering motive. 'If you are satisfied that he did commit the killing,' the judge continued, 'then he is guilty, irrespective of any motive at all. The motive is there for your consideration as one possible explanation of why he did carry out these killings.'

Glancing at the clock, the judge told the jury he would use the remaining half hour to deal with some aspects of the case which he felt were not of prime importance, but which were relevant. The first was the kitchen window: was it closed from the outside on the murder night? Theories about the kitchen window, no matter how interesting, were irrelevant if the jury concluded that Sheila Bamber did not kill herself, and that therefore Jeremy Bamber was guilty. There was also the evidence of the window to the downstairs toilet. This was the window that the prosecution claimed was the one Bamber used to get into the house without being seen on the murder night. There was the evidence of the hacksaw blade found lying near the window, and which had apparently been used to force the catch from the outside. (It had been part of Bamber's explanation to the police that he had indeed forced this toilet window with the hacksaw blade some weeks after the killings when he went to the farm to pick up some documents and found that he had forgotten his door keys.) The judge reminded the jury of the prosecution's view that such an admission showed how easily Bamber could have slipped into the farmhouse to carry out the killings; he also underlined the Crown's assertion that his 'innocent' explanation of how the blade marks got on to the window frame a day or two after being interviewed about the deaths was 'just too much of a coincidence to be credible'. Bamber's explanation, the judge added, was 'one of many examples in this case of there being just too many curious coincidences ... to be acceptable to you'.

Another non-vital but relevant matter concerned June Bamber's bicycle, which Jeremy had taken to his Goldhanger cottage shortly before the killings. There it had been spotted by his cousin, Ann Eaton, who noticed much dried dirt on the walls of the tyres, as though it had been ridden through deep mud. The judge referred to Julie Mugford's evidence that Jeremy had planned to get to and from the farm to murder his family by riding the bicycle from Goldhanger along the sea wall. On the other hand, Jeremy's own explanation was that he had borrowed the bike from his mother in order to lend it to Julie, who didn't drive a car. The judge invited the jury to contrast that explanation with Bamber's own sworn testimony that by August 1985, his relationship with Julie was fast coming to a close. 'What on earth, you may ask, was he doing ... taking his mother's new bike and providing it at his home for use by Julie to cycle when she wanted to from his house, at a time when the relationship was nearing its end?'

'It is no more than one (perhaps) straw in the wind, depending upon what view you take of it, but the prosecution say that there again is an example of just too many coincidences arising on the evidence to be an acceptable explanation . . .'

Finally, there was the question of the gun case and whether or not the .22 Anschutz had been stored in it immediately before the massacre. The rifle with the silencer attached would not fit into the gun case; Bamber had testified that on the evening before the killings, he had left the gun in the kitchen minus the silencer. Anthony Pargeter had visited the farm some nine days earlier and had seen the gun, out of its case and with the silencer attached, standing up in Nevill Bamber's gun cupboard. The silencer was on the gun when it came into contact with the mantelpiece while Nevill Bamber grappled with his killer in the kitchen. Who had put the silencer on? The judge reminded the jurors of the options. 'The defence say: Sheila. The prosecution say: Jeremy. But what has the gun case got to do with it all? . . . It was left without the silencer, and the silencer came to be on it by the time it was involved in the fight, but . . . this appeared to me to be of extremely limited relevance in this case. If you think otherwise,' he added to the listening jury, 'then give it what weight you think fit.'

And with that, and a reminder that the clocks were to be turned back on the following Sunday, 'and it will seem rather later than this on Monday morning', Mr Justice Drake adjourned the trial for the weekend. He resumed his summing-up at 9.45 a.m. on Monday 27 October, taking the jury through a detailed *résumé* of the evidence of Julie Mugford, evidence dismissed by Jeremy Bamber himself as 'a pack of lies by a woman scorned'. 'Well, members of the jury,' the judge remarked at the end of his summary, 'is that whole story a complete pack of lies, a complete fabrication? If she had made it all up, every bit of it a deliberate lie, could she then repeat it at such length and in such detail, and stick to her story under the skilled cross-examination of an experienced advocate? Mr Rivlin complained to you bitterly that she was an impossible witness to cross-examine. Was she? If she showed some degree of emotion when giving evidence, is that a drawback to a skilled Queen's Counsel in cross-examination, or is it something that can be exploited to see whether she maintains her story in the face of persistent skilled questioning? . . .

'Is Mr Rivlin justified in complaining that she was a bad witness? Well, that is for you to decide. You may ask yourself, in view of the fact that she maintained her story throughout, that perhaps his true complaint is that he was unable, in the course of a full cross-examination, to get her once to vary from the story she has always told . . .'

The judge reminded the jury of his earlier warning calling for caution in relying on Julie Mugford's unsupported evidence. 'It is surely a matter of common sense, is it not, that if you were faced with her evidence alone – her evidence against that of Jeremy's – you would be very reluctant and slow to reach any conclusion to find him guilty if there was nothing to support her story at all, although you would be entitled – after bearing in mind my warning – to do so . . . But in this case . . . you have other evidence which you may think of vital importance which you can consider, and see to what extent, in your view, it may fit in with, or destroy, Julie Mugford's evidence.' '

The judge now proceeded to deal in great detail with two crucial pieces of evidence which meshed with Julie

Mugford's story. The first concerned the telephone call that Jeremy Bamber claimed he'd received from his father in the small hours. According to Bamber, the sequence of events was:

1. Before he had a chance to say a word to his father, the line went dead.
2. He tried 'two or three times' to phone his father back, but the line was engaged.
3. Instead of dialling 999, he looked up the number of the police at Chelmsford, and called them. The incoming call was logged as having been made at 3.36, although 'giving the defence the benefit of the doubt', the true timing seems to have been 3.26. Jeremy claimed he was kept hanging on the line for eleven minutes. A police car was dispatched from Witham and Jeremy told to meet it at the farm.
4. He telephoned Julie at Lewisham, feeling he needed 'a friendly ear' and telling her there was 'trouble' at the farm. Julie told him to go back to bed. Jeremy's call seems to have woken most of the occupants at Julie's lodgings, who testified that they heard the phone ringing at 'about 3 a.m.', '3.12 a.m.' and 'two-something'.

If those witnesses are right, the call from Jeremy-Bamber to Julie Mugford was made long before 3.30 a.m. And as the judge pointed out, if Jeremy was wrong in his evidence, and he in fact telephoned Julie well *before* the alleged call from his father – followed immediately by his call to the police – 'it makes a nonsense, does it not, of the whole of his evidence . . . and it would surely undermine the whole of his story?'

There were other inconsistencies. If Nevill had telephoned Jeremy at, say, 3.25 a.m., he did so before receiving any wounds to his face which would have rendered him, almost certainly, unable to talk. In view of the distribution of the cartridge cases, it appeared that Nevill Bamber was wounded upstairs, and later killed by the fatal shots in the kitchen. The judge pointed out that this would have involved Nevill getting out of bed, going down to telephone Jeremy, returning upstairs, being wounded and going downstairs again where he was killed.

The judge invited the jury to consider the timings. Jeremy's call to the police at Chelmsford was made at 3.26 a.m. The police car from Witham arrived at White House Farm at 3.48 a.m. after which, it is certain, no shots were fired. Jeremy himself testified that he called the police *immediately* after his father had telephoned him. There would have been a slight time lapse while Bamber tried to call his father back (using his phone's redial key) and looked up the number of Chelmsford police in the directory. According to the judge, that left Nevill Bamber just over twenty-two minutes to make his stricken telephone call to Jeremy, then to have gone upstairs, to have been shot and wounded in his bedroom, returning downstairs, engaging Sheila in a fight before finally being killed by the fatal shots to the head. Sheila, according to the defence, having shot her parents and twin sons dead, would have had to unscrew the silencer, place it in the gun cupboard and return upstairs to commit suicide by shooting herself in the neck – twice. 'You might like to consider the likelihood of all those things having gone on in the space of just over twenty-two minutes,' mused the judge.

Furthermore, Jeremy Bamber's own account of the night was snagged by possible inconsistencies. On oath at the trial, he denied trying to telephone the police at Witham before calling Chelmsford; two officers to whom he spoke on the night swore that Bamber told them that he had tried to call Witham. PC West, who took Bamber's call at Chelmsford, spoke of his saying that his father sounded 'terrified', and of his sister having a history of psychiatry. According to another officer, Sergeant Bews, Jeremy arrived at the farm saying his father had sounded 'frightened' on the phone, crying: 'Your sister's gone berserk and she's got the gun!' Colin Caffell testified that Jeremy had left him with the impression that Nevill Bamber was already wounded when he telephoned. Yet, on oath and on trial, Jeremy Bamber had said he could not recall his father being injured. Bamber had said: 'When my father spoke to me, it was in his voice but a bit more rushed than normal. I cannot comment on whether he sounded in a panic or terrified. If I said *now* that I remember that, I would be giving the wrong impression. If PC West says I told him that my father sounded terrified, I was probably trying to gee him up because he was not taking me seriously enough.' Mr Justice Drake made no secret of his own feelings. 'Members of the jury, you may again ask yourselves: would you expect the defendant, even now, to remember quite clearly whether his father had sounded terrified or sounded as if he had been wounded?'

Who was to be believed: Jeremy Bamber or Julie Mugford? The prosecution had pointed to inconsistencies in Bamber's story, but the judge was taking a wider view as to whether or not there ever was any telephone call from Nevill Bamber in the middle of the night. 'It is not only on variations in what [Jeremy Bamber] has said that his father said to him, but on those timings which the prosecution say could lead you to the conclusion that story of the telephone call is a false one.'

The judge's second crucial point was: did Sheila kill her parents and children and then commit suicide? The judge invited the jury to consider the evidence that she did. Apart from Jeremy's own protestations of innocence, and his evidence of his sister's mental illness, the only evidence that she killed the others and then herself was the fact that she was found in a locked house, apparently holding the gun in a suicidal attitude. The judge first reviewed the evidence concerning Sheila's mental illness, and whether she was or was not likely to have been the White House Farm murderer. Such evidence fell into two categories: evidence from people who knew or had met Sheila Caffell, and evidence from experts.

Helen Grimster, who met Sheila for the first time the day after she left hospital for the last time, recalled Sheila saying she thought she was a white witch. She felt she had to get rid of evil in the world and said she had contemplated suicide more than once. A nurse, Caroline Heath, who met Sheila socially on 31 July 1985, said Sheila was not well-dressed, was not well made-up and looked a mess, was fidgety and on edge and at times stared blankly into space. Miss Heath had also reported Sheila as saying how she was looking forward to visiting White House Farm with the twins. When Miss Heath met Sheila at a barbecue the following day, she said Sheila looked much better, well dressed, pretty, well made-up and seemed in better spirits. Caroline Heath surmised, correctly, that Sheila was suffering from schizophrenia. Sheila's Iranian friend, Freddie Emami, had said in his statement that when Sheila left hospital in March 1985, he found her quite changed, much slower and more deliberate in her speech, and difficult to talk with.

Then there was the evidence of Jeremy Bamber himself. He said his adopted sister was often difficult to understand because of her illness. At Colin Caffell's party on Saturday 3 August, Sheila had seemed 'a bit vacant'. Asked about her condition on the last full day of her life, 6 August, he had replied: 'Well, she was very similar to what she had been at the party: a bit vacant.' On the other hand, there was the evidence of Julie Foakes, daughter of the farmworker Len Foakes, who had seen Sheila that morning with the twins, walking from one of the nearby woods with a dog scampering at their heels. Sheila had been skipping about with the children 'quite happily'.

Summarizing the evidence of Sheila's friends and acquaintances, the judge said most of them saw signs of Sheila's illness which agreed entirely with the evidence of her psychiatrist, Dr Hugh Ferguson. None of them at any stage knew of any physical violence by Sheila, although on occasions when she was acutely ill – as when Freddie Emami saw her just before she went into hospital in March – they were frightened that she might become violent. All agreed that Sheila was very loving and caring towards her twin sons, but there was evidence that she had sometimes had a difficult relationship with June Bamber. Everyone seemed to agree that Sheila had been very attached to her father, and that he was the person who had a remarkably calming effect on her. Dr Ferguson thought she treated Nevill Bamber as her mentor: a source of help and someone who could calm her when she was in trouble.

The principal medical expert was Dr Ferguson, who first saw Sheila in August 1983. Her illness was psychotic; her state of mind was such that she was liable to misinterpret the world around her, and she was particularly exercised by the idea of her being evil. Sheila was concerned with what she believed was her own ability to project her evil on to others. She thought the Devil had taken her over and that she had the power to project evil, particularly on to her own sons. Sheila's imaginings had included being forced to have sex with the twins, and to join with them in some form of violence. Her disturbed thinking went beyond the twins: she thought other people could read her thoughts and were shocked by what they read.

Sheila had mentioned doing violence to her children. Dr Ferguson also referred to her morbid thoughts: that she was capable of murdering her children, or communicating to them an ability to become evil at a later date. Sheila also had a strong belief that both she and June Bamber had evil in their minds and needed to be cleansed. At that stage, in 1983, Dr Ferguson diagnosed schizophrenia, and this was later confirmed. Although Sheila was deluded, there were no marked signs of hallucinations and no signs of physical violence. During 1984, when Dr Ferguson was seeing Sheila as an outpatient, he warned her against taking drugs, since this would increase the risk of a relapse. (Sheila had admitted being an occasional cannabis user and had sometimes taken cocaine.) On 3 March 1985, she was readmitted to Dr Ferguson's hospital in Northampton, in a very disturbed and bewildered state. She responded readily to treatment, and after twenty-four days her illness had receded to a manageable state. On her release, Dr Ferguson decided to try Sheila on the drug Haloperidol, but in July Sheila asked her GP to reduce the dose from 200 mg to 100 mg a month. The physician asked Dr Ferguson for his opinion, and he wrote back: 'I hardly feel like making any recommendation about Haldol [the brand name of Haloperidol], except to say that if she is coping adequately, then 100 mg monthly will do until she is seen again at the hospital.' In evidence, Dr Ferguson had said the side effects of Haldol could be severe, and might include heavy sedation. But his view was that her illness would not have driven Sheila to murder. 'I don't think that Sheila could or would have killed her father and her twins in particular,' the doctor had said. He had the impression that Sheila was a loving and caring mother, and that her relationship with her father was such that she saw him as a very strong and caring source of support.

Another consultant psychiatrist, Dr Bradley, had said simply that in his experience, people could resort to violence without having done so before, and that people suffering from mental illness, who had no previous experience of violence, could kill. He could not rule out the possibility that Sheila, from what he knew of her condition, could have resorted to violence.

The judge moved on to Jeremy Bamber's own account of his sister's mood on the murder night when the family sat down to a meal in the kitchen of White House Farm. During a discussion of Sheila's problems, Jeremy reported that someone had mentioned fostering, 'not in the sense, apparently, of the children being taken away from Sheila, but in the sense of some local family being found who would help with the children . . .' Asked about Sheila's reaction to this suggestion, Bamber said she replied that she would rather stay in London 'but generally didn't appear to pay much attention'. In the judge's view, there was no evidence that Sheila was excited or disturbed by such a suggestion, or that she was in a highly disturbed state or showing any symptoms at the farm that evening.

When Pamela Boutflour spoke to Sheila that evening on the phone, Sheila did not chat as much as she usually did. Pulling together the evidence about Sheila's mental condition, Mr Justice Drake conceded that she was quite clearly a disturbed woman who from time to time did suffer from relapses, and said things of an odd and sometimes striking nature. Nevertheless, Dr Ferguson had found no reason to think that she was or would be violent, 'and he regards it as totally out of keeping with what he knew of her that she would have killed her sons or her father. And he said that even knowing the extent of her mental illness. Dr Bradley, who had not met her, expresses a different view as a possibility.'

Next, the judge turned to more direct evidence as to whether Sheila actually fired the gun. 'Whoever killed Nevill Bamber clearly fought with him, and there is evidence . . . that the rifle was used to inflict some quite severe injuries on him.' Further, there was evidence that the rifle was found with a damaged stock, the light shade in the kitchen was broken, the silencer had left score marks on the kitchen mantelpiece, and furniture had been overturned. The judge compared Sheila, small and slight, with her father, a farmer who stood six feet four inches tall. Such facts were not conclusive, 'but they point to it being very, very unlikely indeed that she fought and overcame that tough father farmer, who managed to go on fighting, apparently, even with a number of wounds in him.' Sheila's long fingernails remained intact and un-marked and she bore no marks at all of having been in a fight; neither did Jeremy, but he was never examined for any because he was not suspected until much later. But if Jeremy was the killer, he certainly had ample time to clean himself up and make himself presentable before going to the police.

Whoever fired the murder rifle must have reloaded at least twice during the killings, even starting with a full magazine of ten rounds. 'Do you think that Sheila was capable of using that gun and of reloading it twice in the middle of the killings which occurred in the house that night?' asked the judge. The prosecution, he added, said it was just unthinkable. The defence said it was what she did. When Sheila's body was examined, no blood was found on the soles of her feet: surely inconceivable, in the opinion of the judge. The defence suggested that after killing her parents, Sheila washed herself. Tied in with that piece of evidence was the fact that her hands were found to be free of lead marks.

Turning to the time factor, the judge repeated that if Nevill Bamber had telephoned Jeremy just before 3.26 a.m., and no shots were heard after the arrival of the police at the farm at 3.48 a.m., whatever happened must have taken place 'within not much more than twenty-two minutes'. The defence version of events had the suicidal Sheila unscrewing the gun silencer, taking it down to the gun cupboard, hiding it, washing herself so that her feet and hands were clean, fighting with her father, killing her mother, and going to the other bedroom to kill her sons. A murdering Jeremy Bamber, on the other hand, clearly had time to put the silencer in the cupboard, and to return home to wash and clean himself up, having arranged the scene at the farm beforehand so that it looked like suicide.

But what about the evidence that the silencer was on the rifle during the fight with Nevill Bamber in the kitchen? The judge said there was no dispute that the score marks above the mantelpiece were made by the silencer, and that paint from the mantelpiece was found on it. The defence, however, argued that Sheila took the silencer off after fighting with her father in the kitchen. 'Do you think that is a credible theory?' asked the judge.

'Consider what it involves.

'There is some shooting that goes on in the upstairs main bedroom. Then Nevill Bamber is downstairs in the kitchen, where he is killed. At some stage in the kitchen the silencer is on the gun. Then (having killed, at some point, the boys as well) [Sheila] presumably goes to commit suicide with the silencer off and shoots herself twice. And what does she do with the silencer just as she takes it off and is about to end her life? She does not put it down beside her, or throw it to one side. She goes from wherever she was at the time, and walks through the house into the study. She puts the silencer in a box inside the gun cupboard, and then she walks right through the house . . . upstairs . . . and then shoots herself.'

The judge did not bother to veil his view of such 'a fanciful theory'. 'The defence suggestion requires you to consider that,' he said, 'and I am sure it is something you will consider and give it weight if,' he added with a note of contempt, 'you think that it is worthy of any weight.' On the other hand, the judge urged the jury to consider the prosecution's proposition: that the silencer was on the rifle in the kitchen but in the cupboard when found afterwards. 'It is just not credible,' the judge went on, 'that Sheila removed that silencer, walked to the cupboard and walked then back upstairs to the bedroom before she took her own life. The prosecution invite you to say, on that piece of evidence alone, you could conclude that Sheila did not commit suicide. And, if so, it would drive you to the conclusion that it was Jeremy who removed the silencer after she was dead.'

All this, the judge pointed out, was without any mention of the blood in the silencer, blood found inside it possibly down to the sixth or seventh baffle, a distance of some two inches. The blood was analysed and found to be specific to Sheila. John Hayward, the forensic scientist who carried out the analysis, had spoken of the possibility of the blood in the silencer being a mixture of the blood of Nevill and June Bamber, but the chances were remote. If it was, in fact, Sheila's blood, such a finding was of the greatest significance. Sheila could not have moved after the second, fatal, shot. Clearly, if the blood spattered into the silencer from that fatal last shot [a contact wound], she could not have removed the silencer afterwards. It must have been someone else. It must have been Jeremy Bamber.

The judge advised the jury how to approach their task. Start, he said, by considering some of the important facts which were not disputed:

- There was a fight in the kitchen in which either Jeremy or Sheila overpowered the tall, fit Nevill Bamber. Mr Bamber was struck with the rifle, and the rifle – in the kitchen – was fitted with the silencer.
- Sheila was rendered at least unconscious by the second, fatal wound. If the silencer was on the gun at that moment, someone else removed it. That someone must have been Jeremy Bamber.
- When Sheila was found there were no blood marks on the soles of her feet, and no marks on her hands from handling bullets.

The judge now reached his final charge to the jury. Was it a reasonable possibility, or a flight of fantasy, to suggest that after killing her family, Sheila then washed her feet and hands, unscrewed the silencer on the rifle, took it to the cupboard, then went to the bedroom and shot herself? If she did so, the judge observed, she must have relapsed into a state of acute illness. Dr Ferguson, her own doctor, thought this was out of character. And the silencer. Where did she get it from? Why did she put it on? Did Sheila know where it was kept? These were all questions for the jury to consider.

'If you believe that [Jeremy Bamber] may have been telling you the truth when he gave evidence,' the judge concluded, 'then he is not guilty. If you are driven to the conclusion that by a number of approaches the evidence against him is conclusive, then it is your duty to find him guilty.'

The jury stood and filed out of court. It was eleven minutes to one. Everyone remained standing as Mr Justice

Drake left the bench and disappeared through the door to his left. Lawyers gathered in untidy knots in the well of the court, and people in the public seats reached for their packed lunches and flasks. In the rising burble of anxious speculation about the verdict, one or two older legal hands were recalling Mr Justice Drake's zest for sea-angling and wondering whether the jury would now be prompted to take the bait and convict Jeremy Bamber on five counts of murder.

THIRTY-NINE

Geoffrey Rivlin could scarcely conceal his fury. He said he hadn't heard such a summing-up in twenty years at the bar. Even the prosecution lawyers were raising eyebrows. It was the sole topic of conversation as the court broke up for lunch, and Jeremy Bamber was escorted out of the dock through the door in the back wall of the court. How far were judges entitled to comment? Shouldn't they avoid letting the jury know what they think? The lawyers and their officials walked away in groups, exchanging opinions. Some recalled cases in which the judge had summed up heavily for a conviction on the basis of overwhelming evidence, only to be thwarted by an indignant jury feeling that their role had been usurped. Care and circumspection, some murmured, can achieve the same result. A popular hypothesis was that perhaps the judge felt that Arlidge, in his mild-mannered approach, simply hadn't quite brought the crime home to Jeremy Bamber. Possibly, he'd felt the prosecution should have been more aggressive, more positive. 'The great thing about being on the bench,' one lawyer remarked later, 'is that you've spent twenty or thirty years in the arena yourself and you find it difficult to stand back. It's like doing your child's homework: you think you can do better.'

Reporters had dashed from the court when it rose, filing their final takes of copy from the judge's summing-up and talking excitedly to their newsdesks from a bank of telephones in the overcrowded press room. Outside, television crews mooched aimlessly as the correspondents in their sharp suits scribbled out their scripts for pieces to camera. Members of the Eaton and Boutflour families spoke anxiously to each other in the witness room. 'The atmosphere was unbelievable,' one of the detectives recalled. 'The relatives were very tense, all uptight.' Indeed, everyone who had sat through the trial agreed that it had been extraordinarily tense and nerve-racking. Everyone in the court was affected, whatever their role. Witnesses, spectators, court officials, police. 'It was unreal,' one officer reflected. 'The sensational facts of the case, the huge build-up in the media, the character of Jeremy Bamber, his lifestyle, his seeming nonchalance. I mean, how many people in Essex get accused of five murders?'

It was a long wait. The controversy over the judge's summing-up grew more heated and more animated as the afternoon wore on. The defence team were convinced that Arlidge had upset the judge by not being tougher. A more scathing view came from an observer of Arlidge's cross-examination of Bamber, which the critic likened to no more than 'a fairly polite Sunday teatime chat with the vicar'. Low-key, conversational, not an 'as-seen-on-TV' confrontation. 'If a prosecutor is cross-examining someone he's alleging to be a mass murderer, you don't expect him to treat the defendant with kid gloves, which Arlidge seemed to be doing.' One of the lawyers mused that one can never tell the impact counsels' speeches have on a jury, but that one can't help but suspect that if the jury had retired at the close of Rivlin's speech ('a masterful demolition job'), they might well have returned a verdict of not guilty there and then.

The October afternoon slid towards an early dusk with a gentle autumnal glow. For the family, the tension was almost too much to bear. Peter Eaton struggled to keep his cool. At one point he turned despairingly to a detective and asked why the jury was taking so long to bring in the verdicts, and asking, in a studied insult, if all the jurors were former police officers. After everything had been said, and all the evidence brought to light, he simply couldn't understand why the jury wasn't back in five minutes with five unanimous verdicts of guilty.

Outside, it was dark. At two minutes to six, the jury returned to court on the judge's orders. The jury foreman announced that they had reached no unanimous verdict on any of the five murder indictments. Neither was a majority verdict likely in the time available that evening. The judge decided to call it a day, and sent the jury to a hotel for the night. Downstairs in his cell, Jeremy Bamber was keeping an iron grip on his emotions. One observer found him 'disconcertingly composed'. He was discussing what he would do when he was released the following day. He was bandying figures for which he planned to sell his story to the newspapers – somewhat unattractive behaviour, in the opinion of one of his legal team. A group of them sat with Jeremy, trying to buoy up his spirits but feeling increasingly uncomfortable about his obsession with a newspaper deal. The best offer he'd had, he said, was £40,000. Couldn't they get him a better offer than that? After all, he was pointing out, if he was convicted, Julie had been promised £15,000 for her story. She was already ensconced at the Chelsea Holiday Inn in Sloane Street, closeted with two reporters from the *News of the World*.

When Mr Justice Drake arrived at the court on what turned out to be the last day of the trial, his clerk handed him a note from the jury foreman:

> *We need to hear blood expert's evidence regarding the blood in the silencer* (a) *a perfect match of Sheila's blood* (b) *what was the chance of the blood group being June and Nevill's mixing together.*

The judge called counsel together, and noted that

Anthony Arlidge was absent, having left his junior, Andrew Munday, to tidy up any loose ends. After conferring with Munday and Rivlin, the judge called the jury into court shortly after 11 a.m. He reminded them of the evidence of the Crown's blood expert, John Hayward, who testified that in his opinion, the blood inside the sound moderator corresponded with that of Sheila Caffell. There was, he conceded, 'a remote possibility' that it could have been a mixture of Nevill and June Bamber's. Moreover, as an expert, Hayward thought there was nothing in the appearance of the blood he saw in the baffles of the silencer to indicate that the blood belonged to more than one person. Fletcher, the Crown's ballistics expert, had testified that one of Sheila's wounds was a contact wound. So, the judge added, that was entirely consistent with it having been her blood in the end of the moderator. Neither June nor Nevill Bamber suffered contact wounds. But, as Fletcher had conceded to Rivlin in cross-examination, six of the wounds in Nevill Bamber's body were close 'and you could, from very close wounds, get some blood coming back into the moderator'. With that, and an invitation to seek help again if they needed it, the judge sent the jury out again at just after half past eleven.

When the court reassembled for the afternoon sitting, the jury filed back into their seats and the judge took his place on the bench to announce that he had received a second note from the jury. The effect of this note, he went on, would be that he would now direct them on the matter of a majority verdict. He would send them out again, and would take a verdict provided that no fewer than ten were agreed one way or the other. Once again, the court rose and the jury disappeared through a door to the room in which they had now been deliberating for several hours. Once again, the departure of the familiar red-robed figure from the bench signalled a crescendo of chatter from the public seats.

At 2.35, twenty-one minutes after being invited to return a majority verdict, the jury returned to court. Bamber swayed slightly as he stood to hear the verdicts.

Jeremy Bamber, said the foreman, was guilty on five counts of murder. In each case, the verdict had been reached by a majority of ten to two. Two of the women jurors were in tears.

There was an audible shudder for breath as everyone in the court turned their gaze on the young man standing to attention in the dock. Bamber's face registered nothing. He simply swallowed and sat down.

There was an untidy pause, filled by subdued murmuring and the scuttling of some of the reporters towards the doors and their telephones. Mr Justice Drake finished recording the verdicts in his notes, put down his pen, and quietly cleared his throat.

'Well,' he said, glancing quickly round the court before turning his gaze directly towards the dock. 'Stand up, Jeremy Bamber.'

Two prison officers flanking Bamber moved forward, but Bamber got to his feet unaided and stood staring straight ahead as the judge began sentencing. 'When in about March 1985 you stole nearly £1,000 from the caravan site owned by other members of your family, you told your girlfriend, Julie Mugford: "I shall be the prime suspect, but they will never be able to prove it against me." When you planned the killings of five members of your family, you went one better. You used the mental illness of your sister, and planned matters so she became the prime suspect.

'Your conduct in planning and carrying out the killing of five members of your family was evil, almost beyond belief. It shows that you, young man that you are, have a warped and callous and evil mind behind an outwardly presentable and civilized appearance and manner.

'You killed your mother, you killed your father, you killed your sister. Each alone would have been a dreadful crime. But you killed all of them. You fired shot after shot into them, and also into two little boys aged six whom you murdered in your cold blood while they were asleep in their beds.

'I believe you did so partly out of greed,' the judge continued. 'But I take the view you also killed out of an arrogance in your character which made you resent any form of parental restriction or criticism of your behaviour.

'In passing on you the five sentences which are fixed by law for murder I have to consider when I think it likely it will be safe for you to be released from prison to live in the community. And I find it difficult to foresee whether it will ever be safe to release into the community someone who could plan to kill five members of their family, and shoot two little boys aged six while they lay asleep in their beds.

'First of all I pass sentence on you of life imprisonment on each of the counts. And the recommendation I make is that you serve a minimum – and I repeat, a minimum – of twenty-five years.'

Once again, Jeremy Bamber showed no emotion as the sentence was passed. He turned and, without help from either of the prison officers who flanked him, opened the door behind the dock and disappeared from view. He stood for an uncertain moment in the stone-floored ante-room at the top of the stairs. Then at a word from the senior prison officer, he was led quickly down to the cells. In contrast to the tumult that had broken out above – reporters had dashed for their phones and witnesses, lawyers and officials had broken the tension with noisy exchanges of opinion – an odd quietness filled the corridor leading to Jeremy Bamber's cell. At the door, he was stopped by his escort and ordered to remove his striped silk tie. Geoffrey Rivlin arrived with his junior, Edmund Lawson. There were tears in Bamber's eyes. A young woman solicitor from Paul Terzeon's office, following the barristers with an armful of files, was crying softly. Even to case-hardened lawyers, losing a major case after months of hard work is a huge anticlimax and emotions spill over. Apart from trite commiserations, there is little useful to say to a man who has just been locked up for a quarter of a century. Bamber, regaining his composure, spoke briefly about an appeal. Rivlin and Lawson nodded. Bamber seemed remarkably stoical. The lawyers withdrew, with murmurings about future meetings. There was a pause. The prison van was not ready, so Bamber's cell door was closed for a few moments. Through the Judas-hatch in the steel cell door, the young farmer could be seen, seated on the solitary bench, burying his head in his hands and weeping uncontrollably, moaning in stunned disbelief: 'No . . . no . . . no . . .'

FORTY

EXPLANATIONS and excuses began within an hour of the verdict. Essex Police called a news conference. Four senior officers, led by the deputy chief constable, Ronald Stone, sat glumly in a row behind a bristling tangle of reporters' microphones. Yes, at the very outset, Jeremy Bamber had fooled them. No, they had not handled the case in a sloppy way. 'With the benefit of that perfect science – hindsight – it could be said that the judgement of senior officers was misdirected,' he declared. 'The officers read the scene as Jeremy Bamber intended. It was interpreted as murder followed by suicide.' But Ronald Stone rejected Mr Justice Drake's criticism that the investigation lacked care and thoroughness. He was at particular pains to shield the reputation of the man who had headed the original inquiry, Detective Chief Inspector Tom 'Taff' Jones. 'He interpreted the scene he found in a very honest manner,' said Mr Stone, 'and I don't criticize him. But he made a judgement that proved to be misdirected and wrong.' The head of Essex CID, Detective Chief Superintendent Jim Dickinson, agreed. On reflection, he said, Taff Jones had made the wrong judgement. In future, he said, police at the scene of such a crime would be provided with 'all the available assistance' so they could make a more considered judgement.

The reporters challenged the police over the way the house was searched on the morning of the killings and asked how they came to miss the silencer in the gun cupboard. The police response was to insist that an initial full and detailed search of the farmhouse had not been necessary, and that consequently no one looked for a silencer.

In the light of the evidence produced at Bamber's trial, these excuses could hardly have had less effect. Next day's headlines pulled no punches. The *Daily Mail* called the Essex detectives 'The Clouseau squad that let the evil murderer stay at large for too long'. The paper listed twenty 'incredible police blunders' that mired the investigation before Jeremy Bamber's relations turned detective. So did most of the other newspapers. The scale of the police bungling took the breath away, they said, and yet the police were insisting that there would be no inquiry into how and why they had fouled up so badly. 'There are no grounds to justify an inquiry,' said the deputy chief constable, 'and one will not be held.' But within an hour, the government moved to counter boiling public outrage. The Home Secretary, Douglas Hurd, called for an urgent report from Stone's superior, Essex chief constable Robert Bunyard. Mr Hurd made it clear that he expected the report within a matter of days. Members of Parliament were already calling for a full independent and public inquiry to clear the air, and Mr Hurd promised a statement to Parliament after discussing the case with Her Majesty's chief inspector of constabulary, Sir Lawrence Byford.

From Chelmsford Crown Court, Jeremy Bamber was driven in a prison van past a fusillade of flash guns and through the rainy evening streets towards the A12 and London. His destination was Wormwood Scrubs, the maximum security prison in West London, where he was to serve the first part of his sentence.

Meanwhile, in London, in a hotel suite overlooking Sloane Street, Julie Mugford (in the care and custody of the reporters from the *News of the World*) heard the news in a telephone call from her mother. 'She was numbed at first and incredibly relieved,' Mrs Mary Mugford told a local journalist. Julie had suffered pain and torment as she waited for the verdict. After all, a guilty verdict would amount to a complete vindication, while an acquittal would have meant personal disaster. 'She was also very upset – extremely upset,' Mrs Mugford said. 'It's a terrible, terrible feeling when you have been that close to someone and you know all along what you have been saying is true, but you can't really prove it.'

The deal that Julie Mugford had struck with the *News of the World* gave the paper exclusive rights to her story and pictures in return for £15,000, but the deal only stood if Bamber was convicted. (The same paper had secured exclusive rights to Jeremy Bamber's own story had he been found not guilty. That deal would have earned Bamber the sum of £40,000, a figure Bamber himself had complained was hardly adequate given the explosive nature of the revelations he was promising about his relations.)

Julie and her newspaper minders broke off her exclusive interview to gather round a television to watch the evening news. Reports of the verdict and sentence were followed on both major channels by lengthy and detailed background features. The coverage was characterized by a general tone that echoed the strictures of Mr Justice Drake when he branded Bamber as 'evil almost beyond belief'. Colin Caffell, interviewed at his studio surrounded by sculpted figures of his murdered wife and twins, spoke of his 'happy, vibrant children' and their 'very loving and caring mother . . . very beautiful, a bit scatty . . . a bit of a Marilyn Monroe figure really'. Mary Mugford told the BBC of her relief and sadness at the verdict. Her feelings mirrored those of Jeremy Bamber's cousin, David Boutflour, the only member of the immediate family to speak to reporters as he left the court. 'No one wins,' he explained. 'We all lose. We can't bring them back.'

The national newspapers were less reflective. Jeremy's bleakly startled face, caught in a flashbulb instant, stared out from their front pages beneath headlines of the blackest and starkest dimensions. HE DID IT announced the *Daily Mail*. *Today* and the *Daily Express* reprinted the photograph of Jeremy, apparently distraught at the funeral of his shot parents. THE TEARS THAT HID GUILT OF A KILLER was the headline in *Today*. The *Express* found the word that seemed to sum up the 'callous cold-blooded killer': SHAM TEARS OF A MONSTER. The *Daily Mirror* took up the theme, running a picture of Bamber, caught half-blinking by the lens of the camera, alongside the headline EVIL EYES OF MURDER. 'Just for a moment the mask slips and the actor misses his cue. With cold, hooded eyes Jeremy Bamber shows the world his true character – "Evil beyond belief". The monster who slaughtered five members of his family in cold blood was locked up yesterday for at least twenty-five years with the damning words of the judge ringing in his ears.' But the most striking presentation of all was that of the *Daily Star*, which slapped a picture of the rifle used in the massacre across its entire front page. Bamber used this gun to kill five, the headline announced, IN COLD BLOOD!

The monstering of Jeremy Bamber revealed Fleet Street at its most unprepossessing. For more than a year, since Jeremy Bamber's arrest at Dover at the end of September 1985, the press had been fettered by the laws of contempt. These prevented them reporting anything other than bald matters of fact concerning his various appearances in court, and the sketchiest details of the legal process. During the trial, the same contempt laws meant that only the day's evidence could be reported, with none of the lurid background to the case that had been unearthed by some of the more enterprising journalists. As in any notorious murder case, the seasoned crime reporters, those with good contacts among the investigating detectives, soon came to grasp the nature and scope of the case, long before the details were exposed to public gaze. This meant that individual witnesses could be canvassed for co-operation, information and – in the case of the star witness, Julie Mugford – an exclusive deal. Leads could be followed up, such as the scandalous circumstances surrounding Sheila's birth which were revealed exclusively after the trial by Tim Miles, a reporter on the *Daily Mail*. It was he who traced Sheila's natural parents, and who interviewed her natural grandfather, once chaplain to a former Archbishop of Canterbury, at his home in Canada. But most of the tabloids were content to present the story as their own variations on a theme. They saw no more than the evil monster preying on and ultimately betraying the family who had raised him to the sweet and abundant life.

Undeniably, it was good copy. The monstering of Jeremy Bamber illuminated a parable for the age: a young man born to wealth and privilege who reaped a dreadful harvest. It pandered to all the tabloid preoccupations – money, murder, power, drugs and sex – and provided the public with an instant hate figure who personified so acutely many of the darker facets of themselves: envy, vanity, unresolved sexuality and danger. Bamber could be safely consigned to his dungeon and forgotten, abandoned to his own conscience, at liberty only to reflect on his own arrogance and its catastrophic consequences.

Stan Jones, the detective whose first fluttering suspicions had taken hold and who had grilled Bamber for three full days, was sitting behind the barristers in court when the guilty verdicts were announced.

Jones said he had glanced at Bamber in the dock and

observed his expression. 'His face showed absolutely nothing,' Jones remembered. 'An innocent man would have been shouting about lies and rubbish. But with Bamber there was nothing. Anyone on that jury looking at his face could have been in no doubt about the rightness of the verdict.'

Yet two of the jurors had been unconvinced. Not surprising, according to Stan Jones. 'Remember that Bamber was very attractive to women. He doesn't look like a murderer. He's full of charm, he assumes an air of wounded innocence. In court, women who queued for the public seats treated Bamber as though he was a film star. He got mountains of mail from women in the course of the case. He still does.' Jones's own daughter came home from school one day in the middle of the trial and told him that one of her school friends had asked for Bamber's address in prison so that she could write to him. That was a confused schoolgirl's teenage crush, but dozens of adult women were clearly attracted to Jeremy Bamber from the moment his picture first appeared in the newspapers. Jeremy enjoyed the attention they paid him. Some sent him letters accompanied by photographs. Others sent flowers, gifts and money.

Anji Greaves, the blonde beautician who sustained Jeremy Bamber during his twelve months in custody awaiting trial, visited him frequently on remand at Brixton Prison. Bamber, shunned in jail because of his educated accent and privileged background, flaunted his glamorous girlfriend by way of revenge. 'I feel so proud,' he whispered to her on one such visit. 'The sexier you look the better I like it. Everyone is talking about you.' Anji Greaves was incredulous at the trial verdicts. 'I can't believe that someone who blushed like a schoolboy and longed to be hugged all the time could possibly have murdered his family,' she told one reporter. She admitted that Jeremy's conviction had raised doubts about the future of their relationship. 'I feel so much loyalty for Jeremy,' she said, 'but I do not know if I can bring myself to go on visiting now. It could be a life sentence for both of us.'

Other women were quick to take the place of Anji Greaves. Some simply seemed to crave the notoriety of knowing Jeremy. Some seemed to be obsessively in love with him. All were victims of the criminal love syndrome. Psychologists have characterized them as women who need to feel in control of a man. 'They feel they can rehabilitate underdogs and losers,' said sociologist Dr Rosalind Miles in a study of women in love with lifers published in 1992. 'This contrasts with any relationship with a successful man who they feel doesn't really need them.' A man sentenced to life imprisonment can't let a woman down. He can't move away.

A 24-year-old woman named Sabina Butt struck up a relationship with Jeremy Bamber by offering to become his pen friend. She visited him at Wormwood Scrubs in the early months of his sentence, representing herself to tabloid journalists as the heiress of a multi-million-pound manufacturing empire. 'I can't believe he's the evil monster he's made out to be,' said Miss Butt. 'He told me he's innocent and I believe him.' Accordingly, the young woman announced she was pledging the family fortune to finance an appeal. Not long after this, a reporter traced Sabina Butt to the humble council house where she lived. The affair shrivelled on the spot.

Two years into his sentence, Bamber was reported to be having 'steamy jail sex sessions' with a busty 23-year-old blonde called Jayne Beardsley. These, too, ceased when details (including an extract of one of Bamber's letters to 'Dearest Jayne') were published across two pages of a Sunday newspaper.

A third such liaison met a similar fate. In 1991 a pretty 18-year-old retail trainee from Yorkshire, Nikky O'Hare, became interested in Bamber's case and began writing to him. She visited him frequently in prison, and became involved in his efforts to have his case referred to the appeal court. In December 1992, her story appeared in a rival Sunday paper. The young woman claimed Bamber had made her pregnant during 'steamy four-times-a-week sex sessions behind bars' but that she had lost the child through a miscarriage. These 'sessions' had taken place during visiting hours. Miss O'Hare had been given accreditation to visit Bamber as a member of his defence team, and this entitled the couple to meet in a private interview room. 'It was just a ruse for us to have sex,' Bamber was reported as saying. The young woman in question was said to be considering a career in the police force or prison service.

All this titillation obscured Jeremy Bamber's real concerns. A few weeks after his trial, he announced through his lawyers that he planned to launch an appeal against his convictions for murder. He had protested his innocence from the outset, and he was determined that one day – sooner rather than later – he would prove his innocence, and walk out into the waiting world a free man.

FORTY-ONE

JEREMY BAMBER has twice tried and failed to have his case referred to the Court of Appeal. His first application was heard in March 1988 by one of the most senior judges in the Queen's Bench Division, Mr Justice Caulfield, an avuncular Lancastrian of seventy-two who was said to have the most grizzled old wig in the judiciary. He was the judge whose description of Jeffrey Archer's wife Mary as a fragrant, delicate-speaking vision had made headlines in a libel case the year before. Despite his reputation for outspokenness and colourful language on the bench, Mr Justice Caulfield refused the application without comment.

Bamber was, however, entitled to renew his application in the full Court of Appeal and this he did a year later in March 1989. This time, Bamber's trial lawyer, Geoffrey Rivlin QC, argued his case before the Lord Chief Justice of England, Lord Lane, an austere and laconic figure regarded as one of the toughest holders of his office in memory. In his Victorian pine-panelled court in the Strand, Lord Lane sat flanked by two appeal judges, Mr Justice Roch and Mr Justice Henry. On Bamber's behalf, Rivlin made three main submissions: that Mr Justice Drake's summing-up at the original trial was weighted heavily and unfairly against Jeremy Bamber; that the judge repeatedly and unjustly ridiculed Bamber's case, using forceful and extravagant language; and that in his summing-up the judge produced a theory of his own as to the sequence of the killings at White House Farm that undermined the defence case. 'Every man is entitled to a fair trial,' Rivlin declared, 'no matter how heinous the crime.' Bamber, he submitted, didn't have one.

Geoffrey Rivlin claimed that, during Mr Justice Drake's summing up, the case for the prosecution was put as 'overwhelming'. The defence was presented as 'inconceivable, unbelievable, unthinkable and fanciful'. From the first day of the trial until the first day of the summing-up, everyone in the case – prosecution, defence and expert witnesses – had proceeded on the basis that the last person to be killed was Sheila Caffell. According to Rivlin, this acceptance was crucially important, as Bamber's case at the trial was that Sheila committed the murders and then killed herself. But Mr Justice Drake had described the theory of Sheila dying last as speculation. Rivlin submitted that this was 'an extremely dangerous thing to do'. On that ground alone, Jeremy Bamber ought to be granted leave to appeal.

Rivlin criticized the way the judge handled the evidence given by Julie Mugford. Rivlin said he hadn't questioned Julie at the trial about her dealings with the press because he'd been told by the Crown in good faith that Julie didn't intend to sell her story to the newspapers. But immediately after the case, articles appeared in the Sunday papers.

The strictures levelled at the judge by Geoffrey Rivlin could scarcely have fallen on more hostile ears. Lord Lane was notorious for his impatience with criticism of judges. Some reckoned this impatience verged on hypersensitivity. So no one in court should have been unduly surprised to hear the three appeal court judges swiftly reject Rivlin's submissions, and refuse Bamber leave to appeal. Lord Lane ruled there was nothing unsafe or unsatisfactory about the jury's verdicts, and dismissed Bamber's claim that he'd been denied the chance of acquittal because of a summing-up that was biased against the defence. Lord Lane also ruled there had been no material misdirection by Mr Justice Drake. He said it had not been an easy case to conduct. The judge had had to separate the core of the case from peripheral points. Lord Lane said the appeal judges were satisfied that Drake had put the main issues to the jury fully and fairly, and that he had correctly identified the subsidiary issues. Furthermore, Drake had repeatedly told the jury that they could reject any of his comments. Lord Lane said a strong prosecution case inevitably resulted in strong comments. The converse was true in cases where the defence was strong. 'It is quite impossible to say that the language used by the trial judge, read as a whole, is in any way unfair or deprived [Bamber] of his proper chance of an acquittal,' Lord Lane declared. 'There is no proper basis for the criticisms of this summing up, and there is nothing unsafe or unsatisfactory about these convictions. There is no material misdirection.'

Bamber himself was not at the Law Courts in the Strand to hear Lord Lane refuse his application, but remained in his cell on the lifers' wing at Wormwood Scrubs. For the moment, Bamber had exhausted the legal process. Lodging an appeal is an expensive business. Bamber was granted legal aid so that his application for leave to appeal could be presented to Mr Justice Caulfield, sitting alone in chambers. But because Bamber's application was refused, his legal aid had been withdrawn. Unselfishly, his counsel, Geoffrey Rivlin, had worked unpaid for many long, arduous hours drafting the second application, and remained what others on Bamber's defence team characterized as a hands-on leader. 'He had a stronger feeling of injustice than any of us,' said one of the lawyers involved in the case. This seems not necessarily to have been a feeling based on a conviction that Jeremy Bamber was innocent, but one based on the conduct of the trial in general and the summing-up in particular.

Bamber himself, on the other hand, never wavered in his protestations of innocence. His failure to obtain leave to appeal a second time only stiffened his resolve. If Rivlin's grounds of appeal had failed to convince the judges, then Bamber determined to assemble fresh grounds on which to persuade the Home Secretary to refer his case back to the appeal court. This was a massive task. No longer entitled to legal aid, he was unable to pay a solicitor. He had to do most of the work himself, writing letters laboriously in longhand with the help of a few close friends inside and outside prison.

Shortly after the failure of his second appeal application, Jeremy Bamber was moved from Wormwood Scrubs to Full Sutton Prison, a new maximum security jail near York. Most of the other 400 long-term prisoners at Full Sutton had been convicted of offences such as murder, armed robbery, terrorism, burglary, theft and drug-related crimes, but compared with the depressing slopping-out regime at the Scrubs, Bamber found the day-to-day existence at Full Sutton comparatively congenial. His cell contained its own toilet and wash basin, and there were workshops, a gym and educational facilities. There were television facilities, recreation rooms where he could play snooker, darts, pool and table tennis, and a kitchen area where he could cook his own food. An ironic if feeble echo of the broad acres at White House Farm were the small plots of land overlooked by the cell blocks where prisoners were allowed to grow their own vegetables.

But Jeremy Bamber's main preoccupation in the closing months of 1989 was to work his way line by line through every page of every statement, report and deposition that made up his massive case file. His self-imposed task was to tease out mistakes, discrepancies, ambiguities and inconsistencies that together might constitute new grounds of appeal. At the same time, Bamber launched himself on another line of attack. Claiming that he was convicted on the basis of unsound police evidence, he listed more than twenty allegations against Essex Police about the way they handled and investigated his case. Some of these allegations amounted to claims of criminal behaviour, others to breaches of the police disciplinary code. In the face of such serious charges, Essex Police voluntarily referred them to the Police Complaints Authority. The PCA announced that Jeremy Bamber's claims would be investigated by officers of the City of London Police led by Superintendent Barry McKay.

FORTY-TWO

BAD BLOOD lies at the heart of Bamber's campaign for a referral to the appeal court.

The fact is that the Home Office forensic science laboratory at Huntingdon seems to have a questionable record in blood testing. 'The error rate at Huntingdon in the 1980s was appalling,' says one former government scientist. Action was taken. Dr Mike Harris was brought in to get a grip on the blood testing section and to stop the rot. Harris immediately set up a system of double-checking test results, known as corroborative or duplicate grouping. This meant simply that every experiment, test and measurement was done not once but twice. In the late summer and autumn of 1985, when the blood in the Bamber case was being grouped and analysed, the readings, results and measurements were not double-checked. In the Bamber case, it is a central plank of the prosecution case that the blood in the silencer was that of Sheila Caffell and *no one else*. It was because the jury were satisfied that it was (they had been unsure and returned to court specifically to seek clarification from the judge, who sent them out again with a categorical assurance) that they brought in guilty verdicts against Jeremy Bamber. But eight years later, it seems clear that they were not entitled to that assurance. If that is so, the Home Office may be drawn irresistibly to the conclusion that the blood evidence is not entirely safe and that the case should be referred to the Court of Appeal.

The decision will turn on the evidence of one man: John Hayward. In 1985, Hayward was a middle-ranking forensic scientist at Huntingdon, graded in the jargon of the Civil Service as a Higher Scientific Officer. He came to the Bamber case quite by accident. It had originally been assigned to Glynis Howard, but she went sick and the file was handed over to Hayward. The judge quoted Hayward's evidence to the jury: 'I examined the sound moderator. I found traces of blood on the outside . . . Inside there was a considerable quantity of blood in the baffles, deposited in the spaces. I tested it and it corresponds with the group for Sheila, but not anyone else . . . I have been blood testing for nineteen years, and there was nothing in the appearance of the moderator to suggest to me that this was the blood of more than one person.'

As an experienced forensic scientist with nearly twenty years' experience of testing and grouping blood, was John Hayward entitled to claim that there was nothing in the *appearance* of the silencer to suggest to him that this was the blood of more than one person? Perhaps. But in the course of his evidence, Hayward actually issued a large-size *caveat* about coming to conclusions on *the basis of appearance alone*. Leading Crown counsel Anthony Arlidge had asked Hayward about the appearance of the blood inside the moderator. 'There was nothing to suggest to me,' Hayward replied, 'that there was . . . blood from more than one person present, or in my grouping results to suggest that there was more than one.'

Then Arlidge asked him if it was possible to judge blood by appearance at all. 'Not really, no,' said Hayward. '*I certainly would not want to offer an opinion on the basis of appearance alone.*' But the all-important question of appearance seems to have become confused by the time the judge came to sum up. Hayward's qualifying remark was ignored by the judge in turning the case over to the jury. Moreover, when the jury returned for enlightenment, having failed to reach a verdict, Mr Justice

Drake compounded matters, telling them: '[John Hayward said that] in addition to the scientific tests, it is possible, by experience, to form an opinion from the appearance of blood that you are grouping . . .' This is precisely what John Hayward did *not* say. The fact that Mr Justice Drake failed to represent John Hayward's evidence with pinpoint accuracy was underlined further during legal argument in the jury's absence on the morning of the last day of the trial. Again, the judge seems to have misunderstood Hayward's opinion on the efficacy of grouping blood on the basis of appearance alone. '[John Hayward] said that *you can tell from appearance whether there is a mixture*,' the judge declared, 'and nothing in the appearance of the blood inside the moderator suggested to him that there was more than one person's blood.'

Plainly, the judge thought that John Hayward had said one thing where in fact he had said another. The judge had implied that, on the basis of Hayward's evidence, an expert can tell from the *appearance* of bloodstaining that blood from more than one person is present. This is simply not true. Neither did John Hayward ever imply that it was. The position is that an expert like Hayward may be able to tell *from the appearance of blood grouping results* whether a mixture is present.

Bamber's defence lawyers believe the judge was unfair in the way he dealt with the blood grouping evidence in the course of his summing-up. They believe that the misquoting of John Hayward's evidence gave it more weight in the minds of the jury than Hayward himself ever intended. They have sought the opinion of a young, independent expert, Mark Webster, himself a former government forensic scientist. In Webster's opinion, Hayward failed to arm himself with the information necessary to justify his opinions. The notes taken at the time were slender and it is far from clear whether any precautions were taken to prevent a grouping error.

Was the blood found in the silencer tested in a way that would have revealed a mixture? This is the grey area of doubt that now lies at the centre of the Bamber case. If the blood from the silencer was dissolved in water and the solution used in the subsequent tests then there would have been no risk of error even if the blood flake had been heterogeneous, that is, a 'non-mixed' flake of blood from June and Nevill. Tested in solution, such a flake could not possibly have been mistyped as being specific to Sheila. The difficulty now is in establishing whether or not the blood was ever tested in solution. In 1986 John Hayward told Dr Patrick Lincoln, the blood expert then working for the defence, that he had indeed followed this procedure. But in 1993, questioned again by Mark Webster, Hayward said 'he did not think he had done this, and this would not be the usual procedure to follow'. The procedure does not appear to be recorded in John Hayward's notes; if a blood solution was prepared and tested, then it certainly should have been recorded. As Mark Webster points out, the only reason for not testing the blood in solution would have been 'if a scientist had prejudged the issue by forming the opinion that a mixture was not likely . . .'

FORTY-THREE

THE NEW doubts raised about the blood evidence gave Jeremy Bamber's campaign to prove his innocence a boost it badly needed. For the first time since his trial in 1986, his case possessed a proper focus, a real point that transcended the routine bleatings of convicted lifers. During his early years behind bars, Bamber had been courted by a motley collection of campaigners, inside and outside the walls of his prison, who had latched on to his notoriety, dangled there briefly and then (seeing the hopelessness of their cause) let go. His hopes had been raised, only to be dashed in the light of bitter experience. Reporters from the sex-and-sleaze end of the newspaper market had wormed their way into Bamber's confidence (sometimes masquerading as genuinely concerned members of the public offering to help him), grubbed for morsels of sensation, printed them and then abandoned him to his fate. There were the inevitable travellers' tales. (One told how, before his arrest, Bamber had fathered a son by a woman bank robber; the child would grow up, the story went, to stake a claim to the Bamber fortune.) There were times when Bamber himself fell into the trap set by sensation-seeking women, allowing them into his affections, before details of shared intimacies were splashed across double-spreads in downmarket newspapers. The publicity was all highly damaging to his cause. It was only when he was moved from Full Sutton Prison near York to Gartree in Leicestershire in early 1991 that Bamber managed to get a grip on himself, and to think clearly and logically about how to press his case.

Up to that point, more than four years into his sentence, Jeremy Bamber had been content with the scatter-gun approach. He had written to just about anyone in authority within the legal and penal system (and many more outside it) complaining at the manifold injustices (his favourite word at this period) visited upon him as a result of his continuing imprisonment. His relatives had fabricated evidence, manipulated police officers, lied in evidence, perjured themselves in court and conspired to frame him. The police were either buffoons or incompetents, and most of his friends had made up monstrous stories about him which they had either put about surreptitiously or sold to the newspapers. In the spring of 1991, Jeremy Bamber listed a dozen points from the crown case that he contested or rejected outright. He supplied comments on each of them.

1 The phone call to the police

The prosecution fixed the time that Jeremy Bamber called the police at 3.26 a.m. on the morning of the massacre. Jeremy says this timing is wrong. At 3.26, PC Michael West (who took his call at Chelmsford police control room) telephoned Malcolm Bonnet in the information room. Bonnet's (undated) statement: 'At 03.26 a.m. on Wednesday 7 August 1985, I received a telephone call on the internal line.' Jeremy says West made this call to Bonnet after his own call reporting trouble at the farm, so this call 'must have been between 3.15 and 3.20'.

The question of timing here is further muddled because PC West originally logged Bamber's call at 3.36 a.m. Either the clock was wrong, or West misread it, or he simply made a slip when entering the time on the telephone log. Certainly, the log clearly shows the call timed at 03.36. Jeremy suggests two possible answers: either West received another call from someone else ('such as my Dad alerting the police to his situation') or West has 'intentionally manipulated the timing of my call to Chelmsford in an attempt to undermine my evidence, knowing as we do that PC West did not write up this account until 13 September' – five days after Jeremy's arrest at Maida Vale, and more than five weeks after the killings.

2 The phone call from Nevill Bamber
Some accounts of the case have embroidered Jeremy's account of the phone call he claimed to have received from his father in the middle of the night. Jeremy never claimed that in the course of this call he heard a shot and the line went dead.

Jeremy says: 'The phone conversation with my Dad did end abruptly and when I phoned him back the line was engaged. It's hard to guess what happened with his phone. Either the socket was disconnected from the wall, or the handset replaced. I don't specifically recall hearing a dial tone, but there could have been one, though when I phoned back it was definitely an engaged signal which could have been Dad phoning for help elsewhere.' We do know that when the police entered the house, the kitchen telephone receiver was off the hook.

3 The call back
Jeremy told PC West that after receiving the worried call from his father, the line had gone dead and he had tried to call back, only to hear the engaged tone. It's clear that had Nevill Bamber dropped the receiver under attack from Sheila, the line would have stayed open. Jeremy could not have obtained a fresh dialling tone until either the receiver at the farm had been replaced, or two units of phone time had been automatically metered. At that time of night, this would have taken ten minutes.

Jeremy says: 'No one suggests that Dad was attacked while he was speaking to me. The phone may have been replaced in the usual way or the plug disconnected from the wall. This would have cut the connection, thereby allowing me to phone from my house. I recall distinctly getting the engaged tone when I rang Dad back, which indicates that he was either making another call or his handset was off the hook. Even if it is correct that Dad just dropped the phone during his call to me, it is not true that I would have had to wait until two units of phone time had elapsed before getting a fresh dialling tone.'

Jeremy cites the statement of an engineer called Robert Cox, who tested this point on behalf of the police. They wanted to know if Caller A from Tollesbury [Nevill Bamber] had phoned Caller B at Goldhanger [Jeremy], and during the course of the call Caller A had placed the receiver down but not on the hook, would Caller B be able to dial out again? The answer to this question appears to be: yes. Caller B [Jeremy] could have dialled out again provided he had replaced his receiver on the hook for a continuous period of between one and two minutes. Engineer Cox stressed that the period *must* be continuous. If Jeremy had picked up his receiver even for a moment before the 'Force Release' period had expired, this period would begin all over again. The 'Force Release' period can be as long as two minutes.

Jeremy says that although he replaced his handset after the call from his father, 'I don't believe that two minutes elapsed before I tried phoning him back. My return call was probably inside a minute, although I'm guessing. I know I rang back almost straight away. Of course it's all irrelevant if Dad replaced his handset or pressed the cut-off button.'

4 Leaving the rifle out of the gun cupboard

Everyone agrees there were several weapons inside White House Farm on the murder night. These included the murder weapon itself, Jeremy Bamber's own semi-automatic .22 rifle with which he had tried to shoot some rabbits earlier that evening. Jeremy maintains that when he went home to Goldhanger, he left the rifle with the magazine removed on the wooden settle or bench in the scullery between the kitchen and Nevill Bamber's downstairs den. A box of ammunition was left on the side in the kitchen. It was usual for Jeremy (and Nevill) to leave guns lying on the wooden settle before putting them away in the gun cupboard in the den.

'I should have put it away before going home that night,' Jeremy admits, 'but due to rushing out to the barn to collect my next load in my trailer from the combine, when I returned to the house later to ask Dad to pick up the last load, I'd forgotten about the rifle.'

5 Jeremy was a consummate actor, resented being sent away to school, and hated his mother's religious evangelism

Jeremy says: 'I have been in a play only twice in my life: I had a small part at Gresham's Junior School (a non-speaking part as a Roman soldier), and in 1984 I helped out at a local village production when I played a ghost and spoke one line. I have never boasted about my acting ability because I don't have any!

'I never resented being sent away to boarding school. I did find it hard to adjust to being away from Mum and Dad for the first couple of years. This is understandable as I was only eight and a half when I first boarded. I have aired the view that for me, this was too young an age to be away from home, but once I'd got over the first couple of years, I enjoyed school.

'Mum did try and encourage me to be religious, but

she used to with everyone. This did use to get on my nerves at times, more so because I didn't understand why she did it or how her mental illness affected her religious fanaticism. Dad never spoke about his religious beliefs to anyone, nor did he try to convert me or Sheila to his faith. There is no disputing that Mum in her later years became obsessive about Christianity. She was a fanatic. But I have never described Dad in such a way.'

6 *Jeremy boasted that he could easily kill his parents*
Jeremy denies this point-blank, and describes it as 'a complete fabrication'. The remark was reported to the police by Jeremy's uncle, Bobby Boutflour. Jeremy says: 'No such conversation ever took place.'

7 *Jeremy branded his relatives 'a pack of vultures all waiting to see what they're going to get out of it'*
Jeremy admits saying words to this effect. 'By the time of the funeral,' he says, 'I'd already fallen out with the Boutflours and the Eatons. No sooner had the police released the house to me than Ann Eaton, Robert Boutflour and David Boutflour had gone in, stolen my mother's jewellery (they said they took it with Basil Cock's permission), removed all the cash from around the house and taken all the guns, ammunition and various other items.

'I was appalled by their actions, especially when they started claiming that Mum had said they could have this painting and that china set and other items. What shocked me was the way they presumed it was their right to take and lay claim to whatever they fancied. It turned me against offering them the opportunity to choose things they wanted as mementoes from the house.'

8 *Jeremy behaved callously after the deaths of his family, spending the Sunday after the killings drinking pink cham-*

pagne with friends, rather than attending the special service held that Sunday morning at the local church in Tolleshunt D'Arcy at which prayers were said for his murdered family Bamber claims that he knew nothing of the special service, 'And I have never tasted pink champagne. It's possible we drank [white] champagne simply because it was our normal aperitif. It would only have been one bottle, shared between us. Nothing unusual, nothing special.'

9 *The Home Office pathologist quickly realized that Sheila's wounds excluded the possibility of suicide*
Rubbish, says Jeremy Bamber. The pathologist, Dr Peter Vanezis, in his statement to the police, reported: 'One cannot say with any degree of certainty [from the post-mortem examination] whether or not the injuries were produced by another party.'

10 *The pathologist decided that The first 'suicide' shot, to Sheila's throat, would have rendered her incapable – if it had not killed her immediately – of firing a second bullet into her brain*
Bamber refers to Dr Vanezis's statement of 30 September: 'The upper wound to [Sheila's] neck would have been fatal virtually instantaneously. The lower wound had caused substantial haemorrhaging into the soft tissue of the neck, principally from the right external jugular vein. In my view, the injury, although life threatening, would not have caused rapid death as in the other wound. Nevertheless it may have caused the victim to be stunned, although not necessarily to rapidly lose consciousness.'

11 *David Boutflour found Nevill Bamber's silencer in the gun cupboard three days after the killings*
Jeremy Bamber maintains that what Boutflour found was the .22 rifle and silencer belonging to his cousin, Anthony

Pargeter. Bamber says the silencer belonging to his father's rifle was recovered by the police at the crime scene, given the exhibit label SBJ/1, examined and returned to David Boutflour or Ann Eaton. Anthony Pargeter, in his statement dated 10 September 1985, reported: 'Sometime after 10 August I received a telephone call from David Boutflour . . . He told me the silencer had been returned to the family, presumably by the police. He said there was a large scratch on it, some red paint on the knurled end, and what appeared to be blood. I advised David to return it to the police straight away.' Bamber also points to an entry on an official police form dated 13 August: 'Item 22: SBJ/1 Silencer Gun Cupboard'. This denotes the finder as Detective Sergeant Stan Jones. But the silencer exhibited at Bamber's trial bore the exhibit reference DRB/1, denoting the finder as David Boutflour.

12 *There were technical but clear signs that the shots that killed Sheila had been fired with the silencer attached*

Bamber brands this evidence 'highly suspect'. He claims that the silencer was intentionally and maliciously contaminated with traces of red paint from the mantelpiece over the kitchen Aga, a single grey hair and a freshly made scratch mark. 'It is also a fact,' he adds, 'that the small flake of blood found inside the silencer was tested to destruction so that the defence were unable to test it themselves.' Bamber also claims that some of the test results were misreported to give a positive reading on one blood group where a negative reading had been found. (Bamber made this claim on the basis of some of John Hayward's notes. But he underestimated its importance.) Dr Patrick Lincoln, the defence's blood expert, found traces of blood in the threads of the locking nut. The Home Office admit that in the course of tests, blood was dripped into a similar silencer for test purposes. But they can't explain how blood came to be in the threads, since they would be sealed by the act of fitting the silencer to the barrel of the rifle. 'Knowing that the sound moderator supposedly belonging to Dad's rifle was not labelled with an exhibit reference tag, or packaged in a sealed bag,' says Jeremy Bamber, 'it's possible – if not probable – that some mix-up happened at the laboratory between Dad's silencer and the one used in the experiment in the Home Office laboratory.'

FORTY-FOUR

AT THE HEART of Jeremy Bamber's claims of innocence
are his allegations that he is the victim of a conspiracy
involving some of his surviving relatives and the police
officers who handled the original investigation into the
White House Farm tragedy.

The single most damning piece of evidence in the case
was the sound moderator or silencer found, the jury
was told, by eagle-eyed relatives searching White House
Farm three days after the killings on Saturday, 10 August
1985. Bamber says that this silencer did not actually
belong to the murder weapon, but to the .22 rifle owned
by Anthony Pargeter and stored (minus the bolt) in Nevill
Bamber's gun cupboard. Yet, says Bamber, the jury were
under the impression that the silencer spoken of and
produced in court was the one belonging to the .22 semi-
automatic Anschutz rifle found lying across Sheila
Bamber's body.

Jeremy Bamber and a small group of supporters who
are campaigning for his case to be reviewed say the
evidence concerning the silencer is riddled with serious
irregularities.

When was the silencer found? It seems an obtuse
question, but it arises because of a discrepancy in the
notes of Bamber's uncle, Robert Boutflour. Although his
son, David, says the search of the house was made on the
Saturday following the massacre, Robert Boutflour's own
notes (a sort of diary or chronicle of events) record the
discovery of the silencer as having taken place the following day. The entry in Boutflour's record reads: *Sunday 11*

August: The executor, Mr Cock, Ann, David and myself inspect the house. David discovered the silencer and telescopic sights in the gun cupboard . . . Was this simply a slip of the memory?

Assume it was. Much more puzzling, however, is the fact that while several people say they witnessed the finding of the silencer, their accounts of the discovery appear to vary. Assume that the silencer was, in fact, discovered on Saturday, 10 August. There is no dispute that at least four members of Jeremy's family were at White House Farm that day: Ann Eaton, her husband Peter, her brother David Boutflour and her father Robert Boutflour. But an analysis of their statements and trial testimony discloses some surprising contradictions.

How were the guns and ammunition they removed from the gun cupboard transported from White House Farm? David Boutflour, in his statement dated 12 September, told the police that having found the silencer, telescopic sight and ammunition belonging to the murder weapon, 'I took these items together with the other firearms to my sister's house.' But in a further statement on 31 October, he changes his story, saying that the haul was transported in his sister's car. 'The guns,' he stated, 'travelled in Ann's car.' In the intervening six weeks, David Boutflour seems to have shifted responsibility.

Who told the police? Again, there are conflicting answers. David Boutflour (who actually found the silencer, searching the cupboard on his hands and knees) told the police on 17 September: 'I told Ann of my findings and understood that she informed the police.' At Bamber's trial, David Boutflour was not so sure.

He was asked in cross-examination: '. . . you took [the silencer] to your sister's home?'

'Yes,' David Boutflour replied, 'and rang the police immediately to the effect that we had a silencer.'

'You rang to tell them about the silencer?'

'I did not ring them. Somebody did.'

His sister, Ann Eaton, is also vague about who told the police about the silencer. 'Contact was made with the police about the discovery of the blood-and-paint-stained silencer,' was all she said on the subject in a statement on 12 September. Neither does Ann's husband, Peter Eaton, shed much light. 'I believe Ann rang the police to let them know what they had found,' he stated.

David Boutflour's father, Robert Boutflour, witnessed the discovery of the silencer, but didn't return with the others to Oak Farm where it was examined on the kitchen table. In his diary in the entry dated Sunday, 11 August, Boutflour says he told his son to put the silencer in a plastic bag 'for taking to Peter's house and collection by the police'. But he does not record who told the police and when.

Essex Police sent the silencer for forensic examination on at least two separate occasions. The first was on Tuesday, 13 August, the day after it was collected from the Eatons' farm by Detective Sergeant Stan Jones. But the silencer was returned to the police for fingerprint tests, and not sent back to the forensic laboratory at Huntingdon until Friday, 30 August. So the police stored the silencer for seventeen days. It is unclear *how* the silencer was stored, or if the delay might have contributed to the deterioration of any blood on or inside the silencer.

Since his convictions for murder, Jeremy Bamber has employed a small number of people to help him research his case and to gather material which he hopes will persuade the authorities to refer his case to the Appeal Court. At least one of these researchers is a professional investigator, another is a convicted burglar who met Bamber in prison and who is convinced that he is not the killer of White House Farm. Bamber's research team looked closely at hundreds of statements and other documents relating to the case. They claim to have uncovered fresh evidence, in the form of official documentation, which throws the silencer evidence into doubt.

They point out that although the silencer was said to have been found by Bamber's cousin, David Boutflour, it was sent to the forensic science laboratory in Huntingdon with a label bearing the legend SBJ/1. These initials denote Stanley Brian Jones, the detective sergeant who collected the silencer from the Eatons, and the silencer was logged as having been found by Stan Jones in the gun cupboard at White House Farm. This is plainly wrong.

There is another puzzling aspect to the way in which this vital exhibit was labelled. Home Office documents record the silencer as being labelled SBJ/1 when it arrived at Huntingdon on 13 August and again seventeen days later on 30 August. Yet in their statements dated 13/14 November, the forensic officers consistently refer to the exhibit by quoting the legend DRB/1, denoting David Robert Boutflour. Bamber's researchers found that references to DRB/1 in the forensic officers' statements had been altered. The alterations were plain to see, since they had been made using a different typewriter.

On Jeremy Bamber's behalf, his team of researchers compiled a lengthy document detailing 'serious irregularities' in the way exhibits were handled and processed in the course of the investigation. 'What is certain,' one of them reported in 1990, 'is that there appears to have been a deliberate attempt to cover up the inadequacies of the local police force who dealt with the initial investigation.' The silencer recovered from the gun cupboard was certainly a crucial factor in driving the jury towards a conviction. But even more damning was the trace of blood found inside the silencer itself. In their efforts to convince the authorities that Jeremy Bamber's case should be referred to the Appeal Court, Bamber's research team concentrated on the evidence concerning Sheila's blood. They focused on two questions:

- Was the blood in the silencer *specific to Sheila Caffell*? In other words, was the blood hers and hers alone?
- Was the judge, Mr Justice Drake, right to tell the jury, when they returned to court to ask, that the blood *was* specific to Sheila Caffell?

The researchers examined the way in which the forensic scientists and the prosecution reached the conclusion that the blood in the silencer was Sheila's and Sheila's alone. They began by looking at how the sample of blood found in the silencer was analysed. The evidence given to the jury was that a flake of blood the size of a matchhead or pinhead was discovered in the baffle plates inside the silencer. This blood was made up into a solution so that it could be grouped. In all, the blood sample was subjected to five separate tests to try to establish whether it belonged to any of the murdered family. Of these five tests, four gave positive results. These results were then compared to the blood groups of the five murdered people.

This is what they found:

	ABO	PGM	EAP	AK	Hp
Nevill Bamber	O	PGM1 +	EAP BA	AK1	Hp2–1
June Bamber	A	PGM1 +	EAP BA	AK2–1	Hp2–1
Daniel Caffell	O	PGM2 + 1 +	EAP B	AK1	Hp2
Nicholas Caffell	O	PGM2 + 1 +	EAP B	AK1	Hp2
Sheila Caffell	A	PGM1 +	EAP BA	AK1	Hp2–1
BLOOD SAMPLE	A	Nil	EAP BA	AK1	Hp2–1

The tests, it seemed, were conclusive. Sheila's was the only blood which matched up to the test sample. The prosecution at Bamber's trial pointed to these results and claimed that they were consistent with their case that the blood in the silencer matched the blood of Sheila Caffell *and no one else*.

Even so, the jury had seemed unconvinced, asking for confirmation that the blood in the silencer was Sheila's and Sheila's alone. Mr Justice Drake had rehearsed the evidence, but with two important contributions of his own. He said that John Hayward thought there was nothing in the appearance of the blood to indicate that it belonged to more than one person. (Hayward had not said this.) He also provided the jurors with a copy of a schedule listing the blood groups of all five victims. The judge even took the trouble to underline Sheila's blood grouping because, he said, hers was the only blood that matched the test sample. None of the others did.

This schedule was never exhibited in the course of the trial, but the jury were handed copies of this document containing annotations made by the judge. Was this admissible? Was this impartial? Bamber's researchers claim it was not. They point out that the jury had asked to hear the evidence of the blood experts. They say this did not entitle the judge to provide the jury with a document containing entries which he had made himself.

But there was more to it than that. Bamber's research team claim the jury were misled over the whole issue of the blood inside the silencer. They say that the direction to the jury by both the prosecution and the judge to the effect that the blood in the silencer was specific to Sheila was not entirely accurate. In fact, both John Hayward and the judge admitted that the blood could have been a mixture of Nevill and June Bamber's blood, but that this was a remote possibility. They claim that only DNA testing could prove the point beyond any doubt. 'In the absence of DNA testing,' they declared in a report compiled for the Home Office in 1990, 'it would be impossible to differentiate between one person's blood and another. Consequently, the jury . . . have been seriously misled. It is clear that the blood in [the silencer] was *not* specific to Sheila Caffell, but that rather the blood was of a consistency *which may have been a mixture of different people's blood*.' [Author's italics.]

The significance of this claim is stark. If the blood in the silencer was, indeed, a mixture of blood from some (or all) of the other victims, then the evidence does not exclude the possibility that Sheila may indeed have murdered her family before removing the silencer, placing it where it belonged in the gun cupboard, then returning upstairs to take her own life. If that possibility could not be excluded, according to campaigners for Bamber, then his convictions on five counts of murder would be demonstrably unsafe.

FORTY-FIVE

How DID blood get into the silencer in the first place?

At Jeremy Bamber's trial, the prosecution explained the presence of Sheila Caffell's blood in the silencer by placing great emphasis on a phenomenon known as 'backspatter'. When a shot is fired, various gases are generated inside the barrel of the gun. These propellent gases would cause blood and tissue to be blown back into the weapon, or in the Bamber case, back into the hole at the end of the silencer. Backspatter is more likely to occur if the weapon is fired while in contact with the victim's skin, causing a contact wound. At Bamber's trial, it was the prosecution's case that although there were five victims, only blood from Sheila Caffell was discovered on or in the murder weapon or the silencer that was fitted to the end of the barrel. This was in spite of the fact that Sheila may not have been the only victim to have received a contact wound in the course of the killings.

Consider the following sequence of events. Supposing June Bamber is shot and her blood backspatters into the silencer, lodging in the baffles as in figure (a) (overleaf). Her blood group is A (AK2–1). Then Nevill Bamber is shot, and his blood now backspatters down the silencer, also lodging in the baffles as in figure (b). Nevill Bamber's blood is group O (AK1). Supposing that one of the flakes now lodged inside the silencer – an amalgam of June and Nevill's blood – is taken and subjected to tests for grouping. Experiments conducted on behalf of Jeremy Bamber's defence team by independent forensic expert Mark Webster yielded astonishing results. He showed that if half of

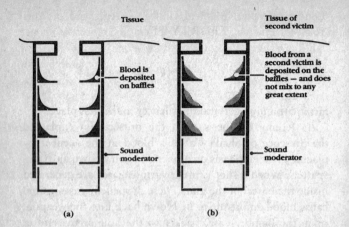

Tissue	Tissue of second victim

Blood is deposited on baffles

Blood from a second victim is deposited on the baffles — and does not mix to any great extent

Sound moderator

Sound moderator

(a)   (b)

the flake is tested and found to give AK1 and the other half is tested and found to give group A, the result obtained *will be indistinguishable from the result which would be obtained from a single source of blood of group A (AK1)*. Only one of the victims of the White House Farm massacre fits such a grouping. And that was Sheila Caffell.

Webster was thus able to show that it may have been possible for scientists running tests on the blood in the silencer to draw a misleading inference from that blood. It seems that such a reading – indicating the presence of Sheila's blood – could have been obtained from sampling different halves of a flake of blood made up of backspatter from June and Nevill Bamber.

Webster's tests conducted in April 1993 were not the first to demonstrate a possible ambiguity in the blood tests. In the course of preparing Jeremy Bamber's defence in 1986, his lawyers had hired one of Britain's pre-eminent blood experts, Dr Patrick Lincoln, senior lecturer in blood group serology in the Department of Haematology at the

London Hospital Medical College. At the end of April 1986, Dr Lincoln visited the Home Office forensic science laboratory at Huntingdon to examine the silencer for himself. He did so in the presence of Detective Inspector Ron Cook of Essex Police and Glynis Howard, one of the laboratory's forensic scientists. Dr Lincoln checked the groupings prepared for the police from blood samples taken from all five victims of the massacre. These were grouped for the ABO, PGM, EAP and AK blood group systems. (For technical reasons it was not possible to type the samples for the Hp [haptoglobin] system, but this was not important: Sheila's blood could be distinguished from that of the other four using the results from the other systems.)

Dr Lincoln stripped the silencer down into its component parts to look for traces of blood. These components included the end piece, the ring collar and seventeen baffle plates. He obtained the strongest positive reactions indicating the presence of blood on the screw thread at the end of the silencer. He detected weak or very weak positive reactions on the ring collar and the first eight baffle plates, to a depth of between 35 and 40 mm into the silencer. No blood was visible to the naked eye.

From the tiny traces of blood on the screw threads at the end of the silencer, Dr Lincoln was able to conduct tests for the ABO blood groups and found evidence of blood group A. This was consistent with the ABO grouping result obtained by Home Office forensic scientist John Hayward on blood from the inside of the silencer. Dr Lincoln also tested for EAP and AK blood group systems but could detect no activity. He thought this was unsurprising in view of the weak reactions he obtained while searching for this blood and the appearance of the swabs when he tried to lift traces of any blood from the silencer.

John Hayward reported obtaining blood from the inside of the silencer which he demonstrated belonged to groups A, EAP BA, AK1, Hp2–1. This blood could have only come from Sheila. None of the other victims' blood fitted these groups. (About 8 per cent of non-related white British people would be expected to have this combination of groups.) But it was not clear whether Hayward had been able to obtain grouping results for all four systems (ABO, EAP, AK and Hp) on a bloodstain from a single area of the silencer or a single baffle plate. Although Hayward collected all his bloodstain material from inside the silencer, it is possible that this came from more than one baffle plate or from more than one area inside the silencer.

If the blood grouping results for the four systems weren't obtained on blood belonging to the same stain, Dr Lincoln reported, the possibility that these bloodstains originated from more than one individual *cannot be excluded*. In such a situation, John Hayward's grouping results (group A, EAP BA, AK1, Hp2–1) could be the result of grouping more than one bloodstain. Moreover, each of these bloodstains need not necessarily have come from the same victim.

Dr Lincoln explained by offering an example. If the bloodstain used for the ABO, EAP and Hp grouping was swabbed from baffle plate number one and came from June Bamber, this bloodstaining would be shown to have groups A, EAP BA and Hp2–1. Suppose the bloodstaining used for the AK grouping tests was taken not from baffle plate number one but from some other area, the possibility that this blood was from a victim other than June Bamber *probably cannot be ruled out*. If this bloodstaining used for the AK testing came from Nevill Bamber, it would produce the AK group AK1. The total result of the grouping of the blood inside the silencer would then be A, EAP BA, AK1 and Hp2–1 – the same combination of groups as the blood of Sheila Caffell.

Could a mistake have been made? Could the Home Office scientists have inadvertently arrived at a wrong conclusion because they used different flakes of blood for different tests or (as Mark Webster suggested) because they used different bits of the same flake which in fact came from different people?

Mark Webster was hired by Jeremy Bamber's defence team in the spring of 1993. Webster was invited to Huntingdon to discuss the case at the Home Office forensic science laboratory. Mark Webster was greeted by Peter Wingad, one of the lab's service managers, and Dr Mike Harris, one of the Forensic Science Service's core experts in blood grouping. To Mark Webster's surprise, John Hayward, the scientist who did much of the original work on the Bamber case, was also there. Hayward left the FSS not long after Bamber's trial to work as an independent forensic scientist. Hayward turned up even though the Home Office had refused to pay for his time. Peter Wingad explained that certain questions relating to the Bamber case could only be answered by John Hayward.

Mark Webster seized his chance and questioned John Hayward about the way in which the blood flake found in the silencer had been grouped. Throughout the case, there was an assumption that the amount of blood found in the silencer was very small; it had been described as 'a flake' no bigger than the head of a pin or a match. Mark Webster was surprised to hear John Hayward revise this estimate. Asked by Webster how much blood was present in the silencer, John Hayward admitted: 'There was a lot.'

'More than one flake?'

'Yes, a number of flakes.'

'The notes refer to a single flake,' said Mark Webster. 'Was only one flake taken for grouping tests?'

Hayward paused. 'That's what it says in the notes.'

Mark Webster asked: 'Was the flake a big one?'

'Yes,' said John Hayward. 'There was a lot of blood in the sound moderator.'

Webster now squared up to the possibility of error. Were precautions taken to make sure that different people working on the grouping tests were actually testing the same material? If one person took one flake for AK testing and another person took another flake for ABO testing – and the two flakes came from different people – wasn't it possible they could end up with the wrong answer? There would be nothing to indicate that what was being tested was actually a mixture. Should the material not have been homogenized in some way, asked Webster, to make sure that everyone was testing the same material?

John Hayward agreed that no procedure had been adopted to preclude this type of error.

Dr Mike Harris intervened. He said the possibility of mixing two samples had been considered during the original investigation. Dr Harris offered an analogy: suppose there was an incident in which more than one person bled, and a single bloodstain was found on a wall or piece of clothing. In such circumstances, it was much more likely that the blood came from one person rather than two or more people because it would be unlikely that blood flying from two or more people would actually land in the same spot.

Mark Webster challenged Dr Harris and his analogy. 'We know that this rifle has been used to kill five people,' Webster said. 'We know that if the silencer is used in a contact shot, then blood will end up inside it. There seems no reason why contact shots to more than one

406

victim should cause blood to land exclusively in different areas of the silencer.

'It seems more logical that the bloodstaining from two different contact shots would be coincident.' Webster turned to Dr Harris. 'A more correct analogy would be using an axe or other weapon to injure several people. The weapon would become stained in the same area with the blood of more than one victim. Under those circumstances there'd be a very real danger of misinterpretation of a mixture.'

But what happened in the Bamber case, in which five people were shot to death, five people who between them possessed four different blood groupings? (The identical twins Nicholas and Daniel had identical blood group characteristics.) Mark Webster re-examined the results of the original grouping tests to see if there was any evidence that the blood analysed at Huntingdon was 'a more or less *homogenous* mixture' of blood from June and Nevill Bamber. (A homogenous mixture is one where blood from two or more sources form an intimate mix, in which the original components are no longer separately identifiable.) June Bamber's blood was group A, AK2–1 and her husband's was group O, AK1. Home Office scientists at Huntingdon looking at the blood from the silencer ran not one set of tests but two. The first test showed high levels of group A substance with no associated group O elements. The second test showed slightly lower levels of group A substance with 'very modest' levels of group O substance. Webster was forced to concede that these results gave no indication that the blood found inside the silencer was a mixture of group A with group O. 'The evidence does not support the hypothesis that the blood flake tested was an homogenous mix of Nevill and June Bamber's blood,' he reported. Quite simply, the idea that such an intimate blood mix could have been mistaken for blood specific to Sheila alone just did not stand up.

Questions remain nevertheless. Did the blood tested by the Home Office forensic scientists came from more than one source? And would the techniques used in the laboratory at Huntingdon have demonstrated this? Mark Webster sought to clarify this during his visit there in April 1993. He reminded those present that the blood grouping evidence and the evidence of the prosecution firearms expert Malcolm Fletcher was the most crucial evidence in the whole of Jeremy Bamber's trial. But Webster also pointed out that the arguments used in court were circular: the Crown's case was that the blood in the silencer was Sheila's alone because the blood tested came from only one individual. This was supported by Malcolm Fletcher's opinion that of all the wounds inflicted on the murder night, only one (the wound to Sheila Caffell) was a contact wound. Meanwhile, Fletcher's opinion that other wounds, such as those to June and Nevill Bamber, were unlikely to be contact wounds was supported by the blood grouping interpretation. Mark Webster pointed out that circular arguments are fine, but only if each link of the argument is strong enough to stand by itself.

Where next? The scientists discussed the possibility of carrying out more tests on any blood which may now – nearly ten years on – still be present inside the silencer. They agreed to take steps to re-examine it, and to see if there was enough blood still inside to allow for further tests. John Hayward was eager to settle the question of whether the silencer contained more than one person's blood by the use of sophisticated, high-sensitivity DNA profiling tests.

The scientists also agreed to look at Mark Webster's hypothesis about two people's blood having been found in the silencer and that what they tested was, in fact, a heterogeneous mixture. (A heterogeneous mixture contains blood that is partially or wholly unmixed.) Webster maintained that it is possible that if two contact wounds are inflicted, two people's blood will end up inside the silencer. It was also possible (in Webster's opinion, even likely) that it would not be apparent just from its appearance that the blood came from more than one victim. In his summing-up at the trial, Mr Justice Drake implied that an expert can tell such things from the way a bloodstain looks. This is simply not true, and John Hayward, the Crown's blood expert, never implied that it was. What the judge should have said is that experts can tell from the appearance of *blood grouping results* whether a mixture of blood may be present.

In essence, the possibility for error exists – in Mark Webster's expert opinion – if different portions of a large flake of blood from two or more victims were tested, or if different flakes were taken for separate tests. It is just possible that the blood groupings accepted by the jury at Bamber's trial may have been flawed because a heterogeneous mixture of blood was misinterpreted. Mark Webster concedes, however, that the chances of this are 'reasonable but small'. Nevertheless, if Webster's hypothesis were proved correct, this would certainly be new evidence on which Jeremy Bamber could launch an appeal against his conviction.

Everything hinges on the blood remaining in the silencer. If enough blood still exists inside it, it may be possible to conduct tests which could settle the matter once and for all. At Bamber's trial, it was said that the possibility of two people's blood mimicking blood from Sheila alone was remote. It may still be possible to conduct experiments that disprove this assertion. On the other hand, Mark Webster pointed out, the same experiments could have the effect of supporting the prosecution case, and showing beyond doubt that the blood in the silencer is and was that of Sheila Caffell and Sheila alone. As Webster himself puts it, the outcome is uncertain.

FORTY-SIX

JEREMY BAMBER'S case forces itself on us because of the unique place he occupies in our darkest imaginings. If he *was* the killer at White House Farm, did it really make him the media monster with the tabloid stare, or was there another person locked within him? If he was *not*, what was he doing in prison?

I first wrote to Bamber in the spring of 1991. He had been moved from Full Sutton to Gartree Prison in Leicestershire to be nearer London; officers from the City of London force were visiting him regularly to conduct interviews with him concerning his claims about the shortcomings of Essex Police.

'I did not murder my family,' Bamber wrote in reply to my first letter, 'or play any part in their deaths.' He said that although he had been protesting his innocence from the day he was arrested, it was only now that he could prove it. The Crown Prosecution Service, which in 1986 had superseded the DPP as the body responsible for prosecuting criminal cases in England and Wales, had suppressed evidence of his innocence, Bamber added, and he was now in a position to prove that key witnesses had lied in court to frame him, and that the silencer had been contaminated in order to undermine his defence. There were, he explained, many other irregularities currently under investigation, 'and it is without doubt that within a matter of months I will be given back my rightful freedom.'

Jeremy Bamber went on to point out that I was by no means the first writer to approach him with a book proposition. Hitherto he had not co-operated with writers because he had nothing to gain from books or articles about him. 'I am a private person who intensely dislikes the media and way they have tried to portray me,' Bamber wrote. Most of what had been written before was no more than hype, hearsay and out-and-out lies. But Bamber added that he might be persuaded to co-operate. The key to that co-operation lay three thousand miles away in the United States.

Bamber discussed his case in prison with a former law student; his fellow inmate suggested that the man he needed to help prove his innocence was America's foremost expert in forensic ballistics, Professor Herbert Leon MacDonell. His pathfinding work in the investigation of the 1969 Black Panther gun battle in Chicago had led one admiring journalist to dub MacDonell the Isaac Newton of ballistics. His approach to scenes-of-crime was known to be coldly clinical, pragmatic and impartial. 'If you don't want the whole truth, don't hire me,' MacDonell told the attorney acting for the Black Panther group when their arsenal was stormed by armed police in a dawn raid. By running lengths of string from the impact craters of various bullets at the scene of the shoot-out, the professor had been able to prove that, contrary to the official version of events, the raiding police had fired first. Since then, MacDonell had been called in to advise on hundreds of criminal cases all over the USA. The professor's speciality was bloodstaining. In a twenty-year career he had become pre-eminent in the properties and behaviour of human blood, and had earned a formidable reputation for his uncannily accurate reconstructions of shoot-outs and massacres. In 1970 he published a short book, *Bloodstain Pattern Interpretation*, which became the leading text in its field.

Jeremy wrote to Professor MacDonell at his Laboratory of Forensic Science in Corning Hospital, New York, enclosing details of his case, and asking for an initial opinion on the evidence concerning the blood in the silencer. The professor's reply galvanized Jeremy Bamber. MacDonell had taken a cursory look and had written back saying that, in his opinion, some of the evidence presented by some of the forensic witnesses was suspect. However, MacDonell pointed out that for his opinion to be of any value, he would need to spend time and effort compiling a proper report. That would cost money. Bamber decided that the time had come for him to exploit the media he so despised. Through an intermediary, he offered a story about new evidence in his case to the *Sunday Sport* newspaper in return for 'expenses'. This money was shared between Bamber and his go-between; Jeremy Bamber planned to spend his share on commissioning a new report from Professor MacDonell. Bamber was sure that a formal report from MacDonell would tip the scales of his case being referred to the appeal court. Tests had shown that (in spite of the judge's direction to the questioning jury) the blood in the silencer was not necessarily specific to Sheila Caffell. Bamber wanted MacDonell to confirm this. Bamber also asked MacDonell for an expert opinion on whether it was possible for more than one weapon to have been used on the night of the killing.

MacDonell was not unhelpful, but it was clear that Bamber's requirements would soon eat up his share of the money from the newspaper. The professor needed a number of documents, including original post-mortem reports, scene-of-crime photographs, measurements and diagrams on which to base an expert opinion. The venture was beyond Bamber's means; as a category A prisoner held in a top security jail, his weekly earnings from his prison duties (he cleaned his landing twice a week) totalled less than £5.

My approach to Jeremy Bamber seeking his co-operation in a book about his case turned out to be timely. We struck a deal: access to Bamber's defence files and his co-operation with requests for information and interviews in return for a report (which *we* would commission) from Professor MacDonell, produced to Bamber's specifications. The documentation requested by the professor was gathered together and dispatched to New York in the late summer of 1992. This included transcripts of the trial evidence of various witnesses, including that of John Hayward, the prosecution's blood expert.

In the meantime, the Police Complaints Authority announced that the investigation into Bamber's complaints against Essex Police had been completed, and that a report had been sent to the Crown Prosecution Service. The casework was voluminous, running to no fewer than 136 statements and a huge file of documents, forensic reports, transcripts of taped interviews and police records and documentation from the original trial. It was now up to the CPS to decide whether criminal charges should be made against individual police officers. At the same time, a report from Essex Police into Bamber's claims of breaches of police discipline was also reviewed by the Police Complaints Authority.

With his interviews with the City of London Police completed, Bamber was moved north to another top security jail, Frankland on the outskirts of Durham, in February 1992. It was there the following August that he was told by the Crown Prosecution Service that as a result of the PCA's investigation, there were no grounds for any criminal proceedings. A few days later came another letter telling him that the PCA had also ruled out any disciplinary action. Jeremy Bamber's reaction was a mixture of boiling rage and disbelief. In his fury, he and four other prisoners went on the rampage at Frankland Prison, smashing up their cells and smearing the walls with giant letters written with excrement that read: FREE BAMBER HE IS INNOCENT. 'I did it out of frustration,' he wrote a few weeks later, 'and my continuing imprisonment for crimes I did not commit.' The wrecking spree and dirty protest cost Bamber fourteen days in a punishment cell. 'My head was done in with the injustice of it all,' Bamber complained.

With Jeremy Bamber, claims of injustice have become a *leitmotiv*. He was making similar complaints when, just over a year after his trial, he applied to succeed to the tenancy at White House Farm following the death of his father. He was secretly taken from Wormwood Scrubs to state his case at a land appeals tribunal in London. Reporters were not told about the hearing. 'Had you been there,' Bamber wrote to the *Evening Gazette* in Colchester, 'you would have learned about the injustices that have been heaped upon me.' (The tribunal reserved a decision pending Bamber's attempt to have his case referred to appeal.)

With the prospective squire serving five life sentences, the tenancy at White House Farm was awarded on a temporary basis to Peter Eaton. Eaton had been installed as manager by Bamber himself shortly after the killings at White House Farm. 'Nevill always wanted his son to take over the farm one day,' Peter Eaton told a reporter a year after the trial. 'Now, because Jeremy can't, perhaps he would wish me to do it.' In September 1989, six months after having his appeal application refused, Jeremy Bamber appeared at another sitting of the land appeals tribunal. This time the sitting was held in the grim surroundings of York Prison. Bamber was driven over from nearby Full Sutton top security jail to announce that he was withdrawing his claim to the tenancy. On Lady Day the following spring, nearly five years after the firestorm that consumed the Bambers, Peter Eaton was formally named as the new tenant at White House Farm.

FORTY-SEVEN

PROFESSOR HERBERT MACDONELL'S report on the shootings arrived on the desk of Jeremy Bamber's new solicitor, Ewen Smith, in the middle of June 1993. MacDonell stressed that what he had done amounted to a preliminary investigation into the blood/ballistics aspects of the shootings, and made no attempt to address all the evidence, reports and photographs that he had been sent in New York. He had concentrated on bloodstain patterns photographed in the main bedroom at White House Farm where June Bamber and Sheila Caffell had met their deaths. From these photographs, and the forensic reports that accompanied them, Professor MacDonell offered a detailed reconstruction of what had happened in this room on the murder night.

June Bamber, he deduced, had been shot in bed. Bullets went through her neck and into the pillow on which she'd been lying. Blood on the top of the pillow came from direct contact with those initial wounds, and was not blood that was dripped or transferred. MacDonell thought this bloodstaining was consistent with June Bamber lying on the pillow for a few moments after being shot. She then appears to have sat on the edge of the bed for a short time before getting up and moving around the bed towards the door to the landing. As she staggered, blood bubbled from her mouth and nose and dripped on to the carpet. The trail could be seen starting at the corner of her pillow and rounding the foot of the bed to where June Bamber was found sprawled on her side by the door. Blood on the carpet beside and beneath the body of Sheila almost certainly came from June as she got out of bed and tried to escape towards the door. There were no small bloodstains on Sheila Caffell's limbs or nightdress that matched those on the carpet around her body.

But what of Sheila? MacDonell turned to the question of whether her bloodstain patterns, clearly seen on a series of colour photographs of the crime scene, suggested suicide or murder. He saw that blood running from Sheila's nose and mouth travelled across her face horizontally. No blood ran down towards her lower body. 'Therefore,' the professor added, 'she could not have been standing or sitting up when she was shot and remained in such a position, or some blood trails would have formed down her face and body.' This contradicts the opinion of John Hayward, who thought Sheila was 'reclining'.

MacDonell reported that Sheila's right arm was moved after she was shot. Her right hand could have been holding her neck after the bullets were fired. One of the photographs suggested that something or someone had smeared blood around the upper entrance wound in Sheila's neck. If Sheila's right thumb or fingers pressed against this wound, they would have become blood-stained. Unfortunately, none of the crime scene pictures showed Sheila's right hand in a perspective that showed blood on her thumb or fingers. A photograph of her right hand taken at the mortuary didn't show any blood inside the hand, but it was not known if the picture was taken before or after the body was washed.

While Sheila's hand was near her neck (or pressed against it), blood ran down from her neck wounds and soaked into the upper right front of her powder blue nightdress. MacDonell saw that this blood had also stained the inner aspects of Sheila's right arm between wrist and elbow. When this arm was positioned to where it was later found, blood from Sheila's fingers – or her killer's fingers – wiped against her nightdress producing bloody fingermarks that could be seen in one of the photographs. A large quantity of blood that had pooled between Sheila's right arm and upper body was released when her arm was moved. This blood ran down over the lateral aspects of Sheila's right arm.

MacDonell pointed to further evidence that Sheila's right arm had moved – or had been moved – after she had been shot. He drew attention to the alternate stain and void elongated fold patterns in Sheila's nightdress. These stains, visible just above her biceps, resulted when blood that had pooled up between her arm and folds in her nightdress was held there by compression. Furthermore, one of the photographs showed that in the time between the shots to Sheila's neck and her body being found either her arm had moved, or the Bible that was found lying near her right shoulder. Also found in or under the Bible was a letter or note, apparently used as a page marker. MacDonell deduced that this piece of paper had been moved from its original position against Sheila's arm when it became bloodstained. When blood ran down over her upper right arm, the bottom of the blood trail produced a small stain on the edge of the paper. But the bottom of this blood trail was no longer aligned with the stain on the paper when the body was photographed. 'So,' MacDonell concluded, 'there has been a shift of the Bible, the arm, or both.'

Another photograph convinced MacDonell that the blood on the carpet around Sheila's body was on the carpet before the Bible was placed on the floor.

Professor MacDonell reported that the rifle found on Sheila Caffell's body had been placed in the position in which police found it. With the silencer fitted, the distance from the end of the silencer to the trigger was some thirty-six inches, too great for Sheila to have shot herself. 'There is no question as to the manner of death of Sheila Caffell,' wrote Professor MacDonell. 'She did not commit suicide but, like the other four victims, was shot to death by someone else.'

So on all major points, Professor MacDonell agreed with the findings of the original forensic investigators. She could not have shot herself with the silencer fitted. Therefore, Sheila Caffell – like the others – was shot to death by someone else.

These conclusions might have settled the issue once and for all, but for Mark Webster's criticisms of the methodology used in grouping the blood in the silencer during the original forensic tests in the Home Office laboratory at Huntingdon. If this methodology could be shown to be flawed, then not only would the whole of the so-called blood evidence be disputed, but other conclusions drawn by the forensic experts from Huntingdon could also be called into question. After all, experts can be wrong. They have been proved to be wrong before.

In 1981, for example, a man called John Preece, serving life for the murder of Helen Wills, was released after the evidence of a former Home Office forensic scientist, Dr Alan Clift, was shown to be unreliable. The Preece case, and other cases involving a second ex-Home Office forensic expert, Dr Frank Skuse, have raised serious doubts about the reliability of expert forensic evidence called on behalf of the Crown. The Home Office itself, which runs the Forensic Science Service, has always rejected calls for an independent inquiry into the FSS.

The Home Office forensic science laboratory at Huntingdon was opened two years before the Bamber case in May 1983 by the then Home Secretary, William Whitelaw. The new laboratory cost £4 million and was built to serve ten police forces in the east of England, from East

Anglia to Leicester, Nottinghamshire and Northamptonshire. When it opened, it employed nearly seventy experts in all branches of forensic science, including biology, chemistry, toxicology, blood serology and the examination of firearms. In theory, the service provided at Huntingdon is equally available to both prosecution and defence teams in a criminal case. But in practice, because of the structural and informal links with the police, the service at Huntingdon (as at the five other regional Home Office laboratories) is identified almost exclusively with the prosecution. Defence lawyers trying to gain access to laboratory resources often find themselves thwarted at every turn. Even obtaining samples for independent testing can be very difficult.

Webster, himself a former Home Office forensic scientist now working as an independent expert, realized that an error in sampling blood from inside the silencer might have led to Hayward drawing a mistaken conclusion over its origin. In early June 1993, Mark Webster was invited to examine a file of papers relating to the original blood grouping tests. Among these papers was a copy of a statement made by John Hayward on 3 October 1986. In this statement, Hayward admitted that on the basis of the results of his grouping tests on the silencer blood, he could not totally exclude the possibility that the blood was a mixture of the blood of June and Nevill Bamber. Hayward added – as he was to say in court – that the possibility was a remote one. In such a mixture he would have expected to detect June Bamber's AK2–1 group, and he did not find it. What caught Webster's attention, however, was a further statement: '. . . the distribution of the blood suggests that the blood has come from a single individual.'

But was John Hayward entitled to make this last observation? Mark Webster was sceptical. This was blood that had found its way into the silencer by means of backspatter. Webster's opinion was that John Hayward 'has not demonstrated that he has any experience of the appearance of blood backspattered into a sound moderator'. Moreover, Webster reported, taking the file of papers as a whole, Hayward's scientific notes were 'inadequate' because they failed to record the detailed appearance of the blood in the silencer. Webster doubted whether Hayward or any other forensic scientist could reliably distinguish between a silencer containing backspattered blood from one shooting and another silencer that had been used to shoot two different people. This was something, Webster maintained, which could and should have been addressed by experimentation.

Is it too late to settle the question of where the blood in the silencer came from? Mark Webster believes that if blood remains in the silencer, sensitive DNA profiling tests could show whether it is a mixture of two people's blood or if any of the blood is male rather than female. Since the trial, it has been assumed that the little blood that was found in the silencer was tested to destruction. This seems not to be so. Although John Hayward told the defence blood expert, Dr Patrick Lincoln, that he had obtained 'a single blood flake' from beneath the first or second baffle plate within the silencer, an official Home Office laboratory diagram refers to 'a large amount of blood' staining the baffle plates when the silencer was dismantled by Malcolm Fletcher at Huntingdon. When Dr Lincoln examined the silencer for himself, he noted that 'the first four, five or six baffles gave reactions showing that there was blood on them.' Mark Webster takes the view that no one has made a proper record of the amount of blood actually inside the silencer, or its exact position.

But at the heart of the matter is the question of

whether the tests at Huntingdon were carried out in such a way as to reveal a mixture of blood rather than blood from Sheila Caffell alone. There are two ways in which blood from two different people may have been mixed together in the deposits of dried blood found inside the silencer. The blood could have formed what scientists call an *intimate* mixture. (This is like adding milk to a cup of coffee or tea; once mixed together, they cannot be separated.) Such a blood mix would have been detected, according to Mark Webster. At the very least, an intimate mixture would not have been misinterpreted as being blood from Sheila alone. The other type of mixture is known as *heterogeneous*. This means that blood from two different sources is present but unmixed, rather like a layer of cream floating on the top of a glass of Irish coffee. With a heterogeneous flake, there is a danger of a sampling error – as described by Mark Webster – causing the blood to be mistyped. But there is a way of preventing this. The procedure is simple. It merely involves dissolving the blood sample in water, and using the *blood solution* in the grouping tests rather than the blood alone.

Did John Hayward follow this procedure? He told Dr Patrick Lincoln that he had. But now there are doubts. On two separate occasions, Mark Webster raised the question with John Hayward, and it seems probable that the blood was *not* tested in solution. On one occasion, Webster tried to pin Hayward down on the question, asking him specifically if he had dissolved the blood flake in water as a precaution against mistyping a mixture of two people's blood. John Hayward's reply confirmed Mark Webster's suspicions. '[Hayward] said that he did not think that he had done this,' Webster reported, '*and this would not be the usual procedure to follow*.'

Is that so? Mark Webster thinks not. He believes that had Hayward and his team not excluded the possibility of the blood being a heterogeneous mixture, they would certainly have tested the sample in solution. 'If a scientist had prejudged the issue by forming the opinion that a mixture was not likely,' Webster reported, 'then perhaps this or a similar procedure would not be adopted.' What seems certain is that no one appears absolutely clear about whether it was done or not. If the blood was tested in solution, the fact should have been recorded in the case notes. But the procedure appears not to have been recorded. Webster hopes that other scientists working in the blood grouping section at Huntingdon may recall what actually happened in the Bamber case.

If blood remains in the silencer, could more tests reveal the presence of a mixture? Mark Webster is certain they could. It would be possible, he says, to measure the likelihood of two separate shootings generating a heterogeneous mixture of blood in a single flake. As for the possibility of such a flake being wrongly grouped, this hinges on the evidence of the former blood expert at Huntingdon, John Hayward, and his recollections of exactly what was and was not done at the laboratory where he worked nearly ten years ago. If the flake tested at Huntingdon in the autumn of 1985 was dissolved in water, then it seems there is no possibility that the blood in the silencer could have belonged to anyone but Sheila Caffell.

But Mark Webster's findings have set alarm bells ringing within the closed and secretive world of the Home Office Forensic Science Service. John Hayward, now an independent forensic consultant, whose evidence propelled the Bamber jury towards their guilty verdict in 1986, has already distanced himself from the judge's attempt to paraphrase his evidence concerning the blood grouping. In mid-1993, presented with the disturbing hypothesis of Mark Webster on behalf of Jeremy Bamber himself, Hayward found himself in a position where he might be forced to admit the possibility of a mistake at Huntingdon. Such an admission would kick away one of the main planks of the Crown's case, and provide Bamber's defence team with compelling new evidence to present to the Home Secretary. Lawyers who have taken up Jeremy Bamber's case have applied to Essex Police to arrange for Mark Webster to examine the silencer to see if any traces of blood remain. So far, Essex Police have refused permission for access to the silencer, saying the blood in it has been tested many times before to everyone's entire satisfaction. This does not impress Bamber's lawyers. 'Either we carry out new tests of our own,' says one, 'or we go straight to the Home Secretary.'

So where next? Jeremy Bamber has an energetic new legal team, headed by the radical young barrister David Martin-Sperry and Ewen Smith, a solicitor with Glaisyers, one of the leading criminal law practices in the Midlands. At the beginning of July 1993, Bamber's lawyers were confident that if it were to be conceded that the original experiments on the silencer might have been flawed, the case for a referral to the Court of Appeal would be unanswerable. But Essex Police were reluctant to let Bamber's new blood expert, Mark Webster, test any blood remaining in the silencer. In the meantime, it seems clear that Professor Lincoln, Bamber's original blood expert, was misled in 1986 when he was told ('by someone else,' says John Hayward) that the blood was tested in solution. This fact alone, which admits the possibility that the blood tested at Huntingdon could have been a mixture of June and Nevill Bamber's blood, could be enough to persuade the C3 division of the Home Office – the department which deals with alleged miscarriages of justice – to reopen the files and to recommend the Home

Secretary to refer the Bamber case to the Court of Appeal.

But it seems unlikely that this will happen overnight. Understaffed and underfunded, C3 has only sixteen civil servants grappling with an estimated 800 cases every year on a budget of just £400,000. Following the well-publicized cases of the Guildford Four, Birmingham Six, Tottenham Three and Judith Ward, C3 has been swamped with petitions seeking referrals. None of the staff at C3 has any legal training, and the process of sifting the cases is lengthy and slow. Very few make it through C3's net. In the year 1988–9, for example, of 536 representations received by the department only three were referred to the appeal court. In 1990, a survey showed that C3 ordered fresh inquiries in fewer than one case in every five it dealt with. Most petitions are rejected outright, refused point-blank because they come from prisoners who simply take issue with the jury's verdict at their trial. What C3 officials look for is new evidence, and that is the strength of the Bamber case. If John Hayward, one of the Crown's principal witnesses at Bamber's trial, is seen significantly to revise his account of the blood tests, C3 may have no alternative but to recommend a referral. When that might happen is another matter altogether. For one thing, C3 itself is doomed.

In July 1993, the long-awaited report of the Royal Commission on Criminal Justice recommended that the department should be scrapped and replaced by an independent appeals tribunal to be known as the Criminal Cases Review Authority. Moreover, under the commission's proposals, the Home Secretary would no longer be responsible for ruling which cases would be referred to the appeal court and which would not. The abolition of C3 with its slow, unresponsive and clumsy machinery was hailed as the most important of the commission's proposed reforms. Some saw it as a direct repudiation of a system based on the presumption that every trial conviction is well-founded. It was, after all, civil servants from C3 who had once recommended the Home Secretary to reject referral applications in the cases of the Guildford Four and the Maguire family. More recently, C3 officials rejected a referral in the controversial Carl Bridgewater murder case, saying they were not convinced about the validity of new evidence. Few will lament C3's demise. The procedures it set in motion were tortuous and lethargic. The Royal Commission wants the new authority to be operationally independent and pro-active. Reformers will want the authority to look at cases like that of Jeremy Bamber in a prompt and open manner. A central worry remains, however. Once the new machinery is in place, the task of conducting a reinvestigation of the case will fall to Essex Police.

Other reforms are on the way. The Royal Commission calls for the creation of a new advisory council to regulate the work of the forensic science services. It also wants the defence to have an enforceable right of access to material held by the prosecution; in Bamber's case, this would mean that Essex Police would be compelled to make the silencer and its contents available to the defence team for examination and analysis. The commission goes further: once a suspect has been charged and is legally represented, it wants the defence to have an enforceable right to observe any further scientific tests. If, as in the Bamber case, material such as blood exists only in minute quantities, the commission recommends that the defence should be entitled to remove some of the material so that defence experts can run their own scientific tests. The prosecution will no longer be allowed to test crucial blood samples to destruction (as was *thought* to have been done in the Bamber case).

FORTY-EIGHT

IT SEEMS such madness. A young man with everything to live for annihilates his family in the dead of night, staging the scene to make it look like the frenzied rampage of a deranged sister. He says that's just what happened, and that he didn't do it. The public, who have never forgotten this terrible act of savagery, thought that justice had finally caught up with Jeremy Bamber, and that the prison system would cage him until the twenty-first century was at least a tenth spent. Most sympathized with Mr Justice Drake's observation that it was hard to know when, if ever, it would be safe to free a man who could shoot dead two six-year-olds sleeping in their beds. But now, barely a quarter of the way through his sentence, Jeremy Bamber has brought himself and his case back to haunt us.

Did he do it? Since the moment suspicion first fell on him eight years ago, he has been telling the world that he did not. At every twist of the investigation, in the face of the blank, uncomprehending and icy rage of his relations, at every turn of the screw at the trial, Jeremy has denied it all. His composure has barely ever slipped. He cracked up in his cell when they took him down after the verdict, and pondered suicide in the black days following his arrest when Julie Mugford, the girl he jilted, denounced him to the police. 'I was feeling very close to the edge,' he wrote to Anji Greaves. 'If I hadn't had your love,' he added, 'I would have called it a day.' Since Anji Greaves, other women, manipulative and capricious, have left Bamber depressed. 'That's the last heavy relationship I get involved with in jail,' he declared, as one of his nubile admirers headed for the gate and the Sunday newspapers. 'It's too much heartbreak when it ends.' The *douleur* seldom lasted. 'Women troubles?' Jeremy wrote four months later. 'What's new? I'd sooner have them than have a womanless life. So I just cope when things get rugged, and buzz with love when everything is sweet.'

There have been spells on Valium, and times when 'I feel as though I'm bashing my head against a brick wall' in Jeremy's efforts to have his case referred to the appeal court. But for a man facing the crushing prospect of permanent imprisonment, he seems extraordinarily resilient. One man who served time with him early in his sentence emerged to tell of Bamber's unwavering faith in his own innocence that transcended all the routine bluster of the newly convicted. Bamber, he said, had sold everyone on the idea, jailers and jailed alike. Other lifers may have ceased their protests, surrendered to the granite regime and opted to serve out their time as quietly as possible. But after seven years facing down accusers, critics and the combined might and majesty of the British penal and legal establishment, Jeremy Bamber still hasn't blinked.

If he is innocent of this terrible crime, then he is nothing less than a martyr to the flawed and ramshackle machine that is British justice. If guilty, then this extraordinary doggedness, this unwavering denial, is no more than his way of dealing with the living death that might otherwise overwhelm him. It could be that these extraordinary reserves of personal fortitude are drawn from the same well of *sang-froid* that fortified him for the firestorm with which he engulfed his family. This is a man, after all, who is said to have devised a murder plot of such horrific dimensions that he first had to put his own nerves to the test by trapping rats and wringing their necks. Or has Jeremy Bamber found and embraced the kind of steadfastness and stoical acceptance that elevates his ordeal to a kind of martyrdom?

'Please beware,' was the advice of Colin Caffell. 'He is an extremely seductive and charismatic person.' It is hard to know quite what to make of a man one knows only from his role in a notorious case, a few snatched conversations in prison visiting rooms and a handful of letters. He has been a disappointing correspondent. When this book was first mooted, I explained that I would need more from him than dates and documents. I wanted to explore the side of Jeremy Bamber that remained hidden, the darker reaches of his life and character that had been missed or ignored by the newspapers. Jeremy demurred. His private life would remain private. 'This way,' he explained to a mutual friend, 'I can distance myself from his book should he not reach the truth of my innocence.' Under sufferance, Jeremy eventually gave me a list of friends and acquaintances he had known before the case, some of whom had spoken to the police and some of whom had not. One, who had been a defence witness, readily agreed to talk. But not one of the others would do so. One of Bamber's old girlfriends threatened legal action if I even mentioned her name. Fear and loathing go hand in hand in Jeremy Bamber's old *milieu*.

He is not at ease, and one would hardly expect him to be. There is evidence that he was genuinely grieved at the monstering campaign waged in the newspapers in the weeks and months following his trial; one man who served time with him early in his sentence remembers real tears and anguished indignation. Jeremy conceals the daily rigours of life as a convicted child killer and camouflages his time inside segregation units with talk of a preference to serve his sentence alone.

Newly convicted in Wormwood Scrubs, he found himself shunned, threatened, despised. 'He was not popular on the wing,' reported Ken Smith in his essay on Bamber for his book *Inside Time*. Jeremy had to struggle to survive. He was attacked and beaten up, but says he hasn't been in a fight now for five years. In any case, he says, asking for protection would make him feel guilty. Neither is he prepared to be seen to knuckle under to the prison system. He has discovered that life as a lifer is doubly hard for a white, middle-class and articulate young man with a private education. Notoriety has its price. Other inmates are jealous because he gets more visitors than they do. They particularly dislike the number of attractive women who visit him. Jeremy has been forced to give up playing chess. His opponents became too competitive. They all wanted to be able to say they beat Jeremy Bamber.

Most of his fellow prisoners are serving long sentences for violent, sordid crimes; they include political terrorists, armed robbers, murderers and rapists who resent Bamber's glamorous image and the abiding media interest. They resent the fact that he receives between twenty and thirty letters a week. Most are to do with his case, but some are from total strangers. He replies to a few. Apart from a letter to his Uncle Bobby Boutflour asking him to repudiate his trial evidence, Jeremy has had no contact with his family for several years. Such communication as is necessary to progress the civil action over the Bamber estate is conducted through formal correspondence composed by lawyers. The family hear about Jeremy's moves towards an appeal by reading the newspapers. They respond to what they read with bewilderment. 'It is beyond my comprehension,' says Bobby Boutflour, 'how any person of average intelligence . . . could have any doubt that he was convicted for these murders on irrefutable evidence.'

431

One can only imagine how they feel. Torn from the background of an idyll of wealthy middle England, the Boutflours and the Eatons were hurled into a nightmare of unimaginable horror, their closest family cut down in cold blood in the dead of night. Policemen bumbled and bungled for weeks. Eventually an adopted kinsman, the greedy young swaggerer who clung to the name of Bamber but rejected all the family's values, was exposed as a ruthless and wicked assassin, stripped of his inheritance, and tried in a feverish atmosphere of sensation and sordidness. Branded a psychopathic monster, Jeremy Bamber had been led away to the deepest, darkest dungeon, perhaps never to breathe free air again. Yet almost as soon as the door had closed behind him, the doubts in the case, amplified by the moves towards an appeal, began to take root. In time the clamour reached such a pitch that the family felt threatened at every turn by what one of them called 'the aspirations of this evil monster, this dangerous maniac'. Jeremy's ceaseless protestations from prison that he had been wrongly convicted were regularly covered by the media. At length Bobby Boutflour wrote begging the coverage to stop. 'It is placing doubts in the minds of people who should know better,' he told me during the course of the investigation into Jeremy's claims by the Police Complaints Authority in late 1991. Boutflour pointed out that his family hadn't been allowed to forget the trauma that had engulfed them six years before. As for Jeremy, whom Boutflour could scarcely bring himself to name (referring to him by his prison number), 'his conviction should not be doubted by any sane person who has bothered to read the trial papers, or even the judge's summing-up.' Others suffered too. Boutflour's grandchildren had to face abuse at school from companions who knew the family link with Jeremy Bamber but little else. The children were receiving counselling at school to cope with the problem.

Blood that should bind families together puts this one asunder. At the sticking point of the case lies the fact of Jeremy's adoption. To the extent that both he and his sister Sheila were adopted, family life at White House Farm was contrived, since no blood ties existed to cement the two generations. Many such families live perfectly normal lives, but it is evident that in the Bamber household, there was friction and unhappiness for many years before the murderous explosion that engulfed it in August 1985. 'Members of a family cannot get rid of each other easily,' observed Margaret Kornitzer in her study of adoption in Britain, *Adoption and Family Life*, 'and generally will suffer a good deal of friction without a major explosion, although not patiently or in silence.' What went wrong behind the handsome neo-Georgian portico at White House Farm? Neither Sheila nor Jeremy was heir to obvious psychopathic traits. In both cases, their natural parents came from good, solid, middle-class stock. Nevill and June Bamber, who adopted them as babes-in-arms, were an attractive couple with wealth and position, living the sweet life amid rolling acres in the prosperous East Anglian grain belt. Yet by modern lights, the decision to allow June Bamber to adopt, given her history of clinical depression, seems surprising. Like other adoption agencies, the Church of England Children's Society (through which both Sheila and Jeremy were placed with the Bambers) guards its case histories closely. But it seems fair to assume that June Bamber was not screened; neither was she offered the kind of counselling and guidance available to adoptive parents in the 1990s.

It is one of the tragic ironies of the whole affair that the Bambers, such decent, kind and generous people, were nevertheless not the best adoptive parents. They were loving but undemonstrative. June seems to have been troubled by the episode when she accidentally dropped the infant Jeremy, striking his head; she reported this to her psychiatrist years later, and there may have been other, undisclosed, examples of tumbles and spills that worried her too. But June was certainly not emotionally neglectful. Rather, she may have tried to smother little Jeremy with the kind of affection grown-up boys remember with acute embarrassment. 'I was a real Mummy's boy,' Jeremy admitted ruefully, 'always hiding behind her skirts if strangers came to call.' At the age of eight and a half, he was sent away to prep school. Like most boys boarding for the first time, he felt bewildered, hurt and resentful. He was fourteen before he felt any benefit. He says he found prison life at Gartree easier than life at Gresham's. Sheila, too, was sent away, failed to settle, but asked in vain to come home. There seems little evidence of any great warmth between the gangling, giggling girl and her straitlaced adoptive mother, unable to deal with her daughter's sexual flowering and damning her as 'the Devil's child' for yielding to her boyfriend in the course of what was, almost literally, a roll in the hay. June Bamber's groping explanation to Sheila of how she came to be adopted ('You didn't grow in Mummy's tummy, but out of all the babies in the world, we chose you') seems inadequate. Remembering such mealiness, Sheila (and Jeremy in turn) may have reckoned that this was not the type of mother to turn to for the kind of advice that inspired confidence. Sheila in particular seems to have resented June's over-protectiveness; Jeremy may have become resentful too, particularly over his family's expectations about his taking over at White House Farm once his father became too old to carry on.

His own aspirations, as a personable young gallivanter, seem to have stretched no further than the totemic Porsche that became the signature of the *jeunesse dorée* of the early Thatcher years. What may have thwarted those aspirations was not necessarily his father's instinctive reluctance to squander money on a noisy car that Nevill would no doubt have considered raffish and ostentatious, but Jeremy's claustrophobic suspicions that he had been adopted and raised for no other purpose than to farm his father's land. Julie Mugford remembered Jeremy's bitter resentment about this. He had railed at his parents for trying to run his life, telling him what to do and complaining that he wasn't working hard enough on the farm.

To Nevill Bamber's blood kin, on the other hand, the farm represented their birthright, their expectations, their future and their children's future. To the family, Boutflours and Eatons descended from the Speakmans and raised on their own massive swathes of Essex flatlands, it meant security and, more importantly, continuity. But in the search for the key to his own identity, and to his sexual ambiguity, it is perhaps not surprising that Jeremy felt trapped, a prisoner within the waving wheatfields of White House Farm. To Jeremy Bamber, the farm represented enslavement to a way of life he feared and despised. To his surviving blood relations, it represented salvation.

FORTY-NINE

LIVES brutally taken, other lives wrecked; everyone within the Bamber family circle was a victim. In old age, Bobby and Pamela Boutflour have still fully to come to terms with the nightmare. To them, Jeremy Bamber, their adopted nephew, remains the monstrous creature that haunts their blackest days and nights. With silver-haired dignity, the Boutflours live each day with the legacy of what they remain convinced is the work of 'this evil criminal'. For them this case is no crusade, but a traumatic daily reminder that their dearest friends were murdered in cold blood and in the dead of night, and the even crueller realization – in Bobby Boutflour's anguished words – 'that they died at the hands of the adopted son that they had raised with love and care from the time that he was a babe in arms'.

There is a sense in which the killings represent the ultimate disintegration of a landed middle-class family; the generation gap that yawned between two hugely decent but strangely ineffectual parents and their adopted children, a dippy daughter and a dangerously disgruntled son. The tragedy might have corroded the family fabric altogether, but for the Boutflours. At an age when they expected the quietness of the fireside, they were engulfed by the kind of catastrophe that might have destroyed folk of lesser mettle. In the numb years that followed, the grief would bubble out at unexpected moments, to the consternation of strangers such as me, unused to seeing a man of seventy-five stop suddenly in mid-sentence and start weeping.

Sheila's former husband, the sculptor Colin Caffell, keeps his own counsel. He told me that he blamed not just Jeremy but the remaining family for 'the many distortions, inaccuracies and downright lies' told about Sheila, both in court and in the newspapers. 'While Jeremy continues to profess his innocence and the cousins, uncles and aunts still defend the reputation of June and Nevill for their part in the tragedy – protecting their "innocence" – the story will be no nearer the truth than the tabloids . . .' Colin Caffell also spoke of 'my own journey of healing and recovery from the experience', a subject which formed the basis of an article in the *Observer* in May 1993 in which he described the therapy he had received at workshops run by the Swiss psychiatrist Elisabeth Kubler-Ross. He attended the first of these in the USA in 1988, three years after the murders, when he remained a prisoner of pent-up hatred and rage for which he could find no means of expression. Caffell explained that he came from a family which had never expressed its feelings well. 'I think that is what first drew me to the Bambers,' he added. 'We had an awful lot in common.' Through his attendance at Kubler-Ross's workshops, Caffell discovered a way to confront and release his anger, and subsequently began to train in therapy techniques himself. 'I finally confronted that dark, destructive, murderous part of myself – or rather it burst out of me in a homicidal rage which scared the living daylights out of me,' he declared. 'But in that moment, I knew and began to understand my brother-in-law.'

In the kitchen at White House Farm the Boutflours' daughter, Ann Eaton, inhabits the scene of the firestorm. She is a woman of curious *insouciance* masking an unexplained inner turmoil. She and her husband Peter are hospitable, hardworking farming folk who have made a life for themselves and their two teenage children, Jane and William, at the farm that Jeremy would have run had he not been convicted of the murders. They love the house, the gardens and orchard, the land that takes an hour to circumnavigate on a brisk evening walk. In the farmhouse kitchen, Nevill Bamber's charnel-house, the Aga is still the warm, welcoming centrepiece of family gatherings. Ann Eaton takes an oblique approach to what she calls 'the tragedy'. There is friction between her and at least one of the detectives on the case who dubbed her 'Miss Marple'. She is wary of sensation-seekers and guards her feelings, especially on the subject of Jeremy, 'the nice, placid little boy who wanted to be like his daddy' but who grew up hankering for the bright lights of London.

Ann Eaton is more comfortable remembering Sheila, the pretty girl cousin with the model figure, the hopelessly impractical Sheila who could neither drive nor cook, whose proudest boast in the kitchen was to say she could rustle up a good baked bean casserole. Ann recalls Sheila the flirt, the girl with the skin of a sixteen-year-old who never needed make-up and yet who worried constantly about the way she looked. She needed people around her for reassurance. 'Don't be a sheep,' Ann told her, but Sheila demurred. 'You have to be in a crowd,' Sheila said. There was Colin, of course, the too-nice dreamer whom she married, a talented artist but with little ambition to succeed. Ann recalls her aunt, June Bamber, trying in vain to persuade the couple to move away from London with its drowsy bohemian enclaves, its drugs and clubs.

It is Sheila's breakdowns that Ann Eaton remembers, the trauma Sheila suffered when June Bamber surprised her in the hayfield with Colin and called her 'the Devil's child' for having sex before marriage. Ann thinks June exploded because, being childless herself, the idea of her adopted daughter having to seek an abortion was simply too much to bear. Ann Eaton believes this incident triggered Sheila's mental problems. Meanwhile Jeremy, the little boy, was looking on, watching and listening.

The case changed Barbara Wilson's life. Nevill Bamber's farm secretary used to think of nothing except bringing up her family and getting them ready for the world. 'I felt if I could put them on the right road, everything would just go on from there and life would be so smooth. That's what the Bambers wanted for their children. But the tragedy has shown that you can't do that.' Grey eyes brim at the memory. 'You can't live solely for your children. The Bambers did, and it was all washed away. Completely. They gave those two children everything they had. And Sheila and Jeremy just smashed them in the face at every turn. Very hard, very sad.'

Barbara Wilson recalls June Bamber in the throes of breakdown, drifting aimlessly around the farmhouse, worrying about her ailing mother-in-law, the failure of Sheila's marriage, the twins' future, Jeremy's ideas about making a career away from the farm and his constant demands for money. Careworn and distracted (Mrs Wilson once found her cooking the family supper in the middle of the day), June Bamber cracked up and spent several weeks at the clinic in Northampton. When she returned to White House Farm, June looked much better. Her sunny disposition and chattiness had returned. It didn't last. As time passed, she became duller, more listless. The eyes lost their sparkle, the lilt in her voice died. She was increasingly given to biblical imagery, and wrote more and more notes and messages. Once again the slide ended at Dr Ferguson's sanatorium in Northampton.

Discharged a second time, June Bamber seemed embarrassed and ill at ease. Religious mania had taken hold. Scribbled pieces of paper littered the house, little homilies and quotes from the scriptures. Barbara Wilson watched as June withdrew from mundane preoccupations. She was being drawn into nature, mesmerized by the beauty of the world, the God-given miracle of creation, the changing seasons, the music of birdsong. She reflected on all this as if in a trance, shutting out everything else. June Bamber spoke only of the nice things she could see and hear. It seemed to be her way of coping, her way of compensating for everything that was going wrong: Sheila in a mess in London, Jeremy on the slide with women. In the end she was noticeably distant, Barbara Wilson recalls, very withdrawn, very weepy. There were always tears in her eyes. She was distressed at how ill and exhausted Nevill appeared, his shambling, sagging gait, his air of resigned defeat. She was worried that he was worried. 'And yet,' she added, 'I don't think Nevill ever shared his premonition with June. I don't think he would have burdened her with that. I don't think she ever knew.'

Now Nevill and June are dead, their ashes buried in a shaded grave in the churchyard at Tolleshunt D'Arcy, marked by a small, simple stone. *Tragically taken from us*, the inscription reads. Sheila's ashes lie buried with the twins at Highgate. Colin Caffell often visits and tends the grave. Only Jeremy is left. Evil almost beyond belief, according to the judge. 'He doesn't pulsate evilness,' says one of his defence team, 'but with Jeremy Bamber there's always that veneer. His coolness under fire, his way of justifying everything. There's a very complex brain at work inside his head.'

At Frankland maximum security prison, behind walls seventeen feet high and fourteen feet thick, they caged him with the hardest of the hard men, IRA and Palestinian terrorists, Mafiosi, London gangsters. 'You'd think I'd have a load of time,' Jeremy wrote in the spring of

1992, 'but I've been here a month on Wednesday and it feels like a week. I'm very happy spiritually right now, physically too, but I'm feeling mentally over the moon, the best for probably over a year as I can see light at the end of the tunnel. It's bright too.' At Easter, I saw him, cleared to visit only under closed conditions (through a plastic screen) now that he had been reverted to Category A security status. At Gartree, in the day room set aside for visits, he had worn a designer sweatshirt, jeans and sneakers; now, in this brutal high-tech fortress, he appeared in striped prison fatigues, explaining he was still on the punishment block at his own request as a protest at his move north. A goatee beard and moustache, he explained, had been grown at the bidding of his current girlfriend.

This, like other visits at Gartree, was upbeat. Jeremy Bamber seemed in good spirits, amiable and comfortable in conversation. At Frankland, Bamber had become interested in the teachings of Islam, and on Fridays attended the weekly Moslem service in the prison chapel. It was one of many changes prison had wrought in him. He admitted he is not the same person he was when his family was killed. He recognized that he was then self-assured to the point of arrogance, and blamed his years at Gresham's for teaching him self-sufficiency and the kind of self-confidence that denies public displays of emotion.

He is busier than ever. He gets and sends between twenty and thirty letters a week. Some are to do with his case. Others are from strangers. He replies to some and not to others. His files and case papers are piled on the floor of his cell, with copies lodged with the prison authorities in case anything is stolen. Early in his sentence he read a book a day. Now he works on his case and reads the newspapers, the *Daily Telegraph* for the crime and the crossword, the *Independent* for world news. Nevertheless, he seems out of touch with the outside world. Jeremy Bamber began his sentence at the height of the Thatcher boom. When I last saw him he had only the slenderest grasp of the extent and depth of the recession. His mind focuses on his case, and it remains the sole preoccupation of his conversation and his letters.

It is perhaps only fair to leave this last word to him, and his unwavering protestation of his innocence.

> *I've tried to understand why Sheila murdered my family and committed suicide* [he writes]. *At times I hate her for it because of the injustice I've suffered because of it. I feel that more than the loss of Mum and Dad, and the tragedy of their lives being cut short, especially so for Dan and Nick. But then I'm still living that injustice from day to day so it's more acute. But I miss them all. Especially Dad. I really miss him a lot because I know he'd have remained my closest friend forever.*
>
> *But then when I read my books on law and medicine, I understand that Sheila wasn't responsible for her actions in murdering our family. She would have spent time in Broadmoor had she not taken her own life, and to an extent I feel guilty for not helping her more and supporting her more while she was ill. If I'd done so, maybe she wouldn't have had a relapse. Maybe she wouldn't have had that brainstorm. Maybe everyone would still be alive. But it's happened, and I've had to bear a heavy burden of injustice for being accused and convicted of murdering them all. I know I didn't. And I know the truth will be told in a court of law soon enough. But I want that for Mum, Dad and Sheila, Dan and Nick as well as for me. Because when I'm cleared, so their memory can finally rest in peace.*

FIFTY

A CONSEQUENCE of the appeal court's decision in March 1989 to refuse Jeremy Bamber leave to appeal against his convictions for murder was that the British government could act to ensure that future murder investigations weren't wrongfooted at the outset. The chief constable of Essex, Robert Bunyard, had acknowledged in his report to the Home Secretary that his detectives had made mistakes in the early stages of the Bamber case investigation; now Her Majesty's chief inspector of constabulary, Sir Richard Barratt, had looked at the lessons of the case and how they might be applied to the police service generally. The Home Secretary, Douglas Hurd, in a written Commons answer, criticized (without naming him) the senior investigating officer, Detective Chief Inspector Taff Jones. He had been guilty of an error of judgement in wrongly concluding that Sheila had committed suicide after shooting the others. Consequently, the detective had failed to follow normal procedures and was reluctant to take account of information which challenged his original theory. However, Hurd added, once the Bamber family began complaining, it was clear that Bunyard and his top officers had taken 'prompt and effective action' to put the investigation on the right lines. Barratt announced eighteen recommendations to tighten up procedures in future murder investigations.

The changes, endorsed by the Home Secretary, included:

- The work of the senior investigating officer to be

- checked by a superior who would question detectives involved in the case and attend major briefings or staff meetings. This would ensure that the progress of the inquiry could not be impaired by the misjudgement of a single officer.
- Detectives to record in writing the fears, concerns or suspicions of people they interview, and pass these on to the senior investigator.
- Once the examination of the crime scene is over, police to tour the premises with someone familiar with it (other than a suspect) to look for anything unusual.
- After the post mortem, bodies to be retained until the coroner receives a written report from the pathologist.
- Chief officers to ensure that detectives have proper guidance and training and are adequately briefed to deal with serious crimes and post mortems.
- Where a pathologist is unable to attend, arrangements to be made for photographs or a video to be made of the crime scene.
- Investigators, when briefing pathologists or other experts, to take care to 'differentiate between the facts relating to the circumstances and conjecture'.
- Where firearms are used, a ballistics expert to attend and pathologists always to attend in cases of multiple deaths.
- A detective superintendent, or more senior officer, to examine the scene before any bodies are moved.

The police accepted these changes without demur. These guidelines now form the framework for every murder investigation conducted in Britain.

INDEX

447